Experts and Practitioners Recommend *Perform Your Best on the Bar Exam Performance Test (MPT)*

A book like this is long overdue. As far as I can tell, the large commercial bar review courses have yet to fully master how to train students to take the MPT. **Mary Campbell Gallagher provides students with a detailed, well-constructed method for succeeding on the MPT and similar exams.**

> —Louis J. Sirico, Jr.
> Professor of Law and Director of Legal Writing
> Villanova University School of Law
> Member, Board of Directors, Legal Writing Institute (former)
> Member, Editorial Board, *Legal Writing:*
> *The Journal of the Legal Writing Institute*

Mary Campbell Gallagher has set a new standard in bar exam preparation materials. One of the reasons so many people have trouble with bar exams is that they don't want to spend time practicing to take the exam by actually taking practice exams under exam conditions. **The tone of the instructions here is calm, straightforward, and authoritative.** The effect is to **instill confidence** in the applicant and persuade the applicant that **with practice, success** is very much possible. I like the way **the instructions are given more than once in different ways**. Providing so much **hands-on practical information** is also helpful, like **tips about using subject headings and about exactly what a passing answer should contain and how it should look, including length. The instruction in this book is simply priceless.**

> —Prince C. Chambliss, Jr.
> President, Board of Law Examiners, Tennessee (former)
> Member, Evans Petree, Memphis, Tennessee (former)
> Author, *Prince of Peace: A Memoir of an African-American Attorney Who Came of Age in Birmingham During the Civil Rights Movement* (2010)
> Author, "Creating Compelling Defense Arguments and Strategies in Personal Injury Litigation," in *Representing Defendants in Personal Injury Cases: Leading Lawyers on Developing a Defense Strategy, Navigating the Discovery Process, and Litigating Disputes* (2011)

This book is excellent practice and guidance for the **California Performance Test, as well as the MPT**.

> —Travis Wise
> Practicing Attorney and California Bar Exam Expert
> Author, *The California Bar Exam Primer*

A NEW CLASSIC
PERFORM YOUR BEST ON THE BAR EXAM PERFORMANCE TEST (MPT)
TEACHES YOU HOW TO RAISE YOUR PERFORMANCE TEST SCORES AND ORGANIZE
YOUR LEGAL RESEARCH ON THE BAR EXAM, IN LAW SCHOOL, AND IN LAW PRACTICE

Successful bar candidates praise
Perform Your Best on the Bar Exam Performance Test (MPT)

The MPT-Matrix™ Method was incredibly helpful, and **I'd never seen anything like it before**.

—Alissa D. Rodriguez, Member, New York Bar

I learned Dr. Gallagher's performance test systems at her Multistate Performance Test Boot Camp, and not only did my practice Pennsylvania Performance Tests improve, but **my solid Pennsylvania Performance Test score helped me pass the Pennsylvania bar exam.**

—Joel Lazovitz, Villanova Law School, Passed Pennsylvania Bar Exam

Your method allowed me to focus on what was important and leave out what wasn't. You gave me the skills to outline and compile the information quickly and completely. **Your method gives the graders exactly what they want to see, in the way they want to see it. Thank you, thank you, thank you!!**

—Kelly Fowler, Passed Utah Bar Exam

I learned that **there is a real method for organizing this abundant material**.

—Gina Redrovan, Ecuadoran-trained attorney, Member, New York Bar

Now I can see **that if I follow this technique, I can gain points on the bar exam**.

—Maria-Fernanda Gallo, Member, New York Bar

Your materials refreshed my memory regarding the structure of briefs, memos, and letters. I also learned a lot about timing, and how much time to spend on reading, outlining, and so on.

—Maya Petrocelli, Member, Massachusetts and New York Bars

I took your MPT course as preparation for the New Hampshire bar exam, which contains two. I passed that exam. When I took the Vermont exam, which also features two MPTs, I took out my MPT materials and was able to get the old mojo back in no time—**the MPT-Matrix™ and indexing approach is really the key. I felt like I was heading in with at least one area totally under control.** Just received word that I passed Vermont as well!

—Merritt Schnipper, Passed New Hampshire and Vermont Bar Exams

PERFORM YOUR BEST ON THE BAR EXAM PERFORMANCE TEST (MPT):
How to Finish the MPT in 90 Minutes "Like a Sport™"

With 12 Actual MPT Tasks, Sample Answers,
Point Sheets, and Complete Analyses

2011 First Edition

A Time-Saving System for Organizing the Results of Legal Research and Succeeding on the Multistate Performance Test (MPT), and on the California and Other Performance Tests, as Well as in Law School and in Law Practice

Mary Campbell Gallagher, J.D., Ph.D.
With assistance from Christine Champey

BarWrite® Press
New York City

Copyright © 2004–2011 by Mary Campbell Gallagher. All content is protected by copyright. All rights are reserved and will be vigorously enforced.

BarWrite® Press
Post Office Box 1308
New York, NY 10028-0010 USA
Staff@BarWrite.com
www.BarWrite.com and www.PerformYourBestontheBarExamPerformanceTest.com

BarWrite® and BarWrite® Press are registered trademarks of Mary Campbell Gallagher & Co., Inc.

Copyright © 2004–2011 by Mary Campbell Gallagher

All rights reserved. No part of this book may be reproduced or transmitted in any form or by any means, electronic or mechanical, including photocopying, recording, or by any information storage and retrieval system, without permission in writing from the publisher.

Dr. Gallagher gratefully acknowledges the assistance of the National Conference of Bar Examiners, the copyright owner, in granting permission to reprint materials from past MPT examinations. Permission to use the NCBE's questions does not constitute an endorsement by NCBE or otherwise signify that NCBE has reviewed or approved any aspect of these materials or the company or individuals who distribute these materials. Materials that have been licensed by the NCBE included Multistate Performance Tests Copyright © 1998, 1999, 2000, 2002, 2003, 2008, 2009 by the National Conference of Bar Examiners. All rights reserved.

Cataloging-in-Publication Data

Gallagher, Mary Campbell.
Perform your best on the bar exam performance test (MPT): how to finish the MPT in 90 minutes "like a sport™": with 12 actual MPT tasks, sample answers, point sheets, and complete analyses/
Mary Campbell Gallagher, J.D., Ph.D.; with assistance from Christine Champey.
-- 1st ed.
p. cm.
ISBN-13: 978-0-9706088-3-3
ISBN-10: 0-9706088-3-7

1. Bar examinations--United States--Study guides. 2. Law--United States--Examinations--Study guides. I. Title.

KF303.G345 2011   340/.076
QBI11-600021
Printed in the United States of America

10 9 8 7 6 5 4 3

ATTENTION: UNIVERSITIES, LAW SCHOOLS, LAW FIRMS, AND PROFESSIONAL ORGANIZATIONS. Quantity discounts are available on bulk purchases of this book for educational purposes or as gifts. For information contact Staff@BarWrite.com.

Contents

Acknowledgments ix

Part I—Learning to Perform Your Best on the MPT

About the Multistate Performance Test 3
What This Book Does 4
Six Steps to Using This Book to Perform
    Your Best on a Performance Test 5
Special Tips for California Bar Candidates 8
Special Tips for Foreign-Trained Attorneys 8
Perform Your Best™ Chart of Past MPT Exams 10

Part II—Understanding the Bar Exam and Your Task on the MPT, with Templates for Main Formats

Introduction to the Bar Examination 13
The Multistate Performance Test
    as a Test of Professional Competence 15
Office Memoranda on the Multistate Performance Test 19
    MPT Template No. 1: Office Memorandum 19
Briefs and Memoranda for the Court
    on the Multistate Performance Test 29
    MPT Template No. 2: Brief or Formal Memorandum
        for the Court 29
Examples of Instructions for MPT Tasks Requiring a Brief
    or Persuasive Memorandum for the Court 39
How to Draft a Letter on the MPT 39
    MPT Template No. 3: Business Letter 41
Sample MPT Task and Office Memorandum for a Will 44
Other Tasks on the MPT 46
How to Use the Case Law in the Library 47
Ethical Considerations on the MPT 48

v

Part III—Applying the Four-Part *Perform Your Best*™ MPT-System™

Time and Organization on the MPT 53
The MPT-System™: Panoramic Overview 55
The MPT-System™: Step-by-Step Lessons 60
Sample *Perform Your Best*™ MPT-Matrix™ 61
I. Step One of the Four-Step *Perform Your Best*™ MPT-System™: Outline the Instructions in the Partner Memo 63
II. Step Two of the Four-Step *Perform Your Best*™ MPT-System™: Complete the MPT-Matrix™ 69
III. Step Three of the Four-Step *Perform Your Best*™ MPT-System™: Create the Work Product 73
IV. Step Four of the Four-Step *Perform Your Best*™ MPT-System™: Re-check Everything 75
Successful Performance Methods: *Perform Your Best*™ Checklist for the MPT 77
NCBE: General Instructions for All Questions 79

Part IV—MPT Tasks with Analyses and Sample Answers

Introduction 83
Perform Your Best™ Task Analysis Chart 84
Twelve Multistate Performance Test (MPT) Tasks
    and Materials from the NCBE, including
    Point Sheets 85

4A *In re Lisa Peel*, Objective memorandum 85
4B *In re Velocity Park*, Objective memorandum 95
4C *Vargas v. Monte*, Persuasive brief 105
4D *Arden Industries v. Freight Forwarders, Inc.*,
      Persuasive brief 115
4E *Ronald v. Department of Motor Vehicles*,
      Persuasive brief 125
4F *Phoenix Corporation v. Biogenesis, Inc.*,
      Objective memorandum 135
4G *In re Emily Dunn*, Will 145
4H *In re Franklin Construction Company*,
      Opinion letter to client 154
4I *In re Gardenton Board of Education*,
      Objective memorandum 164
4J *In re Steven Wallace*, Objective memorandum 171
4K *Kantor v. Bellows*,
      Persuasive letter to opposing counsel 179
4L *Franklin Asbestos Handling Regulations*,
      Persuasive and objective memorandum 188

Twelve *Perform Your Best*™ MPT-Matrixes™, Answers, and Analyses 200

4A *In re Lisa Peel*, Objective memorandum......................200
4B *In re Velocity Park*, Objective memorandum...............210
4C *Vargas v. Monte*, Persuasive brief................................218
4D *Arden Industries v. Freight Forwarders, Inc.*,
      Persuasive brief..226
4E *Ronald v. Department of Motor Vehicles*,
      Persuasive brief..235
4F *Phoenix Corporation v. Biogenesis, Inc.*,
      Objective memorandum..244
4G *In re Emily Dunn*, Will..253
4H *In re Franklin Construction Company*,
      Opinion letter to client..262
4I *In re Gardenton Board of Education*,
      Objective memorandum..272
4J *In re Steven Wallace*, Objective memorandum 282
4K *Kantor v. Bellows*,
      Persuasive letter to opposing counsel 291
4L *Franklin Asbestos Handling Regulations*,
      Persuasive and objective memorandum.................299

Part V—Conclusion.. 309

Part VI—Appendix 311

Acknowledgments

Writing this study guide for performance tests has taken several years, and many people have contributed invaluable help and advice along the way. I thank them all. Hundreds of generous students in the BarWrite® MPT Boot Camp and the BarWrite® 10-Day Coaching Group worked their way through the performance tasks and study materials in this book and cheerfully pointed out to me where they wanted more explanations or help. I hope I have responded fully.

My chief Teaching Assistant for the BarWrite® 10-Day Coaching Group, Christine Champey, discussed the outlines of the book with me over many months. Ms. Champey is a WonderWoman who can polish off an assignment and organize material faster than any other lawyer in New York City. She wrote the first drafts of the sections of the book concerning ethical considerations on the MPT and using case law on the MPT. Sarina Sigel was one of the first bar candidates to try out the *Perform Your Best™* MPT systems on her own bar exam papers, and her excelling on the MPT proved at a decisive early point that my MPT systems would really work under the pressure of the bar exam. For several years, Ms. Sigel then served with great good humor as my Teaching Assistant for the MPT. As I was finishing the book, Ms. Sigel again rose to the MPT challenge, and she made key suggestions for Part 4 of the book, in particular, for the twelve sections in which I analyze each MPT task. My assistant at the BarWrite® office, Candice Franklin, read vital sections and made invaluable suggestions. By happy chance, John Fasesky called from California out of the blue on Thanksgiving Day 2009, I picked up the ringing telephone even though it was a holiday, and he sounded so impressive that I immediately signed him on as an assistant. For nearly a year he did everything from critiquing draft chapters of the book to analyzing his own experience on the California Performance Test to researching webinar software.

Paul Immerman, a member of the New York bar and my longtime colleague in my own writers' group, kindly answered my call for editorial help as I worked on Part 3. Professor Angela M. Doss of the University of Arkansas Law School at Fayetteville made insightful suggestions as the manuscript neared completion, and she offered the kind of assistance every author wishes for by agreeing to test out chapters from the book with the students in her own legal research and writing classes. Professor Yvonne Twiss of Capital Law School in Columbus, Ohio, has been a clear-sighted supporter of my books ever since she first designed the exemplary bar-preparation program at Capital and included my study guide *Scoring High on Bar Exam Essays*. Without being asked, Elizabeth Dutertre applied the skills she'd long honed on the faculty of the Sorbonne, and she saved the book from many infelicities. Other generous academics and deans read and commented on a paper on the MPT that, under its director Mark A. Wojcik, I delivered at the Global Legal Skills V Conference in Monterey, Mexico, in February of 2010, and their comments have influenced the book. They were Mary Lu Bilek, Richard A. Matasar, Shelley Saltzman, Ronald Wright, and Kurt L. Schmoke.

Most important among all my acknowledgments, I owe heartfelt thanks to the late Bill Gehr, president of Legal Books Distributing in Los Angeles. Officially, Bill and his company served as our distributor. Without Bill's insights, efforts, and encouragement, however, neither this book nor its predecessor *Scoring High on Bar Exam Essays* might ever have appeared on bookstore shelves. Bill Gehr was unique in the publishing industry, and possibly in any other industry. He was a national treasure. He passed away, alas, just as this book was being finished. Wherever you are, Bill Gehr, Thank you, Bill Gehr!

Mary Campbell Gallagher, J.D., Ph.D.
New York, NY

Part I
Learning to Perform Your Best on the MPT

About the Multistate Performance Test

Performance tests on the bar examination ask bar candidates to perform a simulated law-office task with the skill of a first-year lawyer. They do not aim to test substantive knowledge of law, but rather to test the skills bar candidates will need to practice law, and thus they may test a wider range of skills than the bar exam essays. This book teaches an easy-to-learn, time-saving, system, the *Perform Your Best*™ **MPT-Matrix**™ **System,** that you can use to achieve a good score on any performance test. Our examples all come from the Multistate Performance Test (MPT), but you can use this system not only on the MPT, but on the California Performance Test (PT), or any other performance test.

The largest numbers of bar candidates currently taking any performance test take either the Multistate Performance Test (MPT) or the California Performance Test (PT). Some 35 jurisdictions now require candidates to take the 90-minute MPT, from which the examples in this book come. The MPT was developed by the National Conference of Bar Examiners (NCBE). As with the other performance tests, its aim is to test an applicant's ability to use fundamental lawyering skills in simulated law office situations. The California Performance Test (PT), historically the first performance test in the United States, allows bar candidates twice as long, three hours, to complete a task. A few other jurisdictions, including Pennsylvania, use their own performance tests.

The NCBE sends each jurisdiction that uses the MPT two 90-minute test items, either or both of which a jurisdiction may select to include as part of its bar examination.[1] When bar candidates, in turn, receive MPT test items on exam day, each item consists of a packet of law office materials and legal materials. The law office materials, called the "File," include a memorandum (the "task memo" or "Partner Memo") from the fictional supervising attorney who is assigning the task the bar candidate must perform. They may also include letters, transcripts of client interviews, or other documents. The Partner Memo is the most important single document in the MPT packet. The legal material, called the "Library," may include cases, hornbook material, statutes, rules, newspaper articles, and any other source in which a lawyer might find legal principles, and explications of legal principles, to use in completing the task.

Since the MPT is not a test of substantive law, the task can come from any area of law. The task can be a brief, a memo, a letter to a client or another attorney, a cause of action for submission to a court, a persuasive memorandum or a brief, a contract provision, a will, a proposal for settlement, a closing argument, or any other task. The chart at the end of Part 1 provides a summary of the types of tasks the MPT has used.[2]

The NCBE also gives jurisdictions administering the MPT a set of Point Sheets for each task. The Point Sheets are neither model answers nor explanations, but rather aids for grading the MPT.

How the MPT is Developed

The NCBE says that "the MPT is developed by a drafting committee that has had extensive experience in writing, editing, and grading performance test items." All MPTs are pretested, critiqued by independent experts, and reviewed by the boards of the states using the test before the drafting committee approves them.[3]

---

[1] NCBE, Jurisdictions Using the MPT in 2011, http://www.ncbex.org/multistate-tests/mpt/mpt-faqs/jurs1/

[2] All of the MPT tasks in this book are released by the National Board of Law Examiners (NCBE), and they are used here by permission of the NCBE.

[3] NCBE, Why NCBE Developed the MPT, http://www.ncbex.org/multistate-tests/mpt/mpt-faqs/why/. Note, however, that for jurisdictions that use the MPT as part of the new Uniform Bar Examination (UBE), grading of the MPT will be uniform. See Part 2 of this book regarding the Uniform Bar Examination.

Perform Your Best on the Bar Exam Performance Test (MPT)

What This Book Does

This book teaches an easy-to-learn, time-saving, system for excelling on any bar exam performance test, including the Multistate Performance Test (MPT), the California Performance Test (PT), and other performance tests. Illustrating its lessons with tasks that have appeared on the Multistate Performance Test (MPT), this book teaches a system, the *Perform Your Best*™ **MPT-Matrix**™ **System**, that you can use to achieve a good score. This system assures that you will focus on the single most important thing you need to do to score high on any performance test, namely, to discover the main issues in your task and understand and follow the instructions in the Partner Memo. The *Perform Your Best*™ MPT-Matrix™ System allows you to stay focused on the instructions in the Partner Memo, to keep control of your research and your time as you structure your work product, to present your work product so that it looks professional and so that your visual presentation helps the grader understand the logical structure of your work, and to complete your work efficiently within the time allowed.

This book provides sample formats you can use on the MPT for the major types of MPT tasks, namely, office memoranda, letters, briefs, and wills. It also refers you to instructions for types of tasks that have appeared on the MPT less frequently, so that you can become familiar with them before the bar exam. It teaches you a new rule for structuring legal documents, which we call the Rule of Three™. This rule will help you organize every MPT work product into parts. Finally, this book demonstrates ways to find touchstones for structuring your work product within the materials in the MPT task itself.

The systems you will learn here will help you even if the subject matter of the MPT you must complete is an area of law you have never seen before and, in fact, even if the type of task you must complete has never before appeared on the MPT.[4]

Here in **Part 1, Learning to Perform Your Best on the MPT**, this book gives you step-by-step instructions for training yourself to perform your best on the MPT.

The other parts of this book are as follows:

Part 2, Understanding the Bar Exam and Your Task on the MPT, places the MPT in the context of the bar exam. You learn formats and techniques for producing the major MPT work products;

Part 3, Applying the Four-Part *Perform Your Best*™ MPT-System™, teaches the four-part *Perform Your Best*™ MPT-System™, including the time-saving MPT-Matrix™. You learn to organize your research materials, organize your work product, and complete a high-scoring draft within the 90 minutes the MPT allows.

Part 4, Twelve MPT Tasks, includes twelve practice MPT Tasks, Sample Answers, Notes on Analyzing the Tasks, and MPT-Matrixes™, plus the NCBE Point Sheets. In Part 4 we give you:

    A. **Twelve (12) actual released MPT tasks.** These come from the National Conference of Bar Examiners and include the File and the Library;

---

[4] For how to outline a legal essay and structure a legal paragraph, consult the book by the same author called *Scoring High on Bar Exam Essays: In-depth Strategies and Essay-Writing Practice that Bar Review Courses Don't Offer, with 80 Full-Length Sample Essays*, 3rd ed. (2006).

B. A Sample *Perform Your Best* MPT-Matrix™ **for each MPT task**. This is the unique time-saving graphic display on which you will plot your research on easy-to-use map coordinates. The sample MPT-Matrix™ for each task shows how you will use the File and Library materials and how the parts of the MPT task fit together;

C. A sample *Perform Your Best*™ **answer for each MPT task**. This shows you what a finished work product might look like: this book does not just give you the NCBE Point Sheets, it gives you sample answers, too;

D. A *Perform Your Best* **note on how to analyze each task**. This analysis explains the MPT task and tells you how to perform your most important job, that is, how to understand and outline the instructions in the Partner Memo. It explains how to create your own MPT-Matrix™, as well as how to apply the Rule of Three, so that the structure of your work product will be clear to the grader and you will complete a higher-scoring answer; and

E. **The National Conference of Bar Examiners (NCBE) grader Point Sheets for each task**. These describe key points the graders may look for.

This book teaches systems for:

A. Managing time;
B. Managing research;
C. Organizing work;
D. Managing research notes and research threads.

Completing the tasks in this book and learning the systems this book teaches will not only prepare you to perform your best on the Multistate Performance Test, it will help prepare you for the masterful practice of law.

Six Steps to Using This Book to Perform Your Best on a Performance Test

In this book, you will learn a system for organizing and drafting a high-scoring MPT work product in 90 minutes. The time-saving *Perform Your Best*™ MPT-Matrix™ System that this book teaches is a system that I have taught, tested, and refined over a period of years in the BarWrite® MPT Boot Camps.[5] Learning this system will not just help you on the bar exam. When you learn to use the system this book teaches, you will become more competent in basic lawyering skills, and that will make it easier for you to meet the demands of practicing law.

This book helps prepare you both for the performance test and for the practice of law by teaching you how to organize and perform basic law office tasks under time pressure. It does not, let us be clear, teach you to achieve the highest level of lawyerly skill. The MPT simply does not call for the highest level

---

[5] In the BarWrite® MPT Boot Camps, bar candidates learn the systems this book teaches for analyzing the key types of MPT tasks, preparing the MPT-Matrix™, and completing MPT tasks on time. The Boot Camps provide abundant opportunity for practice and feedback. For information on all of the classes that BarWrite® offers to help law school graduates prepare for the bar exam, visit the BarWrite® web site, at http://www.BarWrite.com. You can also sign up there for free bar-study materials. To view the BarWrite® Blog, which provides tips for studying for the bar exam, visit http://www.BarWriteBlog.com.

Perform Your Best on the Bar Exam Performance Test (MPT)

of skill. The MPT tests only whether you can perform a law office task at the level of a first-year lawyer, and do it within 90 minutes. When you become a practicing lawyer you will find that it takes much more than 90 minutes to write a sophisticated legal brief. Just drafting the pointed issue statements for your briefs may take you and your colleagues hours or even days. Likewise, you will find as a practicing lawyer that writing an excellent legal memorandum requires a high degree of skill, and that it takes a lot of time. The same is true for writing excellent client letters, for crafting superb wills, and for producing well-drafted causes of action for submission to the court. Together with your law school legal writing courses, this book gives you solid training in the skills you will need in practice. Once you master these skills, you will have the confidence that comes from building on a firm foundation.

The *Perform Your Best*^{TM} system permits you to keep your research materials on one easy-to-access piece of paper, a time-saving graphic display called the MPT-Matrix™. In this book you will also learn how to decide on a clear and simple structure for your work product and then how to make sure that your underlined headings and your spacing of your paragraphs on every page show the grader visually what your organizing structure is.

YOU CAN TRAIN YOURSELF TO PRODUCE A LAWYERLIKE WORK PRODUCT. Many bar candidates will read this book outside a bar review course. With care and commitment, you can use this book to train yourself to produce a lawyerlike work product within the time limits of the Multistate Performance Test (MPT). Exercising a skill is its own reward. As your competence grows, you will increasingly enjoy performing the tasks on a performance test. Here is the SIX-STEP approach to training for the performance test that we suggest.

1. STUDY THE TABLE OF CONTENTS AND READ THE FIRST THREE PARTS OF THIS BOOK. First, study the Table of Contents to survey what this book offers and in what order. Then read the first three parts of this book to understand what the bar exam is, what the MPT is, where the MPT fits into the professional testing framework, the features all MPT tasks have in common, how to use the system this book teaches, and how this book is organized.

Every one of the twelve (12) task chapters in this book includes not only an actual MPT task released by the National Conference of Bar Examiners (NCBE), but also a *Perform Your Best*^{TM} sample answer showing you what an answer might look like, and a note on analyzing the task explaining how to outline and organize that particular MPT task. The time-saving MPT-Matrix™ for each task is a unique feature of the *Perform Your Best*^{TM} treatment of the MPT. It displays graphically how the parts of the File and the Library fit together for completion of the work product. This book also contains twelve (12) NCBE Point Sheets.

Many bar review courses treat the MPT in a cursory manner, giving bar candidates nothing but a few hints and some sample NCBE tasks and NCBE Point Sheets. While the NCBE Point Sheets are helpful for finding out what points the bar exam graders may look for, they are neither sample answers nor explanations of how to outline or analyze the MPT tasks. They do not show bar candidates how to outline the instructions in the Partner Memo or how to organize their answers. That is why for every MPT task, this book provides both a sample *Perform Your Best*^{TM} answer and a *Perform Your Best*^{TM} note on analyzing the task, as well as *Perform Your Best*^{TM} MPT-Matrix™. The NCBE has made some changes to the MPT over the years. Six of the tasks in this book are recent. With practice, most students will find them relatively manageable.

2. READ SLOWLY THROUGH PART 3, THE BASICS OF THE MPT SYSTEM^{TM}. Go back to Part 3 and focus on the basics of the *Perform Your Best*^{TM} MPT System^{TM}. Part 3 teaches you step-by-step how to use the MPT-System^{TM}, including the MPT-Matrix^{TM}. It also tells you how many minutes to spend on each part of the task. This MPT-System^{TM} is different from the systems you have used in law school or a law office. Learning it takes a little patience, but it saves so much time in the end that the effort is more than worthwhile. When you master this system you will not only have a tool you can use to complete the MPT task on time, and so increase your score on the performance test, you will also have skills that will enhance your performance in law practice.

What This Book Does

3. PRACTICE ACTUALLY DOING ONE MPT TASK, WITHOUT CONCERN FOR TIME LIMITS. Pick an MPT task to do. Read the instructions in the Partner Memorandum, go through the File and the Library, create the MPT-Matrix™, and write an answer. Do not concern yourself with time limits. Then look at the *Perform Your Best*™ sample answer and the *Perform Your Best*™ note on analyzing the task. See what the NCBE Point Sheets say about what the graders would give credit for on the task. Note how much longer you took than 90 minutes. Ask why that was.

4. PRACTICE WITH TIME LIMITS. Up until this point, you will have been working without regard to time limits. The reality of performance tests, however, is that staying within the time limits is essential to success. Because one of the greatest challenges on the MPT is managing the time, after you write that first MPT without time limits, you must start practicing within the time limits. You must hold yourself to the time limits Part 3 of this book teaches for accomplishing each part of the process, so that you learn how to finish the entire work product in 90 minutes. No fudging.

For example, observing the time limits in the four-part *Perform Your Best*™ MPT System™, spend 90 minutes reading and completing the MPT task called *In re Lisa Peel*, making the MPT-Matrix™. and drafting the work product. Stick strictly to the time limits. Compare your work with the sample answer. Read the note on analyzing the task. Study the MPT-Matrix™. This will train you in using the BarWrite® MPT-System. It will also introduce you to objective memo-writing, which is one of the principal types of MPT tasks. It will give you experience with common task-structures.

Practice with a stopwatch or a kitchen timer. From this point on, always stick to the time limits when you practice. If you do not finish part of your practice task within the time limit suggested for that part of the task in the four-part *Perform Your Best*™ MPT System™, put down your pen. Look at what you have finished, and compare it with what you ought to have finished. Cut out the unneeded words in your draft and look again. Learn from the experience. Do not assume that you will be able to write more concisely under the pressure of an exam. On the contrary, if you have not been strict in training yourself to write concisely, your old, wordy, habits will come roaring back under pressure.

5. SET YOURSELF A SCHEDULE FOR PRACTICING ADDITIONAL TASKS UNDER TIME LIMITS. To keep up your skills, you should do one practice performance test every week until the bar exam. Observing the time limits in the four-part *Perform Your Best*™ MPT System™ in Part 3, start from scratch and work through the recent MPT task called *Arden Industries v. Freight Forwarders*, and produce the work product, which is a brief. Then read the note on analyzing *Arden Industries*. Finally, study the sample brief for *Arden Industries* that this book provides and compare it with your draft. From working through *Arden Industries* you will learn how to stay on time in preparing a brief on the MPT, and how to organize and format your work for a lawyerlike persuasive work product.

The next week, again sticking to the time limits in the MPT System, produce the work product for another persuasive brief, *Vargas v. Monte*. By now you will have better control of your time, you will understand the constraints of a brief, you will know how to present your work product visually and, using the *Perform Your Best*™ MPT System™, you will be able to draft a good work product. Practice this way every week.

6. USE OTHER TASKS IN THIS BOOK FOR ADDITIONAL PRACTICE OF PARTICULAR MPT SKILLS. YOU MAY FOCUS ON OUTLINING MPT TASKS WITH MPT-MATRIXES™ OR COMPLETING MPT TASKS UNDER TIME LIMITS OR ANY OTHER SKILL. Depending on the level of skill you have achieved so far, you may choose to outline or draft more or fewer of the other MPT tasks in this book. This book will give you abundant opportunity to use your MPT skills on a variety of types of work products, either simply preparing the outlines or else completing the tasks in 90 minutes.

Perform Your Best on the Bar Exam Performance Test (MPT)

Special Tips for California Bar Candidates

This book teaches a unique system for developing the skills that any bar candidate needs to perform well on any performance test, plus ample practice exercises and explanations. The California Performance Test (PT) is a part of the California bar exam that poses a major challenge for many bar candidates. California bar candidates should use this book in addition to the PT materials their California bar review courses or supplemental PT courses provide. This book gives a California bar candidate skill-strengthening exercises and score-boosting analyses. California bar candidates who practice for the California Performance Test using this book in addition to their PT materials will develop and strengthen the skills they need to go into the California PT with confidence. No other book or course material equals the guided practice this book provides.

California bar candidates need to be aware that the chief differences between the Multistate Performance Test (MPT), from which this book draws its examples, and the California Performance Test (PT) are the time allowed and, at least in the past, the number of tasks to be completed within that time. The Multistate Performance Test usually allows 90 minutes for a bar candidates to complete legal research and submit a lawyerlike work product on one task. Whereas earlier PTs required bar candidates to complete two tasks or more in each full three-hour PT period, recently, the California PT has required bar candidates to complete only one task within each three-hour PT period. That task may, however, have more than one part. Thus, each part may resemble an MPT task. Watch for sub-parts.

Candidates for the California bar need to have a system for doing the California Performance Test, whatever the number of tasks they must complete in three hours. This book teaches a system that works for the PT, that is unique, that is easy to learn, and that saves time, and it provides the opportunity for abundant practice. It gives California bar candidates the opportunity they need to do guided practice in reading the instructions, and in exercising the skills of analysis, research, organization, visual presentation, and time management that the Performance Test calls for. Using the tasks in this book will strengthen the skills that are essential for any California bar candidate to perform well on the California Performance Test.

Special Tips for Foreign-Trained Attorneys

Whether you are taking the Multistate Performance Test (MPT), the California Performance Test (PT), or another performance test, if you are a foreign-trained attorney, you can profit from learning the skills that this book teaches and from the ample practice exercises and explanations this book provides. In my more than 20 years of preparing foreign-trained attorneys for the bar exam, I have found that foreign-trained bar candidates typically have excellent educations, and they often have abundant experience practicing law in their home countries. The special challenges for foreign-trained attorneys with performance tests, however, do not arise solely from the fact that performance tests require bar candidates to complete legal research and do legal analysis in a short time. Performance tests ask bar candidates to organize their work in terms of U.S. law office formats that foreign-trained lawyers may not yet have mastered, and they require bar candidates to use very concise language.

What are the formats for the common law office tasks? A foreign-trained attorney may have extensive legal experience in another country but little or no experience working in a law office in the United States. And even with study in a law school in the United States, he or she may not have enrolled in a legal writing course that explained differences among law office formats. This book solves the format problem for foreign-trained lawyers. It provides models and specific instructions for how to produce the performance test versions of the law office formats in most common use in the United States, including briefs, memoranda, letters, and wills.

The chief special challenge for foreign-trained attorneys, however, in my experience, is to adapt their writing style to U.S. expectations so as to meet the strict time limits of performance tests. Good legal writing in the United States sounds more like Hemingway than like Dickens or Proust. The sentences are typically short and to-the-point. Since the time limits on the performance test are tight even for bar candidates accustomed to crisp writing, they can spell catastrophe for bar candidates accustomed to producing literary prose, whether in English or in some other language. A professional interpreter once told me that to express the same idea in French and English typically requires one-third more words in French; likewise for numerous other languages. One-third more words? That could mean not finishing the assigned task at all, and serious trouble on a performance test. And even if English is a foreign-trained attorney's first language, styles of legal writing differ from one country to another, and the conciseness the performance test requires can still pose a challenge.

So if you are accustomed to using more words in legal writing than American legal English uses, beware! No matter how much law you have learned, and no matter how well you perform on the Multistate Bar Exam (MBE), the performance test will require new skills. Pay particular attention to the time limits this book suggests for completing each part of the performance test, especially for producing the draft work product. Train yourself to write one-quarter less than you are accustomed to writing. Practice, practice, practice. Practice with a stopwatch or a kitchen timer. Always stick to the time limits when you practice. If you do not finish a part of your practice task in time, put down your pen. Look at what you have finished, and compare it with what you ought to have finished. Cut out the unneeded words in your draft and look again. Learn from the experience. Do not assume that you will be able to write more concisely under the pressure of an exam. On the contrary, if you have not been strict in training yourself to write concisely, your old habits will come roaring back under pressure. Brevity on the performance test is truly, in the words of Polonius, the soul of wit.

One technique you can use each time you practice drafting a performance test work product is to compare your paragraphs with the paragraphs in the sample work product in this book. Then cut out the extra words in your own paragraphs. Count how many words you have cut. Have you used adjectives or adverbs you did not need? Have you used graceful circumlocutions where American legal writing would go straight to the point? Have you used the passive voice? The passive voice allows for digressions and vagueness. American legal writing prefers the active voice. Change passive to active.

Another technique you can use to train yourself to be concise, even when you are walking around or doing daily tasks, is to speak a sentence of legal prose, and then say the same thing again, but in fewer words, in American legal English. Become accustomed to brevity. Learn to prefer it. This will help you on the essay part of the bar exam as well as on the performance test.

You should use this book in addition to the MPT materials your bar review course provides or, if you are taking the California bar exam, in addition to the PT materials your California bar review course or supplemental PT course provides. This book gives you skill-strengthening exercises and score-boosting analyses. When you practice performance tests using this book, and when you develop your ability to manage the time, you will be strengthening the skills you need to go into any bar exam performance test with confidence and ultimately to become a more competent lawyer.

Perform Your Best on the Bar Exam Performance Test (MPT)

	Persuasive Brief	Objective Memo	Letter to Opposing Counsel	Opinion Letter	Closing Argument	Interro-gatories	Will	Cause of Action
PERFORM YOUR BEST™ CHART OF PAST MPT EXAMS								
July 2010	+	+						
Feb. 2010	++							
July 2009		+	+					
Feb. 2009		++						
July 2008		+						+
Feb. 2008		++						
July 2007	+	+						
Feb. 2007		+		+				
July 2006	+	+						
Feb. 2006	+	+						
July 2005	+			+				
Feb. 2005		++	+					
July 2004	+	+	+					
Feb. 2004	+	++						
July 2003	+	++						
Feb. 2003	+	+	+					
July 2002	+			+			+	
Feb. 2002			+	+	+			
July 2001	++	+						
Feb. 2001	++	+						
July 2000	+	+				+		
Feb. 2000	+	++						
July 1999		+	+				+	
Feb. 1999	+	++						
July 1998		+		+				
Feb. 1998	+	+						
July 1997	+			+				
Feb. 1997	+	+						

Note: Between February 1999 and February 2005, the NCBE offered three MPT tasks, rather than two. In the tasks for February 1999, February 2000, and July 2002, the persuasive arguments were to be included in a memorandum.

Chart © 2010 Mary Campbell Gallagher. All rights reserved.

Part II:

Understanding the Bar Exam and Your Task on the MPT, with Templates for Main Formats

Introduction to the Bar Examination

Every jurisdiction in the United States has its own court system, its own judiciary, and its own bar, that is, the body of attorneys admitted to practice before its highest court.[1] The legal profession has long believed that it has an obligation to the public, and that becoming a member of the bar should be a privilege for which candidates must demonstrate their competence. The courts may govern the process of admission to the bar, or the legislature may govern it, or both. In every state, however, there is now, as there always has been, a specified route for qualification, a rite of passage. In some manner, the candidate has to prove the requisite knowledge of the law, the skill, and the good character to deserve admission. In the days when most candidates for the bar learned law as clerks in the law offices of experienced practitioners, the rite of passage was simpler. Indeed, in his years as a successful private practitioner in Springfield, Illinois, Abraham Lincoln served the Illinois Bar by examining the qualifications of character of some of those who applied. Committees on character still play a role, but now, in addition, we have the bar examination.

Each state bar examination contains essay questions, usually testing the bar candidate on state law. The exam may also contain one or more of the following components: (1) the full-day computer-graded Multistate Bar Examination (MBE); (2) the Multistate Performance Test (MPT); and, in a few states, including New York, (3) an additional test on state law.

Essay questions are the foundation of the bar exam. While most state bar exams now include multiple-choice questions for ease of scoring, all state bar exams use essay questions to measure the candidate's ability to apply his legal knowledge in writing. An essay question can present a fact pattern like one a lawyer might encounter in actual practice. Writing a good essay answer requires mastery of law and the skills of issue analysis, application of law to facts, and deduction of logical conclusions. These are also chief among the legal, logical, and writing skills that a lawyer needs in practice.

Essay questions range from short paragraphs to the extended forty-five minute to one-hour questions of the New York and California bars. All essay questions, however, require mastery of law, application of law to facts, and the drawing of logical conclusions.

The most common subjects on the essay part of the state bar examination include, again, the six basic subjects that appear on the MBE: Contracts and Sales, Constitutional Law, Criminal Law and Procedure, Evidence, Real Property, and Torts. In addition, states frequently test on the staples of daily solo practice, particularly trusts and estates, and domestic relations. Although the law differs from state to state, the legal skills required to write the essays remain the same: knowledge of law, application of law to facts, and drawing of logical conclusions.

Most states make up their own essay questions. Since 1988, however, the NCBE has offered bar examiners the option of using a Multistate Essay Examination (MEE). More than 20 jurisdictions now utilize the MEE, which consists of 30-minute questions. For each administration of the examination, the NCBE makes nine questions available to state bar examiners, from which jurisdictions may select several to administer. States may grade the MEE according to laws of general application or according to state law.

Areas of law that may be tested on the MEE include the following: Business Associations (Agency and Partnership; Corporations and Limited Liability Companies), Conflict of Laws, Constitutional Law, Contracts, Criminal Law and Procedure, Evidence, Family Law, Federal Civil Procedure, Real Property, Torts, Trusts and Estates (Decedents' Estates; Trusts and Future

---

[1] An earlier version appeared in Mary Campbell Gallagher, *Scoring High on Bar Exam Essays: In-depth Strategies and Essay-Writing Practice that Bar Review Courses Don't Offer*, 3rd ed. (New York: BarWrite® Press, 2006).

Perform Your Best on the Bar Exam Performance Test (MPT)

Interests), and Uniform Commercial Code (Contracts; Negotiable Instruments (Commercial Paper); Secured Transactions). Some questions may include issues in more than one area of law.[2]

The Multistate Bar Examination ("MBE") is a national, computer-graded, multiple-choice examination component that comes from the National Conference of Bar Examiners (NCBE). Introduced in July 1972 in a few states, the MBE is now administered in all but two, Louisiana and Washington State.[3] The six subjects the MBE tests are Contracts and Sales, Constitutional Law, Criminal Law and Procedure, Evidence, Real Property, and Torts.

Originally introduced as a means of simplifying the examination-grading process with computer scoring, the MBE must test only on "majority rules," since it is administered in so many jurisdictions. It must somehow distinguish among candidates and create a range of final scores. There has accordingly been a progressive increase in the reading difficulty of the MBE questions.

The most recent addition to the NCBE's arsenal of tests is the Multistate Performance Test (MPT), now administered in more than 30 jurisdictions. The MPT is a simulated law office exercise. On the MPT, the bar candidate is provided with factual and research materials and must perform a law-office task within 90 minutes. The NCBE currently prepares two separate MPT tasks for each administration of the bar exam. States may choose to use one 90-minute task or both.

Examples of tasks the MPT may ask the bar candidate to perform include: a memorandum to a supervising attorney; a letter to a client; a persuasive memorandum or brief; a statement of facts; a contract provision; a will; a counseling plan; a proposal for settlement or agreement; a discovery plan; a witness examination plan; a closing argument.

Thanks to the NCBE's offering so many bar-examination components to the states, the bar examination is becoming increasingly national. Indeed, the NCBE is now offering state bar examiners a Uniform Bar Examination (UBE), consisting of the MBE, the MEE, and the MPT.[4] But local characteristics remain. Anyone who believes that television has leveled all regional differences in the United States has not been reading instructions to state bar applicants and essay questions for state bar examinations. Unlike the homogenized United States of the Multistate exams—commercial, rarefied, and so abstract that even the curriculum of a so-called national law school looks earthy by contrast—the world of state bar examination essay questions is down-to-earth. Shopkeepers, housewives, and ranchers abound. People own used-car lots in small towns and deal at the bank with their classmates from high school. Even local customs for taking the bar examination differ. While taking the California bar exam the author of this book was surrounded by San Diegans wearing shorts, T-shirts, and flip-flops. The rules in Virginia, by contrast, require candidates to appear for the examination dressed as if for an appearance in court: men in coat and tie, women in suits or dresses suitable for trying a case.

With a good knowledge of the law and good lawyering skills, whether learned in law school or in a bar review course, any candidate for the bar can pass the bar examination on the first attempt. The pass rates of first-time candidates for the state bar examinations in 2009, just to touch base with reality, ranged from a low of 67 percent in Wyoming to a high of 95 percent in South Dakota.[5] In most jurisdictions that administer the test twice yearly, the pass rate is higher in the summer than in the winter, partly because repeaters have a lower pass rate than first-time takers, and there are more repeaters in the winter.

Whatever the season, you can pass the bar exam.

---

[2] NCBE, MEE, http://www.ncbex.org/multistate-tests/mee/mee-faqs/description-of-the-mee/

[3] The information in this section comes from the *Comprehensive Guide to Bar Admission Requirements, 2009*, American Bar Association Section of Legal Education and Admissions to the Bar and the National Conference of Bar Examiners, http://www.ncbex.org/comprehensive-guide-to-bar-admissions/, and from the publications supplied to bar candidates in the various jurisdictions.

[4] NCBE, The Uniform Bar Examination (UBE), http://www.ncbex.org/multistate-tests/ube/.

[5] NCBE, Bar Examination Statistics, http://www.ncbex.org/bar-admissions/stats/.

The Multistate Performance Test as a Test of Professional Competence

Performance tests are the most recent additions to the bar examination. Unlike the essays and the Multistate Bar Exam (MBE), performance tests do not aim to test substantive knowledge of law, but rather to test the skills an attorney needs to practice law at the level of a first-year associate. As the NCBE says about the Multistate Performance Test (MPT), each test evaluates an applicant's ability to accomplish a task that a beginning lawyer should be able to do. Whether a bar candidate takes the MPT or some another performance test, the bar candidate's objective on a performance test is always to demonstrate basic first-year lawyering skills.

Performance tests aim to be realistic simulations of law-office tasks. The materials for each MPT include a File and a Library. The File consists of source documents containing all the facts of the case. Instructions for the assignment the bar candidate is to complete, in 90 minutes, are contained in a memorandum from a supervising attorney (the "Partner Memorandum" or "task memorandum"). The File may also include any kind of material that could be found in a law office file, transcripts of interviews, depositions, hearings or trials, letters or email correspondence, receipts, contracts, newspaper articles, medical records, police reports, and lawyers' notes. As in practice, not all of the facts presented are necessary, useful, or even accurate. As in practice, clients, witnesses, and even the supervising attorney may present incomplete or unreliable versions of the facts. The applicant must point out problems with the facts and in some cases indicate where additional helpful facts can be found. This is an aspect of the MPT that can cause bar candidates trouble if they are accustomed only to analyzing the law.

As in a law office, the Library contains cases, statutes, regulations, and rules, some of which may be irrelevant. The applicant is expected to extract from the Library the legal principles necessary to analyze the problem and perform the task. The legal fields are not limited to those on the bar exam essays or on the MBE. The library materials will always provide enough substantive information for finishing the task.[6]

Preparing well for the MPT means improving your lawyering skills, so in the end, the MPT can help make you a better lawyer. Unlike any other part of the bar exam, in addition, the MPT lets you add points on the bar exam without new knowledge of law. Thus, preparing well for the MPT can also give you easily-overlooked extra points and help you pass.

But be warned. On the MPT, reading the instructions carefully and managing time are key. If you misread the instructions, the performance test can be what causes you to fail the bar exam. You can make other mistakes on the MPT, too, and this book will help you avoid them, but the most serious possible mistake is misreading the instructions. On its web site, the NCBE gives a different analysis of which skills the MPT tests.[7]

---

[6] NCBE, Description of the MPT, http://ncbex.org/multistate-tests/mpt/mpt-faqs/description1/.

[7] NCBE, Skills Tested, http://www.ncbex.org/multistate-tests/mpt/mpt-faqs/skills-tested/.

What the Task of Writing the Multistate Performance Test Really Is

Your task on the Multistate Performance Test (MPT) is to act like a first-year lawyer. You are an associate in a law firm, or a junior attorney in a government agency, or a clerk to a judge. The senior lawyer who sends you an assignment in a task memo ("Partner Memo") on the MPT expects you to act like a junior lawyer drafting a work product.

Among the factors the bar examiners will look at in grading the Multistate Performance Test (MPT) are these. Did the bar candidate follow the instructions? Did the bar candidate understand the client's problem and the main legal issue in the case and try to resolve it? Did the bar candidate perform sound legal analysis? Use statutes and other legal resources competently? Spot and resolve ethical issues? Give the work product an orderly structure? Communicate clearly and appropriately? Manage the time?

Remember, your job on the MPT is to produce a draft, not a polished piece of writing. You do not have time for that. Make your motto, "Get in and get out." Trying to produce beautiful writing too often leads to long-winded, pretentious, writing, writing that will not favorably impress the grader. Trying to perfect each sentence or each paragraph of your work as you go along will make you waste your time, and time is your most precious asset on the MPT. *Get in and get out.*

Success on the MPT depends more than anything else on taking exquisite care to understand the instructions in the Partner Memo. Strangely enough, given the fact that you are under enormous time pressure, success on the MPT requires slowing down at the beginning. It means rereading the directions in the task memo several times. It means not plunging into the work until you have some idea of what legal issues the client's problem raises. It means thinking about what kinds of facts and law might help you solve the client's problem before you start looking for the facts and law in the File and Library.

Following the instructions in the task memo is so vital to success on the MPT that this book suggests that even after you have begun work, you should go back and read the directions in the task memo at least twice more. First, go back and read the directions in the Partner Memo again after you have prepared your outline and worked through the File and Library, but before you start to write the work product. That is to make sure you are on the right track. Then read the instructions in the Partner Memo one last time when you re-check everything in the final five minutes before you hand in your paper.

What Students Worry About Although They Do Not Need To

Producing A Lot of Writing

Your job is to produce a draft work product at the standard of a first-year lawyer. You have to try to solve the problem, and you have to finish what you start. You are not being paid by the word, like Charles Dickens. The bar examiners will not grade you on the number of pages you fill. *Get in and get out.*

Producing Polished Writing

Your job on the MPT is to produce a draft work product and finish it in 90 minutes. If you take the time to phrase your sentences beautifully, you may not finish on time. As my MPT teaching assistant Sarina Sigel rightly said, "The MPT will never be your best work." Learn to live with it. The most important things are to understand the task, follow the instructions, and finish the job. *Get in and get out.*

Making Sure You Have the Details Exactly Right

Your work product on the MPT is just a draft. It is not a law review article or a brief you will submit to the Supreme Court of the United States. You will inevitably make mistakes. Leave them, go on, and if you have time at the end, go back and correct them. Except in appellate briefs, do not concern yourself with citation form. Just name the case or the statute. Period. Push on, and finish. Once you have finished the task, you can go back, but not before then. *Get in and get out.*

Producing a Sophisticated Piece of Legal Analysis

The issues in MPT tasks tend to be straightforward, and the bar examiners will normally provide guidance within the File or the Library on how best to do the work. You are only a first-year lawyer. The task memo is asking you to prepare a draft that a first-year lawyer might prepare. The task memo is not asking you to demonstrate the most challenging level of legal work.

Using the Law You Learned in Law School

Far from expecting you to use the law you learned in law school, the drafters of the Multistate Performance Test tell you emphatically not to use the law you learned in law school. If you think you recognize a case in the MPT Library, be careful. The drafters may have changed that case. The MPT asks you to use the skills you learned in law school, but it does not normally ask you to apply specific rules of law you already know.

Impressing the Grader

If your ambition is to dazzle the graders with your work product on the MPT, you will inevitably be disappointed. The MPT is about following directions, managing time, and producing an organized, lawyerlike, draft that responds to the directions. Completing the MPT work product requires competence, not special gifts. The MPT does not allow the needed scope for brilliance. If you insist on aiming for brilliance, you will simply not have time to finish the job, and your grade will suffer.

Students' Most Frequent Challenges on Performance Tests, Especially Following the Directions and Managing Time

While the essays test on the law, and the MPT does not, and while the MPT may require gathering new facts, but the essays do not, both the essays and the MPT require legal analysis, and both have strict time limits. Bar candidates often face the same challenges on both. On either the essays or the MPT, bar candidates may have trouble reading and understanding the task, doing legal analysis, or managing time. This book teaches a system that enables bar candidates to overcome all of these challenges. Practice will make perfect.

Before even beginning to write, bar candidates may guarantee poor results if they don't take the time to understand the instructions in the Partner Memo and the specific problem the hypothetical client presents. Clearly, solving the client's problem is impossible when the bar candidate does not understand what the client's problem is. Resolving the legal question is impossible when the bar candidate has not tried to formulate the main issue.

The MPT system this book teaches makes you take more time than feels necessary to read and reread and understand the Partner Memo, which is the key document describing the client's problem, suggesting the legal issue, and assigning the task. Slow down at the start, to do a better job in the end.

Perform Your Best on the Bar Exam Performance Test (MPT)

Other challenges include being overwhelmed by the sheer amount of paper and the number of different sources and threads of research. Bar candidates may have difficulty organizing the task. The MPT task will provide a number of different documents in the File and a number of different statutes or cases in the Library. Your first hypothesis about the most important issue in the task may turn out to be wrong, which will mean you have a lot of ideas that you cannot use. This book teaches a system for keeping your notes on your research organized and in one place.

Bar candidates may be overwhelmed by the fact that they are being asked to solve a legal problem in an area of law they have never seen before. This book teaches systems for handling the task memo, doing the research, and organizing and writing the work product. These systems work, whether or not you have ever seen the area of law before.

Bar candidates may have trouble organizing the work product. This book teaches you to use law office formats to determine structure and organization. Using standard law office formats makes your work look professional. But the main benefit of using these formats is that it helps you to organize your thinking and your work product. If you know which format your MPT task requires, you will find it easier to structure your work. This book also teaches a guideline I use that I call the Rule of Three™. The number three is often key in speaking and writing. Everyone recalls learning in high school how to write three-paragraph essays. Student debaters learn how to "make three key points." Likewise, legal memoranda on the MPT normally have three main parts: Introduction, Discussion, and Conclusion. Legal briefs on the MPT normally have three main parts: Issues or Summary, Argument, and Conclusion. At least on the MPT, the Discussion part of a memo or the Argument part of a brief usually has its own three parts, as well. The MPT systems this book teaches help you show the grader that your work product has three parts, and that the main section of your work product in turn has the optimal two or three parts.

Bar candidates may also arrive at the bar exam still lacking certain basic lawyering skills. They may lack sufficient skill in basic legal analysis, that is, skill in applying case law and statutes to specific disputes. They may be unable to extract legal principles from statutes and cases and apply them systematically to new facts, rather than merely distinguishing cases from one another on the facts. Likewise, bar candidates may be careless about noting the jurisdiction or relative position in the court hierarchy of the court where a case was decided or about the date of each decision. Or they may be careless about noting differences among cases in which issues were presented. The MPT materials this book contains will provide abundant practice with not only answers but also explanations. Using this book, bar candidate can master the needed skills.

Bar candidates may not be accustomed to producing work products that are visually well organized. On the MPT, however, looks count. The graders may not award extra points for what your work looks like, but the appearance of your work will matter. Visual organization is key. "It's all in there" is not an excuse for organizational chaos. The grader must be able to see the divisions of your work product just by glancing at the pages. You should use section-headings, spaces between sections, numbers, and letters to indicate the parts of your work product. You must not only divide the work product appropriately, you must also demonstrate visually that your work product has those separate parts.

Finally, completing the MPT task on time is a challenge for everyone. Ninety minutes is not much time. For researching and writing a legal memorandum or a brief it is really very little time, even when, as on the MPT, the research materials are already packaged-up for you. The MPT allows no time for staring into space before starting, nor for experimenting with different research systems, nor for following and then abandoning false trails. On the bar exam, the candidate cannot waste time while working on the task but then make that time up by staying late at the office. When the MPT is over, the proctors will collect the papers, and the office will close its doors forever. Every minute counts. You need a good system, and you need to follow the system methodically. This book presents such a system.

Office Memoranda on the Multistate Performance Test

MPT Template No. 1: Office Memorandum

Piper, Morales & Singh
Attorneys at Law
One Dalton Place
West Keystone, Franklin 33322

<u>MEMORANDUM</u>

To: Bar Candidates

From: Mary Campbell Gallagher

Re: Scoring High on MPT Memorandum Tasks

Date: August 12, 2010

INTRODUCTION

The word "Introduction" is centered at the top of the section. You will write two or three sentences, setting out the partner's task assignment and briefly stating what you have accomplished and your conclusions.

DISCUSSION

The word "Discussion" is centered at the top of the section. You will divide the Discussion into two or three sections, following the directions in the task memo. Each section will have a powerful topic heading that uses both law and facts: *Because defendant claimed that his product that was actually made of colored water would cure acne, he may be liable for fraud.*

CONCLUSION

The word "Conclusion" is centered at the top of the final section. The Conclusion part of the memorandum summarizes what the task was and what the writer has accomplished. It presents the writer's conclusions.

Note. The word MEMORANDUM is centered at the top of the page, under the law office letterhead, and underlined. The heading is flush left and has "To," "From," "Re," and "Date."

An Objective Office Memorandum Considers Both Sides of the Question

This section teaches you how to write an office memorandum on the MPT. Every time the Partner Memo asks the bar candidate for a memorandum for that partner, the request is for an office memorandum. The MPT Partner Memo will indicate whether an MPT memorandum should be objective or persuasive. Every time the partner asks for information, or for considerations on both sides of the question, rather than just for arguments on one side, the partner is asking for an objective memorandum. The Partner Memo asking for an objective memorandum usually tells the bar candidate to "evaluate" or to "discuss" or to "analyze." *Write an objective memorandum analyzing whether or not the law applies to our client's case.* Thus, an objective memorandum will normally consider both sides of the question and take an on-the-one-hand/on-the-other-hand approach. To make sure the grader understands that you have grasped what kind of memorandum you are to write, the Introduction to your objective office memorandum should say, "You have asked me to write an objective memorandum." *Important warning:* Where the MPT assignment is to write an objective memorandum, the bar candidate who writes a persuasive argument will be penalized.

A Persuasive Office Memorandum Argues Only One Side of the Question

Where the Partner Memo tells the bar candidate to write an office memorandum that presents arguments, rather than just information, the partner is asking you to write a persuasive office memorandum. For example, the MPT Partner Memo may tell you to write a memorandum for the partner that presents the best arguments in favor of the client's case.

Where the MPT assignment is to write a persuasive memorandum, the bar candidate must argue only one side of the case. The candidate who writes an objective discussion, looking at both sides of the issue, saying on-the-one-hand/on-the-other-hand, will be penalized. You must make it entirely clear to the grader that your work product is either objective or persuasive. The best way, where appropriate, is to state plainly that your memorandum is either objective or persuasive. The Introduction to your persuasive office memorandum can say, "You have asked me to write a persuasive memorandum."

Whether objective or persuasive, office memoranda on the MPT should have the same format, that is, the MPT version of the traditional memorandum format that we have already demonstrated. But here is another key distinction. Be careful to distinguish persuasive office memoranda, on the one hand, from submissions to the court, on the other, including both briefs and memoranda in support of motions. This section of this book is about objective and persuasive office memoranda. The next section of this book is about briefs and memoranda for the court. The formats are different.

Every MPT Office Memorandum Must Display its Own Structure Visually

A lawyer's work product must always look professional. The MPT is a test of the bar candidate's ability to perform law-office tasks competently. Thus, on the bar examination, the task is not just to follow the instructions in the task memo, it is to demonstrate the skills of a first-year lawyer while making the fact of following those instructions so visually obvious that the grader knows just by flipping the pages that the bar candidate has followed instructions. If the partner tells the bar candidate to write a memorandum with three sections, it is not enough for the bar candidate to sit back and think quietly about three different subjects.

Does the Partner Memo say that the Memorandum must have three sections? That means the Discussion part of the MPT work product will have three sections that are both intellectually and visually entirely separate from each other. The three separate sections will be clearly distinct on the page. Each section will have its own persuasive heading, which is underlined, and each section will have a number at the start: Section 1, Section 2, Section 3. In order to display the structure of the work, the careful bar candidate will always number and letter the parts of the work product, leaving abundant white space in between sections.

The MPT is a visual exercise, not just an intellectual exercise. And consider this. Not only does labeling the parts make the work product look professional, it also helps the grader understand your reasoning, so it makes your paper easier to grade.

Using the Most Common Law Office Memorandum Format

Using the most common office memorandum format helps the bar candidate to organize the work and also makes the candidate's memorandum look professional. In the past, MPT tasks were emphatic about requiring correct memorandum format. Some recent MPT memorandum tasks, however, have instructed the bar candidate simply to write what a junior associate would send to the partner who had made the assignment. A bar candidate would be best advised, even with those more flexible instructions, to produce a work product that conforms to the most common law office memorandum format. Graders may not assign extra credit for it, but the traditional memo format looks professional on the page, and appearance is always important on the MPT. That professional-looking work product can only help the bar candidate's relationship with the grader, and it will make the paper easier to grade.

Most important, the most common memo format provides structure for the bar candidate's writing, and having a structure is always useful under time pressure. With the traditional memo format, the bar candidate knows what to write first, second, and third. Although a variety of memorandum formats are in common use in law offices, in all formats, the key sections of the memorandum normally follow the Rule of Three™. With minor variations, the memorandum has these three parts: Introduction, Discussion, and Conclusion.

Note that the format in use in a particular law office may or may not also have a section for Questions Presented and a section for Brief Answers, and it may or may not have a section for Facts, but on the MPT, a memo will usually have just an Introduction, a Discussion, and a Conclusion. Using that structure helps a bar candidate produce a well-organized work product that also looks good.

In the Introduction to the memorandum, a law office memo summarizes the problem to be solved and briefly suggests how the writer has resolved it. *You have asked me to evaluate whether our client has a cause of action in negligence. I have concluded that he probably does, but that further research is necessary.* In the Discussion, the memo takes up aspects of the problem one after another, in turn. In the Conclusion, the memo again states the problem and, based on the factors considered in the Discussion, it states how the writer comes out. *Having evaluated all of the facts in the file and the applicable law, I have concluded that our client may have a cause of action in negligence, and I have suggested further avenues for research.* Thus, the memo begins and ends with a summary paragraph, the Introduction at the beginning and the Conclusion at the end. In between, in the section called Discussion, the memorandum sets out the arguments from law and fact that lead the writer to the Conclusion. So the entire memorandum has three parts. The Discussion section itself often has three parts, as well.

At the end of this chapter is a section that teaches you step-by-step how to use the traditional memorandum format for the MPT.

Perform Your Best on the Bar Exam Performance Test (MPT)

The Logical Structure of the Discussion in the Memorandum

The Structure of the Discussion Part of the Memorandum Must be Clear and Follow the Instructions in the Partner Memo

The bar candidate must always choose a structure for the memorandum to the partner that responds to the instructions in the Partner Memo. The Partner Memo will always state clearly what the bar candidate must accomplish. The bar candidate must organize the content of the work product so that the reasoning of the memorandum makes conformity to the partner's instructions obvious. This chapter contains suggestions for organizing that content. Which topic should you discuss first? Which second? What is the appropriate order for presenting the material? Note that the MPT packet will normally contain one or more documents that help the bar candidate to organize the work product or that provide models to follow.

In deciding how to organize the Discussion, the bar candidate will usually choose from among the following methods of organization:

1. Order according to the conventions of legal analysis, e.g., statutory analysis.
2. If the Partner Memorandum stipulates an order, use the order stipulated.
3. If an Office Memorandum in the File stipulates an order, use that order.
4. If another document in the File requiring a response provides an order, you have the option of following that order.
5. Use the order in the applicable statute or case law.
6. Use logical order: threshold issues first; dispositive issues before other issues; more important issues before less important issues; alternative analyses last.

Normally you will choose from among the following patterns.

1. Order according to the conventions of legal analysis. If the task requires statutory analysis, for example, the memorandum will follow the conventional order for statutory analysis: the writer will take each part of the statute in turn, employ interpretations suggested by applicable cases, use external materials where necessary and permitted, and finally apply the statute to the facts of the case. The MPT task *In re Lisa Peel* requires interpretation of a statute, the Franklin Reporter Shield Act (FRSA). The Partner Memo directs the candidate:

> Please draft an objective memorandum for me analyzing whether we can use the Franklin Reporter Shield Act to move to quash Peel's subpoena.

Case law says that the burden of proving that the FRSA applies is on the party seeking its protection. The FRSA protects only reporters, so the first question in the bar candidate's memo must be whether the client, who is a blogger, qualifies as a reporter under the FRSA.

To define "reporter," the bar candidate will look first to the statute, dividing the first applicable code section into its component parts. Then the bar candidate will interpret those parts by using the cases and then, where necessary and permitted, by using such external sources as newspaper articles and dictionaries. Finally, the bar candidate will apply these authorities to the facts of the case. We demonstrate interpretation of a statute using case law and a newspaper article here:

> Under section 901(a) of the FRSA, a reporter is "any person regularly engaged in collecting, writing or editing news for publication through a news medium." In *Bellows*, where the court took up the similar question whether a photographer is a reporter under the FRSA, the court said that the key to whether a person is a reporter is the person's intent at the inception of news-gathering. According to *America Today*, some bloggers have press credentials. *America Today*, July 5, 2007.

In another variation on statutory analysis on the MPT, the File may contain a proposed code, rather than a statute currently in force. The partner's task memo tells the bar candidate to evaluate each section of the proposed code in turn. The bar candidate will take one code section at a time, employing other statutes, case law, and external sources, in the order listed above. This is the organizing principle in, for example, the MPT task in this book called *In re Gardenton Board of Education*.

2. If the Partner Memo stipulates an order, use the order stipulated. The Partner Memo may, for example, instruct the bar candidate to discuss two questions, one of which involves two sub-questions. The bar candidate must follow the structure the task memo dictates. For *In re Steven Wallace*, for example, the task memo gives two very specific instructions:

> First, analyze the legal and factual bases of the trustee's claim that the painting is an asset of the bankruptcy estate under the Bankruptcy Act and the Franklin Commercial Code (FCC).

> Second, for each of the four defenses under FCC § 2-326(3), discuss how the facts we already know support the defense, identify additional facts that might be helpful to us, state why they would be helpful, and indicate from what sources we might be able to obtain them.

These instructions require the bar candidate to handle the two main questions that counsel would have to answer, in the order that anyone would have to answer them. First, analyzing law and facts, is the painting an asset of the bankruptcy estate? Second, how could counsel put together a factual argument in support of each of the four statutory defenses?

3. If an Office Memorandum in the File stipulates an order, use that order. The Partner Memo may tell the bar candidate to organize the memorandum in accordance with the instructions in an Office Memorandum in the File. That second document will tell the bar candidate how to organize the work product.

4. If another document in the File requiring response provides an order, you have the option of using that order. A second document in the File may require a response. For example, the task may be to evaluate the arguments in opposing counsel's brief. The bar candidate

Perform Your Best on the Bar Exam Performance Test (MPT)

has the option of using the structure of that brief to outline the analysis in the work product. For example, in *Phoenix Corporation v. Biogenesis, Inc.*, the task memo states:

> Please prepare a memorandum evaluating the merits of Phoenix's argument for Amberg & Lewis's disqualification, bringing to bear the applicable legal authorities and the relevant facts as described to me by Ms. Ravel.

The bar candidate must examine Phoenix's brief and will probably decide to follow the same outline Phoenix uses, simply analyzing the arguments against each of the propositions Phoenix asserts. The first topic heading in the Phoenix brief states:

> This Court Should Disqualify Amberg & Lewis from Representing Biogenesis Because It Has Violated an Ethical Obligation Threatening Phoenix with Incurable Prejudice in Its Handling of Phoenix's Attorney-Client Privileged Document.

Thus, the bar candidate's memorandum will analyze the arguments, first, that Amberg & Lewis has not violated an ethical obligation and, second, that Amberg has not threatened Phoenix with incurable prejudice.

Note that in this case, the task is to write an analytic memorandum for the partner, not draft a brief for the court. The subject matter is the arguments in the other side's brief. Drafting a brief would be entirely different. See the explanation below of how to draft a brief or a persuasive memorandum for the court. In sophisticated law practice, incidentally, the brief for the appellant will not dictate the structure of the brief for appellee.

5. Use the order in the applicable statute or case law. The applicable statute or leading case may provide a list of options and, if so, it usually makes sense to evaluate the options in the order given. The instructions in the Partner Memo may, for example, tell the bar candidate to evaluate the client's options in light of a customer's anticipatory repudiation of a contract for the sale of goods. Under UCC 2-610, the client may:

(a) for a commercially reasonable time await performance by the repudiating party; or
(b) resort to any remedy for breach (Section 2-703 or Section 2-711), even though he has notified the repudiating party that he would await the latter's performance and has urged retraction; and
(c) in either case suspend his own performance or proceed in accordance with the provisions of this Article on the seller's right to identify goods to the contract notwithstanding breach or to salvage unfinished goods (Section 2-704).

The bar candidate would normally evaluate the client's options in the order of the subsections of UCC 2-610.

6. Use logical order. Threshold or dispositive issues first; or most important issues first. Normally, a memo or brief will treat threshold issues or dispositive issues, or most important issues, first, suggesting a conclusion for each question. The next following section may begin by assuming that that first conclusion is correct, and discussing the next most important question. The last section may begin with a contrary hypothesis, roughly as follows: "But if that is not the conclusion, ..."

The organizing principles just listed are common not only on the MPT but also in law practice. The purpose of the MPT is to test the bar candidate's ability to perform ordinary law office tasks. The MPT File and Library will normally provide material that will help the bar candidate decide how to organize the MPT task.

Office Memoranda on the Multistate Performance Test

Sample Instructions for Objective Office Memoranda on the MPT

Following are a number of instructions from Partner Memos for MPT tasks that appear in this book. In each one, the bar candidate must write an objective memorandum.

In re Lisa Peel

Please draft an objective memorandum for me analyzing whether we can use the Franklin Reporter Shield Act to move to quash Peel's subpoena.

You need not include a separate statement of facts, but be sure to use the facts in your analysis. Be sure to address both sides of the issue; that is, discuss any facts or law that may prevent Peel from claiming the protection of the FRSA.

Do not concern yourself with any First Amendment issues; another associate is researching those arguments.

In re Velocity Park

To help me advise [our client], please review his proposed waiver and prepare a memorandum:

- analyzing whether the proposed waiver will protect Velocity Park from liability for injuries occurring at the skate park;
- suggesting specific revisions to the proposed waiver, including replacement language as well as any changes in the waiver's design and layout (however, you should not redraft the entire waiver); and
- discussing whether any waiver will be enforceable if signed only by a minor.

Phoenix Corporation v. Biogenesis, Inc.

Please prepare a memorandum evaluating the merits of Phoenix's argument for Amberg & Lewis's disqualification, bringing to bear the applicable legal authorities and the relevant facts as described to me by Ms. Ravel. Do not draft a separate statement of facts, but instead use the facts as appropriate in conducting your evaluation.

In re Gardenton Board of Education

Please prepare a memorandum in which you evaluate the preamble and each of the guideline provisions in the draft of the communications code that Dr. Kantor left with me. Identify the legal issues that can give rise to constitutional challenges to each of the provisions and analyze whether each such provision is likely to be found legally permissible. Make suggestions for deleting, modifying, or adding any items in order to help the Board achieve its goal. Be sure to state your reasons for concluding that each guideline provision is legally permissible or impermissible, as well as the reasons for any suggestions you make. Support your reasons with appropriate discussion of the facts and law.

Perform Your Best on the Bar Exam Performance Test (MPT)

Instruction for a Persuasive Office Memorandum on the MPT

The instructions in the MPT task in this book called *Franklin Asbestos Handling Regulations* ask the bar candidate to draft a memorandum that answers two questions. Most MPT tasks are either persuasive or objective, but not both. This MPT task is unusual in that the memorandum must be both persuasive and objective. The part of your memorandum in which you respond to the first instruction will be persuasive, while the part in which you respond to the second will be objective. The Partner Memo says:

> Please prepare a memorandum for me that:
>
> States the best case for why, in light of the absence of a State Plan, the statutory and regulatory scheme is not preempted in its entirety; and
> Discusses whether each provision of Section 8 of the draft regulations can survive a preemption challenge.

How To Use the Most Common MPT Memorandum Format

A note to the reader. The following memorandum teaches you how to construct the variation of the standard law office memorandum format that has most commonly appeared on the MPT. This memo was written in 2006. Some recent MPT tasks from the National Conference of Bar Examiners have given the bar candidate more latitude with respect to format. For providing the bar candidate with the most useful structure, and for creating the most professional-looking work product, however, this book strongly recommends the format that this 2006 memorandum teaches.

Piper, Morales & Singh
Attorneys at Law
One Dalton Place
West Keystone, Franklin 33322

MEMORANDUM

To: Bar Candidates

From: Mary Campbell Gallagher, J.D., Ph.D.
        President, BarWrite®

Re: Scoring High on MPT Memorandum Tasks

Date: February 12, 2006

Office Memoranda on the Multistate Performance Test

INTRODUCTION

The Multistate Performance Test (MPT) allows bar candidates an extremely short time for researching and writing a memorandum, only ninety minutes. Accordingly, the MPT uses an abbreviated format. It does not usually ask the bar candidate to draft a statement of facts, to frame issues, or to write brief answers. The bar examiners emphasize, however, that using correct memo format is key.

DISCUSSION

As always on the MPT, the memorandum must fulfill the requirements stated in the Partner Memo and the candidate must finish on time. Even though the memo task on the MPT is abbreviated, however, it is vital for the bar candidate to show that he or she knows the correct format. Format is key.

At the top of the memo put in all capital letters, centered, printed and underlined: <u>MEMORANDUM</u>.

Flush with the lefthand margin list the following:

To: Pat Partner

From: Candidate

Re: Charles Client - Arbitration of Securities Claims

Date: February 12, 2006

In your Legal Writing Course, you probably learned a format for the body of the memo something like this:

A. Heading;
B. Issue(s);
C. Brief Answer;
D. Facts;
E. Discussion; and
F. Conclusion.

The MPT, by contrast, usually asks the candidate to use the following radically simplified format:

A. Introduction;
B. Discussion;
C. Conclusion.

In one MPT case called *In re Steven Wallace*, the partner memo asks for a two-part memorandum. What that means is that the Discussion will have two parts. The partner memo specifies what those two parts are. A three-part memorandum is more common. That is why I call it the Rule of Three™.

Perform Your Best on the Bar Exam Performance Test (MPT)

Some MPT point sheets indicate that the grading of a memo on the MPT stresses persuasive writing and correct format:

a. powerful topic headings,
b. persuasive writing,
c. argument from supportive law,
d. distinction of—or attack against—unfavorable law,
e. skillful use of the facts, and
f. careful use of the memo format.

Note, again, that the bar candidate is being graded on "careful use of the memo format."

Read the partner memo carefully for instructions about format. Nothing compels MPT tasks asking for memos to require identical formats. Accordingly, you must read the directions in the partner memo with your usual meticulous care. It is safe to say, however, that there is usually no section in a memo for a Statement of Facts, no section for Issues, no section for Brief Answers. The MPT is short, short, short.

Powerful topic headings are key. Writing a memo requires you to divide your discussion into legal questions and to give the applicable law before applying the law to the facts. Give each section of your Discussion a powerful topic heading. Underline your topic headings. For example: Under FCC sec. 2-326(3), Charles Client's strongest argument is that the contract he entered into with Bee Brokerage required "alternative dispute resolution."

Use the *Perform Your Best*[TM] techniques for writing your memo task. In drafting an MPT memo, you will leave the first page or the first two pages of your bluebook blank. Starting on the second page, you will write the Discussion first, then the Conclusion, forcefully summarizing your arguments in one or two sentences. Finally you will go back to the first page of your blue book and add the opening part of your Memorandum format, including the Introduction. See above.

Thus, the last thing you will write is the Introduction for the MPT memo, on the first page of the memo. You will have left the space for it in your bluebook. The reason for this order of operations is that at the beginning of your writing process, when you are starting to write the memo, you don't yet understand the project well enough to write a good Introduction. That is why you leave writing the Introduction until you are almost finished.

CONCLUSION

A bar candidate can give the bar examiners an MPT memo that will maximize his or her score. Again, the bar examiners have said they are looking for:

a. powerful topic headings,
b. persuasive writing,
c. argument from supportive law,
d. distinction of—or attack against—unfavorable law,
e. skillful use of the facts, and
f. careful use of the memo format.

Fulfill the directions in the Partner Memo, manage your time, and combine attention to these aspects of your work with careful attention to the *Perform Your Best* systems, and you can get a high score on an MPT objective memo task.

Briefs and Memoranda for the Court on the Multistate Performance Test

MPT Template No. 2:
Brief or Formal Memorandum for the Court

FRANKLIN DISTRICT COURT
Arden Industries v. Freight Forwarders

Arden Industries, Inc.,)
        Plaintiff,)
)
       v.)
)
Freight Forwarders, Inc.,)
        Defendant)
)
_____)

Case Number 02-CV-4081
Memorandum in Support
of Plaintiff's Motion for
Summary Judgment

STATEMENT OF FACTS

•

ARGUMENT

•

CONCLUSION

Note. The case caption has the name of the court centered at the top, along with the case name. The name of each part of the brief or memorandum for the court is capitalized and centered. This book gives you a number of sample briefs or memoranda for the court. This format summary reflects one of the MPT's most common formats for briefs or memoranda for the court. This MPT format contains the basic components, but it has fewer parts than the formats set out in the rules of the courts where you will practice.

The Format of Briefs on the MPT is Simplified: MPT Briefs Normally Have Three Parts

In law school, students learn how to format a complete appellate brief. That complete format includes some or all of the following:

Table of Contents
Table of Cases and Authorities
Statement of the Case (procedural history alone or combined with facts)
Issues on Appeal
Statement of Facts
Summary of Argument
Argument
Conclusion

The format for briefs or persuasive memoranda on the MPT will be simpler than the format you learned in law school. The simplest MPT brief has these parts:

Statement of Facts, with or without statement of jurisdictional basis
Argument with persuasive headings
Conclusion

Alternatively, the MPT may ask you to structure an appellate brief as follows:

Statement of the Case
Statement of Facts
Questions Presented
Argument
Conclusion

Writing a Brief on the MPT

Both a brief and a memorandum in support of a motion get submitted to the court or administrative agency. Both are court documents. They become part of the official record of the case. Accordingly, although court formats may vary, at the top of the first page of these court documents is a caption setting out the name of the court or other tribunal and the name of the case, the docket number and the nature of the document. On the MPT the terms "brief" and "memorandum in support of a motion" and "memorandum of points and authorities" are largely interchangeable. Note that occasionally the MPT may tell the bar candidate to submit a persuasive memorandum to an administrative agency without suggesting using the format for a brief. This book strongly recommends using the brief format even in those situations. The traditional format helps the bar candidate organize the work, and it looks more professional.

Either a Brief or a Persuasive Memorandum for the Court Argues Only One Side of the Case

This section of the book teaches you to use the format for MPT briefs and memoranda prepared for the court, rather than for a partner. These documents always argue only one side of the case. They use the brief format.

Counsel may submit a number of briefs or persuasive memoranda in the course of a litigation, whether civil or criminal, whether before a court or in an administrative agency. Litigation has pre-trial, trial, post-trial and, possibly, appellate phases. Once the complaint is filed, there may, for example, be a memorandum in support of a motion to dismiss, or a memorandum in support of a motion for summary judgment. At trial, there may be briefs or memoranda in support of motions to exclude or admit evidence, as well as in support of other motions, such as a motion for a judgment notwithstanding the verdict. Once judgment is rendered, there may be one or more briefs in support of post-trial motions. If the losing party takes an appeal, there will be appellate briefs.

On the MPT, the Partner Memo asking for a brief or persuasive memorandum for the court may, for example, ask the bar candidate to draft a brief or a persuasive memorandum for submission to the court in support of a motion for summary judgment.

Again, Every Work Product Must Present Its Structure Visually and Clearly

Every work product is both visual and verbal. As with other MPT tasks, the key in writing a brief is not just to follow the instructions in the Partner Memo, it is to make your following the instructions so *visually obvious* that the grader cannot possibly miss the fact that you have followed the instructions. If the partner tells the bar candidate to write a brief with three sections, you must not only think about the task as having three parts, you must also clearly number and label the sections of the memo you hand in, "1" and "2," and "3," leaving spaces between the sections, so that no bar exam grader could miss the fact that you have done *exactly* what the Partner Memo told you to do. The MPT is a visual exercise, not just an intellectual exercise. You should underline section headings. You should number and letter the parts of your work product.

Parts of the Brief: How to Write the Statement of Facts on the MPT

The first part of the simplified format for briefs on the MPT is often a Statement of Facts. Sometimes, however, the parties have entered into a Statement of Stipulated Facts. In such cases, the Partner Memorandum will tell you that the introductory section in the brief can be very short, and that you should direct the court's attention to the Statement of Stipulated Facts in the case file. On the other hand, sometimes the partner memorandum will tell you to include a full Statement of Facts. We discuss the full Statement of Facts in the next section.

How to Use a Stipulated Statement of Facts in Your Brief

Here is the text of a Partner Memo telling the bar candidate not to write a new Statement of Facts, but to refer instead to the parties' Stipulated Statement of Facts:

> Prepare the brief in accordance with the guidelines set forth in the attached office memorandum. We have a statement of stipulated facts in this case so, as pointed out in the brief writing guidelines, you should write only a short introductory statement that reminds the court of the nature of the dispute and our goals. In drafting your arguments, however, you must use all relevant facts that support your arguments.

Vargas v. Monte (MPT, July 2003).

Perform Your Best on the Bar Exam Performance Test (MPT)

In accordance with those instructions, the Statement of Facts in the sample work product for *Vargas v. Monte* in this book handles the Stipulated Facts as follows:

STATEMENT OF FACTS

During the period March 2000 to January 2002, defendant removed a total of 700 trees without permission from defendant's property, in an area close to the boundary of her own land. She removed trees both before and after being notified by the Department of the Interior that her logging was illegal. The history of the parties' titles and of the surveys conducted, together with the relevant facts, is set out in the Stipulated Facts and discussed below.

You will also use stipulated facts in writing your brief in another case in this book, *Ronald v. Department of Motor Vehicles*.

How to Write a Full Statement of Facts

"Omit needless words"
—William Strunk Jr. and E.B. White, *The Elements of Style*

Instead of telling you to refer to a statement of stipulated facts, the Partner Memo may instead tell you to draft a full Statement of Facts. Warning. You must be almost absurdly careful about managing time while writing statements of facts. You only have 90 minutes for the entire MPT, and writing the facts can be a huge time drain. Many a bar candidate has exhausted the entire 90 minutes of the MPT writing just a Statement of Facts, and has never completed the MPT task. Don't just jump in and start writing and hope the time will somehow take care of itself.

> **Strategies and Tactics.** Because candidates must complete the entire MPT task within 90 minutes, the wise bar candidate keeps a Statement of Facts as short as possible. One handwritten page of a bluebook is usually enough. The temptation is to let the hand start writing the facts and then lose control of time. Instead, decide in advance how many lines long the Statement of Facts will be and stick with that decision. Here is a trick. Before starting to write, mentally recite the facts to yourself in the shortest form possible. Make sure that your account omits needless words. Then just write down that short version of the facts.

Whether in a separate Statement of Facts or in the Argument, an advocate can often win a case with a skillful use of the facts. Accordingly, the bar candidate must marshal the evidence carefully and use the facts skillfully to make the client's case. Wherever you use the facts, whether in a Statement of Facts or in your Argument, your brief should emphasize favorable facts but also include vital unfavorable facts. As the MPT materials often say, the facts must be stated accurately, but emphasis is not improper.

In *Ronald v. Department of Motor Vehicles*, the Partner Memo says that the brief must argue that the officer lacked probable cause to arrest the firm's client. Here is how our sample work product emphasizes the favorable facts, but also includes unfavorable facts:

The officer conceded that petitioner violated no traffic laws. She left a restaurant where alcohol was served, at 1 a.m., "bar time," and as she drove along afterwards, she wove in her own lane and, as the officer conceded, she did not go over the line into the next lane.

Note that our sample brief includes vital unfavorable facts such as that the firm's client left a restaurant where alcohol was served at 1am, and that she wove in her own lane. It emphasizes, however, the favorable facts that she violated no traffic laws, and she did not go over the line into the next lane. In part, it does so by placing the most favorable fact first, that she violated no traffic laws. In part, it does so by stressing that the officer conceded the favorable facts.

A Statement of Facts should never contain either conclusions or arguments of law. Just the facts, please.

Parts of the Brief: How to Write the Argument on the MPT

The second part of the simplified format for a brief on the MPT is the Argument. The first paragraph of the Argument may be a summary that briefly sets out the issues and tells what action the party wants the court to take.

Headings in a brief are key: they display the architecture of counsel's argument. The section headings in your brief should state the conclusion that you argue in that section, using both law and facts: *Defendant's correspondence with Jones and the testimony of Smith show that defendant took active part in the conspiracy.*

The point sheets that the National Council of Bar Examiners provides for brief-writing tasks often stress the importance of clear, complete, argumentative, section headings.

Recall that one of your jobs is to make the MPT work product easy for the grader to read. How does the grader quickly discover what your argument is? By reading the argument headings. If the MPT File provides instructions for writing the argument section of a brief, it will invariably tell you to divide the argument into two or more parts, each with a strong, persuasive, heading.

Typical MPT brief-writing instructions state that the argument heading "should succinctly summarize the reasons the tribunal should take the position you are advocating." The heading must, that is, contain both law and facts: "A heading should be a specific application of a rule of law to the facts of the case and not a bare legal or factual conclusion or a statement of an abstract principle."

Here are typical examples of proper and improper argument headings, from an MPT task in this book, *Vargas v. Monte*. The first example is improper because it is conclusory. It includes no facts at all:

For example, improper:
THE UNDERLYING FACTS ESTABLISH PLAINTIFF'S CLAIM OF RIGHT.

The second example, by contrast, is proper because it succinctly states both a legal conclusion and the facts on which the conclusion rests:

Proper:
BY PLACING A CHAIN ACROSS THE DRIVEWAY AND BY REFUSING ACCESS TO OTHERS, PLAINTIFF HAS ESTABLISHED A CLAIM OF RIGHT.

Perform Your Best on the Bar Exam Performance Test (MPT)

> **Strategies and Tactics.** Clear argument headings using both law and facts are essential to getting a high grade on the MPT brief-writing task. Here is a trick. Write the paragraphs of your arguments first, leaving abundant white space above each argument, and then when you have finished the arguments, go back and insert the argument headings.

How to Use the Syllogism to Make the Arguments in Your Brief Persuasive

Above all else, an argument must be persuasive. An MPT Office Memorandum with instructions for writing a brief usually tells the bar candidate to "analyze applicable legal authority and persuasively argue how the facts and law support our client's position." This means stating the rule of law, with or without additional supporting rules. Next, applying the law to the facts. Finally, drawing a conclusion based on that law.

One way to master writing paragraphs that make a legal argument is to practice using the Under-Here-Therefore™ system of legal writing taught in *Scoring High on Bar Exam Essays*.[8]

The logical form is the syllogism:

> Under Illinois law, all men are mortal.
> Here, Socrates is a man.
> Therefore, Socrates is mortal.

Here is a paragraph written in response to instructions in the Partner Memo in the MPT task called *Vargas v. Monte*, in this book. It is written in the Under-Here-Therefore™ format.

> Under section 3346 of the Franklin Civil Code, a person is liable for trespass to timber "for wrongful injuries to trees, timber, or underwood upon the land of another, or removal thereof." Here, from March 2000 to January 2002, defendant Carla Monte cut and removed approximately 700 trees from a strip of land owned by plaintiff along the parties' shared boundary. As will be shown, defendant has no defense. Therefore, defendant's actions constituted trespass to timber.

Following is the Office Memorandum from the File for the MPT task *Vargas v. Monte*, stipulating how to write a brief with persuasive subject headings. Note that each argument heading should "succinctly summarize the reasons the tribunal should take the position you are advocating." It should be "a specific application of a rule of law to the facts of the case and not a bare legal or factual conclusion or a statement of an abstract principle."

---

[8] Mary Campbell Gallagher (New York: BarWrite Press, 2006) (3rd edition).

Norman & Longfellow
Attorneys at Law
405 East Gray, Suite 100
Lakeview, Franklin 33071

MEMORANDUM

September 8, 1995

To: All Lawyers
From: Litigation Supervisor
Subject: Persuasive Briefs

All persuasive briefs shall conform to the following guidelines:

All briefs shall include a Statement of Facts. The aim of the Statement of Facts is to persuade the tribunal that the facts support our client's position. The facts must be stated accurately, although emphasis is not improper. Select carefully the facts that are pertinent to the legal arguments. However, in a brief to a trial court, when there is a statement of stipulated facts, the Statement of Facts section of the brief may be abbreviated. In such cases, the lawyer need only write a short introductory statement and direct the court's attention to the statement of stipulated facts.

The firm follows the practice of breaking the argument into its major components and writing carefully crafted subject headings that illustrate the arguments they cover. Avoid writing briefs that contain only a single broad argument heading. The argument heading should succinctly summarize the reasons the tribunal should take the position you are advocating. A heading should be a specific application of a rule of law to the facts of the case and not a bare legal or factual conclusion or a statement of an abstract principle. For example, improper: THE UNDERLYING FACTS ESTABLISH PLAINTIFF'S CLAIM OF RIGHT. Proper: BY PLACING A CHAIN ACROSS THE DRIVEWAY AND BY REFUSING ACCESS TO OTHERS, PLAINTIFF HAS ESTABLISHED A CLAIM OF RIGHT.

The body of each argument should analyze applicable legal authority and persuasively argue how the facts and law support our client's position. Authority supportive of our client's position should be emphasized, but contrary authority should also generally be cited, addressed in the argument, and explained or distinguished. Do not reserve arguments for reply or supplemental briefing.

The lawyer need not prepare a table of contents, a table of cases, a summary of argument, or an index. These will be prepared, when required, after the draft is approved.

Perform Your Best on the Bar Exam Performance Test (MPT)

How to Organize the Argument Section in a Brief Using a Clear and Simple Structure That Responds to the Instructions in the Partner Memo

To be on the safe side in organizing your Argument section, stick with what this book calls the Rule of Three™. Although your argument will sometimes have two parts, normally it will have three parts. Often this will be two main parts, one of which has two sub-parts, making a total of three parts.

Here are the directions in the partner memo for the MPT task *Arden Industries v. Freight Forwarders, Inc*:

> I would like you to draft our brief in support of Arden's position that FFI has neither a security interest nor a carrier's lien in the printing press. In addition to making the affirmative arguments as to why FFI does not have a security interest or carrier's lien, be sure to refute the points made in the November 25, 2002, letter from FFI's attorneys.

You will immediately observe that these instructions reflect the Rule of Three™. There can be three topics in the brief: (1) defendant does not have a security interest; (2) defendant does not have a carrier's lien; and (3) defendant's attorneys' points are in error.

Principles of organization for writing briefs. Briefs and persuasive memoranda argue only one side of a case, whereas objective memoranda examine both sides of a question, but otherwise most of the principles of organization are the same for briefs and persuasive memoranda as for objective memoranda. See the earlier section in this book on Objective Memoranda. Where either task requires analyzing a statute, for example, the writer follows the conventions of legal analysis. That is, the writer starts by examining the statute, taking it apart into elements, then interprets the statute by using the cases in the order of the hierarchy of legal authority, then any non-legal materials, and then finally applies the statute to the facts of the case. Where there are a number of points in issue, to take another principle of organization, the writer may begin with the threshold issues, then any dispositive issues, then other issues in the order of the client's strongest arguments. See the discussion of organizational principles in the section in this book on objective memoranda.

A Partner Memo that assigns a brief-writing task on the Multistate Performance Test often indicates the organizing structure the bar candidate should use on the brief. Usually the Partner Memo tells the bar candidate to write a brief that argues several separate points. One point may be procedural, one substantive, and one evidentiary. Within each point, the bar candidate will structure the argument using one of the organizing principles noted above. The argument may be statutory, and it may apply case law, and it must apply the law to the facts of the client's case. The conclusion of each section must follow logically from the application of the law to the facts.

Briefs commonly make arguments within a framework of civil or criminal procedure, and they often argue the rules of evidence. In litigation, there will always be a framework of civil or criminal procedure and rules of evidence, including burden of proof at trial, and a standard of review in the appeals court.

We can see these principles at work in examples from the Multistate Performance Test. In *Ronald v. Department of Motor Vehicles*, in this book, the partner tells the bar candidate to write a persuasive memorandum arguing three points. The first point is legal, and the second and third points follow from the rules of evidence and procedure. In the MPT task memo, the partner tells the bar candidate to write a persuasive memorandum arguing that:

1. The police officer did not have reasonable suspicion to stop Ms. Ronald;
2. The administrative law judge cannot rely solely on the blood test report to find that Ms. Ronald was driving with a prohibited blood-alcohol concentration; and

3. In light of all the evidence, the DMV has not met its burden of proving by a preponderance of the evidence that Ms. Ronald was driving with a prohibited blood-alcohol concentration.

In *Arden Industries v. Freight Forwarding*, another MPT task in this book, the partner tells the bar candidate to draft a brief in support of their client Arden's position that defendant Freight Forwarding (FFI) has neither a security interest nor a carrier's lien in a certain printing press. The partner's instruction thus breaks the brief into two parts: (1) security interest and (2) carrier's lien. Each part will require interpretation of a statute and application of the statute and case law to the facts. The Partner Memo may appear to add a third part when the partner says, "in addition to making the affirmative arguments as to why FFI does not have a security interest or carrier's lien, be sure to refute the points made in the November 25, 2002, letter from FFI's attorneys." If one uses a three-part structure, the parts are as follows: security interest; carrier's lien; refutation of arguments of opposing counsel. Alternatively, "the points made in the November 25, 2002, letter from FFI's attorneys" can also be refuted in the course of making the two main arguments.

In *Vargas v. Monte*, the partner asks the bar candidate to draft a persuasive brief to the court addressing the liability and damages issues in a case alleging timber trespass. Again, that instruction breaks the brief into two parts: liability and damages. The partner says, "Our goals are to persuade the judge to hold Monte liable for timber trespass and award Vargas the maximum damages allowable by law based on the evidence, explaining why any lower measure of damages is inappropriate." As in *Arden Industries v. Freight Forwarding*, the partner tells the bar candidate to argue against the position of the other side "why any lower measure of damages is inappropriate." Thus, again, the MPT task memo may divide the brief into three parts. Let it be noted that writing the work product in *Vargas* requires interpreting a challenging statute, and that arranging the arguments in optimal order is not easy.

The MPT instructions typically tell the bar candidate not to reserve any arguments for a reply brief or for oral argument. The bar examiners want you to find and use all available arguments that respond to the instructions in the Partner Memo.

Choose a restrained tone of voice for a brief or persuasive memorandum. A brief or a memorandum in support of a motion is restrained and formal in format and tone. These formal court documents always use the third person: *the court, the plaintiff*. A memorandum to a partner, by contrast, although also formal, may use second and even first person: *You have asked me to find out; I have looked at the resources you suggested*.

Further Considerations in Drafting Briefs on the MPT. Remember that ethical considerations apply to persuasive writing. The MPT instructions caution bar candidates to cite unfavorable cases, that is, to cite contrary authority, and to address the arguments in the contrary authority, explaining or distinguishing it. These are ethical principles. Make sure that you not only act in accordance with ethical considerations, but that to the greatest possible extent you also point out plainly that you are acting in accordance with ethical constraints.

Avoid overstatement. A brief that uses emphatic words and strong adjectives belies a weak argument. Briefs are neither emotional nor theatrical. Overstatement may raise ethical issues. Counsel must craft an accurate and neutral presentation of the law and the facts, sufficient to persuade the tribunal and carry the argument. Likewise, counsel must avoid derogatory characterizations either of the opposing party or of opposing counsel and his conduct. Counsel may suggest that opposing counsel might accidentally have overlooked an unfavorable case, but counsel will only irritate the court and appear unprofessional by suggesting that opposing counsel is a liar who is vicious, insulting, and unethical.

37

Parts of the Brief: How to Write the Conclusion of a Brief on the MPT

The Conclusion is the third part of the simplified format for a brief on the MPT. It is another summary of the argument, like the opening paragraph. Be succinct, but do not neglect this final opportunity to argue your client's case. The Conclusion section should include the conclusion of each part of your brief. Here is the Conclusion for our sample brief in *Ronald v. Department of Motor Vehicles.*

CONCLUSION

For the foregoing reasons, petitioner asks the Court to vacate the suspension of her driver's license. The Department has failed to meet its burden of proving that petitioner drove with an impermissible blood-alcohol level by a preponderance of the evidence. The officer did not have a reasonable suspicion justifying his stopping petitioner's car. The blood-alcohol test on which the DMV relies is inadmissible in evidence and suspect. Testimonial evidence before this tribunal supports petitioner's account of events, while the officer's own account is compatible with hers.

Note that briefs always close with the same words: *For the foregoing reasons.* After those words, a brief should always close, as it opens, with a statement of the action the litigant asks to court to take: *petitioner asks the Court to vacate the suspension of her driver's license.* Or: *appellant asks this Court to reverse the judgment of the court below and remand the case.* Every brief is signed with the same words: *Respectfully submitted.* These words go in the signature block above the name of counsel of record. Note that an attorney never writes *Esquire* after his or her own name.

The following Conclusion and signature block come from the sample answer in this book for the MPT task *Vargas v. Monte.*

CONCLUSION

For the foregoing reasons, this Court should hold the defendant liable for trespass to plaintiff's trees. The Court should impose punitive treble damages for the taking of all the trees or, at the least, double damages for the earlier trees and treble damages for the trees defendant took after the Department of the Interior warned her that her conduct was illegal.

Respectfully Submitted,

Jane Norman
Attorney for Plaintiff
Norman & Longfellow
405 East Gray, Suite 100
Lakeview, Franklin 33071

Examples of Instructions for MPT Tasks Requiring a Brief or Persuasive Memorandum for the Court

Following are excerpts from the Partner Memo for MPT tasks requiring a brief or a persuasive memorandum for the court. All appear in this book.

Arden Industries v. Freight Forwarding

I would like you to draft our brief in support of Arden's position that FFI has neither a security interest nor a carrier's lien in the printing press. In addition to making the affirmative arguments as to why FFI does not have a security interest or carrier's lien, be sure to refute the points made in the November 25, 2002, letter from FFI's attorneys.

Follow the guidelines set forth in our office memo on persuasive briefs. However, aside from a very short introduction describing the dispute, do not write a separate Statement of Facts or a statement of Jurisdictional Basis inasmuch as the Stipulated Statement of Facts will be attached to the brief. You will, of course, need to incorporate the relevant facts into your legal arguments to make those arguments persuasive.

Vargas v. Monte

Please draft a persuasive brief to the court addressing the liability and damages issues outlined above. Our goals are to persuade the judge to hold Monte liable for timber trespass and award Vargas the maximum damages allowable by law based on the evidence, explaining why any lower measure of damages is inappropriate.

Prepare the brief in accordance with the guidelines set forth in the attached office memorandum.

For summaries of additional brief-writing tasks, visit the web site of the National Conference of Bar Examiners.[9]

How to Draft a Letter on the MPT

Unlike a memorandum, a business letter is always addressed to someone outside the law firm. It is always sent on firm letterhead.

The Partner Memo on the Multistate Performance Test may tell the bar candidate to draft a letter for the partner's signature. The partner may be writing a letter to another lawyer, perhaps

---

[9] Summaries of MPT tasks are arranged by date at http://www.ncbex.org/multistate-tests/mpt/

opposing counsel. Or the partner may be writing a letter to a non-lawyer, perhaps the firm's client. There is a specific traditional format for the inside address and the signature, which are explained below.

The bar exam graders may assign higher or lower grades depending on whether the bar candidate uses an appropriate style of communication or level of formality in a letter. The bar candidate must be careful to draft a letter for the partner's signature that is appropriate to the recipient. In writing to another lawyer, the partner will be both professional and cordial. Where the recipient is another lawyer, in addition, the partner may choose to cite cases and to use legal terminology. The partner will also be conscious that while cordiality is an aspect of professional courtesy, the letter cannot step over the line between professional courtesy and chumminess. Any document that might make it appear that the partner had too close a relationship with opposing counsel might be used later to support an allegation of conflict of interest.

When the partner is writing to the firm's client or to some other non-lawyer, courtesy is of course still to be expected. The partner will not, however, normally cite cases by name or use legal terminology. The partner will wish to demonstrate an empathetic understanding of the client's situation, and of the problems the client faces. Again, however, the partner will not wish to appear chummy. Professionalism requires not only empathy but also respect and restraint.

MPT Template No. 3: Business Letter

Mumble & Martin
5900 West Madison Street
Chicago, Illinois 60644

October 15, 2010

John Jones, Esquire
Jones and Whittier
5 West Irving Park Road
Chicago, Illinois 60613

Re: Smith v. Smith

Dear Mr. Jones:

    The first sentence or paragraph of the letter introduces the sender and explains the purpose of the letter.

Each section of the letter may have a persuasive section heading.

The conclusion of the letter typically suggests further action.

Yours very truly,

Pat Jones
Managing Partner

Perform Your Best on the Bar Exam Performance Test (MPT)

How to Use the Rule of Three™

Content and Organization of a Letter from the Partner

Body of the Letter. Like other presentations of fact or argument on the MPT, the letter will often have three sections. That is, it will follow what this book calls the Rule of Three™. The Partner Memo or an Office Memorandum in the MPT File may indicate the three main parts. For example, the Partner Memo in *In re Franklin Construction Company* tells the bar candidate to divide the opinion letter as follows:

> Follow the usual office format for opinion letters: (a) a short "Factual Statement"; (b) a "Short Answer" for each issue in which you state the essence of the opinion; and (c) an "Opinion" segment in which you state your conclusions and explain your reasoning, supported by the legal authorities.

In other cases, the letter will have an opening paragraph or sentence, a discussion, and a closing section. In a longer letter, the discussion may have three parts. It will always conform to the instructions in the Partner Memo.

If the MPT file includes an Office Memorandum specifying the format for the particular type of letter required in that task, the bar candidate will stick meticulously to the specified format.

The following rules apply where the MPT File does not provide specific instructions on how to organize the letter.

Opening Section of the Letter. Where the sender and the recipient are not acquainted and the recipient may not be expecting the letter, the opening paragraph or sentence will introduce the sender. *We represent James Jones, who is the former business associate of your client Henry Hobbs.* It will state the purpose of the letter, in accordance with the instructions in the Partner Memo. *Mr. Jones has asked us to seek an agreement with you on his behalf regarding disputed rights to the beachfront property Mr. Hobbs holds in San Diego, California.*

Even where the recipient and the sender are already acquainted, for example, where the recipient is a client, the opening paragraph will usually state the purpose of the letter and indicate the relevant facts. *You have asked our opinion on whether the Delta Music Corporation owes you additional royalties for your CD called "All About Airplanes." You have told us that Delta's accounting reports for your royalties have always failed to include sales of your CD on the internet. We have examined your contract with Delta in order to advise you.*

Discussion. In a longer letter the central part of the discussion may have three parts. These will respond to the instructions in the Partner Memo.

Final Paragraph or Sentence of the Letter. The final paragraph or sentence will usually summarize the content of the letter and suggest a next action. *We believe that we should seek a meeting with Delta's counsel to discuss this matter. Please call me at 415-665-6556 to talk about this possibility and the associated costs, and to discuss the alternatives.*

Typical MPT Partner Memo Instructions for a Letter to Opposing Counsel

Kantor v. Bellows

As the first step in the negotiation process, I want to send a letter to Shawn Martin that:

- argues that Linda is entitled to a share of Bill's enhanced earning capacity;
- addresses counter-arguments that would deny or diminish her share; and
- includes a specific dollar demand that is justified in light of these arguments.

Please draft such a letter for my signature. Be sure to discuss both the legal principles and the facts of our case in making the arguments. Shawn is a thoroughly competent family law practitioner and a straight-shooter. I have no hesitancy in honestly laying out my entire case.

Kantor v. Bellows is one of the MPT tasks in this book.

Typical MPT Partner Memo Instructions for an Opinion Letter Addressed to a Client

In re Franklin Construction Company

Please draft an opinion letter to Mr. Dirksen for my signature advising him on the following questions:

1. Is FCC obligated under either of its two contractual undertakings to pay either MDI or the Venture any part of the money demanded in the letter from MDI?
2. Is FCC obligated under the statutes and case law to pay either MDI or the Venture any part of the money demanded in the letter from MDI?
3. Does FCC have any obligation to undertake efforts to recover the money from the Boyceville Redevelopment Agency?

Follow the usual office format for opinion letters: (a) a short "Factual Statement"; (b) a "Short Answer" for each issue in which you state the essence of the opinion; and (c) an "Opinion" segment in which you state your conclusions and explain your reasoning, supported by the legal authorities. Mr. Dirksen is a sophisticated businessman but he is not a lawyer, so be sure to explain things fully and in language that a layperson can understand.

Perform Your Best on the Bar Exam Performance Test (MPT)

In re Franklin Construction Company is one of the MPT tasks in this book.

Drafting a business letter on the MPT requires the same skills of organization as drafting a memorandum or a brief. The bar candidate will gain extra points by demonstrating mastery of the level of language and the level of legal information that are appropriate to the recipient of the letter.

Sample MPT Task and Office Memorandum for a Will

On the next page is an MPT Office Memorandum setting out will-drafting guidelines, from the File for *In re Emily Dunn,* July 1999 Bar Exam, one of the MPT tasks in this book.

Sample Office Memorandum for Format of a Will

Reilly, Ingersol & Powell, PC

MEMORANDUM

September 8, 1995

To: All Attorneys
From: Robert Reilly
Re: Will Drafting Guidelines

Over the years, this firm has used a variety of formats in drafting wills. Effective immediately, all wills drafted for this firm should follow this format:

Introduction:
    A. Set forth the introductory clause with the name and domicile of the testator.
    B. Include an appropriate clause regarding the revocation of prior testamentary instruments.
    C. Include a clause describing the testator's immediate family (parents, sibling, spouse, children, and grandchildren).

Part ONE: Dispositive Clauses (to be set forth in separate subdivisions or subparagraphs by type of bequest or topic). Bequests should be set forth in the following order, as appropriate:
    A. Specific bequests
        1. Real property
        2. Tangible personal property
        3. Other specific bequests
        4. Any other clauses stating conditions that might affect the disposition of the real and tangible personal property
    B. General bequests
    C. Demonstrative bequests
    D. Residuary clauses

Part TWO: Definitional Clauses. Clauses relating to how words and phrases used in the will should be interpreted.

Part THREE: Boilerplate Clauses. These are clauses relating to the naming of fiduciaries and their administrative and management authority, tax clauses, attestation clauses, and self-proving will affidavits.

Perform Your Best on the Bar Exam Performance Test (MPT)

Other Tasks on the MPT

On the MPT, the bar examiners can test using any area of law. They will always provide you with all the materials you need, no matter which area of law is involved. There have been MPTs concerning, among other things, zoning laws, intellectual property rights, equal access to school athletic programs, and internet blogging.

When you see your MPT topic, remain calm. As Sarina Sigel, my former Teaching Assistant for the MPT, says, put on your game face. Be confident that in the MPT materials the examiners will provide everything you need to complete this portion of the exam. You do not need to arrive at the bar exam knowing anything about that area of law.

You can take precautions, however, so that you are in as strong a position as possible when you face the MPT. As we suggest in Part I of this book, you can complete and outline enough MPT tasks so that that you master the systems this book teaches. It is also wise to familiarize yourself with the general instructions for the MPT from the National Conference of Bar Examiners before you take the bar exam. The instructions can be found both at the end of Part 3 of this book and on the National Conference of Bar Examiners' website.[10]

Cause of Action for Fraud

You will find the summary of *Williams v. A-1 Automotive Center* (July 2008, MPT-2). an MPT task requiring the bar candidate to draft a cause of action (complaint) in a civil action for fraud, on the web site of the National Conference of Bar Examiners.[11] The Library in *Williams* contains three cases discussing the pleading requirements for a cause of action for fraud.

Closing Argument

You will find the summary of *Whitford v. Newberry Middle School District* (February 2002, MPT-3), an MPT task requiring the bar candidate to draft a closing argument, on the NCBE web site.[12]

Interrogatories

You will find the summary of *Pauling v. Del-Rey Wood Products Co.* (July 2000, MPT-1), an MPT task requiring the bar candidate to draft interrogatories, on the NCBE web site.[13]

---

[10] https://secure.ncbex.org/multistate-tests/mpt/MPT2011InformationBooklet/MPT_1B_2011_101110.pdf

[11] NCBE, 2008 MPT Summary, http://www.ncbex.org/multistate-tests/mpt/mpt-summaries/2008-mpt-summary/

[12] NCBE, 2002 MPT Summary, http://www.ncbex.org/multistate-tests/mpt/mpt-summaries/2002/

[13] NCBE, 2000 MPT Summary, http://www.ncbex.org/multistate-tests/mpt/mpt-summaries/2000/

Alternative Dispute Resolution Statement

You will find the summary of *Logan v. Rios* (February 2010, MPT-2), a Multistate Performance Test task in which the bar candidate had to draft an alternative dispute resolution statement, on the web site of the NCBE.[14]

How to Use the Case Law in the Library

In the Multistate Performance Test (MPT) the bar examiners aim to "evaluate your ability to handle a select number of *legal authorities* in the context of a factual problem involving a client."[15] Legal authorities on the MPT are usually of two kinds, statutes and cases. The MPT Library may also contain selections from hornbooks or official commentaries.

In working through the File and Library, you should read the statutes before the cases, since cases usually interpret statutes, rather than the other way around. Book brief the key statute. If there are elements, number them.

Next read through the File, and then survey the cases. Using the cases on the MPT is easier than doing case research in the real world. On the MPT, the Library component of the task materials gives you the only cases you will need. You cannot possibly miss an important case on the MPT. The bar examiners have given you the case law.

Note which jurisdictions the cases come from, which courts decided them, and when. Since the MPT might give you an area of law you have never studied, you must be especially careful in determining the weight of authority. You must be able to pull out the main facts, the rule of law, and the reasoning. You must know whether the case is mandatory or persuasive authority. You must know when the case was decided.

The examiners have not only created the fact pattern in the File, but they have also created the State of Franklin, all of its case law, and the fictitious Fifteenth Circuit of the United States, where Franklin is located. The examiners say that in Franklin, the trial court of general jurisdiction is the District Court, the intermediate appellate court is the Court of Appeal, and the highest court is the Supreme Court.[16] Do not confuse the hierarchy of courts in your own state with the hierarchy of courts in the state of Franklin. In the New York State Unified Court System, for example, the highest court is the Court of Appeals, while the New York Supreme Court is a trial court.

A word of warning. If you begin reading a case in the MPT Library and you notice that it resembles a case you already know, do not assume that the two cases are the same. It is not even fair to the writers to call this a trap, because they warned you in the MPT instructions that you should not assume that cases in the MPT are the same as cases you know. The case law in the MPT Library can be "real, modified, or written solely" for the purposes of the MPT task.

---

[14] NCBE, 2010 MPT Summary, http://www.ncbex.org/multistate-tests/mpt/mpt-summaries/2010-mpt-summary/

[15] NCBE, Instructions Page from the July 2004 Multistate Performance Test and Points Sheets (emphasis added). https://secure.ncbex.org/uploads/user_docrepos/JULY04MPT_010605.pdf

[16] NCBE, July 2004 Multistate Performance Test and Points Sheets, https://secure.ncbex.org/uploads/user_docrepos/JULY04MPT_010605.pdf at iii.

Perform Your Best on the Bar Exam Performance Test (MPT)

Decide on the weight of each case as authority. The two key words are mandatory and persuasive. The main factor that determines whether a case is mandatory or persuasive is which court authored the decision. You will recall that a decision from a higher court in the same jurisdiction is mandatory. It must be followed by the lower courts in that jurisdiction. Likewise, the federal constitution is mandatory law in every jurisdiction.

Decisions of courts in other states, of federal courts applying state statutes of other states, and of lower courts or courts on the same level in the same state, can be persuasive, but not mandatory. A federal or state court may choose to employ a decision as persuasive for any of a number of reasons, including factual similarity or compelling reasoning.

The year the case was decided is also important. If you have two cases that were decided by courts at the same level, read the earlier case first and then the later case. This allows you to see what the general law is and how subsequent cases have interpreted or modified the law. Also note that the MPT Library may not always present the cases in chronological order, so read carefully. Make sure to check on whether a case has been overruled. Unlike Westlaw or Lexis-Nexis, the MPT gives you no red or yellow flag to tell you that the case is no longer good law. The examiners do, however, give you enough information so that you can decide that for yourself.

Whether a case is mandatory or persuasive will dictate the weight of the authority. When you correctly utilize the authorities in accordance with their weight, you demonstrate to the graders that you understand the hierarchy of the law. You will use the case law appropriately in your work product.

Ethical Considerations on the MPT

Ethical considerations may arise in anything that we do as attorneys. The NCBE says that recognizing and resolving ethical dilemmas is tested on the MPT.[17] The relationship between attorney and client, between attorney and opposing counsel, between our families and the parties' families, our prior representation of parties in similar cases, our interests in fee disputes and in the interests at stake in the lawsuit, all are fertile ground for ethical issues on the bar examination. The MPT is a portion of the exam where you are practicing law in a fictional jurisdiction with simulated case law and statutes, but the basic ethical principles you must apply are universal. But note that as fast as the bar examiners put forth an ethical dilemma, they may also provide means for avoiding it or finding a remedy, for example, in the form of a statutory exception that alleviates a possible conflict of interest. Make sure to notice whether the Partner Memorandum mentions an ethical question. If so, take special care to spell out in detail how it will affect your work in aiding the client.

Whether or not the MPT materials include statutes or case law touching on the ethical issue you have noticed, to show the graders that you have recognized this ethical issue, it is important to state clearly, in a separately-labeled section, that there is a possible ethical issue. Explain what the issue is. Use the word "ethical." Make it unmistakably clear that you know you are confronting an ethical issue.

Discuss how the issue could be handled, suggesting what type of disclosure or other resolution is available. The ethical issue may be one where consent of the client suffices, leaving representation unaffected. Where receiving consent from the client will resolve the ethical issue, you must state that fact explicitly and then continue with the remainder of the MPT task.

---

[17] NCBE, Skills Tested, http://www.ncbex.org/multistate-tests/mpt/mpt-faqs/skills-tested/

Examples of Possible Ethical Issues

Conflict of interest. Examples include representing both husband and wife in a divorce proceeding, representing both the buyer and the seller in the sale of property, or representing someone who was an earlier adversary party in a previous transaction. If the present matter is the sale of land and the first matter was a contract for Client A to purchased widgets from Client B, the two transactions may not be materially related. However, if the present matter relates to the business between the two clients in regard to widgets and their business connection, the bar candidate may turn out to be privy to privileged information that could affect the continuing representation of Client A. You must clearly state the fact that there is an ethical issue, and why, and clearly indicate the best resolution.

Representation of Corporation or Its Employees. Your firm represents the corporation. During investigation or discovery, however, an interview with a current employee reveals wrongdoing by the corporation. Perhaps the way the corporation is managing its assets adversely affects the pensions of its employees. This may compromise the defense of that employee, meaning that the employee may have to seek independent representation. In your MPT work product, you must state that there is a question about the attorney's or firm's duty. Whom does it represent, the corporation or the employee?

Drafter versus Beneficiary of a Will. Beware of the attorney drafting the will who is also a beneficiary. This raises a presumption of a conflict of interest. Avoid it.

Attorney's Financial Interests in Conflict With Client's Interests. Cases commonly involve corporations. But students may also have heard about the criminal defendant without the means to pay a lawyer. In order for the attorney-client relationship to survive, that defendant agrees to allow the attorney to acquire all rights to his story and to produce a feature film on his alleged crime and the trial. It would be difficult for an attorney to represent the best interests of the client when the attorney has a financial stake in the legal matter. This raises a red flag. Make sure to describe the ethical issue explicitly and to state whether or not the conflict can be resolved.

Attorney's Ethical Obligations to the Court. Accuracy in both the law and the facts are ethical issues. The attorney drafting a brief must disclose adverse authority, clearly indicating any holdings that are against his position. He or she must also accurately present that adverse authority, neither minimizing its applicability nor over-stating it.

Examples of MPT Tasks Presenting Ethical Issues. *In Re Rose Kingsley* (February 2005, MPT-1) and *Parker v. Essex Productions* (July 2006, MPT-2).

Part III:

Applying the Four-Part *Perform Your Best*™ MPT-System™

Time and Organization on the MPT

The *Perform Your Best*™ MPT-System™ Aids Organization and Ends Legal Research Nightmares. On the bar exam, as in doing research in a law firm, you may become entangled in a research nightmare in which you discover increasing numbers of research paths to follow, you want to take notes, and as you do so, the amount of paper on your desk multiplies. Meanwhile, as in a law office, you may forget what problem you are trying to solve. When you remember what problem you are trying to solve, you cannot remember where you wrote down the notes you took on the research materials that you found earlier, notes that might lead you to the solution. You have piles of notes. You have written the same thing in several different places. But how do these pieces of paper fit together to produce a memorandum? Where are the notes you are looking for? When will you find the time to complete the project? The *Perform Your Best*™ Four-Step MPT System™ eliminates these legal research nightmares.

On the bar exam you will have only 90 minutes to complete the Multistate Performance Test (MPT) or three hours to complete the California Performance Test (PT).

Preparation is the key to confident, accurate, work on any performance test.

Pilots facing an emergency have seconds to react, but they know exactly what to do because they have practiced all of their emergency procedures so many times.

The *Perform Your Best*™ System teaches you exactly what to do on a performance test to produce a lawyerlike answer within the limited time allowed. This part of the book will teach you key procedures and walk you through specific examples.

If you take the time now to learn to use the *Perform Your Best*™ System, including the MPT-Matrix™, you will:

- Save an enormous amount of time on the performance test;
- Understand the issues and be responsive to the instructions in the Partner Memo;
- Create a solid MPT-Matrix™ that shows you how to organize your legal research materials quickly and confidently;
- Finish the performance test on time.

Once you have learned this system, you will be prepared for any performance test.

Seeing the Big Picture

The Multistate Performance Test (MPT) simulates the practice of law. It is therefore an appropriate component of the bar exam, whose purpose is to test whether or not a bar candidate is competent to practice law unsupervised. The MPT, however, allows you only 90 minutes in which to demonstrate your competence. You must therefore plan to work quickly and efficiently. The purpose of the MPT-System™ this book teaches is to help you organize your work, use your time efficiently, and finish your MPT task inside the 90 minutes allowed. Accordingly, one key component of the MPT-System™ is the time-saving MPT-Matrix™. The MPT-Matrix™ is a graphic display that is both a map of your research and a plan for writing your work product. Here in Part 3 we first give you a panoramic overview of the whole MPT-System™. Then we teach you step-by-step how to use the whole MPT-System™, including detailed directions for how to create the time-saving MPT-Matrix™.

Perform Your Best on the Bar Exam Performance Test (MPT)

The first item in the MPT packet is always the general directions from the National Conference of Bar Examiners (NCBE), and these have been the same for all MPT tasks. They explain that the task materials are divided into the File and the Library. The law office task the MPT asks you to perform may be to prepare an oral argument or to write a brief, or any other common task. The directions also inform you that 90 minutes are allowed for completion of the task. They suggest *allowing* at least 45 minutes for reading and outlining the work product. We reprint those instructions at the end of Part 3. Become familiar with them now, and then review them on exam day.

The File and the Library concern the specific MPT task. The File is a collection of documents from the fictitious law office. The most important document in the File and, indeed, in the entire packet, is the Partner Memo ("task memo," "supervisor memo"), a memo from a fictitious supervising attorney. It gives you instructions for completing the particular MPT task. Following these instructions meticulously is key to achieving a good grade on the performance test. The Library is a collection of legal authorities. It may include simulated hornbook materials, statutes, and case law. In sum, the MPT packet always contains the NCBE General Instructions and also: (1) the File, including the Partner Memo, and (2) the Library.

The *Perform Your Best*™ Four-Step MPT System™ addresses all of the challenges of the MPT, including the challenge of organizing research and finishing the work product in 90 minutes. Whether in a law office or on the MPT, organizing legal research is rarely easy.

The *Perform Your Best*™ MPT-System™ Meets the Time-Management Challenge. The MPT requires the bar candidate to demonstrate skills that are important for the practice of law. You must read carefully, follow directions, and organize well. For many bar candidates, however, the biggest challenge of the MPT is managing time. Many bar candidates don't know how long it takes them to do their work. They are totally flummoxed by having to finish an entire law office task, including doing the research and producing the work product, start to finish, in 90 minutes.

Finishing the MPT in 90 minutes is entirely possible, however. The *Perform Your Best*™ Four-Step MPT System™ assures that you can complete the task in 90 minutes:

1. You know how much time to spend on each part of the MPT task.
2. You can keep track of all research on one simple one-page MPT-Matrix™. You need not take extensive notes, so there is no risk of losing your research.
3. You need never read anything in the File or Library more than once.
4. You can keep control of your time and complete the job.

On the MPT, clarity of focus and efficiency are everything. Efficiency means that the MPT does not allow time for meditating on the case, for searching one's memory for similar situations, for writing long introductory sections, or for demonstrating extensive knowledge. The Panoramic Overview below shows you what the time-saving MPT-Matrix™ does. Then the Step-by-Step Lessons will give you detailed directions for creating and using it.

The MPT-System™: Panoramic Overview

The **MPT-Matrix™** is the central, time-saving, device in the *Perform Your Best*™ MPT-System™. To give a rapid overview of this process using a particular example, let us take *Ronald v. Department of Motor Vehicles*, one of the MPT tasks in this book. First, after reading the NCBE general instructions and surveying the Table of Contents, read the Partner Memo. The Partner Memo is the most important document in every task. You must read the instructions in the Partner Memo with exquisite care, take the instructions apart into their smallest pieces, and respond fully to each one. Your task here is to write a persuasive memorandum for submission to an administrative tribunal.

You will start by drawing a blank MPT-Matrix™. Turn your paper sideways, because you will probably need more columns than rows. Your MPT-Matrix™ will take up the whole page. You must draw the matrix by hand, on paper. The computer will not work for this task.

	A.	B.	C.	D.	E.	F.
1.						
2.						
3.						
4.						

Sample Blank MPT-Matrix™

The Partner Memo instructs you to draft a legal memorandum that will persuade the administrative law judge to vacate the suspension of your client's driver's license. The Partner Memo says that your client has already introduced evidence before the administrative tribunal to show that the DMV has failed to prove that her blood-alcohol level exceeded the permissible level. For many other tasks, you will have to tear the Partner Memo instructions apart into many separate topics. Here, however, the partner gives you only three straightforward instructions for what your memorandum must argue.

Down the lefthand column of the MPT-Matrix™ you will list the three instructions from the Partner Memo, giving each one a short name and a number. The Partner Memo instructs you to argue that:

1. The police officer did not have reasonable suspicion to stop Ms. Ronald;
2. The administrative law judge cannot rely solely on the blood test report to find that Ms. Ronald was driving with a prohibited blood-alcohol concentration; and
3. In light of all the evidence, the DMV has not met its burden of proving by a preponderance of the evidence that Ms. Ronald was driving with a prohibited blood-alcohol concentration.

Perform Your Best on the Bar Exam Performance Test (MPT)

Insert these three instructions as a numbered list in the lefthand column of your MPT-Matrix™.

	A.	B.	C.	D.	E.	F.	G.	H.
1. Officer had no reasonable suspicion to stop.								
2. DMV cannot rely on lab test report.								
3. DMV has failed to meet its burden of proof.								

Now write the names of the documents across the top of the MPT-Matrix™, using a capital letter for each one.

	A. Franklin Vehicle Code secs. 352, 353	B. Franklin Evidence Code secs. 1278, 1280, Franklin A.P.A. sec. 115, Franklin Code of Regulations sec. 121	C. Transcript of Administrative Hearing 2/23/09	D. Police Incident Report 12/19/08	E. Crime Lab Test Report 12/29/08	F. *Pratt v. DMV* (Franklin Ct. App. 2006)	G. *Schwartz v. DMV* (Franklin Ct. App. 1994)	H. *Rodriguez v. DMV* (Franklin Ct. App. 1994)
1. Officer had no reasonable suspicion to stop.								
2. DMV cannot rely on lab test report.								
3. DMV has failed to meet its burden of proof.								

The most important single thing you do in a performance task is to read the instructions in the Partner Memo with exquisite care. Normally you will have to tear apart each instruction in the Partner Memo into small pieces, and possibly tear apart a statute, as well. Study the Step-by-Step Lessons in the next section to learn how to do this. The instructions in *Ronald v. DMV* case are unusually straightforward.

Read the File and the Library, starting with the statutes. Now you are ready to read the File and the Library. Always read the statutes first. Cases usually interpret statutes, not the other way around. Except for taking the statutes first, you will read through the entire File and Library in the order in which the documents appear, starting with the File. You will read these materials only once. As you read along, you will underline each part you are going to use in responding to the instructions in the Partner Memo. Then on the MPT-Matrix™ you will note the page number of that information from the File and Library. You will put the page number of the material you are going to use in the MPT-Matrix™ at the intersection of the row for the instruction in the Partner Memo and the column for the document in the File or Library where the material appears. I call this action "indexing." For example, information that appears in the statutes on page P-6, and that you will use to argue that the police officer had no reasonable suspicion to stop your client, will go at the intersection of row 1 and column A. That information responds to the instruction in row 1, using the statute at column A. Thus, the map coordinates are 1-A.

Accordingly, part of the first section of your MPT-Matrix™ will look like this:

	A. Franklin Vehicle Code
1. Officer had no reasonable suspicion to stop.	P-6.

You will need to read through the entire File and Library only once, noting on the time-saving MPT-Matrix™ each place where you will use information to respond to the instructions in the Partner Memo. One of the beauties of the MPT-Matrix™ is that you need never copy the information from the File or Library into a separate note, or take any notes at all.

To illustrate indexing, here is a completed MPT-Matrix™ for *Ronald v. Department of Motor Vehicles*. In what follows, I explain the steps by which you will have noted the page numbers in each line.

	A. Franklin Vehicle Code secs. 352, 353	B. Franklin Evidence Code secs. 1278, 1280, Franklin A.P.A. sec. 115, Franklin Code of Regulations sec. 121	C. Transcript of Administrative Hearing 2/23/09	D. Police Incident Report 12/19/08	E. Crime Lab Test Report 12/29/08	F. *Pratt v. DMV* (Franklin Ct. App. 2006)	G. *Schwartz v. DMV* (Franklin Ct. App. 1994)	H. *Rodriguez v. DMV* (Franklin Ct. App. 1994)
1. Officer had no reasonable suspicion to stop.	P-6		P-2, P-3			P-8, P-9		
2. DMV cannot rely on lab test report.		P-6, P-7	P-2		P-5		P-10, P-11	
3. DMV has failed to meet its burden of proof.	P-6		P-2, P-3	P-4			P-10, P-11	P-13

57

Perform Your Best on the Bar Exam Performance Test (MPT)

What the MPT-Matrix™ shows. The first row of the MPT-Matrix™ indicates that as you were reading through the File and the Library, you noted that on page P-6 you found the Franklin statutes governing driving with a prohibited blood-alcohol percentage, related to reasonable suspicion to stop. On pages P-2 and P-3, you found the facts in the transcript of the administrative hearing relevant to whether or not your client drove with a prohibited blood-alcohol percentage. On pages P-8 and P-9, in the case called *Pratt v. DMV* (Franklin Ct.App. 2006), you found reference to *Terry v. Ohio* (U.S. 1968), establishing the standard for reasonable suspicion, which justifies police stops with less than probable cause. *Pratt* spells out the application of the reasonable suspicion standard to cases under Sections 352 and 253 of the Franklin Vehicle Code.

Map Coordinates. When you want to refer to the place on the MPT-Matrix™ where you noted a page number, you can use the map coordinates. That is, the number of the row, plus the letter of the column. The map coordinates for using the statute regarding driving with an impermissible blood-alcohol level to respond to the first instruction in the Partner Memo are 1-A. This is because you will respond to the instruction in row 1 by using information in column A.

At the same time that you were reading along, putting those page numbers into your MPT-Matrix™, you were also underlining the sections you intended to use for your work product, right where you found them in the documents in the File and the Library. You did not need to copy anything; you just underlined the words you wanted to use, taking care not to underline too many words. Next to that material, you noted the map coordinates in the margin. This is so you can spot the material quickly when you scan that page. I call this "cross-referencing."

To respond to the third instruction in the Partner Memo, for example, you used another section of the Franklin Vehicle Code that you found on page P-6 of the Library. You underlined the words you intended to use where you found them in the statute. In the margin next to that code section in the Library, you noted the map coordinates for the intersection of the row and the column on the MPT-Matrix™ where you have decided to use the material (3-A).

---

§ 353 Administrative suspension of license by Department of Motor Vehicles for prohibited blood-alcohol level on chemical testing

(a) Upon receipt by the Department of Motor Vehicles of a laboratory test report from any law enforcement agency attesting that a forensic alcohol analysis performed by chemical testing determined that a person's blood had 0.08 percent or more of alcohol while he or she was operating a motor vehicle, the Department of Motor Vehicles shall immediately suspend the license of such person to operate a motor vehicle for a period of one year.

(b) Any person may request an administrative hearing before an administrative law judge on the suspension of his or her license under this section. <u>At the administrative hearing, the Department of Motor Vehicles shall bear the burden of proving by a preponderance of the evidence that the person operated a motor vehicle when the person had 0.08 percent or more of alcohol in his or her blood.</u>   3-A.

How to use your time-saving MPT-Matrix™ to draft your memorandum. When you are ready to draft the persuasive memorandum the Partner Memo instructed you to prepare, you will first review the instructions in the Partner Memo again to make sure you are doing exactly what the partner told you to do. Next, you will refer to each row of your MPT-Matrix™, one row after the other. All your research is right in front of you. You have reduced the voluminous pages of the File and the Library to a single sheet of paper. You are not lost in a sea of copied-out material. To quote or refer to your research sources, you only have to go to the pages in the File or Library that you have noted in the MPT-Matrix™. When you look at each page of the File or Library you have noted, in the margin next to the material you intend to use you will have noted the map coordinates for that material in your MPT-Matrix™.

The map coordinates for using the information in the hearing transcript are 1-C, because you will be responding to the instruction in row 1 by using information in column C. The map coordinates for using the *Pratt* case are 1-F, because you will respond to the instruction in row 1 by using information in column F.

The three persuasive section headings in the sample answer in this book are as follows. Each part of the sample persuasive memorandum in this book responds to one of the instructions in the Partner Memo.

    I. The totality of the circumstances fails to provide a reasonable suspicion justifying the officer's stop of petitioner's vehicle.

    II. The blood test report does not satisfy the public records exception to the hearsay rule, and it cannot, by itself, support a finding of driving with a prohibited blood-alcohol level.

    III. The department of Motor Vehicles has not met its burden of proving by a preponderance of the evidence that petitioner was driving with a prohibited blood-alcohol concentration.

Overview

1. Draw the MPT-Matrix™. Use a whole page.
2. Read the NCBE instructions and survey the Table of Contents. Read the Partner Memo and list the instructions (or sub-topics) down the leftmost column, along with instructions from any second document the Partner Memo refers to, giving each instruction or sub-topic a number.
3. List names of the documents in the File and Library across the top of the MPT-Matrix™, and give each one a capital letter.
4. Read the statutes. Read the File and Library, underlining words you will use, noting map coordinates in the margin. (Cross-referencing)
5. Note page numbers of that material in the MPT-Matrix™, at the intersection of the row for the instruction or topic and the column for the document. (Indexing)
6. Review the instructions in the Partner Memo again. Write your work product, using the MPT-Matrix™ as your outline, taking the rows in order from top to bottom.
7. Review the instructions in the Partner Memo one final time, to be sure you are following the instructions. Make sure the format and tone of your work product are correct, and that you have handled ethical issues.
8. Submit Your Work Product.

The NCBE materials for the MPT task *Ronald v. Department of Motor Vehicles* appear in Part 4 of this book. So do the sample MPT-Matrix™, the sample answer, and the analysis of the task.

Perform Your Best on the Bar Exam Performance Test (MPT)

Note that in the MPT-Matrixes™ in Part 4 of this book, this book provides words as well as numbers. It is important to note that your own MPT-Matrixes™ will not contain words. You will use only page numbers in your own MPT-Matrixes™. This book presents both page numbers and words so you can see not only which pages in the File and Library you will use, but also which material you will underline.

For detailed instructions on using the time-saving MPT-Matrix™, read the Step-by-Step lessons in the next section.

The MPT-System™: Step-by-Step Lessons

The key device in the Four-Step MPT System™ is the time-saving MPT-Matrix™. To explain step-by-step how to use the MPT-Matrix™, let's start with a matrix that is not from the MPT and that requires only a simple grid. In the first diagram below, the leftmost column lists some of the rights in the Bill of Rights. Thus, each row in this matrix represents a right, e.g., the right to bear arms. Across the top row of this diagram are the names of constitutional amendments in the Bill of Rights, e.g., Fourth Amendment, Fifth Amendment. That is, the rows in this Matrix are rights, and the columns are amendments. At the intersection of the appropriate row and column there is an "X," indicating that a particular right appears in a particular constitutional amendment.

Example 1. Simple Matrix: Bill of Rights

	First Amendment	Second Amendment	Fourth Amendment	Fifth Amendment
Free exercise of religion	X			
Right to bear arms		X		
Limits on warrantless searches			X	
No forced self-incrimination				X

Legal research, as we all know, is rarely so straightforward. Normally, each research project requires work on a number of sub-topics, and a lawyer often collects many pages of research materials on each one. That's where the *Perform Your Best*™ MPT-Matrix™ is really helpful. Using the MPT-Matrix™ you need never be overwhelmed by your own research.

Sample *Perform Your Best*™ MPT- Matrix™

The MPT-Matrix™ is a map of legal research. To create the time-saving MPT-Matrix™ for legal research, you will enter a list of topics and sub-topics in the leftmost column and a list of documents in the top row. You are creating a grid for your research results. The topics and sub-topics will come from the instructions in the Partner Memo, from a statute, or from any other structuring document. Another structuring document might be an office memo in the File telling you how to structure a brief, or it might even be a code section with several parts. Give each of the topics or sub-topics a number as you list them in the leftmost column. Next, you will list names of the documents in the File and documents in the Library across the top row. You will give each document a capital letter. You are creating a matrix with map coordinates.

Next, you will put the page number of the research material that bears on each sub-topic in the cell at the intersection of the row representing the sub-topic and the column representing the document from the File or Library. We call this process **indexing**. When you are writing your work product, and you are ready to write about the application of research information to a particular sub-topic, you will simply go to the row with the research information you have listed for each sub-topic, moving from top to bottom in your MPT-Matrix™. The page number will be right there. As you read, you will also note your map coordinates in the margin on the pages of the File and Library. We call that second process **cross-referencing**.

The next sections of this book explain all of the steps in the MPT-System™ in detail. To describe these steps we use a limited technical vocabulary, such as "index" and "cross-reference," in a special sense. We explain all terms in what follows.

Example 2. *Perform Your Best*™ MPT-Matrix™: *In re Steven Wallace*, MPT, July 1999. Analyze the legal and factual bases of the trustee's claim that the painting is an asset of the bankruptcy estate under the Bankruptcy Act and the Franklin Commercial Code (FCC).

	A. Meeting	B. Receipt	C. *Walker on Bankruptcy* (hornbook)	D. Franklin Commercial Code	E. *First National Bank*	F. *In re Levy*
1. Legal basis under the Bankruptcy Act			7			
2. Factual basis under the Bankruptcy Act	2	4				
3. Legal basis under the Franklin Commercial Code				8	11	
4. Factual basis under the Franklin Commercial Code	2	4				

At-a-Glance: Summary of the Four-Part Perform Your Best™ MPT System™

I. **Step One. Outline. Five (5) minutes.** Refresh yourself on the general instructions from the NCBE, look at the Table of Contents, and skim the entire File and Library quickly to see what is there. **Outline the instructions in the Partner Memo and any other key document.** List topics down the leftmost column of your MPT-Matrix™ and number them.

II. **Step Two. Thirty-five (35) minutes. Complete the MPT-Matrix™.** Complete the framework of the *Perform Your Best* MPT-Matrix™ by noting the names of the documents in the File and the Library across the tops of the columns in the Matrix and giving each one a capital letter. Then fill in the MPT-Matrix™ by reading straight through the File and Library materials, starting with the statutes, entering page numbers of useful material at the intersection of the appropriate rows and columns in the MPT-Matrix™ (**indexing**). As you go along, you will also be noting those MPT-Matrix™ map coordinates in the margins of the File and Library next to the material you will use (**cross-referencing**).

III. **Step Three. Forty-five (45) minutes. Create the work product. Check again to make sure that you are following the directions in the Partner Memo and any other key documents.** Then write at least one sentence for each section of your work product. Finally, complete your work product.

IV. **Step Four. Five (5) minutes. Re-check everything. Check that the work product follows the instructions in the Partner Memo.** Check that the format and tone are correct, that you have dealt with all ethical issues, and that each part of the work product has a persuasive heading that is underlined. Proofread.

Reminder: Managing Time is Key on the MPT

TIME IS KEY. Since you have just 90 minutes in which to complete the MPT task, you must plan to move smartly along. The system this book teaches provides benchmarks for managing time. When you come to the end of the time allowed for each part of the task, stop. Time management is key on the MBE. Quality counts. But time is key, whether you like your work or not, because you must finish the job. Remember, you are writing a draft, not polished work.

Word to the Wise

You will never feel happy with your work on the MPT. The MPT will never be your best work.

—Sarina Sigel

I.
Step One of the Four-Step *Perform Your Best*™ MPT System™: Outline the Instructions in the Partner Memo

I. Step One. Outline. Five (5) minutes. Refresh yourself on the general instructions from the NCBE, look at the Table of Contents, and skim the entire File and Library quickly to see what is there. Outline the instructions in the Partner Memo and any other key document. List topics down the leftmost column of your MPT-Matrix™ and number them.

The Partner Memo is the most important document in the MPT packet. It provides the framework for the entire work product. When you first open the task packet, refresh yourself on the general instructions from the NCBE, look at the Table of Contents, and skim the entire File and Library quickly to see what is there. **Read and analyze the Partner Memo with exquisite care.** Take more time than you think necessary. Your grade depends on it. Later you should reread the instructions in the Partner Memo at least twice more. You should reread the instructions in the Partner Memo again before you start to write your work product. Finally, you should check the instructions in the Partner Memo one final time before you hand in your finished work product. Fulfilling the instructions in the Partner Memo is the key to success.

The first step in the MPT-System™ is to outline the instructions in the Partner Memo.

5 Minutes

I. Step One. Outline. Five minutes. First, refresh yourself on the general instructions from the NCBE, look at the Table of Contents, and skim the entire File and Library quickly to see what is there. Note on your scrap paper the kind of task you are being asked to complete; e.g., letter to client, objective memo, or brief. Note the parties and whom you represent. Note whether your client is the plaintiff or the defendant or some other party.

Next, outline the instructions in the Partner Memo and any other key document. "Outline" here means listing the topics and sub-topics, that is, the smallest parts of the instructions, vertically, in the leftmost column of the MPT-Matrix. It includes listing the smallest parts of any other key document, including a statute.

When you list items, make sure that you separate all of the smallest elements of the instructions out of the sentences in which the partner has given directions. If the Partner Memo asks for both legal and factual analyses, make "legal" one item, and "factual" a separate item, on a separate line. You will have a list of perhaps six to twelve separate items. If the instructions require analyzing part of a statute, take it apart, too.

- Take the instructions in the Partner Memo apart carefully.
- If the instructions require analyzing part of a statute, take the statute apart, too.
- You should have a list of six to twelve items in your outline.
- Be certain you know what the Partner Memo requires you to do.

Perform Your Best on the Bar Exam Performance Test (MPT)

The key to success on the MPT is understanding the issues in the case and following the instructions in the Partner Memo. This time-saving MPT-Matrix™ system means making a painstaking outline of the instructions in the Partner Memo, using both the smallest parts of the instructions in the Partner Memo and the key parts of any other key document, and following the instructions with care. The Partner Memo will often specify not merely separate tasks for you to accomplish but separate objectives within each task or separate aspects of each task. Do not rush over these distinctions. Give these little parts their own rows. List them down the lefthand column of the MPT-Matrix™.

> *Hint:* Turn your page sideways so that it is wider than it is high. In a very narrow column down the lefthand side of your outline page, note the separate smallest constituent parts of what the Partner Memo tells you to do (No. 1, above). Leave big spaces vertically. Assign a number to each row.

The Partner Memo for *In re Steven Wallace*, MPT, July 1999, tells the bar candidate to evaluate the legal and factual bases of the trustee's claim that a painting is an asset of the bankruptcy estate under the Bankruptcy Act and the Franklin Commercial Code (FCC).

1. Painting is an asset of bankruptcy estate.
    a. Under Bankruptcy Act
        i. Legal basis
        ii. Factual basis
    b. Under the Franklin Commercial Code
        i. Legal basis
        ii. Factual basis

Memo Items	A.	B.	C.
1. Bankruptcy Act: Legal basis			
2. Bankruptcy Act: Factual basis			
3. Franklin Commercial Code: Legal basis			
4. Franklin Commercial Code: Factual basis			

Do not expect to remember anything important from the Partner Memo without writing it down. *Write it down.* Do not write it down on another piece of paper. *Write it down on your outline* on your *Perform Your Best*™ MPT-Matrix™.

Another sort of instruction in a Partner Memo, from another MPT task:

> Give arguments why the statute is unconstitutional as written and make suggestions for redrafting it, stating both legal and factual reasons for your suggestions.

1. Step One of the Four-Step Perform Your Best™ MPT System™

This instruction is most emphatically not just asking one thing. Rather, it requires:

1. **Arguments** why statute is unconstitutional as written;
2. Suggestions for **redrafting**, stating both
   a. **Legal** and
   b. **Factual** reasons for your suggestions.

> *Word to the Wise*
>
> If you do not treat a topic or sub-topic as a separate item in your outline of the Partner Memo, you will not write about it separately in your work product. Accordingly, you will not get credit for handling it. Dissecting the Partner Memo with scrupulous care is essential to getting a good grade on the MPT.

Other documents. As you are outlining from the Partner Memo, read any other instructions or any other document that the Partner Memo refers to. Do so with similar exquisite care. If the Partner Memo indicates that another document contributes to the framework for your work product, add its parts to your outline. This other document may be a law firm memo, perhaps one setting out the format that the firm uses for wills. Or this key document may be a statute, perhaps, as in *Steven Wallace*, one setting out four defenses, each with four parts. Or it may be a letter from opposing counsel. Whatever that document is, take it apart just as carefully as you take apart the Partner Memo.

> *Word to the Wise*
>
> **BE NEAT. Leave yourself a lot of space in your MPT-Matrix™. Make sure your outline is legible.** If you cannot read your own outline while you are working, you will not be able to use it. Always leave abundant white space.

Perform Your Best on the Bar Exam Performance Test (MPT)

Example of Outline of Partner Memo Directions plus Additional Document

Partner Memo Plus Statute: *In re Steven Wallace* (MPT, July 1999)

Piper, Morales, & Singh
Attorneys at Law, One Dalton Place
West Keystone, Franklin 33322

MEMORANDUM

To: Applicant
From: Eva Morales
Date: July 27, 1999
Subject: Steven Wallace—Painting Titled "Hare Castle"

Steven Wallace, a long-time friend of mine, recently retired as Chair of the English Department at the University of Franklin to pursue full time what has until now been his avocation as an artist. He came in yesterday to get my advice and brought the documents I've included in the file. On reviewing the file, I can see that there are other facts we need in order to advise him properly.

About a year ago, Steven left one of his paintings, a canvas he had titled "Hare Castle," with Lottie Zelinka, an art dealer friend of his, with the understanding that she would try to sell it for him. Ms. Zelinka is the owner of Artists' Exchange, an art gallery here in West Keystone. Ten days or so ago, Ms. Zelinka returned the painting to Steven. A few days ago, he received a letter from Martin Feldner, a bankruptcy practitioner here in town. Mr. Feldner represents Charles Sims, the court-appointed Trustee in Bankruptcy. The letter advises Steven that Ms. Zelinka has filed for bankruptcy and demands that Steven turn "Hare Castle" over to the Trustee in Bankruptcy. Naturally, Steven is upset by this turn of events and wants to know how to respond.

Please draft for me a two-part memorandum:

First, analyze the legal and factual bases of the trustee's claim that the painting is an asset of the bankruptcy estate under the Bankruptcy Act and the Franklin Commercial Code (FCC).

Second, for each of the four defenses under FCC § 2-326(3), discuss how the facts we already know support the defense, identify additional facts that might be helpful to us, state why they would be helpful, and indicate from what sources we might be able to obtain them.

To prepare the outline for *In re Steven Wallace*, you will have to look not just at the instructions in the Partner Memo but also at the statute, FCC §2-326(3). You will find sub-topics in both places. Read and reread the instructions. How many sub-topics can you find?

The two key instructions come at the end of the Partner Memo:

> Please draft for me a two-part memorandum:
>
> First, analyze the legal and factual bases of the trustee's claim that the painting is an asset of the bankruptcy estate under the Bankruptcy Act and the Franklin Commercial Code (FCC).
>
> Second, for each of the four defenses under FCC § 2-326(3), discuss how the facts we already know support the defense, identify additional facts that might be helpful to us, state why they would be helpful, and indicate from what sources we might be able to obtain them.

1. Step One of the Four-Step Perform Your Best™ MPT System™

Here is the first instruction again, regarding the first part of the memorandum. This time, the sub-topics are in boldface type:

> First, analyze the **legal** and **factual bases** of the trustee's claim that the painting is an asset of the bankruptcy estate under the **Bankruptcy Act** and the **Franklin Commercial Code (FCC)**.

Turning those smallest parts or sub-topics into a list:

1. Painting is an asset of bankruptcy estate
   a. Under Bankruptcy Act
      i. Legal basis
      ii. Factual basis
   b. Under the Franklin Commercial Code
      i. Legal basis
      ii. Factual basis

As we have already noted above, this one sentence in the Partner Memo yields four (4) separate sub-topics. A bar candidate who neglects to analyze the instructions in the Partner Memo will sacrifice numerous points on the MPT.

Now, let's look at the second sentence of the instructions in the Partner Memo:

> Second, for each of the four defenses under FCC § 2-326(3), discuss how the facts we already know support the defense, identify additional facts that might be helpful to us, state why they would be helpful, and indicate from what sources we might be able to obtain them.

In order to prepare this part of the outline, you will have to look not just at the Partner Memo but also at the statute, FCC §2-326(3). If you look at the statute, you will find that there are indeed four defenses. But note that the instructions in the Partner Memo suggest that you may have to provide four points under each one of those defenses: (i) How the facts we know support the defense; (ii) Additional facts that might be helpful; (iii) Why they would be helpful; and (iv) From what sources we might be able to obtain them. Here are those directions from the Partner Memo with the smallest elements in boldface type:

> Second, for each of the **four defenses** under FCC § 2-326(3), discuss **how the facts we already know support the defense**, identify **additional facts that might be helpful** to us, state **why they would be helpful**, and indicate from **what sources** we might be able to obtain them.

Thus, under the Franklin Commercial Code, there are sixteen (16) possible topics:
   a. First defense: Compliance with sign law
      i. **How facts support**;
      ii. **Additional helpful facts**;
      iii. **Why helpful**;
      iv. **Possible sources**

b. **Second defense:** Creditors generally know person conducting the business to be substantially engaged in selling the goods of others.
   i. **How facts support;**
   ii. **Additional helpful facts;**
   iii. **Why helpful;**
   iv. **Possible sources**
c. **Third defense:** Complies with filing provisions of UCC Article 9.
   i. **How facts support;**
   ii. **Additional helpful facts;**
   iii. **Why helpful;**
   iv. **Possible sources**
d. **Fourth defense:** Person making delivery used or bought the goods delivered for personal, family, or household purposes.
   i. **How facts support;**
   ii. **Additional helpful facts;**
   iii. **Why helpful;**
   iv. **Possible sources**

In fact, when you do the *In re Steven Wallace* task, you will find that there are not really sixteen possibilities. It is unlikely, for example, that an artist who has just started exhibiting his work professionally has complied with the filing provisions of UCC Article 9. Nonetheless, *In re Steven Wallace* is an example of a common MPT pattern, in that one of the organizing documents that must form part of the framework for the work product is a statute, in this case, FCC §2-326(3). And that statute has many sub-parts.

In making an outline from a Partner Memo *plus* another document, the bar candidate should be careful to include all the required parts of that other document in the outline with the parts of the Partner Memo, taking care, again, to make sure that the directions have been broken into the smallest parts. For *In re Steven Wallace,* many of the possible responses to the Partner Memo's four questions about the defenses under the statute must appear in this outline.

Making an MPT-Matrix™ for any other MPT task is the same in principle as making an MPT-Matrix™ for *In re Steven Wallace.* The process is the same every time. You may conceivably be asked to complete an MPT task on the exam that is so straightforward as to make this painstaking process unnecessary. But how can you be sure the task is so straightforward unless you at least try to break the instructions down into their smallest parts? And no matter how straightforward the task is, success begins with painstakingly reading the instructions in the Partner Memo.

Step I. Outline What the Partner Memo Asks For:

i. Read the Partner Memo carefully at least twice;
ii. Break the instructions in the Partner Memo down into their smallest parts;
iii. Write each small topic or sub-topic on a separate line of the leftmost column of the MPT-Matrix™;
iv. Follow previous three steps with other organizing documents.

II.
Step Two of the Four-Step *Perform Your Best*™ MPT System™: Complete the MPT-Matrix™

II. **Step Two. Thirty-five (35) minutes. Complete the MPT-Matrix™.** Complete the framework of the *Perform Your Best* MPT-Matrix™ by noting the names of the documents in the File and the Library across the tops of the columns in the Matrix and giving each one a capital letter. Then fill in the MPT-Matrix™ by reading straight through the File and Library materials, starting with the statutes, entering page numbers of useful material at the intersection of the appropriate rows and columns in the MPT-Matrix™ (indexing). As you go along, you will also be noting those MPT-Matrix™ map coordinates in the margins of the File and the Library pages in your MPT packet (cross-referencing).

35 Minutes

II. **Step Two. Thirty-five (35) minutes.** Complete the framework of the time-saving MPT-Matrix™ by noting the names of the documents in the File and the Library across the tops of the columns in the MPT-Matrix™ and giving each one a capital letter. Remember that your paper should be turned sideways. You may need more than one piece of paper. You will use a number of columns, one for each document. You will not necessarily use every document in the File in your work product, but at this stage, you don't know that yet. Once you have completed the framework of your MPT-Matrix™, you are ready to start filling it in.

Fill in the MPT-Matrix™ by reading straight through the File and Library materials, starting with the statutes, entering page numbers at the intersection of the appropriate rows and columns in the MPT-Matrix™ (indexing). As you go along, you will also be noting those MPT-Matrix™ coordinates in the margins of the File and the Library pages in your MPT packet next to the material you will use (cross-referencing). By noting all of your research on one page, you avoid having to try to find notes you have copied from the File and the Library. By making a note of your map coordinates in the margin in the File and the Library next to the material you will use, you are assuring that you can find the material to use it when you need it. Once you have finished reading through the File and the Library indexing and cross-referencing at the same time, writing the work product will be easy.

(1) How to Index Your Research on the MPT-Matrix™

Indexing is entering page numbers of useful material at the intersection of the appropriate rows and columns in the MPT-Matrix™. As you read quickly through the File and the Library, note on your MPT-Matrix™ the page number from the File or Library of each item you are going to use in your work product. Write that page number in the column for that File or Library item, and in the same row as the topic from the Partner Memo to which it applies. The intersection of the column and the row in your MPT-Matrix™ give you map coordinates for that item.

Perform Your Best on the Bar Exam Performance Test (MPT)

Thus, suppose that the first item in the Partner Memo tells you to find the law on a given issue, and as you are reading through your MPT packet you find the law in item D of the Library, at page 10. You will note the number 10 at the intersection of the appropriate row and column. It will be in the column for Library-D and in the row for Partner Memo item number 1, which is "the Law." Your map coordinates are D-1:

	A File	B File	C Library	D Library
1. Law				10
2. Facts				

Suppose, again, that the instructions in the Partner Memo tell you to analyze the legal and factual bases of the trustee's claim that the painting is an asset of the bankruptcy estate under the Bankruptcy Act and the Franklin Commercial Code (FCC). Here, again, are the page numbers for the material noted in the appropriate rows and the columns.

Note that in the MPT-Matrixes™ in Part 4 of this book, there are words as well as numbers. Your own MPT-Matrixes™ will not contain words. They appear in this book only for illustrative purposes, to point you to the material you will have underlined in the File and the Library.

(2) How to Cross-Reference the Pages of the File and Library

Good **cross-referencing** is one key to success with complex MPT problems.

Cross-referencing is needed because when you start writing your work product, you will need to go from your MPT-Matrix™ back to the page you have indexed from your File or Library and use that material in your work product. You don't want to have to read the whole page over again to find the words you need. Accordingly, you must put something on that page in the File or Library to point you quickly to the material you are going to use. That is the purpose served by cross-referencing.

Cross-referencing works like this. While you are indexing the items in your left-hand column to the pages in the Library across the top row, writing a page number in the cell at the intersection of the appropriate row and column, you will also be underlining a few words that you want to use on that key page in the File or Library, and putting the appropriate map coordinates next to those words in the margin of your MPT booklet.

That's why you made the MPT-Matrix™ work like a map, with numbers down the leftmost column and letters across the top row. At the same time you are indexing to the MPT-Matrix™, you will be noting map coordinates in the margin next to the underlined words in the File or Library that point you to the material you want to use. That is cross-referencing.

To repeat, as you read your material you are both indexing and cross-referencing as you go along. You will index by placing a page number on the MPT-Matrix™. Meanwhile, on that page of the research materials in the MPT packet, you will also have cross-referenced by underlining the material you are going to use and writing the map coordinates in the margin of your MPT booklet. Everything in your File and Library will be both indexed and cross-referenced.

At the end of this step, your MPT-Matrix™ will be indexed to your Library and File, on the one hand and, on the other, your File and Library will also be entirely cross-referenced to your MPT-Matrix™.

Thus, when you start writing your work product, applying the next part of the MPT System™, you will be working row-by-row from the top of your columns on the MPT-Matrix™ to the bottom, using the research material indexed in each column as you write out your work product. You can easily check back in the MPT task booklet to get the exact words when you need them, because your research is both indexed and cross-referenced.

70

2. Step Two of the Four-Step Perform Your Best™ MPT System™

Some Rules for Reading, Indexing, and Cross-Referencing

- When you read the Library, always read statutes first.
- Bookbrief the elements of key statutes.
- Work through your File and Library materials just once, indexing and cross-referencing as you move along.
- Resist the temptation to work inefficiently.

When you read the Library, always read statutes first. If there is a key statute in the Library, take care to read and understand it first, before you read the cases. Likewise, if a court case quotes an important statute that is not provided to you anywhere else, read it as soon as you can, carefully. Cases usually interpret statutes, not the other way around. Understanding the statutes takes precedence over understanding the cases.

In the case *In re Steven Wallace*, for example, the statutes are the Bankruptcy Act and the Franklin Commercial Code. The Partner Memo assignment requires analysis of both the Bankruptcy Act and the Franklin Commercial Code. You will read those statutes first.

Bookbrief the elements of key statutes. If you are going to apply a key statute, you will apply it one element at a time, using the *Under-Here-Therefore*™ system for legal writing.[1] Accordingly, you will be best prepared to complete the MPT task if you have a list of those separate elements in front of you. As you read the key statute, find the most important section for your task. Break it into elements. List those elements. Neatly. You must be able to read your own writing.

In *In re Steven Wallace*, for example, the Partner Memo forces the bar candidate to separate out the four defenses under FCC § 2-326(3).

Read through your File and Library materials just once. You are going to read through your whole File and Library from start to finish only once. While you read you will index and cross-reference at the same time. That is one of the virtues of the MPT-Matrix™ system. You will not repeat any work. You will not have to re-read. You will not have to take the time to make separate notes in which you copy out sections of the File or Library. Your work will always be economical. And you will always be able to find what you are looking for.

Resist the temptation to work inefficiently. Here are two temptations to resist. First, resist the temptation to read everything first, and then go back and index it. The 90 minutes for the MPT simply do not allow you enough time to repeat your work. Just read and index and cross-reference, all at the same time. Likewise, resist the temptation to read through the whole File for line 1 of your MPT-Matrix, then go back and read the whole File for line 2, and so on. Again, the MPT simply does not allow you enough time. Just move swiftly along, reading once and indexing as you go along.

Read carefully, noting all dates and other numbers. Underline everything in the text that contains a number. That goes for dates, document numbers, and amounts. Note the date of every case, and note every day or time-limit in key statutes.

---

[1] The *Under-Here-Therefore*™ method for legal writing was originally taught in Mary Campbell Gallagher, *Scoring High on Bar Exam Essays: In-depth Strategies and Essay-Writing Practice that Bar Review Courses Don't Offer, with 80 Full-Length Sample Essays*, 3rd ed. (2006).

Summary of Indexing and Cross-Referencing:

Indexing. As you go through your MPT Library, you may note that a line from Case A at page 8 will help you to respond to the direction in the Partner Memo that you have noted as MPT-Matrix™ line 1. You will index it by writing the number 8 at the intersection of the appropriate row on your MPT-Matrix™ for Item 1, and in the column for Case A. Your map coordinates are thus A-1.

Cross-referencing. At the same time, you will underline a few words from the passage on page 8 that you are referencing, and in the margin of that Library page, you will write your map coordinates: A-1. Then when you start writing your work product, and you want to write a section in response to the first direction in the Partner Memo, you can go to page 8 and quickly find that material.

* * * * *

Sample Blank MPT-Matrix™						
	A.	B.	C.	D.	E.	F.
1.						
2.						
3.						
4.						

III.
Step Three of the Four-Step *Perform Your Best*™ MPT System™: Create the Work Product

III. Step Three. Forty-five (45) minutes. Create the work product. Check again to make sure that you are following the directions in the Partner Memo and any other key documents. Then write at least one sentence for each section of your work product. Finally, complete your work product by referring to your *Perform Your Best*™ MPT-Matrix™.

5 Minutes

Part Three-A. Five minutes. Leave the first page of your bluebook blank, so you can go back and insert the first part of the format for a brief or a memo or letter, or the first part of the format for whatever your assignment is.[2]

Read the instructions in the Partner Memo. Refresh yourself on what the issues are and what your task is and renew your sense of where your work product is going. Make sure you have a firm understanding of the roadmap you have created in your MPT-Matrix™.

Starting with page two, go quickly through the bluebook and write at least one full sentence for each major topic at the top of a bluebook page, either on every page or on every other page. If this sentence is your strong, persuasive, section heading, so much the better. No matter how incomplete your treatment of the topic seems to you, quickly write something for every single section heading. This gives you a framework in the bluebook or on the computer. You will not be plunging into a vacuum on your blank pages.

And let's be tactical. By writing at least one sentence for each topic before you get involved in the process of creating your work product, you make it more likely that you will get some credit for every single part of your work than if you leave a blank page, since there is always a risk of not finishing the work product. Remember, too, that the graders may be using a checklist. You want to be as sure as you can be that your checklist, namely, your MPT-Matrix™ or outline, is as much like their checklist as possible. You also want to make sure that you get some credit for every single section of the work product.

One key to managing this work is to leave a large amount of space between items so that you have enough room to construct your entire work product under these key sentences. For each topic, therefore, *leave a minimum of one page in your bluebook*.

40 Minutes

Part Three-B. Forty minutes. Re-read the instructions in the Partner Memo, again make sure you understand the key issues, pause to reflect on the big picture and to make sure that you are responding to the big picture, and then briskly complete your work product.

---

[2] If you are using a computer or a typewriter, apply these instructions to your typed page.

> *Word to the Wise*
>
> **Format is key for giving yourself a structure and for creating the best professional impression.** Make sure that the grader can see the logical structure of your work product just by looking at your pages.

Give yourself a structure by choosing a standard law office format for your task: memo, brief, and so on. Your work product will usually have three main parts. Note how many sub-sections your work product will have. Divide your time available by the number of subsections. You will normally write only a few sentences for each sub-section. Remember. No sub-section should require much more than one bluebook page, or the equivalent on the computer. Control your time.

After you have written all your paragraphs, at the end, if you have not already done so, go back and insert a short clear persuasive heading for every section. Your section headings should state succinctly your conclusion or argument for each section, using both law and facts. Incorporate in each section heading the key word or words from your topic outline. Underline your heading, leave space above it, and otherwise make it obvious to the grader's eye what your section headings are. The grader must be able to follow your argument visually. Wait! You aren't quite finished yet.

IV.
Step Four of the Four-Step *Perform Your Best*™ MPT System™: Re-check Everything

IV. Step Four. Five (5) minutes. Re-check everything. Check that the work product follows the instructions in the Partner Memo, that the format and tone are correct, that you have identified and dealt with all ethical issues, and that each part of the work product has a persuasive heading that is underlined. Proofread.

5 Minutes — Take five (5) minutes to re-check everything. Re-check the instructions in the Partner Memo, and re-check your format.

1. Go back through your work product.
2. Make sure that you have used all of the material in your MPT-Matrix™.
3. Make sure that you have handled every single topic down the lefthand column of your MPT-Matrix™.
4. Quickly check over the beginning and end of your work product. Is the format correct?
5. Does your memorandum state what the task is at the beginning? Does your brief state at the beginning what you wish the court to do?
6. Do you state that you have completed your task, or restate what you wish the court to do, at the end?
7. Have you used the correct tone for the task? Neutral tone and third-person for a brief, showing courtesy and deference to the court; professional and cordial tone for a letter to a client, using first- and second-person.
8. **Read the Partner Memo again.** Be certain that you have done exactly what the partner told you to do, that you have addressed each topic, and that you have answered all of the partner's questions.
9. Proofread.

Make sure that the format is correct and complete for whatever task you have been assigned: memo, brief, and so on. It is not enough that your work product does what it is supposed to do. Your format must make it visually obvious that you have done so.

Make sure that your *tone* is correct for the task. If you wrote a brief, did you use a neutral tone, use the third person, and show deference to the court? If you wrote a letter to a client, did you use a cordial but professional tone? Reread the Partner Memo again to make sure that you have done exactly what the partner asked you to do, that you have hit all the topics, and that you have stated plainly what you have done. Proofread.

Good work! You have done a good job on your MPT task, and you have completed it within the 90 minutes allowed!

At-a-Glance: Summary of the Four-Part Perform Your Best™ MPT System™

I. **Step One. Outline. Five (5) minutes.** Refresh yourself on the general instructions from the NCBE, look at the Table of Contents, and skim the entire File and Library quickly to see what is there. **Outline the instructions in the Partner Memo and any other key document.** List topics down the leftmost column of your MPT-Matrix™ and number them.

II. **Step Two. Thirty-five (35) minutes. Complete the MPT-Matrix™.** Complete the framework of the *Perform Your Best* MPT-Matrix™ by noting the names of the documents in the File and the Library across the tops of the columns in the Matrix and giving each one a capital letter. Then fill in the MPT-Matrix™ by reading straight through the File and Library materials, starting with the statutes, entering page numbers of useful material at the intersection of the appropriate rows and columns in the MPT-Matrix™ (**indexing**). As you go along, you will also be noting those MPT-Matrix™ map coordinates in the margins of the File and Library next to the material you will use (**cross-referencing**).

III. **Step Three. Forty-five (45) minutes. Create the work product. Check again to make sure that you are following the directions in the Partner Memo and any other key documents.** Then write at least one sentence for each section of your work product. Finally, complete your work product.

IV. **Step Four. Five (5) minutes. Re-check everything. Check that the work product follows the instructions in the Partner Memo.** Check that the format and tone are correct, that you have dealt with all ethical issues, and that each part of the work product has a persuasive heading that is underlined. Proofread.

Successful Performance Methods

Perform Your Best™ Checklist for the MPT

1. Do note the time the MPT exam begins. Write it down on your bluebook, along with the time the MPT exam will end. Write down the time you will finish outlining (after 5 minutes), the time you will finish the MPT-Matrix™ (another 35 minutes), the time you will finish the work product (another 45 minutes) and re-check everything. Write down the time you will finish. Stay on track to complete the MPT inside 90 minutes.
2. Do bring your own office supplies. Even if you are typing the exam, bring pencils, pens, and an eraser. Remember not to use colored pens or highlighter on your work product.
3. Do put your name down on your work product as "Applicant" or "Bar Candidate." Do not put your own name on your work product.
4. Do refresh yourself on the general instructions from the NCBE before beginning to work. To give you a head start, they are reprinted below.
5. Do skim the Table of Contents and the MPT packet to see what is there before starting to work.
6. Do complete the framework for the MPT-Matrix™ before starting to outline the instructions in the Partner Memo.
7. Do read the instructions in the Partner Memo as though your legal career depended on them, because it may. Read the partner's key instructions at least three times before beginning your outline. Follow the partner's instructions about how to use the case law or how to structure documents. Do follow all of the partner's instructions about what to do and what not to do. Some instructions appear again and again in the MPTs. But pay attention, because the instructions you receive may be different.
8. Do follow all the steps outlined in this chapter for the MPT-System™. Do stick to the time limits.
   a. Outline. Five (5) minutes.
   b. Complete the MPT-Matrix™. Thirty-five (35) minutes.
   c. Create the work product. Forty-five (45) minutes.
   d. Re-check everything. Five (5) minutes.
9. Do read the statutes before the cases.
10. Do refresh yourself again on the instructions in the Partner Memo before you start to write your work product. Do make sure you remember what the issues are. Make sure you understand the road map in your MPT-Matrix™.
11. Do write at least one sentence for each section of your work product before beginning to write the whole project. Leave abundant space for filling in your discussion in each section.
12. Do divide your entire outline into sub-sections and divide the number of sub-sections into the amount of time you have. Stick to the time limits per sub-section.
13. Do give citations for all cases you use. If you are using a case that is included in another case, cite to both.

14. Do limit your quotations. But always quote the key words of any statute you are relying on, and use quotation marks. Do not paraphrase key portions of a statute. In the unlikely event that it is absolutely necessary to quote 50 or more words, indent the quote as a block quote and do not use quotation marks.

15. Do check whether the statute you would like to use was effective at the time of the incident discussed and that it is effective now.

16. Do be careful in handling the weight of the case law. Be careful that you have applied the law in accordance with the hierarchy of authorities. This includes distinguishing various court levels and jurisdictions, as well as noting whether a case has been overruled or distinguished.

17. Do make clear what the law is, whether it is in a statute or in a case or in some combination.

18. Do state explicitly that the Partner Memo has asked you to draft an objective memorandum, or that the Partner Memo has asked you to draft a persuasive memorandum, and that that is what you are doing.

19. Do tell the grader explicitly when you are confronting an ethical issue. Use the words "ethical issue" and explain clearly how you will resolve it.

20. Do give careful citations for all authorities. If you are using three cases, cite all three by name. If each case cites two other cases, and you use those cases, then cite those cases by name, and also cite the cases in which they appear. While Bluebook form may not be required on the MPT, your citations must be clear. Underline case names if you are handwriting the exam; italicize case names if you can, if you are using a computer. You may use abbreviations of case names and omit page numbers.

21. Do pay attention to footnotes in cases and briefs. They are there for a reason. Some courts and attorneys put their most important points in their footnotes.

22. Do make your work look professional. Make your work product look like a memorandum or a brief or a letter. Do use the MPT versions of the standard law office formats provided in this book. Your work product will never contain colored ink or highlighter. And please, no boxes around words. Do not abbreviate, except for names of statutes and case references.

23. Do underline the persuasive headings of the sections of your work product and number them. Do number and letter the sub-sections of your work product. Present your organization visually, so the grader can tell how you have organized your work just by looking at your pages.

24. Do include both law and facts in all of your persuasive headings. Underline your persuasive headings. Use numbers and letters.

25. Do remember that the visual structure of your work product is as important as the intellectual structure.

26. Do use headings and section titles. You must make your organization clear not just in your words but also visually, in the way you present your work product on the page. You should hand in the work product of a well-organized bar candidate with whom any grader would be happy to practice law.

27. Do handle the facts with care. Do not get carried away stating the facts. Remember, you must finish in 90 minutes. But your skill in using the facts is key to a successful performance on the MPT. Make it clear to the grader that you are using the facts to make an argument, that you are not just restating the facts. Underline key facts, use quotation marks where you quote from the fact pattern, and if longer quotes are absolutely necessary, set them out in indented paragraphs, where appropriate.

28. Where possible, do state the applicable standard for the court. If you are writing a memo in support of a motion for summary judgment, if you can, start by stating the standard for summary judgment. If it is a motion to dismiss, if possible, start by stating the standard for a motion to dismiss. If you are writing an appellate brief, if you can, start by stating the standard of review.

29. Do review everything in your work product before handing it in. Have you followed the instructions in the Partner Memo? Is your structure visually clear? Is the tone appropriate? Have you explicitly recognized any ethical issues and stated clearly how you propose to resolve them? Does every part of the work product have a persuasive heading?

30. Do proofread your work product before you hand it in.

NCBE: General Instructions for All Questions

1. You will have 90 minutes to complete this session of the examination. This performance test is designed to evaluate your ability to handle a select number of legal authorities in the context of a factual problem involving a client.

2. The problem is set in the fictitious state of Franklin, in the fictitious Fifteenth Circuit of the United States. In Franklin, the trial court of general jurisdiction is the District Court, the intermediate appellate court is the Court of Appeal, and the highest court is the Supreme Court.

3. You will have two kinds of materials with which to work: a File and a Library. The first document in the File is a memorandum containing the instructions for the task you are to complete. The other documents in the File contain factual information about your case and may also include some facts that are not relevant.

4. The Library contains the legal authorities needed to complete the task, and may also include some authorities that are not relevant. Any cases may be real, modified, or written solely for the purpose of this examination. If the cases appear familiar to you, do not assume that they are precisely the same as you have read before. Read them thoroughly, as if all were new to you. You should assume that the cases were decided in the jurisdictions and on the dates shown. In citing cases from the Library, you may use abbreviations and omit page references.

5. Your response must be written in the answer book provided. In answering this performance test, you should concentrate on the materials provided. What you have learned in law school and elsewhere provides the general background for analyzing the problem; the File and Library provide the specific materials with which you must work.

6. Although there are no restrictions on how you apportion your time, you should be sure to allocate ample time (about 45 minutes) to reading and digesting the materials and to organizing your answer before you begin writing it. You may make notes anywhere in the test materials; blank pages are provided at the end of the booklet. You may not tear pages from the question booklet.

© 2010 National Conference of Bar Examiners.

Part IV:
MPT Tasks with Analyses and Sample Answers

Introduction

Part 4 of *Perform Your Best*™ contains 12 tasks from the Multistate Performance Test (MPT), released by the National Council of Bar Examiners (NCBE). Use these tasks to strengthen your lawyering skills. As you practice, you will find yourself becoming proficient at reading and outlining the Partner Memo, completing your research, and writing your MPT work product within the time allowed. With sufficient practice, you should be able to complete any work product competently inside 90 minutes.

For each task, Part 4 gives you not merely the task itself and the NCBE Point Sheets but also guidance to help you succeed on other MPT tasks. In Part 4 you will find:

(1) The NCBE materials for each MPT task, including the File and the Library;
(2) The *Perform Your Best*™ MPT-Matrix™;
(3) The *Perform Your Best*™ Sample Answer;
(4) The *Perform Your Best*™ Note on Analyzing the Task.

An MPT-Matrix™ shows graphically how the materials in the File and the Library work together. Your own MPT-Matrix™ will contain only page numbers for the passages you want to use. Each MPT-Matrix™ in Part 4, however, contains words as well as page numbers. This is so that you can see exactly what material has been chosen.

Each "Sample Answer" shows you one way to respond to the instructions in the Partner Memo. These sample answers are illustrations, not models. Keep in mind that a bar candidate need not write long answers or hit all possible points in order to do well on the MPT. This book gives answers that are sometimes fuller than a bar candidate can write within the 45 minutes recommended for the MPT. And the NCBE Point Sheets often provide additional legal points. Each "Note on Analyzing" explains how to read and outline the instructions in the Partner Memo and how to structure your answer.

This book explains recommended steps for self-teaching in Part 1. Take this opportunity to strengthen your professional competence. Do not merely glance at an MPT task, jot a few notes, and then look at the sample answer or the "Note on Analyzing" that task. Do the work. Then, when you have completed each task, set your MPT-Matrix™ side-by-side with the *Perform Your Best* MPT-Matrix™. See how you could have found more issues in the instructions in the Partner Memo. Then look at your answer alongside the sample answer. You will learn one choice for visual presentation. Remember, you want the bar exam grader to see the logical structure of your work just by looking at the pages.

Read the "Note on Analyzing." Did you understand how to read the instructions in the Partner Memo and outline the task? Have you used an appropriate law office format? Does your work product have three parts? Do your persuasive headings contain both law and facts? Are they powerful?

Use these MPT tasks in Part 4 to gain the skills in legal research, organization, and presentation that you will use on the MPT on the bar examination. Supplement these MPT tasks with any MPT tasks you receive in your bar-preparation course. Once you are admitted, you will use many of the same techniques in your legal practice.

The chart on the next page systematically analyzes these 12 tasks and indicates the type of task, the context, the purpose, and the type of legal analysis the task calls for. This information appears again at the top of every "Note on Analyzing" the tasks.

Perform Your Best™ Task Analysis Chart

Name of MPT Task	Type of Task	Context	Purpose	Type of Legal Analysis
A. *In re Lisa Peel*	Objective memorandum	Litigation	Evaluate potential of client's case	Statutory interpretation
B. *In re Velocity Park*	Objective memorandum	Contract drafting	Analyze proposed document	Document and case analysis, suggestions for re-drafting
C. *Vargas v. Monte*	Persuasive brief	Litigation	Submit to court	Statutory and case law analysis and application
D. *Arden Industries v. Freight Forwarders, Inc.*	Persuasive brief	Litigation	Submit to court	Statutory and case law analysis, applying terms to facts
E. *Ronald v. Department of Motor Vehicles*	Persuasive brief	Litigation	Submit to agency	Statutory and case law analysis and application
F. *Phoenix Corporation v. Biogenesis, Inc.*	Objective memorandum	Litigation	Evaluate merits of opposing party's arguments	Statutory and case law analysis and application
G. *In re Emily Dunn*	Will	Will drafting	Draft will with explanations, to use in meeting with client	Will in correct will format: code and case law analysis and application
H. *In re Franklin Construction Company*	Opinion letter to client	Contract dispute	Advise client on how to respond to demand letter	Contract, statutory and case law analysis and application
I. *In re Gardenton Board of Education*	Objective memorandum	Code analysis and drafting	Analyze proposed school district speech code, section-by-section, and suggest revisions	Statutory interpretation with suggestions for deleting, adding or re-drafting sections
J. *In re Steven Wallace*	Objective memorandum	Litigation	Advise client on how to respond to demand from trustee in bankruptcy	Statutory and case law analysis and application, with suggestions for factual investigation
K. *Kantor v. Bellows*	Persuasive letter to opposing counsel	Litigation	Set out client's case for opposing counsel, make proposal for settlement	Statutory, case law and factual analysis, argument
L. *Franklin Asbestos Handling Regulations*	Persuasive and objective memorandum	Litigation	Frame best arguments and evaluate regulations, section-by section	Statutory interpretation and case law analysis and application

MPT Task 4A:
In re Lisa Peel

FILE

Black, Fernandez & Hanson LLP
Attorneys at Law
Suite 215
396 West Main Street
Greenville, Franklin 33755

MEMORANDUM

To: Applicant
From: Henry Black
Re: Peel subpoena
Date: February 26, 2008

Our client, Lisa Peel, has just been subpoenaed by the local district attorney to testify before a grand jury. The subpoena directs her to bring notes concerning any and all persons interviewed regarding an item she posted on her Web log (blog). These notes will reveal the identities of her sources for the information she posted on her blog. Peel promised to protect the confidentiality of her sources. She seeks our advice on whether she has grounds to resist the subpoena.

I am somewhat familiar with the Franklin Reporter Shield Act (FRSA). However, I do not know if the FRSA applies to Peel and her blog. Please draft an objective memorandum for me analyzing whether we can use the FRSA to move to quash Peel's subpoena.

You need not include a separate statement of facts, but be sure to use the facts in your analysis. Be sure to address both sides of the issue; that is, discuss any facts or law that may prevent Peel from claiming the protection of the FRSA.

Do not concern yourself with any First Amendment issues; another associate is researching those arguments.

TRANSCRIPT OF INTERVIEW WITH LISA PEEL
February 22, 2008

Atty: Lisa, nice to see you. What can I do for you?

Peel: You can make this subpoena go away.

Atty: Tell me more. Why don't you start at the beginning?

Peel: A couple of years ago, I retired from teaching, and my husband and I moved to Greenville here in Montgomery County. To find out more about my new community, I started attending the meetings of several public bodies—the library and school boards, the park district board, and the town council. The more I went, the more I got to know people, and the more I became part of the scene. People got to know and trust me. Soon, I realized that there was a lot going on that the public should know about.

Atty: Did you think about getting the local newspaper involved?

Peel: Most of the towns in this county are too small to support a daily paper. So there is only one daily paper covering all of Montgomery County. The publisher believes the paper should boost the local communities, and he discourages the reporters from doing any stories and investigations that might portray the communities in a bad light.

Atty: So what did you do?

Peel: About a year ago, I started an Internet blog. As you know, often the owner of the blog starts a discussion and others can post comments. On my blog, I posted the agendas of the Greenville town council, library and school boards, and sometimes the planning commission. After the meetings, I posted the minutes, my summary of the minutes, and my own commentary about how these decisions would affect the town. Within weeks, over 400 people visited the blog, and about a quarter of them commented on what I wrote or added questions that others would respond to. I actually had citizens engaged in learning what their government was doing.

At first I updated the blog only occasionally. Then it generated so much interest that I decided to update it more often.

Atty: How often do you update it?

Peel: I generally post new items on Friday, but sometimes I may not get around to it until later in the weekend. I have movie reviews and gardening tips on the blog and also share news of my family. I post pictures of my pets and places where I've traveled. I'll also post announcements about the library's bake sale and events like that.

Atty: Do your readers pay for access to your blog?

Peel: No, it's free. At first, I kept the blog wide open; anyone could access it and post anything—anonymously if they wanted to. But then I decided that letting anyone post anything might not be wise. So now, anyone can access it at no cost. But if you want to post a comment or a question, you have to register. Registering is also free. In the past two months, I've had over 3,500 registrants in this town of 38,000 people, and people have visited the site more than 15,000 times. I've also picked up a couple of local businesses, which pay me to post their ads on my blog.

Atty: So, tell me about the subpoena.

Peel: One day, I got a call from an individual familiar with the school district administration. This person told me that the Greenville School District was losing the use of $10,000 worth of audiovisual and computer equipment purchased with district funds because the stuff was going to the home of the assistant superintendent. Well, $10,000 isn't a lot of corruption, I concede, but it is public money and it was intended to buy equipment for schoolchildren.

So I investigated and got confirmation from a couple of sources. I wrote a piece about what I found out and posted it on my blog. I brought you a hard copy of the posting. Now the Montgomery County District Attorney wants to know the sources of my information.

Atty: Why not reveal your sources?

Peel: To get to the truth, especially the truth about public corruption, I have to talk to people on the inside. But insiders will never talk to me if they think their names will become public because they're worried about losing their jobs. So I get inside information from confidential sources, let people know about it by getting the word out, and suddenly the government starts investigating or the public starts asking questions.

Atty: Do you get paid for this work?

Peel: Not much. The little income that comes from the sponsors' ads, I use for my expenses: computer upgrades, copy costs, telephone costs, gas for traveling, that sort of thing.

Atty: Do you know why the district attorney subpoenaed you?

Peel: I have a couple of guesses. Now that I've exposed this scandal, he has to investigate. I suspect he is embarrassed to learn about this from my blog. Also, the district attorney is just being lazy. Think about it—how many people are in a position to know about this going on at the school? He just needs to start asking the right people and the information will come out. But, regardless of the reason, I have to protect my sources. I may be retired and this blog may be my hobby, but right now it is the only avenue for real news in this county.

Atty: I'm somewhat familiar with the Franklin Reporter Shield Act—we may have an argument that you are protected by it, but I doubt that "blogs" or "bloggers" are specifically mentioned in the Act. I am also concerned that you've never worked as a reporter before.

Peel: But I work just like a real reporter. I attend public meetings, read agendas, minutes, budgets, etc. I make calls to the officials and other staff members and interview them. I then post the official agendas and minutes, along with my summaries and comments. The amount of time varies, but I usually spend 12–15 hours a week on my blog.

Atty: I see your point. Well, we'll do some research and get back to you soon.

Peel: Thanks. I look forward to hearing from you.

Greenville Citizen Blog Posting

GREENVILLE CITIZEN BLOG—IT'S YOUR GOVERNMENT

$10,000 in School Equipment Diverted from Schools to Home of Assistant Superintendent

January 4, 2008: Greenville, Franklin
by Lisa Peel

The Greenville School District approved the purchase of $70,000 worth of new audiovisual and computer equipment for the schoolchildren of the Greenville School District this year, but not all of the equipment is in the schools. As the equipment arrived at the district offices, selected items were redirected to the home of Assistant Superintendent Frank Peterson, according to several sources closely associated with the school district. Sources estimate that Peterson has school district equipment worth over $10,000 at his home at the present time.

According to sources, who would speak only on the condition of anonymity, Peterson took selected items home "to test them out." But instead of returning these materials to the school, he kept them at his home.

At this time Peterson reportedly has at home two fully equipped desktop personal computers with two color printers, two laptop computers, one high-performance scanner, and a digital camera. He also has a classroom multimedia system in his home. That's $10,000 worth of public school equipment that he's using to create his own multimedia studio!

When asked for a response on Peterson's alleged activities, Greenville School Board President Annette Gross said, "We have policies in place to ensure that the public's dollars are spent according to budget."

Citizens should immediately ask President Gross for a full accounting of the purchases and for an investigation of Assistant Superintendent Peterson.

Subpoena Duces Tecum

IN THE DISTRICT COURT FOR MONTGOMERY COUNTY
STATE OF FRANKLIN

In re Grand Jury Investigation   Grand Jury Case Number 08-7703

SUBPOENA DUCES TECUM

TO:

Lisa Peel
9853 S. Elm Street
Greenville, Franklin 33755

YOU ARE COMMANDED TO APPEAR before the Grand Jury duly empaneled in the above-captioned case at the Montgomery County Courthouse, Room 346, March 10, 2008, at 10:00 a.m. YOU ARE COMMANDED TO PRODUCE all reports, files, notes, and other documentation regarding Greenville School District equipment in the possession of Assistant Superintendent Frank Peterson, including all files, notes, reports, and any other documentation taken of or from any and all persons interviewed for or sources described or quoted in the GREENVILLE CITIZEN BLOG operated by Lisa Peel and dated January 4, 2008.

Subpoena requested by the Montgomery County District Attorney's Office.

DATE ISSUED: February 20, 2008

Elliot Wallace
———————————
Elliot Wallace
District Attorney

NOTICE:
FAILURE TO COMPLY WITH THIS SUBPOENA MAY RESULT IN FINES OR IMPRISONMENT OR BOTH.

LIBRARY

AMERICA TODAY

Article from America Today

July 5, 2007

BLOGS COMPETING WITH NEWSPAPERS AND NETWORKS

Blogs—slang for Web logs—started out as online personal diaries or journals but have rapidly become part of the everyday Web vernacular and are replacing news websites for many readers.

Blog owners or "bloggers" establish Web pages on which they post news items, commentary, information, and links to other sources for readers. Readers are often invited to respond. For example, the blogger might post a movie review, and ask readers to post their opinions. Or the blogger might comment on the latest appropriations bill before Congress and encourage readers to share their views with their representatives.

According to recent surveys, at least 8 million adults in the United States have created blogs, and 30 percent of Americans read one or more blogs regularly. Blogs cover every topic imaginable—technology, sports, medicine, art, entertainment, business, news, and politics. Of course, many blogs still serve as forums for sharing personal experiences, from weddings to the contents of a blogger's junk drawer.

Journalists and politicians have learned the power of blogs and recognize that they are now a force to be reckoned with. For example, during the 2006 Congressional campaigns, bloggers challenged many of the candidates' statements. Several major bloggers have received press credentials for political events. Most major news outlets have several staff bloggers.

Blogging software is easy to use and inexpensive. Blogging is said to give a voice to those not given attention in the traditional media. It is just this ease of blogging that makes some professional journalists uncomfortable. "The blogger is the reporter, editor, and publisher. Where is the check on the blogger to ensure the truth?" asked Al Rains, Franklin Newspaper Association director. "Blogging isn't reporting, it's just writing. Any hack can offer half-baked commentary on the news of the day and post it online. How is that different from the millions of people who post items on their MySpace or Facebook pages?"

Other journalists see blogging as just another development in journalism—from newspapers to radio to TV to cable news, talk radio, and YouTube. "More means of sharing the news and inviting commentary is better than fewer means. I trust the public to learn from many sources and decide for themselves," says Tanya Browne, a journalism professor at Franklin University. "With so much media consolidation, there are many voices, especially local ones, that will be heard only through these 'alternative' forms of journalism."

Franklin Reporter Shield Act

§ 900 Preamble

The primary purpose of this Act is to safeguard the media's ability to gather news. It is intended to promote the free flow of information to the public by prohibiting courts from compelling reporters to disclose unpublished news sources or information received from such sources.

§ 901 Definitions

As used in this Act:

(a) "reporter" means any person regularly engaged in collecting, writing, or editing news for publication through a news medium.

(b) "news medium" means any newspaper, magazine, or other similar medium issued at regular intervals and having a general circulation; a radio station; a television station; a community antenna television service; or any person or corporation engaged in the making of newsreels or other motion picture news for public showing.

(c) "source" means the person from whom or the means through which the information was obtained.

§ 902 Nondisclosure of source of information

No court may compel a reporter to disclose the source of any information or any unpublished material except as provided in this Act.

Dictionary Definitions

The American Heritage Dictionary of the English Language (4th ed., 2000)

Blog: *noun* [shortened form of Web log], a website that contains an online personal journal with reflections, comments, and often hyperlinks provided by the writer.

Circulation: *noun*, movement in a circle or circuit; ...free movement or passage; the passing of something, such as money or news, from place to place or person to person; the condition of being passed about and widely known, distribution; dissemination of printed material, especially copies of newspapers or magazines among readers; the number of copies of a publication sold or distributed.

Publication: *noun*, the act or process of publishing printed material; the communication of information to the public.

Publish: *verb*, to prepare and issue material for public disclosure or sale; to bring to public attention; to announce.

Reporter: *noun*, a writer, investigator, or presenter of news stories; a person who is authorized to write and issue official accounts of judicial or legislative proceedings.

In re Bellows

Franklin Court of Appeal (2005)

During Terrence Johnson's trial for murder, Johnson served a subpoena *duces tecum* upon respondent Peggy Bellows, a newspaper photographer employed by the *Springfield Review*. The subpoena required Bellows to produce certain photographs that she took during a police search of Johnson's residence prior to his arrest. When Bellows refused to produce the photos, the trial court found her in civil contempt and sentenced her to jail. This appeal followed.

The sole issue on appeal is whether Bellows is a reporter whose unpublished photographs are protected by the Franklin Reporter Shield Act (FRSA). In Franklin, reporters have a statutory, qualified privilege protecting their sources and unpublished material from compelled disclosure. FRSA § 902. It is the burden of the party claiming the privilege to establish his or her right to its protection. *Wehrmann v. Wickesberg* (Fr. Sup. Ct. 2002).

We note at the outset that testimonial privileges, in general, are not favored because they "contravene a fundamental principle of our jurisprudence that the public has a right to every man's evidence." *United States v. Bryan*, 339 U.S. 323 (1950). The preamble to the FRSA, on the other hand, states that the FRSA seeks to promote the free flow of information to and from the media by protecting the media's confidential sources. Hence, competing interests must be addressed in determining the FRSA's scope.

We have found few cases that discuss who, beyond members of the traditional media, has status to claim the journalist's privilege. In 2002, the Franklin Supreme Court rejected using the FRSA to protect the identities of those paying for newspaper ads disguised as journalism. *St. Mary's Hospital v. Zeus Publishing* (Fr. Sup. Ct. 2002). The full-page ads recounted a hospital's alleged illegal labor practices and urged a boycott. Similarly, the Columbia Supreme Court rejected the argument that defamatory messages posted on a sports Internet bulletin board (GolfNet) could be construed as "news" or as being "published at regular intervals," and therefore held that the poster of the messages was not protected by the Columbia Reporter Shield Act. *Hausch v. Vaughan* (Col. Sup. Ct. 1995).

In contrast to these cases, the Franklin Supreme Court did grant FRSA protection to a freelance writer for a magazine, *Kaiser v. Currie* (Fr. Sup. Ct. 2004), and to the author of a medical journal article, *Halliwell v. Anderson* (Fr. Sup. Ct. 2002), holding that neither could be compelled to divulge their sources of information.

What we glean from these cases is that the test does not grant "reporter" status to any person simply because that person has a manuscript, a computer, a Web page, or a film. Rather, it requires an intent at the inception of the newsgathering process to disseminate investigative news to the public. Thus in *Hoey v. Fellenz* (Fr. Ct. App. 1989), the court held that the FRSA did not shield two reporters from having to testify about a crime that they happened to witness on their way home from work—when they witnessed the crime, they had no intent to disseminate news to the public. As we see it, the privilege is available only to persons whose purposes are those traditionally inherent to the press: gathering news for publication.

The FRSA defines a reporter as "any person regularly engaged in *collating*, writing, or editing news for publication through a news medium." § 901(a) (emphasis added). Johnson claims Bellows is not covered by the FRSA for the simple reason that the Act doesn't mention "photographers." He claims that had the legislature intended to protect photographers, it would have included photographers in the statute.

Franklin law concerning statutory construction is clear. The principal rule of statutory construction is to ascertain and give effect to the legislature's intent. To determine the legislature's intent, courts first look to the statute's language. A court must give the legislative language its plain and ordinary meaning and construe the statute as a whole, giving effect to every word therein. When interpreting a statute, words and phrases must not be viewed in isolation but must be considered in light of other relevant provisions of the statute.

Where the language of the statute is clear and unambiguous, the only legitimate function of the courts is to enforce the law as enacted by the legislature. Courts should not depart from the plain language of the statute by reading into it exceptions, limitations, or conditions which conflict with the intent of the legislature. No rule of statutory construction authorizes the courts to declare that the legislature did not mean what the plain language of the statute says.

The record is clear from testimony of the *Springfield Review* editor that Bellows is employed as a photographer for the newspaper and that her permanent assignment is to "photograph newsworthy events." There is no dispute that the *Springfield Review*, a daily newspaper with a daily circulation of more than 100,000 readers, is a news medium. The record is also clear that, in her capacity as a photographer, Bellows does not write or edit.

The question then is whether she collects news by photographing newsworthy events. Where the legislature has supplied a definition, we are constrained to use only that definition. However, the legislature does not define the term "collecting" in the FRSA. In interpreting "the plain and ordinary meaning" of a word, where the legislature has not defined the term, courts may use a dictionary to assist in determining the plain and ordinary meaning. Turning to Merriam Webster's Collegiate Dictionary 720 (10th ed. 1998), we find that collecting means "to bring together, gather, assemble." Taking photographs of events is one way to gather or assemble news. Bellows, by photographing newsworthy events, is regularly engaged in the gathering or assembling of news, and her activities fall within the statutory meaning of "collecting" news for publication.

Furthermore, extending the protections of the FRSA to photographers is consistent with the purpose of the Act. When it enacted the FRSA in 1948, the legislature stated the purpose of the Act as encouraging the free and unfettered flow of information to the public. The more recent amendments to the FRSA extend the protections to undisclosed materials as well as sources. See FRSA § 900. This provision protects the discretion of journalists to determine when and how to publish their materials.

Accordingly, Bellows meets the statutory definition of a reporter as she is a person regularly engaged in collecting news for publication through a news medium. Bellows is protected by the FRSA.

Reversed.

Lane v. Tichenor

Franklin Supreme Court (2003)

The sole question on appeal is whether the term "recreational purpose," as used in the Franklin Landowner's Recreational Immunity Act ("the Act"), § 730, includes hayrides. Lane brought this action against Tichenor for damages sustained during a hayride on Tichenor's land. On Tichenor's motion, the trial court dismissed the case and the appellate court affirmed.

The Act provides that landowners owe no duty of care to keep their premises safe for entry or use by any person for recreational purposes. The stated purpose of the Act is to "encourage owners of land to make land and water areas available to the public for recreational purposes by limiting their liability toward persons entering thereon for such purposes." § 730(1). Thus, the Act provides immunity only if the land is entered upon or used for a "recreational purpose."

The Act defines the term "recreational purpose" as follows: "[r]ecreational purpose' includes any of the following, or any combination thereof: hunting, fishing, swimming, boating, snowmobiling, motorcycling, camping, hiking, cave exploring, nature study, water skiing, water sports, bicycling, horseback riding, and viewing or enjoying historical, archaeological, scenic or scientific sites, or other similar activities." § 730(2)(c).

Lane argues that because hayrides are not listed among the items defined in the Act, the legislature meant to exclude them from the definition of "recreational purpose," and therefore the Act does not apply here. Tichenor responds that the term "other similar activities" indicates the legislature's intent to broadly define the term "recreational purpose."

In interpreting a statute, the court is constrained to ascertain and give effect to the intent of the legislature. The statutory language is the best indication of the drafters' intent. Where that language is unambiguous, courts must enforce the law as enacted. Each word in the statute, as well as the punctuation used, is to be examined. Where the statute enumerates various covered activities, such enumeration implies the exclusion of all others.

However, in this case the statutory language is not clear, and the enumeration is neither exclusive nor exhaustive. While the legislature provided a list of activities intended as a definition of "recreational purpose," the question is what the legislature meant by "other similar activities." The question, more precisely, is whether hayrides fit within the phrase "other similar activities."

Where the language of a statute is unclear, the court may avail itself of external aids to interpret the statute. One such aid is the rules of construction of statutes, also called the canons of statutory interpretation. These rules or canons guide the court in ascertaining the intent of the legislature.

One canon, *ejusdem generis*, states that when general words follow particular and specific words in a statute, the general words must be construed to include only things of the same general kind as those indicated by the particular and specific words.

When we examine the items specifically enumerated in the Act, we find that the quality or characteristic common to all of them is the enjoyment of nature. While some may find enjoyment in fishing or hunting, others will find enjoyment in viewing historical or scientific sights, and still others in horseback riding or motorcycling. All of these activities take place outdoors and involve nature: the study of nature, the enjoyment of nature, or even travel through a natural setting.

Applying that quality to the present situation, a hayride is just another form of the enjoyment of nature. It is hard to see how hayrides are significantly different from horseback riding, motorcycling, or bicycling—all of which involve transporting oneself or others across the outdoors for enjoyment. One can imagine a group climbing onto a farm wagon, traveling along in the open, watching the stars, and communing with nature.

Lane further argues that while we should not apply this canon of construction at all, if we do, we must conclude that the quality common to all the enumerated or specific activities is that they occur by day.

In this case, the hayride was conducted at night. However, we note that camping occurs overnight and that some fishing does as well. A starlit night far away from the lights and noise of a city, the crisp night air of an October evening, the snap and crackle of fall leaves accompanied by the sounds of night birds, the moonlight faintly illuminating old trees and fallen leaves, can all be enjoyed on a hayride at night under cover of darkness.

Because we hold that hayrides fall within the term "other similar activities" of the Act, we conclude that the trial court properly dismissed the case.

Affirmed.

THE MPT
MULTISTATE PERFORMANCE TEST

In re Lisa Peel

POINT SHEET

The MPT point sheet, grading summary, and grading guidelines describe the factual and legal points encompassed within the lawyering task to be completed. They outline all the possible issues and points that might be addressed by an applicant. They are provided to the user jurisdictions for the sole purpose of assisting graders in grading the examination by identifying the issues and suggesting the resolution of the problem contemplated by the drafters. These are not official grading guides. Applicants can receive a range of passing grades, including excellent grades, without covering all the points discussed in these guides. The model answer is included as an illustration of a thorough and detailed response to the task, one that addresses all the legal and factual issues the drafters intended to raise in the problem. It is intended to serve only as an example. User jurisdictions are free to modify these responses in the same way to receive good grades. Applicants need not present their grading materials, including the suggested weights assigned to particular points. Grading the MPT is the exclusive responsibility of the jurisdiction using the MPT as part of its admissions process.

Copyright ©2008 by the National Conference of Bar Examiners.
All rights reserved

In re Lisa Peel

DRAFTERS' POINT SHEET

In this performance test item, applicants are employed by a law firm. Applicants' task is to prepare an objective memorandum evaluating whether a motion to quash will be successful with respect to a subpoena served on the firm's client, Lisa Peel. Peel operates an Internet Web log or "blog," which functions much as a newspaper, reporting news items and commentary; she is not a professional reporter. She recently posted to her blog a report that Greenville School Assistant Superintendent Frank Peterson was using school district equipment in his home. The report was based on information from anonymous sources. Soon after the story was posted, Peel was served a subpoena duces tecum by the district attorney and ordered to appear before a grand jury and to bring notes and other documents concerning the sources of her information. Peel seeks the law firm's advice on whether there are grounds to resist the subpoena.

Applicants must analyze whether Peel is entitled to claim the protection of the Franklin Reporter Shield Act (FRSA), which provides that a reporter cannot be compelled to reveal his or her sources of information except as provided by the Act. The instructional memo instructs applicants not to address any First Amendment issues. To complete the assigned task, applicants must parse and interpret the statute and, in particular, the definitions of "reporter" and "news medium."

The File consists of the instructional memo from the supervising partner, a transcript of the interview with Peel, a copy of the item posted on the blog, the subpoena, and a news article about blogs. The Library consists of excerpts from the FRSA, several dictionary definitions, and two cases bearing on the subject.

The following discussion covers all of the points the drafters intended to raise in the problem. Applicants need not cover all of them to receive passing or even excellent grades. Grading is entirely within the discretion of the user jurisdictions.

I. Overview

The task is to draft an objective memorandum assessing whether there are grounds to quash the subpoena. The work product should resemble a legal memorandum such as one an associate would prepare for a supervising partner. The key issue is whether Peel qualifies as a "reporter," as defined in the Act; if so, she cannot be compelled to reveal the sources of her report, except as provided in the Act.

This is primarily an exercise in statutory interpretation. Applicants should thus examine the definitions provided in the Act, determine the elements of the definition that must be met if Peel is to be protected by the Act, and reach a conclusion regarding whether Peel's blogging activities meet each element. With respect to the key definitions in the Act, it is expected that applicants will arrive at the following conclusions:

- A "reporter" is any person regularly engaged in collecting, writing, or editing news for publication through a news medium.
- Peel regularly engages or involves herself in collecting, writing, or editing the news, specifically, by attending meetings, analyzing public information, interviewing public officials, and writing summaries of and commentaries on their activities.
- The news written by Peel is published through a news medium.
- A "news medium" is any newspaper, magazine, or other similar medium issued at regular intervals and having a general circulation.
- Peel's blog is a publication issued at regular intervals and with a general circulation. Therefore, it qualifies as a news medium within the meaning of the Act.

II. Relevant Facts

Applicants are instructed to incorporate the relevant facts into their analysis. Some applicants may wish to set forth the facts at length. Others may wish to state only enough facts to set the scene and import other facts as necessary into their discussion of the issues.

A thorough discussion of whether Peel's blogging activities bring her within the Act's coverage would include the following facts:

- Peel began an Internet blog in which she publishes information about public bodies, including the agendas and minutes of public meetings, summaries of the meetings, and her own comments about the importance of these meetings.
- Peel attends meetings, obtains public documents, prepares summaries of the meetings and documents, and writes commentaries about the business of several public bodies. Peel's activities generally take about 12 to 15 hours per week.
- Peel's blog, the Greenville Citizen Blog, has at least 3,500 persons who are registered as readers. In order to post comments to the blog, readers must register with the blog; registration is free. There are likely many additional readers who are not registered.
- Peel usually posts items to the blog every Friday.
- There is no town newspaper and the only newspaper available is a countywide one that does not publish anything critical of the local communities.
- On January 4, 2008, Peel posted a news item to the blog reporting that Greenville School Assistant Superintendent Frank Peterson was keeping school district audiovisual and computer equipment, worth approximately $10,000, in his home for his personal use.
- The blog posting about Peterson is based on information provided by confidential sources.
- The district attorney has subpoenaed Peel to appear before a grand jury and to bring notes concerning the source of her information about Frank Peterson.

III. Analysis

Applicants are told to analyze applicable legal authority and explain how the facts and law support their conclusions. The instructional memo emphasizes that both sides of the issue should be addressed; that is, applicants should discuss not only those facts that support a motion to quash but also those facts that weigh against the motion's success. Applicants should take care to address each of the elements of the definition of a reporter found in the Act. One format is for each element of the definition to be the subject of separate heading followed by analysis related to that heading. Alternatively, applicants may organize their work product in other ways. The headings appearing below are exemplars only and are not intended as the only acceptable headings.

<u>Whether Peel engages in the activities of a reporter for the purposes of the FRSA</u>

At the outset, applicants should note that the person claiming the privilege under the FRSA has the burden to establish his or her right to its protection. *In re Bellows* (Franklin Ct. App. 2005). Thus, in order to successfully resist the subpoena, the burden is on Peel to demonstrate that her blogging activities come within the ambit of the FRSA.

- The FRSA defines a reporter as "any person regularly engaged in collecting, writing, or editing news for publication through a news medium." FRSA § 901(a). Some of the terms in the statutory definition are further defined by statutes and others are not defined. Each of them must be interpreted.
- In interpreting the FRSA, the court must ascertain and give effect to the intent of the legislature. Ordinarily the best indicator of the legislature's intent is the plain and ordinary meaning of the words used in the statute. Where the language is unambiguous, the court must rely on that language, giving effect to all the words in the statutory provision at issue. Where the legislature has defined terms, the court must use the definitions provided in the Act. *Bellows*.
- NOTE: Applicants who rely on the dictionary definition of the term "reporter" have misconstrued the nature of statutory interpretation as explained in *Bellows*. The court is clear that where the legislature has defined a term, the court must rely on that definition.
- Peel collects, writes, and edits news.
  - To collect news means to "gather or assemble" it. *Bellows*.
  - Peel gathers and assembles the news by obtaining public documents from public bodies, attending their meetings, and interviewing public officials.
  - Peel writes and edits the news by preparing summaries of minutes and other public documents and commentaries on the activities of several public bodies and posting them to her blog.
- The term "news" is not defined in the Act. The plain and ordinary meaning of the term "news" involves activities of public bodies and the use of public monies.
  - Many of Peel's blog postings involve activities of public bodies.
  - However, Peel's blog is not entirely devoted to news items. She posts recipes, gardening tips, and items about her family, as well as her vacation and pet photos, presumably none of which would be considered newsworthy.
- The FRSA describes a reporter as someone who "regularly engages" in newsgathering activities. FRSA § 901(a). The term "regular" is not defined. However, common usage of the term would include weekly activities of attending meetings and posting items to the blog.
- In addition, in *Bellows*, the court emphasized that the protections of the FRSA will be extended only to those individuals and organizations having "an intent at the inception of the newsgathering process to disseminate investigative news to the public."
  - Clearly Peel has the intent when she is attending civic meetings and interviewing officials to disseminate the news to the public via her blog. *Cf. Hovey v. Fellenz* (cited in *Bellows*) where two reporters were not entitled to claim the protection of the FRSA when they witnessed the commission of a crime on their way home from work.
  - Nevertheless, Peel has no training as a reporter and she is not employed by the traditional media. By contrast, the person deemed a "reporter" for FRSA purposes in *Bellows* was a professional news photographer.
  - Likewise, *Kaiser v. Currie* and *Halliwell v. Anderson*, two cases cited in *Bellows* as examples of situations in which the Franklin courts have granted FRSA protection, involved persons writing for traditional media: a magazine and a medical journal.

Whether Peel's blog qualifies as a "news medium" under the FRSA.

- A reporter collects, writes, or edits news for publication through a news medium. FRSA § 901(a). Thus applicants must determine whether Peel's blog is a "news medium" for purposes of the FRSA.
- The term "news medium" is defined in the FRSA as "any newspaper, magazine, or other similar medium issued at regular intervals and having a general circulation…." FRSA § 901(b).

- Neither the term "Web log" nor "blog" is listed in the statute. Thus applicants must discuss whether an Internet blog like Peel's meets the definition of a "news medium."
- The examples of news media provided in the statute are not an exhaustive or exclusive listing, because the definition includes the term "other similar medium." *See Lane v. Tichenor* (Franklin Sup. Ct. 2003).
- Arguably, the use of the term "other similar medium" indicates the intent of the legislature to interpret "news medium" in a broad manner.
- One canon of statutory construction, *ejusdem generis*, is helpful in interpreting the term "other similar medium." The canon states that when general words follow particular and specific words in a statute, the general words must be construed to include only things of the same genera, kind as those indicated by the particular and specific words. *Lane*.
  - In this case, one key quality common to the particular and specific words listed (i.e., newspapers and magazines) is that they are publications that occur on a regular basis.
  - However, it is also possible that the court may focus on the fact that newspapers and magazines are primarily print media.
  - Arguably, an indication in the statute that the legislature intended the term "news medium" be interpreted in a broad manner is the long list of various forms of media listed in the statute; these media are not limited to print media, but encompass a broad range of means of communication. FRSA § 901(b).
  - And applicants could note that it is now common for newspapers and magazines to have online versions.
- There is a strong argument that, like the listed forms of news media in § 901(b), Peel's blog is published at regular intervals and has a general circulation.
  - The word "publish" means "to prepare and issue material for public disclosure or sale; to bring to public attention; to announce." *American Heritage Dictionary*.
  - Peel posts items to the blog in order to bring them to the attention of the public. This is analogous to the printing and distribution of a newspaper or magazine.
  - Indeed, she states that, because of her blog, "I actually had citizens engaged in learning what their government was doing." (*Interview*)
- As a general rule, Peel posts new items to the blog on a regular basis—she tries to post new items every Friday. But sometimes it may be later in the weekend before new posts are on her website.
- Thus, Peel's blog lacks the reliability of most traditional media (e.g., the morning newspaper or 11:00 p.m. news broadcast).
- Nonetheless, Peel's blog can be distinguished from the Internet bulletin board in *Hauseh v. Vaughan* (Col. Sup. Ct. 1995). In that case, the Columbia Supreme Court, interpreting the Columbia Reporter Shield Act, held that messages posted to an Internet bulletin board, which were posted intermittently, failed to meet that Act's requirement that to be a news medium, the claimed "news" had to be "published at regular intervals."
- Peel's blog is updated every week.
- And, unlike an Internet bulletin board, Peel's blog is not designed to be primarily a forum for readers to post messages for others to read. (In fact, she modified her blog so that only registered users could post comments.) Her blog is intended to inform members of her community about local government activities.
- The term "circulation" is not defined in the Act, but the dictionary defines "circulation" as "the condition of being passed about and widely known, distribution; …the number of copies of a publication sold or distributed." *American Heritage Dictionary*.

- In order to post to the blog, a reader must register with the blog. This is an act like subscribing, although there is no cost. The current registration for the blog totals over 3,500, or almost 10 percent of the Greenville population.
- The large number of visitors (15,000) to Peel's blog indicates that, in addition to the more than 3,500 registered readers, there are numerous regular or intermittent readers.
  - This relatively large readership is consistent with the statistics showing that millions of Americans either operate, read, or otherwise participate in blogs. *See America Today* article.
- Additionally, the fact that the legislature used a broad range of means of communication or types of media when defining "news medium" suggests that an Internet blog is a news medium.
  - Words in statutes are not to be viewed in isolation but in light of other relevant provisions of the statute. *Bellows*.
  - Other news media included in the Act are radio, television, community antenna television, and newsreels. FRSA § 901(b).
- Including a blog in the definition of "news medium" is consistent with the inclusion of more "modern" forms of communication in the Act.
  - Even though "blogs" and "bloggers" did not exist when the Franklin legislature enacted the FRSA in 1948, they are now, as indicated in the *America Today* article, a journalistic force to be reckoned with.

<u>Whether including Peel's blogging activities within the coverage of the FRSA serves the legislative intent underlying the Act.</u>
- The intent of the legislature in enacting the statute was discussed in *Bellows*.
  - The Franklin legislature, in 1948, stated that the purpose of the Act was to encourage the free flow of information. See FRSA § 900 ("The primary purpose of this Act is to safeguard the media's ability to gather news. It is intended to promote the free flow of information to the public . . . .").
  - The purpose of promoting the free flow of information to the public applies here where Peel's blog is dedicated to that purpose, where the item posted on the blog reported on misconduct by a public official, where there is no town newspaper, and where the only newspaper in the county does not engage in investigative journalism.

IV. Conclusion

- Even though Peel is not a professional reporter employed by traditional media, because she is regularly engaged in collecting, writing, and editing the news for publication on her blog, which is a news medium, being published at regular intervals and having a general circulation, she should be deemed a reporter under the FRSA.
- Because she is a reporter under the FRSA, she cannot be compelled to reveal the identity of the source of the information for the article that appeared in the blog.
- Therefore, it is probable that a motion to quash the subpoena based on the FRSA privilege will be successful.

FILE

MPT Task 4B:
In re Velocity Park

Hall & Gray LLP
Attorneys at Law
730 Amsterdam Ave.
Banford, Franklin 33701

MEMORANDUM

To: Applicant
From: Deanna Hall
Re: Liability waiver for Velocity Park
Date: February 26, 2008

Our client, Zeke Oliver, is about to open his new business venture, "Velocity Park," an outdoor skateboarding park (also referred to as a "skate park"). To reduce his liability to those who may be injured while skateboarding, Zeke has brought in a waiver form that he proposes to use. To help me advise him, please review his proposed waiver and prepare a memorandum:

- analyzing whether the proposed waiver will protect Velocity Park from liability for injuries occurring at the skate park;
- suggesting specific revisions to the proposed waiver, including replacement language as well as any changes in the waiver's design and layout (however, you should not redraft the entire waiver); and
- discussing whether any waiver will be enforceable if signed only by a minor.

CLIENT INTERVIEW—ZEKE OLIVER
February 22, 2008

Atty: Zeke, come on in. How are things coming along with your new business?

Zeke: I am totally pumped! The construction is right on schedule, and on April 30, 2008, Velocity Park, Banford's first and only skateboarding park, will be open to the public!

Atty: Great. So what can I help you with today?

Zeke: Well, my brother told me that I should require everyone who uses the skateboard park to sign a liability waiver so if someone gets hurt, they can't sue me. I found an entry form from a triathlon in the state of Columbia that I entered last year. It had some stuff about waiving liability, so I just made some changes and added the Velocity Park logo. I was all set to send it to the printer, but then I thought that I should have you look it over first.

Atty: A liability waiver is an excellent idea. And you're right—waivers aren't necessarily interchangeable from one situation to another. Before we discuss your proposed waiver form, let's talk a bit about who will be using the skateboarding park and what activities they will be able to do there.

Zeke: Okay. According to my market research, I expect that most of Velocity Park's visitors will be teenagers and young adults. There will be a minimum age of 10 for using the park. It will have all the basic stuff skateboarders love: a large concrete bowl, a beginners' area, and jumps, sliding rails, and two half-pipes, so advanced skaters can do ollies, kickflips, grinds, and other stunts. I plan to hold skills clinics and offer private lessons. Also, I've hooked up with a couple of skateboard manufacturers to sponsor some competitions, although I don't have anything definite yet. By the way, I've brought a newspaper article that mentions the park.

Atty: Thanks. Will you charge admission for the park? What about equipment rentals?

Zeke: Admission will be $10 for a three-hour block of skateboarding. I want it to be affordable for teenagers. Right now, I have no plans to rent equipment, but the park will have a shop to sell boards, helmets, T-shirts, and accessories. Of course, there will be a concessions area for soft drinks and snacks.

Atty: I assume that skateboarders get a fair number of bumps and bruises. Do you have any particular concerns about injuries at your park?

Zeke: Injuries are just part of skateboarding. Usually they're nothing more than scrapes, bruises, and the occasional sprained wrist from taking a fall. There will be signs posted stating that skateboarders have to wear helmets while using the park.

Atty: Where will skateboarders fill out your waiver form? I notice that it's two pages—that's a fair amount of reading for a teenager waiting to get into the park.

Zeke: Hey, I thought I was doing well to have only a two-page waiver. If I included everything I wanted to, it would be five pages. Anyway, the waivers will be handed out where skateboarders pay the admission fee, and whoever is staffing the cash register will collect them. I suppose some kids may not read it closely, especially if they're anxious to get in and skateboard, but short of reading the waiver to them, I don't know how to get around that. Also the waiver can be printed off of the park's website.

Atty: Will your staff be trained to deal with medical emergencies?

Zeke: I'm in the process of putting together a first-aid station, but kids won't get much more than a bandage there. For anything more serious, staff will be trained to call the skateboarder's emergency contact or an ambulance. I'm not too worried about serious injuries. In my experience, skateboarders have a good sense of what tricks they can do safely. Besides, it's so much better to have kids skateboarding in a park designed for that purpose than on the streets.

Atty: Where do most skateboarders go now in Banford?

Zeke: It's really sad. As soon as the kids find a good place, like a parking lot or cul-de-sac with a nice incline, they get chased out by the neighbors. The city council doesn't like skateboarders either. It's voted to ban skateboarding downtown. That's why I'm opening the park. Unless kids can get to another town in the area with a skateboard park, there's no place to skateboard, apart from streets and driveways in the outlying neighborhoods. Eventually, if Velocity Park succeeds, I'd like to partner with the city of Banford to operate the park and make it free, but until then, I've got my work cut out for me just to make Velocity Park recoup its costs.

Atty: With your business experience, I'm sure it will turn a profit in no time. I'll review this liability waiver and see if it meets your needs. Then we'll meet next week to discuss it.

Zeke: Thanks. I appreciate it. I really need to have this taken care of before the park opens.

DRAFT LIABILITY WAIVER

VELOCITY PARK
SKATEBOARDING
FOR A 21st CENTURY WORLD

1500 North Street
Banford, Franklin 33712
(555)555-1805

Welcome to Velocity Park! Before you hop on your skateboard and start work on your grinds, kickflips, and ollies, be sure to read and complete this form.

Admission Fees

$10 per skateboarder for a three-hour session in the park. $20 gets you an all-day pass. Unlimited monthly passes available for $75.

Hours of Operation

Monday-Friday, noon-8 p.m.
Saturday-Sunday, 10 a.m.-8 p.m.
Hours of operation subject to change without notice. Unanticipated closures will be posted at www.velocityparkskate.com.

Park Rules

- Must be 10 years of age or older to enter the skate park.
- Only skateboards and in-line skates may be used in the skate park.
- To enter and remain inside the skate park, you must wear a helmet.
- Inspect your equipment to make sure it is in good working order.
- Be considerate of fellow skateboarders, especially those who are younger and/or less skilled.
- No food, drink, or smoking allowed inside the skate park except in designated areas. No alcohol or drugs allowed.
- Skate park visitors must abide by staff instruction at all times.
- Velocity Park is not responsible for lost or stolen items.
- Failure to abide by these rules may result in expulsion from Velocity Park.

1. I understand and appreciate that participation in a sport carries a risk to me of serious injury and/or death. I voluntarily and knowingly recognize, accept, and assume this risk and hereby forever release, acquit, covenant not to sue, and discharge Velocity Park, its employees, event sponsors, and any third parties from any and all legal liability, including but not limited to all causes of action, claims, damages in law, or remedies in equity of whatever kind I have or which hereafter accrue to me, whether such injuries and/or claims arise from equipment failure, conditions in the park, or any actions of Velocity Park, its employees, third parties, or other skateboarders. Velocity Park is not responsible for any incidental or consequential damages, including, but not limited to, any claims for personal injury, property damage, or emotional distress. This release is binding with respect to my heirs, executors, administrators, and assigns, as well as myself.

2. I have been informed of Velocity Park Rules and agree to abide by them.

3. In connection with any injury I may sustain, or illness or other medical condition I may experience during my participation in skateboarding or attendance at Velocity Park, I authorize any emergency first aid, medication, medical treatment, or surgery deemed necessary by attending medical personnel if I am not able to act on my own behalf.

4. In consideration of permission to use the skate park facility, I agree that Velocity Park, its agents, and its employees may use my appearance, name, and likeness in connection with my use of the facility in any Velocity Park publication, including news releases. I further agree that I am not entitled to any compensation for such use of my appearance, name, or likeness.

Name (please print): _____ Sex:_____ Age:_____

(Signed): _____ Date: _____

Emergency Contact Information

Name: _____ Phone No.: _____

Address: _____

How did you hear about Velocity Park?

_____

Would you like e-mail updates about Velocity Park events?   Yes   No

If yes, e-mail address: _____

LIBRARY

ARTICLE FROM THE BANFORD COURIER

The Banford Courier
February 2, 2008

SKATEBOARDING: OLD AND NEW INJURIES ON THE RISE

Each year in Franklin, skateboarding results in about 500 visits to hospital emergency rooms, with some 50 skateboarders (usually children and adolescents) requiring hospitalization, usually because of head injuries. Nationally, in 2007, some 15,000 emergency room treatments were skate-board-related. Wrist injuries are the most common, either sprains or fractures. Although rare, deaths from falls and collisions with motor vehicles can occur.

Protective gear, such as helmets, slip-resistant closed-toe shoes, and wrist guards can greatly limit the number and severity of injuries. However, according to J.P. Clyde, a professional skateboarder, injuries could be further reduced if skateboarders paid more attention to the surfaces they ride on. "Studies by the U.S. Consumer Product Safety Commission found that 35 percent of all skateboarding-related injuries could have been avoided if skateboarders really paid attention to the skating environment," he said. "One-third of injuries happen because there's a flaw in the riding surface, whether it's a street, a parking lot, or a skate park. Innocuous objects like pebbles, twigs, bottle tops, or other debris can cause a skateboarder to take a spill. Cracks, potholes, and ruts also pose hazards to the unwary skateboarder."

Dr. Sanford Takei, a sports medicine specialist, agrees. "Beginning skateboarders—those who have been riding for less than a week—account for one-third of skateboarding injuries overall," he said.

"Obviously, beginners fall more often and may not know how to fall correctly. When experienced riders are injured, it is usually from falls caused by rocks and other irregularities in the riding surface."

But what really has parents in Banford up in arms is a new trend in skateboarding-related injuries: injuries that occur when teenagers mix alcohol or marijuana and skateboards. There has been a rise in reports of teenagers gathering in the Library Mall, drinking alcohol and then skateboarding on home-made ramps and trying risky stunts. Maggie Alden, a student at Banford High School, said that she quit skateboarding in the Mall after seeing a rider fall and break his nose after colliding with another skateboarder. "Those guys are clueless about where they're going," Alden said. "Someone is always trying to start a fight or take someone else's skateboard," she added.

For his part, Zeke Oliver, owner of Velocity Park, which will be Banford's first skate park when it opens in April, appeared relaxed about the risks of skateboarding injuries and aggressive skateboarders. "Look, skateboarding is only going to grow in popularity," he said. "It's a great way for kids to get outside, blow off some steam, and get some exercise."

Franklin Statutes—Civil Actions

§ 41 Contracts involving minors; limitations on authority of minor.

This section is intended to protect minors and to help parents and legal guardians exercise reasonable care, supervision, protection, and control over minor children.

* * * *

(a) A minor cannot make a contract relating to real property or any interest therein.

(b)(1) The contract of a minor may be disaffirmed by the minor himself, either before his majority or within a reasonable time afterwards, unless the contract at issue is one for necessaries, such as food or medical care.

(b)(2) Where a minor enters into a contract, whether one for necessaries or not, said contract may be enforced against that individual if, upon reaching the age of majority, the individual expressly or implicitly ratifies the contract.

(b)(3) Subsections (b)(1) and (b)(2) shall not apply to contracts made on behalf of a minor by the minor's parent or guardian.

Lund v. Swim World, Inc.

Franklin Supreme Court (2005)

Tim Lund sued Swim World, Inc., for the wrongful death of his mother, Annie Lund, who suffered a fatal head injury at its facility. The trial court granted summary judgment to Swim World, ruling that the waiver signed by Lund released Swim World from liability. The court of appeal affirmed. For the reasons set forth below, we reverse.

Swim World is a swimming facility with a lap pool open to members and visitors. On May 3, 2001, Lund visited Swim World as part of a physical therapy program. Because Lund was not a Swim World member, she had to fill out a guest registration card and pay a fee before swimming.

The guest registration, a five-inch-square preprinted card, also contained a "Waiver Release Statement," which appeared below the "Guest Registration" section, requesting the visitor's name, address, phone number, reason for visit, and interest in membership. The entire card was printed in capital letters of the same size, font, and color. The waiver language read as follows:

WAIVER RELEASE STATEMENT. I AGREE TO ASSUME ALL LIABILITY FOR MYSELF, WITHOUT REGARD TO FAULT, WHILE AT SWIM WORLD. I FURTHER AGREE TO HOLD HARMLESS SWIM WORLD, AND ITS EMPLOYEES, FOR ANY CONDITIONS OR INJURY THAT MAY RESULT TO ME WHILE AT SWIM WORLD. I HAVE READ THE FOREGOING AND UNDERSTAND ITS CONTENTS.

The card had just one signature and date line. Lund completed the "Guest Registration" portion and signed at the bottom of the "Waiver Release Statement" without asking any questions.

After swimming, Lund used the sauna in the women's locker room. The bench she was lying on collapsed beneath her, causing her to strike her head against the heater and lose consciousness. Lund was rushed to the hospital but died the next day as the result of complications from her head injury.

The complaint alleged that Swim World was negligent in the maintenance of its facilities and that its negligence caused Lund's death.

Summary judgment is granted when there is no genuine issue of material fact and the movant is entitled to judgment as a matter of law. *Samuels v. David* (Franklin Sup. Ct. 1991). The case at bar turns on the interpretation of Swim World's waiver form and whether it relieves Swim World of liability for harm caused by its negligence.

Waivers of liability, also known as exculpatory contracts,[1] are permitted under Franklin law except when prohibited by statute or public policy. As no statute bars the contract at issue, we proceed to a public policy analysis of the exculpatory clause.

Public policy can restrict freedom of contract for the good of the community. Thus, claims that an exculpatory contract violates public policy create a tension between the right to contract freely without government interference and the concern that allowing a tortfeasor to contract away responsibility for negligent acts may encourage conduct below a socially acceptable standard of care.

We examine the particular facts and circumstances of the case when determining whether an exculpatory contract is void and unenforceable as contrary to public policy.

---

[1] The words "release," "waiver," and "exculpatory agreement" have been used interchangeably by the courts to refer to written documents in which one party agrees to release another from potential tort liability for future conduct covered in the agreement.

Exculpatory contracts are generally construed against the party seeking to shield itself from liability. In *Schmidt v. Tyrol Mountain* (Franklin Sup. Ct. 1996), we set forth two requirements for an enforceable exculpatory clause: "First, the language of the waiver cannot be overbroad but must clearly, unambiguously, and unmistakably inform the signer of what is being waived. Second, the waiver form itself, viewed in its entirety, must alert the signer to the nature and significance of what is being signed." *Id.* We also noted that a relevant consideration in the enforceability of such a clause is whether there is a substantial disparity in bargaining power between the parties.

Thus, a release having language that is so broad as to be interpreted to shift liability for a tortfeasor's conduct under all possible circumstances, including reckless and intentional conduct, and for all possible injuries, will not be upheld. Likewise, release forms that serve two purposes and those that are not conspicuously labeled as waivers have been held to be insufficient to alert the parties' that he is waiving liability for other parties' negligence as well as his own.

In *Schmidt*, an action on behalf of a woman who fatally collided with the base of a chairlift tower while skiing, the plaintiff alleged that the defendant ski resort negligently failed to pad the lift tower. The resort moved for summary judgment, relying on the exculpatory clause in the ski pass signed by the skier. The waiver read, in part: "There are certain inherent risks in skiing and I agree to hold Tyrol Mountain harmless for any injury to me on the premises."

The court in *Schmidt* held that the release was void as against public policy. First, the release was not clear; it failed to include language expressly indicating the plaintiff's intent to release Tyrol Mountain from its own negligence. Without any mention in the release of the word "negligence," and the ambiguity of the phrase "inherent risks in skiing," the court held that the skier had not been adequately informed of the rights she was waiving.

As to the second factor, the form, in its entirety, did not fully communicate its nature and significance because it served the dual purposes of an application for a ski pass and a release of liability. Furthermore, the waiver was not conspicuous, in that it was one of five paragraphs on the form and did not require a separate signature. In addition, we noted that there was a substantial disparity in bargaining power between the parties.

Following *Schmidt*, we hold that Swim World's exculpatory clause violates public policy. First, the waiver is overly broad and all-inclusive. The waiver begins: "I AGREE TO ASSUME ALL LIABILITY FOR MYSELF, WITHOUT REGARD TO FAULT...." Here, it is unclear what type of acts the word "fault" encompasses; it could potentially bar any claim arising under any scenario.[2] We reject Swim World's claim that negligence is synonymous with fault and conclude that the word "fault" is broad enough to cover a reckless or an intentional act. A waiver of liability for an intentional act would clearly violate public policy. *See* Restatement (Second) of Contracts § 195(1) (term exempting party from tort liability for harm caused intentionally or recklessly is unenforceable on grounds of public policy).

Exculpatory agreements that, like this one, are broad and general will bar only those claims that the parties contemplated when they executed the contract. Here, we must determine whether the collapse of sauna bench was a risk the parties contemplated when the exculpatory contract was executed. If not, the contract is not enforceable.

---

[2] While including the word "negligence" in exculpatory clauses is not required, we have stated that "it would be helpful for such contracts to set forth in clear terms that the party signing it is releasing others for their negligent acts. *Schmidt*.

Here, given the broadness of the exculpatory language, it is difficult to ascertain exactly what was within Lund's or Swim World's contemplation. Nevertheless, it appears unlikely that Lund, when she signed the guest registration and waiver form, would have contemplated receiving a severe head injury from the collapse of a sauna bench.

Further, Swim World's guest registration and waiver form failed to provide adequate notice of the waiver's nature and significance. Like the contract in *Schmidt*, the form served two purposes: it was both a "Guest Registration" application and a "Waiver Release Statement." The exculpatory language appeared to be part of, or a requirement for, a larger registration form. The waiver could have been a separate document, giving Lund more notice of what she was signing. Also, a separate signature line could have been provided, but was not. Clearly identifying and distinguishing those two contractual arrangements could have provided important protection against a signatory's inadvertent agreement to the release.

Another problem with the form is that the paragraph containing the "Waiver Release Statement" was not conspicuous. The entire form was printed on one card, with the same letter size, font, and color. It is irrelevant that the release language is in capital letters; *all of* the words on the form were in capital letters. Further, the only place to sign the form was at the very end. This supports the conclusion that the waiver was not distinguishable enough such that a reviewing court can say with certainty that the signer was fully aware of its nature and significance.

Finally, we consider the bargaining positions of the parties. This factor looks to the facts surrounding the execution of the waiver. We hasten to add that the presence of this factor, by itself, will not automatically render an exculpatory clause void under public policy.

Here, the record suggests that there was an unequal bargaining position between the parties. Lund had no opportunity to negotiate regarding the standard exculpatory language in the form. In his deposition, Swim World's desk attendant testified that Lund was simply told to complete and sign the form; the waiver portion was not pointed out, nor were its terms explained to her. No one discussed the risks of injury purportedly covered by the form. The desk attendant further testified that Lund did not ask any questions about the form but that there was pressure to sign it because other patrons were behind Lund waiting to sign in. These facts undeniably generate, at a minimum, a genuine dispute of material fact regarding the parties' disparity in bargaining power.

For these reasons we conclude that the exculpatory clause in Swim World's form violates public policy, and, therefore, is unenforceable.

Reversed.

Holum v. Bruges Soccer Club, Inc.

Columbia Supreme Court (1999)

Pamela Holum registered her seven-year-old son, Bryan, for soccer with Bruges Soccer Club, Inc. (the Club), a nonprofit organization that provides local children with the opportunity to learn and play soccer. Its members are parents and other volunteers. As part of the registration process, Mrs. Holum signed a release form whereby she agreed to release "the Club from liability for physical injuries arising as a result of [Bryan's] participation in the soccer club."

Bryan was injured when, after a soccer practice, he jumped on the goal and swung on it. The goal tipped backward and fell on Bryan's chest, breaking three ribs. Bryan's parents, Phil and Pamela Holum, sued the Club, alleging negligence on their own behalf and on behalf of Bryan. The trial court granted summary judgment to the Club, holding that the release signed by Bryan's mother barred the Holums' action against the Club.

The court of appeal affirmed in part and reversed in part. It held that the release barred Mr. and Mrs. Holum's claims. However, it went on to hold that the release did not bar Bryan's claim. Thus, while the parents' claims were barred, Bryan still had a cause of action against the Club, which a guardian could bring on his behalf, or which he could assert upon reaching the age of majority.

We agree with the court of appeal that the release applies to the injuries at issue. As to whether the release executed by Mrs. Holum on behalf of her minor son released the Club from liability for Bryan's claim and his parents' claims as a matter of law, we conclude that the release is valid as to all claims. Accordingly, we reverse that portion of the court of appeal decision holding that the release would not prevent Bryan from asserting a claim for his injuries.

We first consider whether the release is valid. In Columbia, with respect to adults, the general rule is that releases from liability for injuries caused by negligent acts arising during recreational activities are enforceable, whether the negligence is on the part of the participant in the recreational activity or the provider of the activity, in this case, the Club. This approach recognizes the importance of individual autonomy and freedom of contract.

For that reason, the release agreement is valid as to the parents' negligence claim. Mrs. Holum acknowledged that she read the agreement and did not ask any questions. Mr. Holum did not sign the release, but he accepted and enjoyed the benefits of the contract. In fact, when the injury occurred, he was at the practice field, thereby indicating his intention to enjoy the benefits of his wife's agreement and be bound by it. It is well settled that parents may release their own claims arising out of injury to their minor children. Accordingly, we find that Bryan's parents are barred from recovery as to their claims.

Here, however, the release was executed by a parent on behalf of the minor child. The Holums contend that the release is invalid on public policy grounds, citing the general principle that contracts entered into by a minor, unless for "necessaries," are voidable by the minor before the age of majority is reached. The Club, however, argues that the public interest justifies the enforcement of this agreement with respect to both the parents' and the child's claims.

Organized recreational activities provide children the opportunity to develop athletic ability as well as to learn valuable life skills such as teamwork and cooperation. The assistance of volunteers allows nonprofit organizations to offer these activities at minimal cost. In fact, the Club pays only 19 of its 400 staff members. Without volunteers, such nonprofit organizations could not exist and many children would lose

THE MPT
MULTISTATE PERFORMANCE TEST

In re Velocity Park

POINT SHEET

The MPT point sheet, grading summary, and grading guidelines describe the factual and legal points encompassed within the lawyering task to be completed. They outline all the possible issues and points that might be addressed by an applicant. They are provided to the user jurisdictions for the sole purpose of assisting graders in grading the examination by identifying the issues and suggesting the resolution of the problem contemplated by the drafters. These are not official grading guides. Applicants can receive a range of passing grades, including excellent grades, without covering all the points discussed in these guides. The model answer is included as an illustration of a thorough and detailed response to the task, one that addresses all the legal and factual issues the drafters intended to raise in the problem. It is intended to serve only as an example. Applicants need not present their responses in the same way to receive good grades. User jurisdictions are free to modify these grading materials, including the suggested weights assigned to particular points. Grading the MPT is the exclusive responsibility of the jurisdiction using the MPT as part of its admissions process.

Copyright ©2008 by the National Conference of Bar Examiners.
All rights reserved

---

the benefit of organized sports. Yet, the threat of liability deters many individuals from volunteering. Even if the organization has insurance, individual volunteers could find themselves liable for an injury.

Faced with the threat of lawsuits, and the potential for substantial damage awards, nonprofit organizations and their volunteers could very well decide that the risks are not worth the effort. Hence, invalidation of exculpatory agreements would reduce the number of activities made possible by the services of volunteers and their sponsoring organizations.

Therefore, although when his mother signed the release Bryan gave up his right to sue for the negligent acts of others, the public as a whole received the benefit of these exculpatory agreements. Because of this agreement, the Club can offer affordable recreation without the risks and overwhelming costs of litigation. Bryan's parents agreed to shoulder the risk. Accordingly, we believe that it is in the public interest that parents have authority to enter into these types of binding agreements on behalf of their minor children. We also believe that the enforcement of these agreements may promote more active involvement by participants and their families, which, in turn, promotes the overall quality and safety of these activities.

A related concern is the importance of parental authority. Parents have a fundamental liberty interest in the care, custody, and management of their offspring. Parental authority extends to the ability to make decisions regarding the child's school, religion, medical care, and discipline. Invalidating the release as to the minor's claim is inconsistent with parents' authority to make important life choices for their children.

Mrs. Holum signed the release because she wanted Bryan to play soccer. In making this family decision, she assumed the risk of physical injury on behalf of Bryan and the financial risk on behalf of the family as a whole. Apparently, she determined that the benefits to her child outweighed the risk of physical injury. The situation is comparable to Columbia Stat. § 2317, which gives parents the authority to consent to medical procedures on a child's behalf. In both cases, the parent weighs the risks of physical injury to the child and its attendant costs against the benefits of a particular activity.

Therefore, we hold that parents have the authority to bind their minor children to exculpatory agreements in favor of volunteers and sponsors of nonprofit sport activities where the cause of action sounds in negligence. These agreements may not be disaffirmed by the child on whose behalf they were executed. We need not decide here whether there are other circumstances, beyond the realm of nonprofit organizations, which will support a parent's waiver of a child's claims.

Accordingly, we hold that the release is valid as to the claims of both the parents and the minor child.

Affirmed in part and reversed in part.

In re Velocity Park

Drafters' Point Sheet

This performance test requires applicants, as associates at a law firm, to analyze the provisions of a liability waiver for a recreational activity. The client, Zeke Oliver, owns Velocity Park, set to be the first skateboarding park in Banford, Franklin, when it opens in April. Zeke has asked the law firm for advice regarding an appropriate liability waiver that users of the skate park will be required to sign in order to use the park.

In analyzing whether the waiver that Zeke provided is enforceable under Franklin law, applicants are expected to address both the waiver's language and its format. Applicants also must grapple with the issue of whether liability waivers signed only by minors will be enforced to bar actions for negligence arising from the minor's skateboarding injuries.

The File contains the task memorandum from the supervising partner, a client interview transcript, a liability waiver Zeke assembled by taking language from a triathlon entry form/liability waiver, and a newspaper article about the risks of skateboarding. The Library includes a Franklin statute regarding civil actions, a Franklin case, and a case from Columbia.

The following discussion covers all of the points the drafters intended to raise in the problem. Applicants need not cover them all to receive passing or even excellent grades. Grading is entirely within the discretion of the user jurisdictions.

I. Format and Overview

Applicants' work product should resemble a legal memorandum such as an associate would write to a supervising partner. Applicants should analyze the waiver Zeke has proposed, identifying problems with its content and design that may preclude it from being found enforceable by a court. Applicants are told not to rewrite the entire waiver. However, if certain language is overbroad or ambiguous, applicants should suggest replacement language that better conforms to the standards set forth in the cases and explain why the changes are necessary for an enforceable waiver. Further, applicants should recognize that the reach of a waiver is tied to the characteristics of the activity (and potential injuries) at issue. Thus they should incorporate the relevant facts from the client interview and the news article in their analysis of the issues. The task memorandum does not require applicants to organize their answers in any particular order, but the order presented below is a logical manner in which to address the issues.

Applicants should conclude that (1) Zeke's proposed waiver contains significant content and format defects, and (2) while the precise issue has not been addressed by Franklin courts, it is unlikely that a court will enforce an exculpatory contract executed by a minor in this situation.

II. Discussion

In Franklin, a party may use an exculpatory contract to limit its liability exposure, but a court may refuse to enforce such a contract on the grounds that its terms violate public policy. A court considers two factors when determining whether an exculpatory contract is enforceable: whether the waiver of liability language is overly broad and ambiguous and whether the exculpatory clause is conspicuous such that it notifies the signer of the nature and significance of what is being waived. Courts will also consider a third, nondispositive factor: whether there exists a substantial disparity in bargaining power between the parties. *Lund v. Swim World, Inc.* (Franklin Sup. Ct. 2005).

A. Whether the Velocity Park Waiver Is Overly Broad and Ambiguous

Franklin courts construe the language of an exculpatory contract against the party seeking to enforce the contract. *Lund*. To survive a public policy challenge, the exculpatory contract must include a description that "clearly, unambiguously, and unmistakably inform[s] the signer of what is being waived." *Id.* (quoting *Schmidt v. Tyrol Mountain* (Franklin Sup. Ct. 1996)). In *Lund*, the deceased swimmer had signed a waiver in which she agreed "to assume all liability for myself, without regard to fault." The Franklin Supreme Court concluded that, by using only the word "fault," the exculpatory clause was overly broad because it could be construed as waiving any and all claims, even those for the defendant's intentional or reckless acts and omissions.

The key to determining whether the exculpatory language is overly broad is whether the risks that the parties contemplated at the time the waiver was executed can be ascertained. In *Lund*, the court held that the waiver's broad language prevented it from concluding that, at the time Lund signed the waiver, she anticipated the risk of a severe head injury when a sauna bench collapsed under her. Not only did the Swim World waiver refer generally to "fault," it failed to spell out any particular risks for which Lund was waiving the right to sue Swim World.

Here, the Velocity Park waiver fails to satisfy *Lund*'s requirement that exculpatory contracts "clearly, unambiguously, and unmistakably inform the signer of [the rights he or she is waiving]." The relevant paragraphs of the proposed waiver read as follows:

1. I understand and appreciate that participation in a sport carries a risk to me of serious injury and/or death. I voluntarily and knowingly recognize, accept, and assume this risk and hereby forever release, acquit, covenant not to sue, and discharge Velocity Park, its employees, event sponsors, and any third parties from any and all legal liability, including but not limited to all causes of action, claims, damages in law, or remedies in equity of whatever kind I have or which hereafter accrue to me, whether such injuries and/or claims arise from equipment failure, conditions in the park, or any actions of Velocity Park, its employees, third parties, or other skateboarders. Velocity Park is not responsible for any incidental or consequential damages, including, but not limited to, any claims for personal injury, property damage, or emotional distress. This release is binding with respect to my heirs, executors, administrators, and assigns, as well as myself.

2. I have been informed of Velocity Park Rules and agree to abide by them.

1. **The language of the waiver is overbroad.**

   a. Exculpatory clauses are strictly construed against the party seeking to shield itself from liability. *Lund*.

   b. The waiver at issue ostensibly releases Velocity Park from liability "from any and all legal liability, including but not limited to all causes of action, claims, damages in law, or remedies in equity of whatever kind...."

   c. The phrase "any and all legal liability" would presumably cover injuries resulting from intentional and reckless acts, as well as from negligence. As stated in *Lund*, a release that is "so broad as to be interpreted to shift liability for a tortfeasor's conduct under all possible circumstances, including reckless and intentional conduct, and for all possible injuries, will not be upheld."

   - Waivers are not effective to bar liability for intentional acts. *See Lund* (citing Restatement of Contracts (Second) § 195(1)).
   - The word "negligence" need not appear in a waiver for it to be enforceable, but the better practice is to clearly state that by signing the waiver, the party is releasing others from negligence claims. *Lund*, fn.2.

d. Thus, Zeke's waiver is too broad to inform a skateboarder of the precise rights waived.
e. Further, the waiver attempts to be a release of claims against not just Velocity Park and its employees, but also against "any third parties."
   - This attempt to extend the waiver to unknown third parties is most likely unenforceable under *Lund*.
f. The exculpatory clause also contains repetitive and confusing language (e.g., "[I] hereby forever release, acquit, covenant not to sue, and discharge Velocity Park..."), making it more likely that the average skateboarder at the park—according to Zeke, most Velocity Park visitors will be teenagers and young adults—will not carefully read or understand the agreement before signing it.

2. **The waiver fails to alert the signer to the risks involved in skateboarding.**
   a. Overbroad and general exculpatory agreements will be construed to bar only those claims that the parties contemplated when they executed the contract. *Lund*. A waiver that only vaguely refers to the activity at issue will not be deemed sufficient to inform the signer of the risks of the activity and the rights being waived. In *Schmidt v. Tyrol Mountain*, cited in *Lund*, a waiver's reference to the "inherent risks in skiing" was insufficient to inform the skier of the risks she was assuming.
   b. The Velocity Park waiver states that the signer "understand[s] and appreciate[s] that participation in a sport carries a risk to me of serious injury and/or death."
      - This language is even more vague than the language in *Schmidt* ("the inherent risks in skiing"); it gives no information to the signer about particular risks associated with skateboarding.
   c. Thus the waiver should be revised to include language expressly informing the signer of specific skateboarding injury risks and possible causes.
      - *The Banford Courier* article states that the most common skateboarding injuries are wrist sprains and fractures, but serious head injuries may also occur.
   d. Applicants could redraft the Velocity Park waiver as follows: "I understand and appreciate that skateboarding carries a risk to me of injury from falls or collisions with objects or other skateboarders, including but not limited to bruises, abrasions, sprains and fractures (especially to the wrist), and head injuries, and that these injuries could be severe or even result in substantial disability or death."
      - A revised waiver could also mention something to the effect that using the half-pipes, jumps, etc., increases the risk of harm to the skateboarder.
      - A thorough waiver might also state that falls are likely due to debris on or irregularities in the riding surface (thus insulating Velocity Park for claims based on a skater falling because he or she ran over a piece of trash).
   e. The waiver also should clearly and expressly convey the risks of skateboarding in a park with other skateboarders.
   f. Applicants might note that many park users will be teenagers, so the language of the waiver should use terms understandable to someone of a relatively young age, even if the form will have to be signed by parents (*see* discussion *infra* II.D.).
   g. Moreover, given the rise in injuries associated with aggressive behavior in skateboarders (e.g., risky stunts, fights), the waiver should include language denying liability for injuries caused by Velocity Park's negligent failure to supervise skateboarders.
   h. Applicants could also note that there are other injuries that even a well-drafted waiver may not cover because they were not within the parties' contemplation when the waiver was executed. (For example, a skateboarder gets food poisoning from a hot dog sold by the Velocity Park concession stand.)

B. Whether the Velocity Park Waiver Is Conspicuous

Second, a liability waiver must "alert the signer to the nature and significance of what is being signed." *Lund*. The exculpatory clause must be conspicuous to the signer; its format must visually communicate that the waiver language is important.[3] In *Lund*, the court noted that documents that serve two purposes generally are not sufficiently conspicuous, especially when there is only a single signature line, because the importance of the exculpatory clause may not be clearly distinguishable from the rest of the document. Further, the exculpatory clause in *Lund* was not conspicuous because it was in the same size, font, and color as the rest of the form.

1. *Lund* provides specific examples of how a dual-purpose document may be improved.
   a. The waiver could be a separate document.
   b. There could be a separate signature line for the exculpatory clause.
2. Zeke's form serves many purposes and the exculpatory clause is not conspicuous.
   a. The form contains information on park hours, prices, and rules. It also has paragraphs whereby the skateboarder agrees to waive liability, consents to the use of his or her likeness, authorizes medical treatment, provides emergency contact information, and agrees to receive park e-mails.
   b. There are headings for the sections regarding fees, hours, and park rules, but there is no heading for the exculpatory clause or the medical care and use of likeness paragraphs (although these paragraphs are numbered).
   c. The exculpatory clause is in a *smaller* font than is the first part of the form.
   d. There is only one signature line; arguably, the exculpatory clause, consent to medical treatment, and use of likeness parts warrant separate signatures.
   e. The clause does not have any language to the effect of "I have read this form and understand that by signing it I am waiving important rights." (Even the waiver in *Lund* contains the sentence "I have read the foregoing and understand its contents.") Adding such language would emphasize to the skateboarder the nature and significance of the waiver.

C. Whether There Is a Disparity in Bargaining Power Between the Parties

The third public policy factor addressed in *Lund* is the question of whether there is a substantial disparity in bargaining power between the parties. In making this determination, the court will consider "the facts surrounding the execution of the waiver," including whether the signer has an opportunity to negotiate its terms. *Lund*.

1. In *Lund*, there was no opportunity to negotiate the waiver's terms; Lund either signed or didn't swim.
2. The Swim World employee did not alert Lund that the entrance form included a liability waiver, let alone explain its terms to her.
3. The court also noted that there was not enough time to read Swim World's form and make a reasoned decision about the consequences of signing it, because there were other Swim World patrons waiting in line to check in.
4. The court concluded that, at a minimum, there was a genuine dispute of material fact regarding the parties' disparity in bargaining power.

---

[3] Applicants are not expected to redraft the entire waiver or attempt to recreate it in a better format in their answer books (e.g., by redrafting the waiver language using a larger font). However, as directed by the task memo, they should suggest those changes that should be incorporated into the waiver's design and layout.

5. Regarding the expected circumstances of skateboarders' execution of Zeke's proposed waiver, a substantial disparity of bargaining power could be found.
   - As in *Lund*, skateboarders will have to sign the exculpatory contract to use the park; there is no "opt-out" provision.
   - Velocity Park would-be patrons, similar to the deceased in *Lund*, may be under pressure to sign the waiver as quickly as possible so as not to delay the entry of other skateboarders waiting in line.
6. Applicants should suggest that park employees alert skateboarders and their parents (*see* below) to the form's liability waiver portion, warning them to carefully read it.
7. They should also suggest that all patrons (and their parents) be told that if they have any questions about the waiver, they should ask park employees, who should be familiar with the waiver's terms.
8. Also, Zeke should be sure to fully staff the park at peak times (e.g., opening and after school) when there might be many impatient kids and parents waiting in line.
9. Applicants thus should suggest measures Zeke can take to minimize a substantial disparity in bargaining power between the parties. However, even if there is some disparity (i.e., patrons are not allowed to opt out of signing), it is unlikely that the presence of this one negative factor would lead a court to find an otherwise enforceable waiver void as against public policy. *See Lund*. Indeed, the *Lund* court appears to give more weight to the first two factors: whether the language is overbroad and ambiguous, and whether the form notifies the signer to the significance of what is being waived.

D. Whether a Waiver Is Enforceable If Signed Only by a Minor

1. *Lund* does not address whether a release signed by a minor, or by a parent on a minor's behalf, would be contrary to public policy. Thus, it appears that the enforceability of waivers against minors is an issue of first impression in Franklin.
2. The relevant case law on this issue is a Columbia case, *Holum v. Bruges Soccer Club, Inc.* (Col. Sup. Ct. 1999). *Holum* discusses the effectiveness of a waiver signed by a parent on behalf of her minor child as a condition of the child's participation in a soccer club. The court held that enforcing the waiver against the parents and the child was in the public's interest, largely because the defendant was a nonprofit soccer club that relied on volunteers to offer soccer to many children at low cost. The court reasoned that protecting the club and its volunteers from liability was critical to the existence of such recreational activities because volunteers might be reluctant to help if doing so meant subjecting themselves to liability. The court said that enforcing the club's liability waiver allocated the risk of injury from the club to parents, thereby benefiting the community as a whole by making soccer more accessible to all children.
3. The court in *Holum* also emphasized that parents have authority to make decisions regarding the welfare of their children, comparing the club's waiver to the parents' statutory right to consent to medical procedures involving their children. The court assumed that a parent signing a release of future claims would be in a position to consider the alternatives and make a reasoned decision that the cost of waiving the right to sue was outweighed by the benefit to the child of being able to participate in the activity.
   a. In *Holum*, the mother signed a release on behalf of her seven-year-old child. Most of the patrons at Velocity Park will be teenagers. Applicants will have to address how *Holum* applies to an activity which, unlike the soccer club, is not sponsored by a volunteer-driven organization.

E. Application of *Holum* to the proposed Velocity Park waiver form

1. Zeke's proposed waiver has a single line for the skateboarder's signature, and places for indicating sex and age. Zeke says in his interview that 10 is the minimum age to use the park and that he expects most skateboarders to be teens or young adults. In short, a substantial number of park patrons will be minors.
2. Also, because beginning skateboarders account for one-third of skateboarding injuries, liability for claims by underage skateboarders is a real concern.
3. The fact that Velocity Park is a for-profit enterprise weighs against enforcing a release that purports to waive a minor's right to sue for negligence under *Holum*.
   a. While Zeke states that, at some point, he would like to partner with the City of Banford and make the skate park free, Velocity Park will clearly open as a for-profit business.
   b. Thus, the rationale that enforceable liability waivers ensure volunteer participation and the provision of community-based recreation (so central in the *Holum* holding) is not a consideration here.
   c. That does not mean that Velocity Park won't benefit Banford: it gives skateboarders a supervised space in which to skate and one that was expressly designed for that purpose. Thus, it will be an improvement over teens skateboarding in neighborhood cul-de-sacs and the Library Mall.
   d. Applicants must recognize that *Holum*, a Columbia case, is persuasive only.
   e. However, the *Holum* court based its holding equally on the fact that parents have authority to make life choices for their children and that they assume the risk of injury to their child in exchange for the privilege and benefit of participation in low-cost recreational sports.
4. Applicants must grapple with the Franklin statute regarding enforceability of contracts entered into by minors. It seems clear that under § 41, a liability waiver signed by an underage skateboarder, without being co-signed by a parent or guardian, will not be enforceable.
   a. For example, under § 41(b)(1), a minor can disaffirm a contract, unless the contract was for necessaries (e.g., food). Because skateboarding is not a necessary, an under-18 skateboarder could sign but then disaffirm a Velocity Park waiver. On the other hand, the waiver could be enforced against the skateboarder if he or she ratifies the agreement after turning 18 by, for example, continuing to use the park. (The assumption here is that once a waiver is signed, Velocity Park keeps it on file and a skateboarder doesn't need to sign a new one every time he or she uses the park.)
5. Applicants should note that under *Holum*, parents in Columbia can waive claims on their own behalf and on behalf of their children for negligence that results in injuries to their children. Given that exculpatory contracts in Franklin will be enforceable if they meet the standards for scope and clarity in *Lund*, applicants should suggest that the Velocity Park waiver be signed by the parents of any skateboarder who is under 18. This will help insulate Velocity Park from negligence claims by injured skateboarders' parents.

Note: Applicants could receive extra credit for observing that, strategically, even if it is uncertain whether a waiver will be enforced, some provisions may be desirable to discourage people from suing the park after an injury.

MPT Task 4C:
Vargas v. Monte

FILE

[MPT Task July 2003 Bar Exam]

Norman & Longfellow
Attorneys at Law
405 East Gray, Suite 100
Lakeview, Franklin 33071

MEMORANDUM

To: Applicant
From: Jane Norman
Date: July 29, 2003
Subject: Vargas v. Monte

We have nearly completed the bench trial of the *Vargas v. Monte* timber trespass case. Our client, Les Vargas, brought this action against adjoining landowner Carla Monte for wrongfully cutting and removing trees from his property. He is seeking an award of statutory treble damages. The parties have presented their evidence at trial, and the judge has now requested briefs on the issues of whether, based on the evidence adduced at trial, (1) defendant Monte is liable for timber trespass and, if so, (2) whether single, double, or treble damages, or some combination thereof, should be assessed against her.

Please draft a persuasive brief to the court addressing the liability and damages issues outlined above. Our goals are to persuade the judge to hold Monte liable for timber trespass and award Vargas the maximum damages allowable by law based on the evidence, explaining why any lower measure of damages is inappropriate.

Prepare the brief in accordance with the guidelines set forth in the attached office memorandum. We have a statement of stipulated facts in this case so, as pointed out in the brief writing guidelines, you should write only a short introductory statement that reminds the court of the nature of the dispute and our goals. In drafting your arguments, however, you must use all relevant facts that support your arguments.

Norman & Longfellow
Attorneys at Law
405 East Gray, Suite 100
Lakeview, Franklin 33071

MEMORANDUM

September 8, 1995
To: All Lawyers
From: Litigation Supervisor
Subject: Persuasive Briefs

All persuasive briefs shall conform to the following guidelines:

All briefs shall include a Statement of Facts. The aim of the Statement of Facts is to persuade the tribunal that the facts support our client's position. The facts must be stated accurately, although emphasis is not improper. Select carefully the facts that are pertinent to the legal arguments. However, in a brief to a trial court, when there is a statement of stipulated facts, the Statement of Facts section of the brief may be abbreviated. In such cases, the lawyer need only write a short introductory statement and direct the court's attention to the statement of stipulated facts.

The firm follows the practice of breaking the argument into its major components and writing carefully crafted subject headings that illustrate the arguments they cover. Avoid writing briefs that contain only a single broad argument heading. The argument heading should be succinctly should be a specific application of a rule of law to the facts of the case and not a bare legal or factual conclusion or a statement of an abstract principle. For example, improper: THE PLAINTIFF HAS ESTABLISHED PLAINTIFF'S CLAIM OF RIGHT. Proper: BY PLACING A CHAIN ACROSS THE DRIVEWAY AND BY REFUSING ACCESS TO OTHERS, PLAINTIFF HAS ESTABLISHED A CLAIM OF RIGHT.

The body of each argument should analyze applicable legal authority and persuasively argue how the facts and law support our client's position. Authority supportive of our client's position should be emphasized, but contrary authority should also generally be cited, addressed in the argument, and explained or distinguished. Do not reserve arguments for reply or supplemental briefing.

The lawyer need not prepare a table of contents, a table of cases, a summary of argument, or an index. These will be prepared, when required, after the draft is approved.

STATEMENT OF STIPULATED FACTS

1. Plaintiff Les Vargas owns property covering several hundred acres of land in Cleveland County, Franklin.
2. Adjoining the Vargas property is a several-hundred-acre parcel of land owned by defendant Carla Monte.
3. Prior to 1880, the two parcels were part of a larger tract of land owned by the United States Government.
4. In 1879, the original survey of this area was conducted by licensed surveyors for the U.S. General Land Office ("USGLO"). The original survey was undertaken for the purpose of subdividing the area into smaller parcels, which were then sold.
5. In 1880, the USGLO transferred to Vargas's and Monte's ancestors their respective parcels. The Vargas family bought the west half and the Monte family bought the east half.
6. As part of the 1879 survey, the one-quarter-mile-long common boundary running north and south between the Vargas and Monte parcels was established and marked.
7. The 1879 survey established section corners that were monumented using wooden posts set in mounds of stone. The lines between these corners were marked by blazing trees along the common boundary. A blaze is a chest-high, smooth surface cut on a tree.
8. Between 2000 and 2002, the boundary line between the parties' properties was resurveyed by the U.S. Department of the Interior, Bureau of Land Management ("BLM"), as part of a larger resurvey of portions of the county. The BLM resurvey is the only licensed survey conducted of these parcels since the original USGLO survey.
9. From March 2000 to January 2002, Carla Monte cut and removed approximately 700 trees from a strip of land along the parties' shared boundary.

EXCERPTS FROM TRIAL TESTIMONY OF PLAINTIFF LES VARGAS

Direct Examination by Jane Norman, Counsel for Plaintiff:

* * *

Q: How long have you and Carla Monte shared a common property boundary?
A: Well, we each inherited our parcels from our families, who had owned them for generations. So I guess that makes us lifelong neighbors in a sense.

Q: Was the boundary line between your and Ms. Monte's properties clearly delineated before the BLM resurvey?
A: Not at all. There were conflicting blaze marks at various points along the property line, and even some trees sprayed with paint and tagged with construction tape. Members of both families had tried to figure out where the true boundary was, but they eventually gave up.

Q: So, how did you and Ms. Monte deal with the uncertainty surrounding the property line?
A: Well, both of our parcels are big enough that we never really got around to sorting it out. When I heard about the BLM resurvey, I figured that we'd finally know once and for all where the true boundary line was.

* * *

Q: How would you describe your relationship with Carla Monte?
A: Well, I thought it was pretty neighborly until I found out she was cutting down my trees.

EXCERPTS FROM TRIAL TESTIMONY OF STAN LINHART

Direct Examination By Jane Norman, Counsel for Plaintiff:

* * *

Q: As a licensed surveyor for the United States Department of the Interior, Bureau of Land Management, were you involved in the BLM resurvey of Cleveland County?

A: Yes, I was the lead surveyor and the point of contact for local landowners.

Q: Are you familiar with the parcels owned by plaintiff Les Vargas and defendant Carla Monte?

A: I am. The Vargas and Monte parcels were surveyed as part of the BLM resurvey.

* * *

Q: Did you have contact with Ms. Monte during the fall of 2001?

A: Yes. We were surveying a stretch of the boundary between the Monte and Vargas parcels when I spotted Ms. Monte and her crew cutting down trees west of the property line, in fact more than 100 feet onto the Vargas parcel. I noticed that she had already cut about 300 trees. When I pointed out to Ms. Monte that she was logging trees on the Vargas parcel, she told me that the trees were on her property.

Q: What specifically did she say to you?

A: She said her grandfather and Vargas's grandfather had agreed on the boundary. Then she pointed to some old blaze marks and paint stains about 20 feet farther west inside the Vargas property and said that the parties had relied on these markings for years. When I pointed out that the true boundary line was more than 100 feet east of the point where she was logging, she said it wasn't fair for BLM to come in and try to change the boundary lines after all these years.

Q: Did the conversation end there?

A: No. I warned her that the boundary markers she was relying on weren't accurate, and I cautioned her against continuing to log there until BLM could complete its resurvey.

Q: Do you know whether Ms. Monte continued logging in that area after you told her this?

A: The very next day I saw her in the same area cutting down more trees on the Vargas property. When I returned to the area a few weeks later to double check some of our survey work, I saw additional evidence of logging by Ms. Monte farther along the shared boundary line, including more stumps on the Vargas side of the property line. By that time, I had already notified Mr. Vargas, and I figured this was something that the two property owners would have to work out.

Q: Can you describe the condition of the boundary line between the Monte and Vargas properties prior to the BLM resurvey?

A: Well, before the resurvey, the boundary line was a real mess and nobody knew exactly where it was located.

Q: Why is that?

A: Because the section lines blazed on trees during the original survey back in the 1800s had deteriorated. Previous attempts had been made to locate and perpetuate the original survey monuments. Over time, these attempts created errors and conflicting blaze marks and other evidence concerning the property boundaries. This problem wasn't limited to the boundary line between the Vargas and Monte properties. It was a widespread and well-known problem throughout the county, which is why we were called in to do the resurvey.

* * *

Q: When did you discover this?

A: Sometime during the fall of 2001, when I got a call from a BLM surveyor by the name of Stan Linhart.

Q: Did you do anything as a result of Mr. Linhart's call?

A: Yes. I went out to the boundary between the two properties and saw that dozens of my trees had been chopped down. Everywhere I looked, I saw stumps where there used to be beautiful, mature ponderosa pines.

Q: What, if anything, did you do after you discovered that your trees had been destroyed?

A: I tried to reach Carla, but she never returned my calls. I left messages on her machine asking her to stop destroying my trees. I also posted some signs that said "No Trespassing."

Q: Did your efforts have any effect?

A: When I went back about a month later to check on things, I discovered that even more of my trees had been cut down and hauled off. I couldn't believe that Carla had continued to log in this area and that she'd cut down more of my trees even after I posted the "No Trespassing" signs. That was when I decided to take legal action.

Q: Does Carla Monte have your permission to cut down any of your trees?

A: Absolutely not. In fact, she knew that I'd turned down some lucrative logging contracts with logging companies that wanted to harvest trees on my property.

Q: How did she know this?

A: Well, over the years I told her about a few of the offers I'd received from logging companies. She told me I was silly to turn down these big money offers. She said that if I ever changed my mind, I should let her know because, since she was in the logging business, she wanted the logging rights to my land.

* * *

Cross-Examination by William Warren, Counsel for Defendant:

* * *

Q: Mr. Vargas, isn't it true that your family and the family of Ms. Monte had a longstanding agreement about the boundary of the two properties?

A: No, she and I never agreed on the exact boundary. As the landscape changed over the years, it was more and more difficult to determine the exact location of the dividing line. But we knew within a few feet or so where our property line was, especially in the area where she chopped down my trees.

Q: Showing you what has been marked as Defendant's Exhibit A for identification, can you identify it?

A: Well, it looks like a letter with a hand-drawn map from my grandfather, Amos Vargas, to someone by the name of Ben Monte.

Q: You recognize the handwriting of your grandfather, Amos Vargas, don't you?

A: Yes, it seems to be his writing. It looks like his letters that we have in the family collection.

Q: And your grandfather wrote this letter in 1906, didn't he?

A: Well, all I know is the letter says it was written on April 18, 1906.

* * *

Cross-Examination by William Warren, Counsel for Defendant:

* * *

Q: As the surveyor of the boundary between the Vargas and Monte properties, you are aware of the natural features in the area, aren't you?

A: Of course.

Q: So you know where Bella Creek is, correct?

A: Yes.

Q: And that creek bed shifts, doesn't it, Mr. Linhart, depending on whether it's the wet or dry season?

A: Yes, that makes sense.

Q: And over time, creek beds can shift several hundred feet, depending on changing natural conditions, right?

A: Well, several hundred feet may be a stretch but, yes, creek beds have been known to move.

Q: Well, 50 or 100 feet over 100 years wouldn't be a stretch, would it, Mr. Linhart?

A: No, that could happen.

Q: OK. Are you aware of a large outcropping near the north end of the Vargas-Monte properties, known by most local folks as "the big rock"?

A: Yes.

Q: And "the big rock" is north of Bella Creek, right?

A: Right.

Q: And the distance between the bend in Bella Creek and "the big rock" is well over 1,000 feet, isn't it?

A: At least 1,000 feet.

Q: And the area where you saw Ms. Monte logging trees along the Vargas-Monte boundary is between the bend in Bella Creek and "the big rock," correct?

A: That's correct.

EXCERPTS FROM TRIAL TESTIMONY OF DEFENDANT CARLA MONTE

Direct Examination by William Warren, Counsel for Defendant:

* * *

Q: Ms. Monte, whose trees did you believe you were cutting down?

A: I thought I was on my side of the boundary line and that the trees belonged to me.

Q: Why did you believe the trees belonged to you?

A: Because I followed the existing blaze marks made by our families over the years and the marks conform to the 1906 agreement between my grandfather, Ben Monte, and Amos Vargas. The Vargas parcel is west of mine, and I made sure I stayed east of the existing blaze marks, which are based on the line between the bend in Bella Creek and "the big rock."

Q: Showing you Defendant's Exhibit A, can you identify this?

A: Yes. It's a copy of a letter to my grandfather from Amos Vargas. There's a hand-drawn map on the letter showing the boundary between the two properties. It's among the family papers passed along to me by my dad before he passed on.

Q: Did you and Mr. Vargas ever discuss the boundary between your properties?

A: We had a few discussions over the years about the poor condition of the boundary line. I thought that he would not object to my logging along the common border, as long as I stayed east of the existing blaze marks.

* * *

Cross-Examination by Jane Norman, Counsel for Plaintiff:

* * *

Q: Ms. Monte, isn't it true that you knew before you began logging along the Monte-Vargas boundary line that BLM was in the process of resurveying property lines in this area?

A: Yes, I did receive a notification letter from BLM before I began my logging operations.

Q: And you own literally hundreds of acres of land in Cleveland County, don't you?

A: Yes.

Q: And there was nothing to prevent you from logging another section of your land away from the boundary line, was there?

A: Well, the trees that we cut were ready for thinning, and the logging trucks had easy access. But, in any event, I only cut down trees that belonged to me.

Q: But you didn't know for a fact that the trees you harvested were on your property, did you?

A: Based on everything I knew at the time those were my trees.

Defendant's Exhibit A for Identification

April 18, 1906

Benjamin Monte
Route 2, Box 4
Belleville, Franklin

Dear Ben,

I know it's been a while since you and I last talked about the north-south boundary line between our parcels in Cleveland County, but I just want to put in writing what I think is the understanding you and I have about that matter.

When you and I were walking the property last summer we looked for the old markers, but we couldn't figure out where they were or where the line ran. The rock piles weren't there, and we could see some scars on some of the older trees but who's to say if they were blaze marks or what.

I know we talked about you and me just arbitrarily setting the boundary and agreeing that that would be it. The line we more or less decided on was a line from the southern boundary, proceeding north along Bella Creek, which is dry most of the year but changes course a bit during the winter months, to where it bends to the west, along the deer path, continuing north to the big rock on the northern boundary. I've drawn a map at the bottom of this letter.

So, as far as I'm concerned, let's agree on that. Okay? If I don't hear back from you, I'll assume it's okay with you.

Your friend,

Amos Vargas
Amos Vargas

United States Department of the Interior

Bureau of Land Management
Franklin State Office
1000 Government Way
Belle Garden, Franklin 33021

May 27, 2000

Carla Monte
14562 Cedar Ridge Drive
Belleville, Franklin 33025

Dear Landowner:

The Bureau of Land Management is conducting a land survey within Cleveland County to determine the boundaries. Records indicate that you are a landowner in the area of our survey and we wish to make you aware of our presence.

Should it become necessary to enter your lands during the course of this survey, Stan Linhart of our Maddock Field Station will attempt to contact you personally for prior permission.

Please notify Mr. Linhart of any locked gates you may have, or if you have questions regarding this survey. He may be contacted at the following address:

Maddock Field Station
332 Clarksburg Drive
Diamond Springs, Franklin 33022

Sincerely,

Cecilia S. Chen
Cecilia S. Chen
Chief, Survey Branch

LIBRARY

Franklin Civil Code

§ 3346. Injuries to timber, trees, or underwood; treble damages; double damages; actual detriment

(a) For wrongful injuries to timber, trees, or underwood upon the land of another, or removal thereof, the measure of damages is three times such sum as would compensate for the actual detriment, except that where the trespass was casual or involuntary, or where the defendant had probable cause to believe that the land on which the trespass was committed was his own or the land of the person in whose service or by whose direction the act was done, the measure of damages shall be twice the sum as would compensate for the actual detriment.

(b) The measure of damages to be assessed against a defendant for any trespass committed while acting in reliance upon a survey of boundary lines which improperly fixes the location of a boundary line, shall be the actual detriment incurred if the trespass was committed by a defendant who relied upon a survey made by a licensed surveyor.

(c) Any action for the damages specified by subdivisions (a) and (b) of this section must be commenced within five years from the date of the trespass.

Anderson v. Flush

Franklin Court of Appeal (1953)

Maggie Anderson brought this action to recover statutory treble damages for injuries to 39 trees in her orchard. She alleges the injuries were caused by the deliberate action of Todd Flush while moving a house along Levin Avenue, a public street, in the course of his house-moving business. The trial judge awarded double, not treble, damages. Anderson appeals the trial court's denial of treble damages. Flush also appeals, claiming that, although he damaged Anderson's trees, double damages are not mandatory and should not have been awarded.

Levin Avenue is bordered on one side by Anderson's orchard and on the other by that of John Koh. The trees in Koh's orchard bordering the avenue are interspersed with telephone poles while those of Anderson's orchard are not. Between the orchards, the paved portion of Levin Avenue is only about 15 feet wide. The damaged trees are on Anderson's property, but their branches extended over the street.

Flush observed that it would be necessary to touch the bordering trees on at least one side of Levin Avenue. He chose to strike those of Anderson because of the telephone poles on Koh's property. He thought that the house would brush by the limbs without causing any extensive damage to the trees. He sawed off some limbs to prevent them from breaking farther back near the trunks and from causing permanent damage to the trees.

The purpose of Civil Code § 3346 is to protect trees and timber. The trial court held that Flush's actions were wrongful and the double damages provision of § 3346 was mandatory. We agree.

There are three measures of damages depending on the nature of the trespass: (1) for willful and malicious trespass, the court may impose treble damages but must impose double damages; (2) for casual and involuntary trespass, the court must impose double damages; and (3) for trespass in reliance on a survey, actual damages.

Under § 3346 the trial court has discretion to determine the circumstances under which to award treble damages. Because treble damages are punitive, the defendant must have acted willfully and maliciously.

While § 3346 leaves the imposition of treble damages to the discretion of the court, it places a floor upon that discretion. Double damages must be awarded whether the trespass be willful and malicious or casual and involuntary. The trial court was required to impose no less than double damages.

We must determine whether the trial court abused its discretion in refusing to award treble damages. It is undisputed that the branches of Anderson's trees extended over the street. Since the street is dedicated to public use to its full width irrespective of the paved portion, the trial court was justified in deciding that Flush did not act with malice or a reckless disregard of Anderson's rights. Flush, faced with the dilemma of inflicting what he believed would be slight damage to Anderson's orchard, damage to telephone poles, or blocking a public street for a substantial period of time, acted reasonably to minimize the damage. The trial court did not abuse its discretion in refusing to impose treble damages. Affirmed.

Hardway Lumber v. Thompson
Franklin Court of Appeal (1971)

Hardway Lumber appeals from a judgment awarding it double damages based on the value of timber wrongfully removed from its land, contending the trial court erred in not awarding treble damages pursuant to § 3346 of the Franklin Civil Code.

Hardway entered into a 10-year contract with defendant Henry Thompson for the sale of timber on Hardway's land. Five years into the contract, Hardway properly rescinded the agreement by filing a notice with the Recorder of Deeds. While the recording provided constructive notice, it is undisputed that Thompson was never given actual notice of the rescission. Shortly after the rescission, Hardway discovered that Thompson was logging timber on its property. Hardway sued, seeking treble damages.

The trial court concluded (i) Thompson was not aware that Hardway had rescinded the logging contract; (ii) at the time Thompson removed the timber, he believed he had a right to do so; and (iii) Thompson was not acting with malice or ill will toward Hardway.

Although § 3346 does not expressly so provide, Franklin courts have held that to award treble damages, the plaintiff must prove that the wrongful act was willful and malicious. Since a defendant rarely admits to such a state of mind, it must frequently be established from the circumstances. Malice may be found when a defendant performs an act with reckless disregard of or indifference to the rights of others.

For example, in *Guernsey v. Wheeler* (Franklin Court of Appeal 1966), the defendant had a contract permitting him to log on a parcel of land known as Sherman's Trust. Prior to removing trees, he was told repeatedly there were conflicting descriptions as to the precise location of Sherman's Trust, but he nonetheless logged a large number of trees. The trial court rejected his claim that he had probable cause to believe he was logging the land covered by his contract. We held that because the trespass was neither casual nor involuntary but was instead committed with a reckless disregard of and indifference to the rights of the owner, treble damages were appropriate.

In the present case, the trial court found that Thompson's acts were not in bad faith; that his motives were not to vex, harass, annoy, or injure Hardway; and that the trespass was committed while attempting to harvest what he thought was his own timber. The trial court did not abuse its discretion. Affirmed.

Blackjack Lumber Company v. Pearlman
Franklin Court of Appeal (1986)

Blackjack Lumber Company brought this action against Frank Pearlman to recover statutory damages for timber trespass under Franklin Civil Code § 3346. Pearlman invoked the doctrine of agreed boundary as a defense. The trial court found that predecessors of the parties had agreed upon a boundary between their respective parcels, and decided in Pearlman's favor.

At issue is the boundary line between the northern and southern halves of Section 35. In 1961, Tom Majors purchased the north half from the Union Lumber Company. Majors was uncertain as to the boundary line between the two parcels. In 1962, non-licensed Union Lumber personnel undertook an informal survey of the boundary line and blazed trees (i.e., notched them with an axe) as they went across the boundary line. Majors observed the informal survey as it progressed and agreed with the line that was drawn.

In 1970, Pearlman bought the south half of Section 35 from Union Lumber and agreed with Majors that the line blazed by Union Lumber in 1962 was the boundary line. In 1973, Majors sold the north half to Blackjack Lumber. By this time, Pearlman had flagged the blazed line and the flags were clearly visible on the ground. In 1980, Pearlman conducted logging operations on his property and logged up to the blazed line. On one occasion, Pearlman asked and received Blackjack's permission to install a landing north of the blazed line for convenience in conducting his operations.

In 1982, Blackjack hired a licensed surveyor to survey the boundary line between the two halves of Section 35. This survey showed the boundary to be several hundred feet to the south of the line blazed in 1962.

In cases of uncertainty, courts look with favor upon private agreements fixing and marking boundary lines. This judicially created rule is known as the doctrine of agreed boundary. It is intended to secure repose and prevent litigation. The essential elements of the doctrine are (1) uncertainty about the true boundary line; (2) an agreement between adjoining landowners as to the boundary; (3) an agreed-upon boundary that is identifiable on the ground; and (4) acceptance and acquiescence to the agreed-upon boundary for a period at least equal to the statute of limitations.

The doctrine of agreed boundary applies even where the parties intend to set the boundary along the true property line but fail to do so, due to a mistake. Moreover, there is no requirement that the true location be unascertainable. Here, it is clear neither Majors nor Union Lumber knew the true location of the boundary line.

The trial court found that, after the line was established by Union Lumber, both Union and Majors accepted the marked line, and their successors likewise accepted it for 20 years as the correct location of the boundary line between the two parcels. Acceptance of the line by both Majors and Union Lumber and their successors is sufficient evidence to show an agreement between Majors and Union Lumber that the blazed line was in fact the agreed-upon boundary line between their respective properties. Therefore, we find that the elements for the doctrine of agreed boundary have been satisfied, and the trial court's judgment is affirmed.

THE MPT

MULTISTATE PERFORMANCE TEST

Vargas v. Monte

POINT SHEET

The MPT point sheet, grading summary, and grading guidelines describe the factual and legal points encompassed within the lawyering task to be completed. They outline all the possible issues and points that might be addressed by an applicant. They are provided to the user jurisdictions for the sole purpose of assisting graders in grading the examination by identifying the issues and suggesting the resolution of the problem contemplated by the drafters. These are not official grading guides. Applicants can receive a range of passing grades, including excellent grades, without covering all the points discussed in these guides. The model answer is included as an illustration of a thorough and detailed response to the task, one that addresses all the legal and factual issues the drafters intended to raise in the problem. It is intended to serve only as an example. Applicants need not present their responses in the same way to receive good grades. User jurisdictions are free to modify these grading materials, including the suggested weights assigned to particular points. Grading the MPT is the exclusive responsibility of the jurisdiction using the MPT as part of its admissions process.

Copyright ©2008 by the National Conference of Bar Examiners.
All rights reserved

Vargas v. Monte

DRAFTERS' POINT SHEET

This performance test requires applicants to draft a persuasive brief in the context of a pending bench trial. The setting is a timber trespass action brought by landowner Les Vargas against neighboring landowner Carla Monte, seeking statutory treble damages for wrongfully cutting down and removing trees from Vargas's land. The parties have presented their evidence at trial, and the judge has requested additional briefing on the issues of liability and damages. Specifically, the judge has asked the parties to address whether, based on the evidence adduced at trial, defendant Monte is liable for timber trespass and, if so, whether single, double, or treble damages, or some combination thereof, should be assessed against her.

The File contains the following materials: (1) instruction memo to the applicants from the supervising attorney; (2) the firm's Memorandum regarding Persuasive Briefs, containing instructions on the format and general contents of the brief; (3) the Statement of Stipulated Facts; (4) a partial trial transcript containing excerpts of testimony; (5) Defendant's Exhibit A, a letter from Vargas's grandfather to Monte's grandfather; and (6) a notification letter to defendant Monte regarding a government resurvey of the boundary lines between the parties' properties. The Library contains the relevant timber trespass statute and the case law necessary to complete the assignment.

Applicants are expected to use these materials to write a well-organized, persuasive argument explaining why the court should impose liability against Monte and award treble damages to Vargas. The following discussion covers all of the points the drafters intended to raise in the problem. Applicants need not cover them all to receive passing or even excellent grades. Grading decisions are entirely within the discretion of the graders in the user jurisdictions.

I. Format and Organization

Applicants are expected to follow the instructions in the instruction memo and the firm's Memorandum regarding Persuasive Briefs:

- The brief should be written in a persuasive, as opposed to objective, style. Applicants who write an objective memo in which they take an on-the-one-hand/on-the-other-hand narrative approach will have failed to follow the instructions.

- In accordance with the Memorandum regarding Persuasive Briefs: (1) the brief must contain a Statement of Facts (which means that applicants must extract the relevant facts from the File and concisely present them in a way that favors the plaintiff's position); (2) the headings should be persuasive and should apply the facts to the legal principles; and (3) the argument section of the brief should incorporate the facts and contain logical and persuasive arguments.

- Applicants are instructed to incorporate the case law that supports their position into the argument section of the brief, to distinguish cases that are not helpful, and to explain why a lower measure of damages would be inappropriate.

- Based on the facts and cases, applicants should conclude that Monte is liable for (1) at least double damages with respect to trees removed from Vargas's property prior to her encounter with the BLM survey team, and (2) treble damages for trees removed from that point onwards, when she continued logging with actual notice of the trespass.

II. Statement of Facts

As emphasized in the Memorandum regarding Persuasive Briefs, applicants should extract from the File the facts that are relevant to their brief and present them in the light most favorable to the plaintiff. There is no one right way to present the facts. Some applicants may choose to front-load most of the facts in their Statement of Facts, while others may choose to present only an overview of the case and deal more extensively with the facts in the argument section. Either way, a complete and thorough treatment of the facts should cover the following areas:

- The parties' status as adjoining landowners.
- The parties own adjoining tracts of land that share a common north-south boundary approximately a quarter-mile long.
- The parcels have been owned by the parties' respective families since 1880.
- Prior to that time, both parcels were part of a larger tract of land owned by the United States Government.
- The survey-related history of the two properties.
- Only two licensed surveys have ever been conducted with respect to the parties' boundary lines: (1) the original USGLO survey in 1879; and (2) a recent resurvey conducted by the Bureau of Land Management (BLM).
- The condition of the boundary line prior to the BLM resurvey of the two properties.
- The collective testimony of the witnesses establishes that at the time of the BLM resurvey, the boundary between the parties' properties was confused by conflicting evidence.
- Monte's knowledge of the BLM resurvey and the attendant risk of logging near property lines prior to commencing logging.
- Monte received a notification letter from BLM regarding the impending resurvey (copy included in the File).
- The absence of an agreement between the parties regarding the location of their shared boundary, notwithstanding Monte's reliance on the 1906 letter.

- Vargas testified that the parties' families were unable to ascertain the true boundary line, and that he and Monte "never really got around to sorting it out."
- Monte claims to have relied upon a letter from Vargas's grandfather to her own grandfather regarding an agreed-upon boundary. However, as discussed below, the letter is far from clear, indicating that the original survey markers were indiscernible and that what was "more or less" agreed to was a shifting boundary line approximately 1,000 feet long that followed a creek that changed course from season to season and other natural landscape markers that also may have shifted over time.
- Monte continued logging even after learning that she was trespassing and despite warnings received from BLM surveyor Linhart and Vargas.
- Monte was specifically informed that she was trespassing more than 100 feet onto plaintiff's land. She was further told that the old boundary markers she was relying on were not accurate. She disregarded these warnings and continued logging the same stretch of land the very next day.
- Monte also disregarded Vargas's phone messages and the "No Trespassing" signs.
- Although Monte testified that she relied on the 1906 letter in conducting her logging operations, there is no evidence that the parties or their families agreed with or abided by the shifting, natural boundaries described in the letter.
- The extent of the trespass:
- Between March 2000 and January 2002, Monte harvested approximately 700 trees from a strip of land along the parties' shared boundary line. According to the testimony of BLM surveyor Linhart, several hundred of those trees belonged to Vargas.

III. Argument

The argument section of the brief should be broken into two sections (liability and damages), each containing one or more headings. Better applicants will address the issue of liability before turning to the question of whether plaintiff is entitled to single, double, or treble damages, since damages cannot be imposed absent liability. However, regardless of how they choose to organize the brief, applicants should cover the following points:

- BECAUSE THE PARTIES NEVER AGREED TO THE BOUNDARY LINE AND BECAUSE THE BOUNDARY WAS NOT IDENTIFIABLE, DEFENDANT MONTE CANNOT RELY ON THE AGREED BOUNDARY DEFENSE.
- Under Franklin law, the doctrine of agreed boundary is a complete defense to an action for timber trespass. (Blackjack Lumber Company v. Pearlman)
- The necessary elements of the doctrine are (1) uncertainty about the true boundary line; (2) an agreement between adjoining landowners as to the boundary; (3) an agreed-upon boundary that is identifiable on the ground; and (4) acquiescence to the agreed-upon boundary for a period at least equal to the statute of limitations.
- Here, Monte cannot satisfy the second and third elements of the doctrine, and thus the fourth element also is not met.
- On cross-examination, Vargas specifically denied that the parties had reached any agreement allowing Monte to harvest trees along the boundary of their properties. Vargas further stated on direct that neither the parties' families, nor the parties themselves, ever resolved the uncertainty surrounding the boundary line.
- Monte did not directly contradict this testimony. Although she claimed to have relied on the 1906 letter, there is no evidence that Vargas even knew of the letter's existence prior to trial, let alone

that the parties had agreed to abide by it. The letter is unilateral in nature and ends with the cryptic comment: "If I don't hear back from you, I'll assume it's okay with you." Monte has the burden of establishing the existence of an agreement, and she clearly has not satisfied that burden.
- Moreover, even if the court could conclude that an agreement existed, the requirement that the boundary be identifiable certainly has not been met. To the contrary, it is undisputed that the parties' shared boundary line was anything but "identifiable" prior to the BLM resurvey. BLM surveyor Linhart described the property line as "a real mess" and went on to state that "nobody knew exactly where it was located." Similarly, Vargas testified in some detail about the conflicting blaze marks, paint, and construction tape on trees along the boundary. Even Monte conceded in her own testimony that the boundary line was in "poor condition." Significantly, the natural boundary markers identified in the 1906 letter and relied upon by Monte were shifting in nature. Therefore, it cannot be said that there was any "identifiable" boundary upon which the parties could have agreed.
- Thus, for this reason alone, the doctrine of agreed boundary does not apply, and Monte is not insulated from liability.
- HAVING FAILED TO SATISFY THE ELEMENTS FOR THE AGREED BOUNDARY DEFENSE, MONTE IS LIABLE FOR TIMBER TRESPASS BECAUSE SHE CUT DOWN AND REMOVED TREES FROM VARGAS'S PROPERTY WITHOUT HIS PERMISSION.
- Franklin Civil Code § 3346 imposes strict statutory liability for trespass, even where the trespass is "casual or involuntary," committed by a defendant who had " probable cause to believe" that the land belonged to him, or committed in reliance on a licensed survey.

- It is clear that Monte did not have Vargas's permission to cut the trees. Indeed, Monte knew that Vargas opposed any logging on his property. Thus, Monte is liable for timber trespass.
- There are three measures of damages depending on the nature of the trespass: (1) for willful and malicious trespass, the court may impose treble damages but must impose double damages; (2) for casual and involuntary trespass, the court must impose double damages; and (3) for trespass under authority, actual damages. Anderson v. Flush. Each situation should be discussed in turn by the applicants.
- **BECAUSE MONTE DID NOT RELY ON A LICENSED SURVEY, THE COURT CANNOT LIMIT VARGAS'S AWARD TO SINGLE DAMAGES.**
- Pursuant to Franklin Civil Code § 3346, single damages (i.e., the "actual detriment" caused by the trespass) are appropriate where a defendant commits trespass in reliance on a survey that improperly fixed the location of a boundary line, provided the survey was conducted by a licensed surveyor.
- Although the original USGLO survey was conducted by licensed surveyors, Monte did not rely on the lines established thereby and there is no evidence to suggest that the original survey improperly fixed the location of the parties' shared boundary. Therefore, single damages are not an option.
- **MONTE'S TRESPASS WAS WILLFUL AND MALICIOUS, AS OPPOSED TO CASUAL OR INVOLUNTARY, IN THAT SHE HARVESTED TREES ALONG THE PARTIES' SHARED BOUNDARY LINE DESPITE REPEATED WARNINGS AND THEN CONTINUED LOGGING WITH ACTUAL KNOWLEDGE OF THE TRESPASS.**
- The issue of whether Monte should be ordered to pay double versus treble damages is the primary tension in this test item. Applicants should devote the lion's share of their argument to analyzing this issue, persuading the court why Monte's conduct justifies an award of treble damages, and distinguishing the double damages case law in the Library.
- Under Franklin law, where the reliance-on-survey-by-licensed-surveyor provision does not apply (Civil Code § 3346(b)), an award of double damages is mandatory whether the trespass is willful and malicious, or casual and involuntary. Anderson.
- Although Franklin Civil Code § 3346 does not specifically address the intent required for an award of treble damages, the cases make clear that such an award is left to the discretion of the trial court and shall not be made absent a finding that the defendant's conduct was willful and malicious. Anderson; Hardway Lumber v. Thompson.
- Malice implies an act conceived in a spirit of mischief or with indifference toward the obligations owed to others. Malice may consist of a state of mind determined to perform an act with reckless or wanton disregard of or indifference to the rights of others. Since a defendant rarely admits to such a state of mind, it must frequently be established from the circumstances surrounding his or her allegedly malicious acts. Hardway Lumber.
- The *Anderson* and *Hardway Lumber* cases, both upholding double damage awards, are distinguishable in several respects.
- In *Anderson v. Flush*, (1) the defendant damaged trees while attempting to move a house along a public street and was faced with the Hobson's choice of continuing down the street with his load or blocking traffic; (2) the defendant took precautions to minimize the injury to plaintiff's trees; and (3) the defendant found himself in a situation where he could have reasonably believed that he had a right to inflict injury to the plaintiff's trees.
- Similarly, in *Hardway Lumber*, the defendant had entered into a logging contract with the plaintiff landowner and was unaware that the plaintiff had rescinded the contract. Thus, the court concluded that the defendant could have reasonably believed that he had a right to harvest the plaintiff's trees.
- Here, in contrast: (1) Monte was not attempting to use public space; (2) there was no Hobson's choice (Monte owns hundreds of acres and was not compelled to log this particular section of her property); (3) Monte had no logging contract with Vargas and could not have reasonably believed that she had the right to log trees on Vargas's land; and (4) Monte continued cutting down Vargas's trees even after being informed by BLM surveyor Linhart that she was in clear trespass and despite Vargas's phone messages and "No Trespassing" signs.
- Indeed, Monte affirmatively knew that Vargas had resisted efforts to log his land.
- Moreover, Monte was in the logging business and would certainly have had a greater appreciation for the need to avoid trespassing.
- More generally, with respect to both the *Anderson* and *Hardway* opinions—and this is a subtle point that many applicants may not catch—timber trespass cases are reviewed under an abuse of discretion standard, which means, as a practical matter, that it is unlikely that the Franklin Court of Appeal would set aside a particular judgment so long as there is evidence in the record to support it. The *Anderson* and *Hardway* decisions are fact-specific outcomes that should not dictate a particular result in this case.
- The evidence in the File strongly suggests an absence of any effort on the part of Monte to minimize the risk of trespass. The facts establish that at least from the point of her encounter with the BLM survey team, Monte acted with the scienter needed to support an award of treble damages. For instance, we know from Vargas's testimony that Monte was interested in obtaining logging rights to Vargas's land. Monte's unwillingness to heed the warnings of BLM surveyor Linhart, her complete disregard for the "No Trespassing" signs posted by Vargas, her comments to BLM surveyor Linhart about it not being "fair" for BLM to move the boundary line, and her continued logging in the area with actual notice of the trespass suggest a reckless, willful disregard of Vargas's rights.
- Given these facts, the circumstances of this case are much more analogous to the facts in the *Guernsey v. Wheeler* decision cited in Hardway. Here, as in Wheeler, we have a defendant who has disregarded repeated warnings, who has failed to take the steps necessary to eliminate or at least substantially reduce the risk of trespass, and whose motives were suspect. Therefore, as in Wheeler, an award of treble damages is justified and supported by the evidence in the record.

FILE

MPT Task 4D:
Arden Industries
v.
Freight Forwarders, Inc.

[MPT Task February 2000 Bar Exam]

Swann, Rubin & Chanturia LLP
Attorneys at Law
One Belden Place
Taverly, Franklin 33056
(555) 965-3100

Office Memorandum

To: Applicant
From: Lara Chanturia
Date: February 27, 2003
Subject: Arden Industries, Inc. v. Freight Forwarders, Inc.

We represent Arden Industries, Inc. (Arden) in a suit we filed for declaratory and injunctive relief against Freight Forwarders, Inc. (FFI). The dispute is over whether FFI has a security interest and a carrier's lien on a printing press shipped by Arden through FFI. We succeeded in getting a temporary injunction preventing FFI from selling the printing press during the pendency of our suit. Because the material facts are not in dispute, the parties have agreed to file cross motions for summary judgment. To expedite matters, we have entered into a Stipulated Statement of Facts, which you will find in the File.

I would like you to draft our brief in support of Arden's position that FFI has neither a security interest nor a carrier's lien in the printing press. In addition to making the affirmative arguments as to why FFI does not have a security interest or carrier's lien, be sure to refute the points made in the November 25, 2002, letter from FFI's attorneys.

Follow the guidelines set forth in our office memo on persuasive briefs. However, aside from a very short introduction describing the dispute, do not write a separate Statement of Facts or a statement of Jurisdictional Basis inasmuch as the Stipulated Statement of Facts will be attached to the brief. You will, of course, need to incorporate the relevant facts into your legal arguments to make those arguments persuasive.

Swann, Rubin & Chanturia LLP
Attorneys at Law

MEMORANDUM

To: All Attorneys   September 8, 1995
From: Leslie Rubin
Subject: Persuasive Briefs

All persuasive briefs, including Briefs in Support of Motions, whether directed to an appellate court, trial court, or administrative officer, shall conform to the following guidelines.

All briefs shall include a concise statement of the Jurisdictional Basis for the case and Statement of Facts, emphasizing facts that favor our client's position.

The Argument section of the brief follows the Statement of Facts. Each distinct point in the Argument should be preceded by a carefully crafted subject heading that encapsulates the argument it covers and succinctly summarizes the reasons the tribunal should take the position you are advocating. A heading should be a specific application of a rule of law to the facts of the case and not a bare legal or factual statement of an abstract principle. For example, improper: THE DEFENDANT DID NOT PROPERLY PERFECT HIS SECURITY INTEREST. Proper: THE DEFENDANT DID NOT HAVE A PERFECTED SECURITY INTEREST BECAUSE HE FAILED TO FILE A PROPERLY EXECUTED FINANCING STATEMENT IN THE OFFICE OF THE SECRETARY OF STATE.

The argument under each heading should analyze applicable legal authority and state persuasively how the facts and the law support our client's position on the proposition stated in the heading. Authority supporting our client's position should be emphasized, but contrary authority should also be generally cited, addressed, and explained or distinguished. Do not reserve arguments for reply or supplemental briefs.

There is no need for the lawyer to prepare a table of contents, a summary of the argument, or the index. These will be prepared, where required, after the draft is approved.

Marshall, Danbury & Markowitz LLP
Attorneys at Law
12895 Clearwater Way
Markleeville, Franklin 33058
(555) 442-1280

November 25, 2002

Albert Ripple, President
Arden Industries, Inc.
6400 Adams Highway
Taverly, Franklin 33056
Re: Freight Forwarders/Arden Industries

Dear Mr. Ripple:

I write on behalf of our client, Freight Forwarders, Inc. (FFI). Arden Industries, Inc. (Arden) is in arrears on five unpaid past invoices rendered by FFI totaling $122,725. FFI has in its possession the printing press it shipped for Arden last week. We believe that press has a value of $200,000.

We have advised FFI that it has a valid security interest and carrier's lien in the printing press in its possession. Thus FFI is entitled to sell the press and apply the proceeds to the amount Arden owes it. FFI's carrier's lien arises under § 7-307 of the Franklin Commercial Code. Its security interest arises from the language in Section 15 on the back of FFI's invoices. That is the same language that has appeared on the invoices since Arden and FFI began doing business together some five years ago. Therefore, the "course of dealing" between Arden and FFI includes the agreement that Arden's goods shipped through FFI constitute collateral for amounts owing on the invoices. Actually, we have litigated this question successfully before, and we refer you and your attorneys to Freight Forwarders, Inc. v. Wendover Mfg. Co., U.S.D.C., (D. Olympia 1997).

If Arden does not bring its account current within 10 days, FFI will sell the printing press and apply the proceeds to the arrearages.

Very truly yours,

Arlo P. Danbury

Arlo P. Danbury

STIPULATED STATEMENT OF FACTS

FRANKLIN DISTRICT COURT

Arden Industries, Inc.,)
Plaintiff,)
) Case Number 02-CV-4081
v.) **Stipulated Statement of Facts**
)
Freight Forwarders, Inc.,)
Defendant.)

Defendant, Freight Forwarders, Inc. (FFI), asserts that under the Franklin Commercial Code it has a perfected security interest and/or carrier's lien in the Model Z Swift-Print printing press (Model Z) manufactured by plaintiff, Arden Industries, Inc. (Arden). FFI has retained possession of the Model Z it shipped on behalf of Arden, which owes FFI arrearages on earlier FFI shipping invoices. To support FFI's position that it has a perfected security interest in the Model Z and is thus entitled to sell the press to satisfy Arden's arrearages, FFI argues: (1) the effect of Section 15 of its shipping invoices; (2) the long course of dealing between the parties; (3) the fact that it has possession of the Model Z; and (4) otherwise by operation of law. Arden denies that FFI has a security interest or carrier's lien under the Franklin Commercial Code. In anticipation of filing cross motions for summary judgment, the parties stipulate that the following undisputed facts are the only material facts necessary to resolve the summary judgment motions.

1. The court has jurisdiction over this action, in which the parties seek a declaration of their respective rights, i.e., whether FFI has a valid security interest and/or carrier's lien in certain goods of Arden.
2. Arden and FFI are both duly formed and existing corporations of the State of Franklin.
3. Arden is a manufacturer of printing presses.
4. FFI is a common carrier that transports goods in interstate commerce.
5. Starting in 1998, Arden began using FFI's services to transport Arden's finished printing presses from Arden's manufacturing plant in Taverly, Franklin, to purchasers of the presses throughout the United States and overseas. In all cases, Arden retained title to the goods until delivery to the customer.
6. Each shipment of goods was initiated by a telephone call from Arden's shipping manager to FFI's offices. The shipping manager would inform FFI's dispatcher that a press was ready for shipment and give the dispatcher the name, address, other necessary destination information, and a description of the items being shipped.
7. FFI's dispatcher would prepare an invoice on an FFI form, describing the goods along with origination and destination information. FFI's driver would pick up the goods at Arden's dock and leave a copy of the invoice with Arden's shipping manager.
8. Facts numbered 6 and 7, above, describe the full extent of the steps the parties took to arrange each shipment.
9. There were never any negotiations or discussions between the parties regarding the terms of shipment. Arden understood that it would be charged and would pay the invoice price, which conformed to FFI's published transportation rates, net 30 days.
10. There were no writings or contractual undertakings, other than the invoices FFI presented to Arden for each shipment. Arden never signed any documents related to the parties' shipping transactions.
11. During the first year of the business relationship, FFI presented Arden with a form long-term shipping services contract that contained terms and conditions that would govern the relationship, including language identical to the language quoted below from Section 15 of FFI's form invoice (see Fact No. 13). Arden declined to enter into that contract.
12. During the five years in which the parties transacted business with each other, FFI provided shipping services for Arden on 137 separate occasions, always carrying printing presses to Arden customers. On each occasion, FFI presented Arden with an invoice covering the shipment.
13. Each FFI form invoice contained the following language in small print on the reverse side:

Section 15: General Lien on Any Property. The Company shall have a general lien on any and all property (and documents relating thereto) of the Customer in the Company's possession, custody, or control or en route, for all claims for charges, expenses, or advances incurred by the Company in connection with any shipments of the Customer. If such claim remains unsatisfied for thirty (30) days after demand for its payment is made, the Company may sell at public auction or private sale, upon ten (10) days written notice, sent certified or registered mail with return receipt requested to the Customer, the goods, wares, and/or merchandise, or so much thereof as may be necessary to satisfy such lien. The Company shall apply the net proceeds of such sale to the payment of the amount due the Company. Any surplus from such sale shall be transmitted to the Customer. The Customer shall be liable for any deficiency in the sale.

14. By inserting the Section 15 language in the invoice form, FFI intended to create a security interest in its customers' goods to secure payment of its freight charges.
15. Arden never intended to grant FFI a security interest in the goods it shipped via FFI.
16. Arden never signed any security agreements or UCC financing statements explicitly granting FFI a security interest in any property.
17. FFI never filed any documents with the Secretary of State's Office evidencing its claim to a security interest.
18. Although no Arden employee remembers ever having read the language of Section 15 of the invoices, Arden at all times had constructive knowledge thereof.
19. No FFI employee ever explicitly directed the attention of anyone at Arden to the language of Section 15 of the invoices.
20. Until this dispute arose, there never have been any discussions between Arden and FFI regarding the meaning and effect of Section 15 of the invoices.
21. Arden never objected to or otherwise expressed any intent not to be bound by the provisions of Section 15 of the invoices.
22. Arden owes arrearages to FFI on five unpaid invoices in an amount totaling $122,725. FFI made demand for payment thereof more than 30 days ago and the amount remains unpaid.
23. FFI is in possession of the Model Z printing press manufactured by Arden and shipped via FFI on November 18, 2002, which press has a market value of approximately $200,000.
24. Arden owes arrearages on five invoices covering earlier shipments, not including the invoice for shipment of the Model Z in FFI's possession.

25. The goods covered by the invoices that are in arrears were delivered by FFI in the ordinary course of business to the destinations designated in those invoices and those goods are no longer in FFI's possession.

26. Despite several earlier payment delinquencies by Arden, FFI has never before claimed or attempted to enforce a security interest or carrier's lien in Arden's property.

27. This is the first and only occasion on which a dispute has arisen between the parties on the meaning and effect of Section 15 of the invoices.

Date: January 27, 2003

Swann, Rubin & Chanturia LLP   Marshall, Danbury & Markowitz LLP

By *Lara Chanturia*   By *Arlo P. Danbury*
Lara Chanturia   Arlo P. Danbury
Attorneys for   Attorneys for
Arden Industries, Inc.   Freight Forwarders, Inc.

LIBRARY

Franklin Commercial Code

Article 1 (General Definitions)

§ 1-201. General Definitions The following definitions apply to all articles and divisions of this code.

* * * *

(3) "Agreement" means the bargain of the parties in fact as found in their language or by implication from other circumstances, including course of dealing, usage of trade, and course of performance....

* * * *

§ 1-205. Course of Dealing....

(1) A course of dealing is a sequence of previous conduct between the parties to a particular transaction, which is fairly to be regarded as establishing a common basis of understanding for interpreting their expressions and other conduct.

* * * *

(3) A course of dealing between parties gives particular meaning to and supplements or qualifies terms of an agreement.

* * * *

Article 7 (Warehouse Receipts, Bills of Lading and Other Documents of Title)

§ 7-307. Lien of Carrier

(1) A carrier has a lien on the goods covered by a bill of lading for charges subsequent to the date of its receipt of the goods for storage or transportation (including demurrage and terminal charges) and for expenses necessary for preservation of the goods incident to their transportation or reasonably incurred in their sale pursuant to law.

* * * *

(3) A carrier loses its lien on any goods which it voluntarily delivers or which it unjustifiably refuses to deliver.

* * * *

<u>Franklin Commercial Code Comment:</u> This section, as opposed to creating a general security interest in collateral, is intended to give carriers a specific statutory lien for charges and expenses [on the goods covered by the particular bill of lading].... But since carriers do not commonly claim a lien for charges in relation to other goods or lend money on the security of goods in their hands, provisions for a general lien or a security interest...are omitted.

* * * *

Article 9 (Secured Transactions) [REVISED]

§ 9-102. Definitions

* * * *

(3) "Security Agreement." Security agreement means an agreement that creates or provides for a security interest.

* * * *

§ 9-203. Attachment and Enforceability of Security Interest; ...Formal Requisites

* * * *

(b) A security interest is enforceable against the debtor and third parties with respect to the collateral only if:

(1) value has been given;

(2) the debtor has rights in the collateral or the power to transfer rights in the collateral to a secured party; and

(3) one of the following conditions is met:

* * * *

(B) the collateral...is in the possession of the secured party under Section 9-313 pursuant to the debtor's security agreement....

* * * *

§ 9-310. When Filing is Required to Perfect Security Interest

(a) Except as otherwise provided in subsection (b) ... a financing statement must be filed to perfect all security interests....

(b) The filing of a financing statement is not necessary to perfect a security interest:

* * * *

(6) in collateral in the secured party's possession under Section 9-313.

* * * *

§ 9-313. When Possession By or Delivery To Secured Party Perfects Security Interest Without Filing

(a) A secured party may perfect a security interest in...goods by taking possession of the collateral.

Freight Forwarders, Inc. v. Wendover Mfg. Co.

United States District Court, (D. Olympia 1997)

Freight Forwarders, Inc. (FFI) brought the action below in the Chapter 11 proceedings of Wendover Mfg. Co. (Wendover) seeking to enforce an alleged security interest in goods of Wendover that were in FFI's possession. Applying the Uniform Commercial Code as adopted in the State of Olympia and as interpreted by the courts of that state, the Bankruptcy Court found that FFI did not have a security interest in the goods because there was no signed, written agreement to which an enforceable security agreement was referable, i.e., that the invoices sent by FFI were not part of an agreement. This was error on two counts: first, although there must be a writing that expresses an intent to grant a security interest, it need not be a signed writing when the collateral is in the possession of the creditor; and, second, as we note below, the terms of the invoices granting a general lien were part of the parties' contract.

FFI provided ocean freight shipping services for Wendover for more than five years. There was no integrated signed contract that specified the terms under which the services would be furnished.[1] Each freight shipment was accompanied by an invoice sent to Wendover for the services provided. Each invoice described the property being shipped. Wendover did not sign any of the invoices. On the reverse side of every invoice was a paragraph 15, entitled "General Lien on Any Property," stating:

> The Company shall have a general lien on any and all property (and documents relating thereto) of the Customer in the Company's possession, custody, or control or en route, for all claims for charges, expenses, or advances incurred by the Company in connection with any shipments of the Customer.

Over the five years of the business relationship, FFI had sent over 1,000 invoices to Wendover for services provided. FFI never filed with the Secretary of State any UCC financing statement purportedly asserting a security interest.

On the day Wendover filed its Chapter 11 Bankruptcy petition, 14 containers of ocean freight were in transit with FFI bound for Wendover. At the same time, FFI was attempting to collect payment for ocean freight shipments previously delivered to Wendover. In FFI's action in the Bankruptcy Court, it alleged that it had a security interest in Wendover's ocean freight and that it was holding the 14 containers to satisfy its earlier claims for delinquent payments on freight services.

As a general rule, there are two fundamental requirements to finding an enforceable security interest. First, there must be a security agreement. Second, a security interest must attach to be enforceable. Where the creditor has not obtained from the debtor an authenticated security agreement, a security interest does not attach and, therefore, is not enforceable unless: "the collateral is in possession of the secured party under Section 9-313 pursuant to the debtor's security agreement...." UCC § 9-203(b)(3)(B).

This case deals only with the question whether the first of those requirements (existence of a security agreement) is met. FFI correctly argues that the invoice language became a security agreement by the assent of the parties and through a course of dealing over a five-year period. With respect to contracts for the services of a carrier, invoices evidencing the contractual relationship between the parties need not be signed to bind them. A shipper who receives a carrier's invoice or bill of lading without objecting after having an opportunity to inspect it and who permits the carrier to act

---

[1] Early in their business relationship, FFI presented to Wendover a bid proposal for future shipping services. The proposal contained the same language that is now in dispute. Wendover did not enter into or execute the bid proposal.

on it by completing the shipment has accepted it as correctly stating the contract and has assented to its terms.

The Uniform Commercial Code does not prescribe the words necessary to create a security agreement. The only definition of a security agreement in the UCC is in § 9-102(3): "Security agreement means an agreement that creates or provides for a security interest." All that is required is language showing the parties' intent to enter into a relationship in which an interest in property secures payment or performance of an obligation between them. Here, the invoice language describing a "lien" on the debtor's property "for all claims for charges, expenses, or advances" clearly expresses the intention to create an interest in property to secure payment to FFI. Moreover, the existence of an agreement is reinforced by the parties' course of dealing. Although a course of dealing is frequently used to supplement or qualify the terms of a written agreement, UCC § 1-205(1) expressly provides that the existence of an agreement may be implied:

A course of dealing is a sequence of previous conduct between the parties to a particular transaction which is fairly to be regarded as establishing a common basis of understanding for interpreting their expressions and other conduct.

Throughout their five-year business relationship, FFI sent many invoices to Wendover for shipping services. Each invoice contained the language that expressed an intention to create a general lien. In addition, there is evidence that such terms and conditions are standard in the industry. This course of dealing establishes that the parties had a common basis of understanding for interpreting the conditions of their relationship.

The UCC requirements for an enforceable security interest are present: the invoice is an agreement that expresses an intention to create a security interest; it describes the property that secures the payment; and it is undisputed that the property is in the creditor's possession. Accordingly, FFI has an enforceable security interest.

Reversed.

Data Systems v. Link Associates
Franklin Supreme Court (1998)

The trial court directed a verdict in favor of Link Associates (LA) in this case brought by Data Systems (DS). The court of appeal affirmed. DS now files this appeal. At issue in this case is whether the "box-top license," printed on LA's product packaging and disclaiming all warranties, was part of a contract between the parties.

DS developed and marketed a multiuser computer system designed for use by small offices and retail establishments. DS selected LA's "Advanced Multiuser" software program as the operating system for DS's design.

DS sold 142 systems and immediately began receiving complaints from a number of its customers that the Advanced Multiuser software was defective. LA worked with DS, rendering technical assistance in an effort to correct the problems, but the parties could not agree on whose responsibility the problems were and they were never able to correct the technical problems. As a result, 12 of DS's customers filed suit against it. DS brought this suit for declaratory relief and indemnification against LA.

DS initially contacted a sales representative of LA concerning the Advanced Multiuser program. Based on the representations of LA's sales representative, DS decided to use Advanced Multiuser as the operating system for its product. It was understood between DS and LA that Advanced Multiuser would be resold by DS to its customers. DS ultimately purchased and resold 142 copies.

The pattern of the transactions between DS and LA was, typically, that DS would telephone LA and place an order, usually for 20 copies at a time. LA, while still on the telephone, would accept the order and agree to ship promptly. After the telephone order, DS would send a purchase order detailing the items to be purchased, the price, and the shipping and payment terms. LA would ship the order along with an invoice, which would contain terms essentially identical to those on DS's purchase order. No reference was ever made during the telephone conversation or on the purchase orders or invoices regarding a disclaimer of any warranties.

Printed on each package containing a copy of Advanced Multiuser was a "box-top license."[1]

The trial court directed a verdict in favor of LA, finding that the box-top license was part of the contract between DS and LA and that all warranties were disclaimed.

On appeal DS contends that the contract for each copy of the program was formed when LA agreed over the telephone to ship the copy at the agreed price.

LA contends that, even if DS never explicitly agreed to it, the box-top terms are a part of the contract by reason of the course of dealing between the parties. Essentially, LA argues that the repeated expression of those terms by LA eventually incorporates them into the contract.

---

[1] The "box-top license" provided:
(1) The customer has not purchased the software itself, but has merely obtained a personal, nontransferable license to use the program;
(2) LA disclaims all express and implied warranties except that the disks contained in the box are free from defects;
(3) The sole remedy available to a purchaser is to return any defective disk for replacement and, specifically, the license excludes any liability for damages, direct or consequential, caused by use of the program;
(4) The box-top license is the final and complete expression of the terms of the parties' agreement; and
(5) "Opening this package indicates your acceptance of these terms and conditions. If you do not agree with them, you should promptly return the package unopened to the person from whom you purchased it within 15 days of the date of purchase, and your money will be refunded to you by that person."

Under Franklin Commercial Code (FCC) § 1-205(1), which applies to all transactions that are subject to the FCC, "A course of dealing is a sequence of previous conduct between the parties to a particular transaction which is fairly to be regarded as establishing a common basis of understanding for interpreting their expressions and other conduct." The implication of this language is that the parties to any agreement covered by the Code must have consistently taken action with regard to a particular issue. In this case the parties have never before taken any action with respect to the terms of the box-top license.

There is a split of authority on the question whether terms repeated in a number of written confirmations eventually become part of the contract even though neither party takes any action with respect to the issue addressed by those terms. This court sides with the majority and holds that the mere repetitive transmission of such confirmations, without more, does not make the terms of the confirmations part of the contract. (Contra, *Freight Forwarders, Inc. v. Wendover Mfg. Co.*, U.S.D.C., (D. Olympia 1997).)

In *Wendover*, the court correctly understood that in order to create an enforceable security interest, there must first be an agreement to create the security interest. We disagree, however, with that court's conclusion that there existed a course of dealing under § 1-205 (which is equally applicable to Article 9) sufficient to constitute an agreement.

Whereas the *Wendover* court relied solely on the definition in § 1-205(1), we believe the correct focus is on FCC § 1-205(3), which provides that, "A course of dealing between parties gives particular meaning to and supplements or qualifies terms of an agreement." Thus, course of dealing evidence may supplement the agreement by providing evidence of the parties' intentions, but it may not be used to create an agreement. Where the only action taken has been the repeated delivery of a particular form by one of the parties, there is no "agreement" to "supplement" or "qualify."

For two reasons, we hold that the repeated sending of a writing that contains certain standard terms, without any action with respect to the issues addressed by those terms, cannot constitute a course of dealing that would incorporate a term of the writing into the agreement of the parties.

First, the repeated exchange of forms by the parties only tells DS that LA desires certain terms. Given LA's failure to obtain DS's express assent to these terms before it will ship the program, DS can reasonably believe that, while LA desires certain terms, it has agreed to do business on other terms, i.e., only those terms expressly agreed upon by the parties.

Second, the seller in these multiple transaction cases will typically have the opportunity to negotiate the precise terms of the parties' agreement. The seller's unwillingness or inability to obtain a negotiated agreement reflecting the terms strongly suggests that, while the seller would like a court to incorporate terms if a dispute were to arise, those terms are not part of the parties' commercial bargain.

Indeed, the evidence shows that, by allowing DS to resell the license to its customers and working with DS to attempt to resolve the technical problems, LA itself ignored the "nontransferable license" and "replacement/money-back only" terms of the box-top license. This is strong evidence that LA was satisfied to do business on terms inconsistent with those of the box-top license.

Course of conduct is ordinarily a factual issue. But we hold as a matter of law that the unilateral actions of LA in repeatedly sending a writing cannot by itself establish a course of dealing between the parties.

Reversed.

Shellac's Drayage v. Pavel's Hardware Supply
Franklin Court of Appeal (1996)

Per Curiam. The issue in this appeal is whether a common carrier can properly claim a lien under Franklin Commercial Code § 7-307 as to goods in its possession when the debt relates to charges incurred by the shipper for past deliveries.

Pavel's Hardware Supply regularly shipped goods via Shellac's Drayage and fell behind in payment for Shellac's services. Shellac's began requiring advance payment before it would accept Pavel's goods for shipment.

In connection with a particular prepaid shipment, Shellac's notified Pavel's that it was holding the goods in that shipment, under lock and key in a boat at its dock, and intended to sell them pursuant to Shellac's carrier's lien rights under § 7-307 and apply the proceeds to sums owed on past shipments.

The court below enjoined the sale and eventually ruled properly that Shellac's had no carrier's lien as to the current shipment.

Franklin Commercial Code § 7-307 confers upon a common carrier a "lien on the goods covered by a bill of lading for charges subsequent to the date of its receipt of the goods for…transportation…." But, under § 7-307(3), "A carrier loses its lien on any goods which it voluntarily delivers…." The Official Code Comment makes it clear that the lien is not a general lien on other goods; i.e., the lien is limited to the goods in possession and can only be asserted to cover charges owed for transportation of the goods in possession, not to cover charges owed for goods previously transported and no longer in possession.

Affirmed.

THE MPT

MULTISTATE PERFORMANCE TEST

Arden Industries v. Freight Forwarding

POINT SHEET

The MPT point sheet, grading summary, and grading guidelines describe the factual and legal points encompassed within the lawyering task to be completed. They outline all the possible issues and points that might be addressed by an applicant. They are provided to the user jurisdictions for the sole purpose of assisting graders in grading the examination by identifying the issues and suggesting the resolution of the problem contemplated by the drafters. These are not official grading guides. Applicants can receive a range of passing grades, including excellent grades, without covering all the points discussed in these guides. The model answer is included as an illustration of a thorough and detailed response to the task, one that addresses all the legal and factual issues the drafters intended to raise in the problem. It is intended to serve only as an example. Applicants need not present their responses in the same way to receive good grades. User jurisdictions are free to modify these grading materials, including the suggested weights assigned to particular points. Grading the MPT is the exclusive responsibility of the jurisdiction using the MPT as part of its admissions process.

Copyright ©2008 by the National Conference of Bar Examiners.
All rights reserved

Arden Industries v. Freight Forwarders

DRAFTERS' POINT SHEET

In this test item, applicants work for a firm that represents Arden Industries, Inc. (Arden) in a dispute with Freight Forwarders, Inc. (FFI). Arden, a manufacturer of printing presses, owes FFI about $120,000 on past due invoices for transportation services. FFI recently undertook to transport an Arden printing press worth $200,000 and asserts that it has a security interest and a carrier's lien in the press under the Franklin Commercial Code (FCC). FFI has notified Arden that it intends to sell the press and apply the proceeds to satisfy Arden's past indebtedness to FFI.

Arden's attorneys have obtained an injunction to prevent the sale, and the parties have entered into a Stipulated Statement of Facts in anticipation of filing cross motions for summary judgment. Applicants' task is to draft Arden's brief in support of its motion for summary judgment.

The File consists of the office memo regarding persuasive briefs instructing applicants on the basics of writing a brief and the Stipulated Statement of Facts, which has a mix of relevant and irrelevant facts.

The Library contains excerpts from the Franklin Commercial Code (which is identical to the UCC) and the case law that is necessary for resolution of the problem.

The following discussion covers all of the points the drafters intended to raise in the problem. Applicants need not cover them all to receive passing or even excellent grades. Grading decisions are within the discretion of the graders in the user jurisdictions. The formulations of the headings used in the Discussion section (below) are examples only and other headings are possible.

I. **Overview:** Applicants' work product should resemble a brief and should follow the instructions in the memorandum regarding persuasive briefs.

- As stated in the memo from the partner, applicants need not write an extended statement of facts because the Stipulated Statement of Facts will be appended to the brief.
- They should, however, write a brief introductory statement that informs the court of the nature of the dispute, e.g., that the parties have stipulated to the facts and that the dispute involves a commercial law question: whether FFI has either a valid security interest or a carrier's lien in an Arden printing press in FFI's possession.
- The Argument section of the brief should be broken down into descriptive headings.
- The headings should be more than mere abstract statements.
- The argument should proceed logically from the proposition stated in the heading.
- The law should be applied to the facts in making the arguments.
- Applicants must follow the partner's instructions by:
  - making the affirmative arguments why FFI has no security interest or carrier's lien;
  - refuting the points raised in the letter from FFI's attorneys, including a distinction of the Wendover case.
- It does not matter whether applicants set up separate sections in the brief to make these points or whether they deal with them in the appropriate parts of their affirmative arguments. Either approach is acceptable.

II. Discussion: There are several ways applicants can organize the brief, but they must present the following arguments:

- Under Franklin law, there was no security agreement because:
  - there is no writing in which Arden expressly granted a security interest to FFI; and
  - there was no "course of dealing" incorporating Section 15 of the invoices into the parties' contract.
- There is no carrier's lien to the printing press in FFI's possession because the indebtedness relates to earlier invoices.
- The Wendover case is distinguishable on at least two bases:
  - Franklin courts are not bound by the case law of the State of Olympia, which is the law applied by the Bankruptcy Court in Wendover; and
  - the Franklin Supreme Court has given the same UCC provisions a different interpretation.
- Note: Aside from distinguishing Wendover, applicants may occasionally draw on that case for support as well.

- **THIS COURT SHOULD GRANT ARDEN'S MOTION FOR SUMMARY JUDGMENT BECAUSE FFI HAS NO SECURITY INTEREST IN ARDEN'S PRESS, EITHER EXPRESS OR BY COURSE OF DEALING.**

A. There is No Written Agreement by Which Arden Expressly Granted to FFI a Security Interest in Any Property.

- The FCC defines a security agreement only as "an agreement that creates or provides for a security interest." See FCC §9-102(3) and Wendover.
- The fact that the printing press is in FFI's possession obviates the need for a signed security agreement. FCC §9-203.
- Although a signed writing might not be an absolute requirement for a security interest (see Wendover), the facts make it clear that Arden never signed or otherwise expressly assented to grant FFI a security agreement in any of the documents related to the shipping transactions.
- Under FCC §9-203(b)(3)(B), the collateral must be in the secured party's possession "pursuant to the debtor's security agreement."
- If there is no "debtor's security agreement," FFI's possession does not perfect a security interest.
- Early in the relationship of the parties, FFI presented Arden with a form contract that contained language by which Arden would have granted FFI a lien, but Arden declined to sign it.
- The only place any language is found that can be interpreted as granting a security interest to FFI is in Section 15 of the invoices.
- FFI unilaterally presented that language, but Arden never expressly adopted it.
- Indeed, the stipulated facts state that Arden never intended to grant a security interest to FFI.
- The parties did business in such a way that they never discussed Section 15 or otherwise alluded to it in the course of setting up their many transactions. The facts show that:
  - All shipping arrangements were made and agreed to over the phone;
  - No one at FFI ever explicitly made Arden aware of the existence of Section 15; and
  - The parties never negotiated or discussed the terms of the shipment other than price and payment terms.
- Thus Arden never expressly granted or intended to grant a security interest.

B. There Was No Course of Dealing Between the Parties by Which the Language of Section 15 of the Invoices Became Part of the Contract Between the Parties.

- At this point, applicants must draw on the holding of the Franklin Supreme Court in Data Systems, which is dispositive on this point.
- That holding is directly opposed to the Olympia court's holding in Wendover.

- The clear holding of Data Systems is that, "[T]he repeated sending of a writing that contains certain standard terms, without any action with respect to the issues addressed by those terms, cannot constitute a course of dealing that would incorporate a term of the writing into the agreement of the parties."
- Applying the reasoning of the Data Systems court to the facts of this case, the analysis would appear to be the same:
- A course of dealing can be used to supplement or qualify the agreement of the parties.
- However, it cannot be used to create the agreement.
- As the court reasoned in Data Systems, notwithstanding FFI's failure to obtain Arden's express assent to the Section 15 terms, FFI continued to use invoices with that language for five years. This practice did not create an agreement between FFI and Arden, but merely showed that, while FFI desired certain terms, it was willing to do business on the terms only agreed to expressly.
- That is to say, FFI willingly continued to do business with Arden notwithstanding the arrearages and without resorting to Section 15 of the invoice.
- The fact that FFI was never able to negotiate an agreement expressly containing the terms of Section 15 is also strong evidence that those terms were not part of the parties' agreement.
- Early in their relationship, FFI tried to get Arden to sign a long-term contract including the Section 15 language, but Arden refused to enter into such a contract.
- Moreover, the implication of a course of dealing is that "the parties to any agreement covered by the Code must have consistently taken action with regard to a particular issue."
- The facts make it clear that this is the first time the effect of Section 15 had ever been discussed or put in issue between FFI and Arden.

- Despite Arden's earlier delinquencies, FFI had never before claimed or attempted to enforce a lien on Arden's property.
- Thus, it cannot be said that the parties had a course of dealing by which they had a common basis for understanding that this was part of their agreement when they never before took any action on it.
- The Wendover case is not controlling, principally because it arises in another jurisdiction and the Franklin Supreme Court disagrees with its holding.
- The Wendover court simply takes a different approach:
- Where Data Systems views the contract as containing only those terms upon which the parties specifically agreed to over the phone (FFI will transport the goods and Arden will pay the published transportation rates), Wendover finds that the invoice is the operative part of the contract and becomes an express part of it through an unobjected-to course of dealing.
- The cases focus on different subsections of FCC §1-205, which is the course-of-dealing definition:
- Data Systems focuses principally on §1-205(3), which states that a course of dealing "supplements or qualifies terms of an agreement" and concludes that, if there is no agreement, there is nothing to supplement or qualify.
- By contrast, Wendover focuses on §1-205(1), which defines it as "establishing a common basis of understanding for interpreting their expressions and other conduct" and concludes that invoices can fulfill that function.

- **THIS COURT SHOULD GRANT ARDEN'S MOTION FOR SUMMARY JUDGMENT BECAUSE FFI DOES NOT HAVE A CARRIER'S LIEN UNDER THE FRANKLIN COMMERCIAL CODE; THE PAST DUE INVOICES RELATE TO CHARGES FOR GOODS NO LONGER IN FFI'S POSSESSION.**

- Section 7-307 of the FCC gives a common carrier "a lien on goods covered by a bill of lading for charges subsequent to the date of its receipt of the goods for…transportation.…"
- Drawing on the Code Comment and the Shellac's case, applicants should have no trouble concluding that such a lien applies only to goods in the carrier's possession and only for charges incurred in transporting those goods.
- The facts in the File make it clear that, "The arrearages owed by Arden are on account of five invoices covering earlier shipments, not the invoice covering the shipment of the Model Z Swift-Print press in FFI's possession."
- Thus, FFI has no lien against the press in its possession.

III. Conclusion: Under the law of the State of Franklin, FFI has no security interest or carrier's lien in the Arden printing press in its possession.

MPT Task 4E:
Ronald v. Department of Motor Vehicles

FILE

LAW OFFICES OF MARVIN ANDERS
1100 Larchmont Avenue
Hawkins Falls, Franklin 33311

M E M O R A N D U M

To: Applicant
From: Marvin Anders
Date: February 24, 2009
Subject: Ronald v. Department of Motor Vehicles

Our client, Barbara Ronald, was arrested and charged with driving a motor vehicle with a prohibited blood-alcohol concentration. A blood test taken after her arrest indicates that she had a blood-alcohol concentration of 0.08 percent. Pursuant to § 353 of the Franklin Vehicle Code, the "Administrative Per Se" Law, the Franklin Department of Motor Vehicles (DMV) suspended her driver's license even though she has not yet had a criminal trial for driving with a prohibited blood-alcohol concentration.

Section 353 permits a driver whose license has been suspended to request an administrative hearing to vacate the suspension. The evidentiary portion of Ms. Ronald's hearing was yesterday. We must submit written argument to the administrative law judge on the issues we raised by the close of business today. Because this is an administrative proceeding—not a criminal prosecution for driving with a prohibited blood-alcohol concentration—the rules are different, particularly the rules of evidence. For example, the DMV may introduce hearsay evidence that would be inadmissible in court. Also, under § 353, the DMV need prove only that Ms. Ronald was driving with a prohibited blood-alcohol concentration only by a preponderance of the evidence.

Please draft a persuasive memorandum for the administrative law judge arguing that:
1. The police officer did not have reasonable suspicion to stop Ms. Ronald;
2. The administrative law judge cannot rely solely on the blood test report to find that Ms. Ronald was driving with a prohibited blood-alcohol concentration; and
3. In light of all the evidence, the DMV has not met its burden of proving by a preponderance of the evidence that Ms. Ronald was driving with a prohibited blood-alcohol concentration.

Do not write a separate statement of facts. However, be sure to use the law and the facts to make the strongest case possible on each issue, anticipating and addressing the arguments that the DMV may be able to make in its favor.

TRANSCRIPT OF FEBRUARY 23, 2009, ADMINISTRATIVE HEARING

Administrative Law Judge (ALJ): We're here for the hearing on the one-year suspension of Barbara Ronald's driver's license pursuant to Franklin Vehicle Code § 353. Attorney Jennifer Newman appears on behalf of the DMV. Marvin Anders on behalf of Ms. Ronald. Ms. Newman, you've got the burden; you go first.

Newman: Thank you. The DMV requests that the clerk mark as Exhibit 1 a Hawkins Falls Police Department Incident Report, by Officer Barry Thompson, regarding the incident involving Ms. Ronald on December 19, 2008. The DMV also requests that the Hawkins Falls Police Department Crime Laboratory § 353 Blood Alcohol Test, dated December 29, which is the document that triggered Ms. Ronald's driver's license suspension on January 9, be marked and admitted as Exhibit 2.

ALJ: Any objections to the admission of the police report and crime lab test results?

Anders: We don't object to admitting the police report. However, since the officer is here, I'll call him as a hostile witness and examine him on some details. We do dispute that he had reasonable suspicion to stop Ms. Ronald. We're also challenging the sufficiency of the § 353 test results as inadmissible hearsay, and we'll argue that they are not enough to support a finding that Ms. Ronald was driving with a blood-alcohol level of at least 0.08 percent.

ALJ: Ms. Newman?

Newman: It's the DMV's position that you should, at a minimum, consider the § 353 test results as evidence and that they are, in fact, enough to meet our burden, and that Officer Thompson did have reasonable suspicion to stop Ms. Ronald.

ALJ: The police report is admitted. Since this is an administrative hearing, I'll receive the § 353 test results, and you can argue their impact in a written memorandum.

Newman: With that, the DMV rests.

Anders: Your Honor, Ms. Ronald wants to testify briefly, and I'd like to call her.

[Witness takes the stand and is sworn and identified.]

Anders: Ms. Ronald, can you tell us what happened on the night of the incident?

Ronald: Yes. I went to the Lexington Club for a late supper. I had worked 18 hours at the Palace Hotel, where I'm the manager, dealing with a host of problems that came out of nowhere. I had to go somewhere to unwind, and I was hungry. I had a salad and a piece of grilled fish and some white wine—no more than two glasses, just as I told the officer. I wasn't under the influence of anything. I was just drained. I left the Lexington Club after midnight. As I was driving down Highway 13, I saw a car following me so closely that I couldn't see it in my side mirrors. I became frightened, and I guess I must have begun to weave in my lane as I paid more attention to the car in my rearview mirror than to the road ahead. I was actually relieved when I saw the police lights. I immediately pulled over to the shoulder. I told the officer about the wine because I had nothing to hide. I was just very, very tired.

Anders: How do you think you did on the field sobriety tests that Officer Thompson had you perform—the coordination and balancing tests?

Ronald: Well, the officer told me I did not perform well. I myself think I did quite well, particularly since I'd been working for 18 hours. I was also wearing high heels, my arthritis was acting up, and traffic was whizzing by the side of the road where the officer had me perform the tests.

Anders: Thank you, Ms. Ronald. Your witness.

Newman: Ms. Ronald, how can you be sure you weren't under the influence of alcohol?

Ronald: I've worked in the hospitality business all my life. I've seen many people under the influence of alcohol. I know how they act. I simply wasn't acting that way.

* * * *

Anders: I'd like to call Officer Barry Thompson as a hostile witness. [Officer enters the room, takes the stand, and is sworn and identified.] Officer, do you remember your arrest of Ms. Ronald?

Thompson: Yes, I do.

Anders: After you first noticed her car, you followed her closely for nearly a mile. True?

Thompson: I wasn't tailgating her, but yes, I wanted to observe her carefully.

Anders: You had your high-beam headlights on?

Thompson: Yes. Again, to get a good look.

Anders: She wasn't going over the speed limit, was she?

Thompson: I don't recall.

Anders: If she had been, you would have mentioned it in your report?

Thompson: I probably would have.

Anders: You said that her vehicle was weaving back and forth in its lane, correct?

Thompson: Yes.

Anders: But not until after you started following her?

Thompson: Yes.

Anders: I saw her weaving and it was 1:00 a.m., the time bars were closing.

Anders: Did Ms. Ronald's vehicle ever travel out of her traffic lane?

Thompson: I didn't see her cross into another lane, but she wasn't driving straight, either.

Anders: You stopped her car on U.S. Highway 13, a major truck route, is that right?

Thompson: Yes.

Anders: Wasn't it quite busy that night?

Thompson: I suppose so. It usually is.

Anders: After you stopped her, you had her step onto the shoulder close to Highway 13?

Thompson: Yes.

Anders: She was wearing fairly high heels, wasn't she?

Thompson: Yes.

Anders: Did you allow her to take her shoes off?

Thompson: She never asked to take her shoes off.

Anders: You asked her to stand on one foot?

Thompson: Yes.

Anders: And to walk a straight line while right next to Highway 13, the truck route?

Thompson: On the shoulder, off the highway.

Anders: Okay, Officer. Let me ask: you didn't smell alcohol on her breath, did you?

Thompson: I don't recall.

Anders: I have nothing further.

Newman: I have no questions.

Anders: We rest. [Witness steps down.]

ALJ: I've got another hearing scheduled. Written arguments are due by the close of business tomorrow.

HAWKINS FALLS POLICE DEPARTMENT INCIDENT REPORT # 48012

Incident Date: December 19, 2008 **Arrest Time:** 1:15 a.m. **Incident Type:** Driving with blood-alcohol level of 0.08 percent or more (Fr. Veh. Code § 352) **Personal Injuries:** None
Incident Location: U.S. Highway 13 at Bellaire Blvd. **Conditions:** Dark, clear, dry
Suspect: Barbara Ronald, white female, weight 145 lbs, height 5'9", d.o.b. 9/15/1951, age 57
Suspect's Identification: Franklin driver's license, #W23152
Suspect's Address: 110 Merrill Crest Drive, Hawkins Falls, FR 33309
Motor Vehicle: License Plate: Franklin JSP-256   **Make/Model/Year:** Jaguar XJS V12 1992

Detailed Description of the Incident: This officer first observed suspect's vehicle pulling out from the Lexington Club parking lot at 1:00 a.m. at U.S. Highway 13 and Montview Way. The vehicle began to travel south on U.S. Highway 13; followed suspect in patrol car and observed her vehicle weaving back and forth in her lane. There was no debris or other material in the roadway that could explain such weaving. I activated the patrol car's overhead emergency lights, and suspect pulled over to the right shoulder near the corner of U.S. Highway 13 and Bellaire Boulevard about 1.4 miles from the Lexington Club; approached driver's window to ask for identification; as suspect handed over her driver's license, her eyes appeared bloodshot and watery; she said that she had been weaving back and forth because she had been scared by my headlights and was trying to see who was following her; on questioning, she admitted to having consumed two glasses of white wine.

I asked suspect to exit her vehicle and observed that her gait was unsteady. Based on these observations, I asked suspect to perform a series of field sobriety tests. When asked to walk a straight line and then stand on one foot, suspect performed poorly, lost her balance, and was distracted. As a result of her poor performance on the field sobriety tests, objective symptoms of intoxication, and poor driving, I formed the opinion that she had been driving with a blood-alcohol level of at least 0.08 percent, and placed her under arrest at 1:15 a.m.

I transported her to headquarters; she consented to a blood test. I then transported her to Mercy Hospital for the blood draw. We arrived at 2:05 a.m. and waited until a blood sample could be drawn by a technician at 2:50 a.m. I booked the blood sample into the evidence locker under HFPD No. 48012.

Reporting Police Officer: Barry Thompson, Badge No. 4693
Report Date/Time: December 19, 2008, 8:29 a.m.

EXHIBIT 1

HAWKINS FALLS POLICE DEPARTMENT
CRIME LABORATORY
VEHICLE CODE § 353 BLOOD ALCOHOL TEST RESULTS

This is to certify under penalty of perjury under the law of the State of Franklin that on December 21, 2008, I tested a sample of the blood of Barbara Ronald, entered as HFPD No. 48012, on the HemoAssay-Seven Chemical Testing Instrument. I attest that my analysis of the Ronald sample reflected a blood-alcohol concentration of 0.08 percent.

Daniel Gans signed by *Charlotte Swain*
Daniel Gans
Forensic Alcohol Analyst
(Fr. Bur. of Inv. Cert. #802)

Charlotte Swain
Charlotte Swain
Senior Laboratory Technician

I certify that this is a true and accurate copy of forensic alcohol test results performed at the Crime Laboratory of the ___Hawkins Falls Police Department___, pursuant to F.C.R. § 121.

Tony Bellagio
Tony Bellagio
Records Custodian
Dated: December 29, 2008

EXHIBIT 2

LIBRARY

Ronald v. Department of Motor Vehicles
Franklin Vehicle Code

§ 352 Driving with a prohibited blood-alcohol percentage

It is unlawful for any person who has 0.08 percent or more of alcohol in his or her blood to operate a motor vehicle.

§ 353 Administrative suspension of license by Department of Motor Vehicles for prohibited blood-alcohol level on chemical testing

(a) Upon receipt by the Department of Motor Vehicles of a laboratory test report from any law enforcement agency attesting that a forensic alcohol analysis performed by chemical testing determined that a person's blood had 0.08 percent or more of alcohol while he or she was operating a motor vehicle, the Department of Motor Vehicles shall immediately suspend the license of such person to operate a motor vehicle for a period of one year.

(b) Any person may request an administrative hearing before an administrative law judge on the suspension of his or her license under this section. At the administrative hearing, the Department of Motor Vehicles shall bear the burden of proving by a preponderance of the evidence that the person operated a motor vehicle when the person had 0.08 percent or more of alcohol in his or her blood.

(c) Any party aggrieved by a decision of an administrative law judge may petition the district court in the county where the offense allegedly occurred for review of the administrative law judge's decision.

Franklin Code of Regulations

§ 121 Forensic blood-alcohol testing

Forensic blood-alcohol testing may be performed only by a forensic alcohol analyst who has been trained in accordance with the requirements of the Franklin Bureau of Investigation. A forensic blood-alcohol analysis signed by such a forensic alcohol analyst and certified as authentic by a records custodian for the laboratory in which the analysis was performed may be admitted in any administrative suspension hearing without further foundation.

Franklin Administrative Procedure Act

§ 115 Hearsay evidence; admissible at administrative hearing

Hearsay evidence shall be admissible at an administrative hearing. If hearsay evidence would be admissible in a judicial proceeding under an exception to the hearsay rule under the Franklin Evidence Code, it shall be sufficient in itself to support a finding. If hearsay evidence would not be admissible in a judicial proceeding under an exception to the hearsay rule under the Franklin Evidence Code, it may nonetheless be used for the purpose of supplementing or explaining other evidence.

Franklin Evidence Code

§ 1278 Hearsay definition

Hearsay is a statement, other than one made by the declarant while testifying at a judicial proceeding, offered in evidence to prove the truth of the matter asserted.

§ 1279 Hearsay rule

Hearsay is not admissible except as provided by this Code.

§ 1280 Hearsay rule: public-records exception

Evidence of a writing made as a record of an act, condition, or event is not made inadmissible by the hearsay rule when offered in any judicial proceeding to prove the act, condition, or event, if (a) the writing was made by and within the scope of duty of a public employee, (b) the writing was made at or near the time of the act, condition, or event, and (c) the sources of information and method and time of preparation were such as to indicate its trustworthiness.

Pratt v. Department of Motor Vehicles

Franklin Court of Appeal (2006)

The Department of Motor Vehicles (DMV) seeks review of a district court decision vacating the suspension of Jason Pratt's driver's license for the offense of driving a motor vehicle with a prohibited blood-alcohol concentration (PBAC). The DMV asserts that the court erred in concluding that Pratt's deviations within one lane of travel, with nothing more, failed to provide the police officer with reasonable suspicion to justify an investigative stop of the vehicle.

On February 2, 2004, Plymouth police sergeant Tom Kellogg was on patrol on Mill Street. There is no line or marking delineating the traffic lane from the parking lane on this street. The parking lane is bounded by the curb. Sergeant Kellogg testified that, at approximately 9:30 p.m., he was traveling southbound on Mill Street and observed Pratt's car traveling northbound, but that the car was "canted" such that it was driving at least partially in the unmarked parking lane.

After Pratt's car passed, Sergeant Kellogg turned around and began following it. He observed the car traveling in an "S-type" pattern—a smooth motion toward the right part of the parking lane and back toward the centerline. He stated that Pratt's car moved approximately 10 feet from right to left within the northbound lane, coming within one foot of the centerline and to within six to eight feet of the curb. Pratt's car repeated the S-pattern several times over two blocks. The movement was neither erratic nor jerky, and Pratt's car did not come close to hitting any other vehicles or to hitting the curb. Sergeant Kellogg testified that the manner of Pratt's driving suggested that the driver was intoxicated, so he turned on his emergency lights and pulled Pratt's car over. As a result of the evidence obtained after the stop, Sergeant Kellogg arrested Pratt for violating § 352 of the Franklin Vehicle Code and the DMV suspended Pratt's driver's license.

At the administrative hearing, Pratt's primary defense was that Sergeant Kellogg had no reasonable basis to stop his vehicle. The administrative law judge (ALJ) held that Sergeant Kellogg's testimony of Pratt's "unusual driving" and "drifting within one's own lane" provided reasonable suspicion to justify the stop. Pratt sought review of the ALJ's decision in the district court. The district court reversed, holding that slight deviations within a single lane do not give rise to reasonable suspicion that a driver has a PBAC.

The issue is whether the traffic stop violated Pratt's constitutional rights because it was not based on reasonable suspicion. Although investigative stops are seizures within the meaning of the Fourth Amendment, in some circumstances police officers may conduct such stops even where there is no probable cause to make an arrest. *Terry v. Ohio* (U.S. 1968). Such a stop must be based on more than an officer's "inchoate and un-particularized suspicion or 'hunch.'" *Id.* Rather, the officer "must be able to point to specific and articulable facts which, taken together with rational inferences from those facts, reasonably warrant" the stop. *Id.* The DMV has the burden of establishing that an investigative stop is reasonable. *See Taylor v. Dept. of Motor Vehicles* (Fr. Sup. Ct. 1973).

The DMV contends that Sergeant Kellogg had reasonable suspicion to stop Pratt. It argues that, in and of itself, repeated weaving within a single lane (absent an obvious innocent explanation) provides reasonable suspicion to make an investigative stop. While we agree that the facts of the case give rise to a reasonable suspicion that Pratt was driving with a PBAC and that the investigative stop was reasonable, we reject a bright-line rule that weaving within a single lane alone gives rise to reasonable suspicion. Rather, our determination is based on the totality of the circumstances.

In *State v. Kessler* (Fr. Ct. App. 1999), a police officer observed the defendant's car traveling slowly, stopping at an intersection with no stop sign or traffic light, turning onto a cross street, and accelerating "at a high rate of speed" (but under the speed limit). The officer then saw the car pull into a parking lot where the driver opened the door and poured out a "mixture of liquid and ice" from a cup. When the officer identified himself to the driver, the driver began to walk away, at which point the officer made an investigative stop. We held that the stop was based on a reasonable suspicion, even though any of these facts alone might be insufficient to provide reasonable suspicion.

The DMV contends that repeated weaving within a single lane alone gives an experienced police officer reasonable suspicion to make an investigative stop. That view, however, conflicts with *Kessler*. Further, the DMV's proffered bright-line rule is problematic because movements that may be characterized as "repeated weaving within a single lane" may, under the totality of the circumstances, fail to give rise to reasonable suspicion. This may be the case, for example, where the "weaving" is minimal or happens very few times over a great distance. Because the DMV's proffered standard can be interpreted to cover conduct that many innocent drivers commit, it may subject a substantial portion of the public to invasions of their privacy. It is in effect no standard at all.

However, driving need not be illegal to give rise to reasonable suspicion. Thus, we adopt neither the bright-line rule proffered by the DMV that weaving within a single lane may alone give rise to reasonable suspicion, nor the bright-line rule advocated by Pratt that weaving within a single lane must be erratic, unsafe, or illegal to give rise to reasonable suspicion. Rather, we maintain the well-established principle that reviewing courts must determine whether there was reasonable suspicion for an investigative stop based on the totality of the circumstances. As the building blocks of fact accumulate, reasonable inferences about the cumulative effect can be drawn.

Sergeant Kellogg did not observe any actions that constituted traffic violations or that, considered in isolation, provided reasonable suspicion that criminal activity was afoot. However, when considered in conjunction with all of the facts and circumstances of the case, Pratt's driving provided Kellogg with reasonable suspicion to believe that Pratt was driving while intoxicated.

Moving between the roadway centerline and parking lane is not slight deviation within one's own lane. The district court also incorporated by reference Sergeant Kellogg's testimony regarding Pratt's drifting and unusual driving. Our read of Sergeant Kellogg's testimony does not support the view that Pratt's weaving constituted only slight deviation within one lane. After initially stating that he did not have an estimate of how many times Pratt's vehicle weaved, on cross-examination Sergeant Kellogg stated that Pratt's vehicle weaved "several" or "a few" times over several feet. The manner and frequency of Pratt's weaving are not the only specific, articulable facts here. When Sergeant Kellogg first observed Pratt's vehicle, it was "canted into the parking lane" and "wasn't in the designated traffic lane." Finally, we note that the incident took place at 9:30 at night. While this is not as significant as when poor driving takes place at or around "bar time," it does lend some further credence to Sergeant Kellogg's suspicion that Pratt was driving while intoxicated.

When viewed in isolation, these individual facts may not be sufficient to warrant a reasonable officer to suspect that Pratt was driving while intoxicated. However, such facts accumulate, and as they accumulate, reasonable inferences about the cumulative effect can be drawn. We determine, under the totality of the circumstances, that Sergeant Kellogg presented specific and articulable facts, which, taken together with rational inferences from those facts, gave rise to the reasonable suspicion necessary for an investigative stop. Accordingly, the stop did not violate Pratt's constitutional right to be free from unreasonable searches and seizures.

Reversed.

Schwartz v. Department of Motor Vehicles

Franklin Court of Appeal (1994)

On October 21, 1992, at 2:25 a.m., Dixon City Police Officer James Pisano observed Gil Schwartz's vehicle straddling the south-bound lanes of Valley Road at 60 miles per hour. Officer Pisano stopped Schwartz's vehicle at that time and, after making contact with him, noted that Schwartz had slurred speech, bloodshot eyes, a strong odor of alcohol, and an unsteady gait. Officer Pisano then administered field sobriety tests on which Schwartz performed poorly. Officer Pisano then arrested Schwartz.

Officer Pisano had Schwartz's blood drawn at 3:45 a.m. at the Dixon City hospital. The blood-alcohol lab test disclosed a blood-alcohol concentration of 0.129 percent. The lab test results were immediately noted on the lab's internal records but, because of an error, not on the official § 353 report until November 29, 1992, over a month after Schwartz's arrest and blood draw.

Pursuant to § 353 of the Franklin Vehicle Code, the Department of Motor Vehicles (DMV) suspended Schwartz's driver's license. Schwartz challenged the suspension at an administrative hearing. At the hearing, Officer Pisano testified and the administrative law judge (ALJ) received the lab test report offered by the DMV showing Schwartz's blood-alcohol concentration. Schwartz did not offer any evidence of his own, but raised several evidentiary objections, including that the lab test report was hearsay. The ALJ overruled his objections, concluded that the lab test report came within the public-records exception to the hearsay rule, Fr. Evid. Code § 1280, found that the DMV had proved by a preponderance of the evidence that Schwartz had operated a motor vehicle with a blood-alcohol concentration of at least 0.08 percent, and upheld the suspension.

Schwartz petitioned for review in the district court, seeking to overturn the ALJ's decision. The court concluded that the lab report did not come within the public-records exception to the hearsay rule because the results of the test were not recorded close in time to the performance of the test, as required, but more than a month later. The court thus ruled that the suspension was not supported by a preponderance of the evidence. The DMV appeals.

Under § 353 of the Franklin Vehicle Code, the ALJ was bound to uphold the suspension if he found by a preponderance of the evidence—that is, if he found it more likely than not—that Schwartz was driving with a blood-alcohol concentration of 0.08 percent or more. The DMV has now conceded that the § 353 analysis in this case does not satisfy the public-records exception to the hearsay rule because of the late recording of the results. Therefore, we must consider what weight to give it.

Pursuant to Franklin Administrative Procedure Act § 115, if the blood-alcohol analysis satisfies an exception to the hearsay rule, it may conclusively establish a violation of § 352. If not, additional evidence is needed to support such a finding.

In this case, the lab test report supplements Officer Pisano's testimony. Although a chemical blood-alcohol test report is one means of establishing that a driver's blood-alcohol concentration was 0.08 percent or more, it is not the only means. Both parties are free to introduce circumstantial evidence bearing on whether the driver's blood-alcohol concentration was at least 0.08 percent. Officer Pisano testified that he observed Schwartz driving in an erratic and dangerous manner, and that Schwartz had bloodshot eyes, gave off a strong odor of alcohol, had an unsteady gait and slurred speech, and performed poorly on field sobriety tests. This evidence that Schwartz was driving while heavily intoxicated provided sufficient support for the ALJ's finding that Schwartz was driving with a blood-alcohol concentration of at least 0.08 percent.

We emphasize that our decision does not justify license suspensions based solely on circumstantial evidence. A police officer's observations, standing alone, cannot establish that a driver's blood-alcohol concentration is at least 0.08 percent or more. Here, however, the record contains a blood test report, which (though inadmissible in court because it does not meet the public-records exception) may still be used in an administrative proceeding "for the purpose of supplementing or explaining other evidence." Franklin APA § 115.

Thus, the ALJ could properly consider whether this blood test report, together with the police officer's observations, supported a finding on the critical fact of blood-alcohol concentration. We conclude that the ALJ's decision is properly supported by the record in this case.

Reversed.

Rodriguez v. Department of Motor Vehicles

Franklin Court of Appeal (2004)

Following suspension of his driver's license by the Department of Motor Vehicles (DMV), Peter Rodriguez sought review in the district court seeking to vacate the suspension. The district court vacated the suspension, and the DMV appeals. We affirm.

Rodriguez was stopped by Town of Ada Police Officer Mac Huber on June 20, 2003, after failing to stop at a stop sign. When Officer Huber observed that Rodriguez was exhibiting symptoms of intoxication, he arrested him. Rodriguez submitted to a blood test, which purportedly showed a blood-alcohol concentration of 0.17 percent.

The DMV suspended Rodriguez's driver's license. At the hearing on the suspension held pursuant to the "Administrative Per Se" Law (Fr. Veh. Code § 353), the DMV submitted Officer Huber's written police report describing in perfunctory fashion the circumstances of the stop and the arrest. The DMV also submitted a one-page document entitled "blood-alcohol test results," which stated that Rodriguez's blood had been tested and found to contain "0.17 percent alcohol." The blood-alcohol test report was on letterhead from the "Town of Ada Police Department Crime Laboratory." The report bore the signature of "Virginia Loew, Criminalist."

Rodriguez challenged the sufficiency of the blood-alcohol test report under § 115 of the Franklin Administrative Procedure Act. He contended that the DMV had failed to show that the blood-alcohol test report satisfied the public-records exception to the hearsay rule because the DMV did not establish that the report had been prepared by a person with an official duty to perform a forensic alcohol analysis, as required by § 121 of the Franklin Code of Regulations. The administrative law judge (ALJ) rejected the challenge to the report and found that Rodriguez was driving with a blood-alcohol level of 0.08 percent or more, a finding based solely on the report.

Section 115 of the Franklin Administrative Procedure Act provides: "Hearsay evidence shall be admissible at an administrative hearing. If hearsay evidence would be admissible in a judicial proceeding under an exception to the hearsay rule under the Franklin Evidence Code, it shall be sufficient in itself to support a finding. If hearsay evidence would not be admissible in a judicial proceeding under an exception to the hearsay rule under the Franklin Evidence Code, it may nonetheless be used for the purpose of supplementing or explaining other evidence."

Rodriguez maintains that there is not sufficient evidence to support the ALJ's finding that he was driving with a blood-alcohol level of at least 0.08 percent because the report purporting to show his blood-alcohol concentration at 0.17 percent was hearsay that would not have been admissible at a judicial proceeding under the public-records exception.

As the proponent of the blood-alcohol test report, the DMV bore the burden of establishing the foundation for the public-records exception, which entailed findings that (1) the forensic alcohol analysis was performed within the scope of the public employee's duty, (2) the results were recorded close in time to the performance of the analysis, and (3) the analysis and results were generally trustworthy. See Fr. Evid. Code § 1280.

The DMV claims that it established the proper foundation for the public-records exception to the hearsay rule regarding the blood-alcohol test report because under § 664 of the Franklin Evidence Code, "[i]t is presumed that official duty has been regularly performed."

We generally agree with the DMV that when a blood-alcohol test is performed within the scope of a public employee's duty, under § 664 of the Franklin Evidence Code it is presumed that the results were recorded close in time to the performance of the blood test and that the test and its results were generally trustworthy, inasmuch as the public employee's duty imposes such requirements.

We disagree, however, with the DMV that Rodriguez's blood-alcohol test was performed within the scope of duty of the public employee in question. Indeed, we conclude that the public employee here was not authorized to perform the forensic alcohol analysis in the first place.

The performance of forensic alcohol analysis is subject to strict regulation by § 121 of the Franklin Code of Regulations. Section 121 authorizes only "forensic alcohol analysts"—to perform forensic alcohol analysis—and none others, including "criminalists."

On this record, it is evident that the blood-alcohol test here was performed by a public employee who was not authorized to perform forensic alcohol analysis. Virginia Loew is identified solely as a "criminalist"—and criminalists, as is evident, are not authorized to perform such blood-alcohol analyses.

The DMV argues that *Schwartz v. Department of Motor Vehicles* (Fr. Ct. App. 1994) permits the ALJ to consider an otherwise inadmissible blood test report, together with other circumstantial evidence, including a police officer's observations of the driver. But *Schwartz* involved very different facts. The DMV in that case conceded that the blood test report did not come within the public-records exception to the hearsay rule. Because the blood test report, by itself, was insufficient to support a finding, the DMV took great pains to establish the police officer's observations in detail. Here, by contrast, the DMV provided only cursory proof of the officer's observations. Indeed, this case illustrates a danger in the *Schwartz* ruling, especially if it permits the DMV to "rescue" testing by an unqualified person with unscientific testimony. For these reasons, we reject the DMV's reliance on *Schwartz*.

In this case, it follows that the DMV failed to meet its burden of establishing the necessary foundation for the public-records exception to the hearsay rule with respect to the blood-alcohol test report. A police report void of detail and a blood test report that lacks proper foundation, even in combination, do not add up to the necessary quantum of evidence. Consequently, the DMV failed to prove by a preponderance of the evidence that Rodriguez had an excessive blood-alcohol concentration, and the district court did not err in granting Rodriguez's petition and vacating the suspension of his driver's license.

Affirmed.

THE MPT
MULTISTATE PERFORMANCE TEST

Ronald v. Department of Motor Vehicles
POINT SHEET

The MPT point sheet, grading summary, and grading guidelines describe the factual and legal points encompassed within the lawyering task to be completed. They outline all the possible issues and points that might be addressed by an applicant. They are provided to the user jurisdictions for the sole purpose of assisting graders in grading the examination by identifying the issues and suggesting the resolution of the problem contemplated by the drafters. These are not official grading guides. Applicants can receive a range of passing grades, including excellent grades, without covering all the points discussed in these guides. The model answer is included as an illustration of a thorough and detailed response to the task. It is intended to serve only as an example. Applicants need not present their responses in the same way to receive good grades. User jurisdictions are free to modify these grading materials, including the suggested weights assigned to particular points. Grading the MPT is the exclusive responsibility of the jurisdiction using the MPT as part of its admissions process.

Copyright © 2008 by the National Conference of Bar Examiners.
All rights reserved

Ronald v. Department of Motor Vehicles
DRAFTERS' POINT SHEET

In this performance test, applicants work for a sole practitioner who represents Barbara Ronald. The Franklin Department of Motor Vehicles (DMV) suspended Ronald's driver's license for one year under § 353 of the Franklin Vehicle Code for driving with a blood-alcohol level of 0.08 percent or more in violation of § 352 of the same code. Ronald requested an administrative hearing to challenge the suspension. The evidentiary portion of the administrative hearing occurred on February 23, 2009. By the close of business on February 24, counsel must submit written arguments to the administrative law judge (ALJ). Applicants have a single task, to draft a persuasive memorandum arguing that (1) the officer did not have a reasonable suspicion warranting the stop of Ronald's vehicle; (2) the ALJ cannot rely solely on a blood test report to make a finding that Ronald was driving with a blood-alcohol concentration of at least 0.08 percent; and (3) in light of all the evidence, the DMV has not met its burden of proving that Ronald was driving with a blood-alcohol concentration of that percentage.

The File contains the memorandum from the supervising attorney, the administrative hearing transcript, the police report, and the § 353 test results. The Library contains a selection of Franklin statutes, administrative code provisions, and three cases.

The following discussion covers all of the points the drafters intended to raise in the problem. Applicants need not cover them all to receive passing or even excellent grades. Grading decisions are entirely within the discretion of the user jurisdictions.

I. Overview

Applicants' task is to prepare a persuasive memorandum setting forth three arguments for why the ALJ should vacate the suspension of Ronald's driver's license for driving with a prohibited blood-alcohol concentration. No specific format is given for the task. Applicants are instructed not to draft a statement of facts. However, applicants are told to incorporate the relevant facts into their arguments. In addition, applicants should anticipate the arguments that the DMV may make in support of the suspension.

Because this is an administrative proceeding, and not a criminal matter, applicants should recognize that the DMV has a lower burden of proof: it need prove that Ronald violated § 352 only by a preponderance of the evidence. With respect to the three issues, it is expected that applicants will make the following points:

1. The officer did not have a reasonable suspicion justifying the stop of Ronald's vehicle and the contrary case law (*Pratt v. Department of Motor Vehicles* (Fr. Ct. App. 2006)) is readily distinguishable.
2. The blood test report would not be admissible hearsay in a judicial proceeding as it does not fall within the applicable exception to the hearsay rule—the public-records exception. Therefore it cannot, by itself, support a finding that Ronald was driving with a prohibited blood-alcohol concentration.
3. The remaining evidence (the police report and testimony), coupled with the limited weight accorded to the blood test report, falls far below what is required (and thus the DMV cannot meet its burden of proof) to show that Ronald was driving a motor vehicle with a prohibited blood-alcohol concentration.

II. Analysis

A. Officer Thompson did not have reasonable suspicion to stop Ronald.

In *Pratt v. Department of Motor Vehicles* (Fr. Ct. App. 2006), the court discussed the circumstances under which a weaving automobile presents reasonable suspicion justifying a traffic stop.

- Driving does not have to be illegal to give rise to reasonable suspicion.
- Rather, reasonable suspicion exists when an officer can "point to specific and articulable facts which, taken together with rational inferences from those facts, reasonably warrant" the stop. *Pratt*, quoting *Terry v. Ohio* (U.S. 1968). Rejecting a bright-line rule for such situations, the court held that there was reasonable suspicion for stopping the defendant in *Pratt* based on his erratic driving.
- Under the totality of the circumstances test, the court concluded that Pratt's driving created a reasonable suspicion. Pratt's driving went beyond slight deviation within one lane—his vehicle moved from the parking lane to within one foot of the center-line and then to within six to eight feet of the curb. This conduct occurred several times. In addition, when first observed, Pratt's vehicle was not in the designated driving lane but was "canted" in the parking lane. And the incident occurred at 9:30 at night. Taken together, these facts and the reasonable inferences therefrom provided the officer with a reasonable suspicion to stop Pratt.

Applying the *Pratt* standard to the *Ronald* facts

Applicants should argue that the ALJ should reject the DMV's assertion that there was reasonable suspicion for the traffic stop of Ronald's vehicle.

- First, there was no traffic violation.
  - Officer Thompson admitted that had Ronald been speeding, he would have noted so in his report.
  - Ronald's vehicle never crossed into another lane.
- Second, there is an innocent explanation for the weaving of Ronald's vehicle.
  - Ronald testified that when she noticed that a vehicle was following her closely (so closely that she could not see it in her side mirrors), she became frightened and began "to weave in my lane as I paid more attention to the car in my rearview mirror than to the road ahead."
  - And she was very tired, having just finished working an 18-hour shift.
- By contrast, in *Pratt*, the defense did not offer any innocent explanation for Pratt's erratic driving.
- Further, unlike the situation in *State v. Kessler* (Fr. Ct. App. 1999) (discussed in *Pratt*), there are no actions by the driver that provide additional facts supporting reasonable suspicion. In *Kessler*, the driver did not break any traffic laws, but did stop at an intersection where there was no traffic signal, accelerated at a high rate of speed, and then pulled into a parking lot where the driver then poured a "mixture of liquid and ice" from a cup onto the ground. When the officer identified himself to the driver, the driver began to walk away and at that point the officer executed a *Terry* stop.
- Officer Thompson's account of the stop does not contradict or undercut Ronald's testimony that she began to weave in her lane because she was frightened by the car following her. In fact, his testimony corroborates her description of the stop.
- A fair reading of both Officer Thompson's testimony and his police report supports the conclusion that Ronald did not begin to weave in her lane until Thompson began following her.
- Unlike *Pratt*, where there was detailed testimony describing the extreme nature of how the defendant weaved in his lane, here there are no details about the weaving beyond Officer Thompson's statement that "I didn't see her cross into another lane, but she wasn't driving straight, either."
- Also, Officer Thompson testified that he used his high-beam lights. This would distract Ronald and make it difficult for her to see who was following her so closely.
- While it is relevant that Officer Thompson saw Ronald's vehicle leave the Lexington Club at 1:00 a.m., the time that bars close in Hawkins Falls, without more, that fact is not enough to constitute reasonable suspicion for the traffic stop.
- Granted, in *Pratt*, the court noted that it is more suggestive of intoxication when poor driving occurs "at or around 'bar time.'"
- In short, there are only three facts weighing in favor of reasonable suspicion: that Ronald had left a restaurant where alcohol was served, that she was driving around "bar time," and that she was weaving within her lane (but only after being closely followed).
- Applicants should argue that when viewed in light of the totality of circumstances—Ronald broke no traffic laws, and began weaving only after Officer Thompson began to follow her so closely that his vehicle could not be seen in her side mirrors, and he had high-beam lights on—the facts fall far short of establishing reasonable suspicion for the traffic stop.

B. **The blood test report cannot, by itself, support a finding that Ronald was driving with a prohibited blood-alcohol concentration (0.08 percent or more).**

- The relevant facts regarding the test of Ronald's blood are undisputed:
  - On December 19, 2008, at 2:50 a.m., a sample of Ronald's blood was drawn at Mercy Hospital in Hawkins Falls.
  - On December 29, 2008, the Crime Laboratory of the Hawkins Falls Police Department issued a "Vehicle Code § 353 Blood Alcohol Test Results" stating that Ronald's blood sample was subjected to a chemical test on December 21 and reflected a blood-alcohol concentration of 0.08 percent. The document bears the signature of Charlotte Swain, who is identified by the title of "Senior Laboratory Technician," and the name "Daniel Gans," who is identified by the title of "Forensic Alcohol Analyst." Gans did not sign the document. Rather, his name was signed by Swain.
- The burden is on the DMV to prove by a preponderance of the evidence, that is, to prove that it is more likely than not, that Ronald was driving with a blood-alcohol concentration of at least 0.08 percent. Fr. Veh. Code § 353(b); *Schwartz v. Dept. of Motor Vehicles* (Fr. Ct. App. 1994).
- The ALJ should give limited weight to the § 353 lab report as evidence that Ronald had a prohibited blood-alcohol concentration.
- The § 353 lab report is hearsay: it is an out-of-court statement offered to prove the truth of the matter asserted—that Ronald was driving with a blood-alcohol concentration of 0.08 percent or more. *See* Fr. Evid. Code § 1278 (defining hearsay).
- The DMV asserts that the § 353 lab report should be considered as evidence and that, by itself, the lab report is sufficient to prove by a preponderance of the evidence that Ronald was driving with a prohibited blood-alcohol concentration.
- The § 353 lab report does not fall within an exception to the hearsay rule and therefore cannot, by itself, support a finding at an administrative proceeding.
  - Under § 115 of the Franklin Administrative Procedure Act, if hearsay evidence would be admissible in a judicial proceeding under an exception to the hearsay rule, it is sufficient to support a finding at an administrative hearing. *See Rodriguez v. Dept. of Motor Vehicles* (Fr. Ct. App. 2004).
- Thus, the question is whether the § 353 lab report comes within the public-records exception of § 1280 of the Franklin Evidence Code. *Rodriguez*; *Schwartz*. Section 1280 provides: "Evidence of a writing made as a record of an act, condition, or event is not made inadmissible by the hearsay rule when offered in any judicial proceeding to prove the act, condition, or event, if (a) the writing was made by and within the scope of duty of a public employee, (b) the writing was made at or near the time of the act, condition, or event, and (c) the sources of information and method and time of preparation were such as to indicate its trustworthiness."
  - The report of a forensic alcohol analysis, when performed by an authorized person, comes within the public-records exception of § 1280 of the Evidence Code by virtue of the presumption of § 664 as described in *Rodriguez*, that the "official duty has been regularly performed."

- However, under § 121 of the Franklin Code of Regulations, forensic alcohol analysis "may be performed only by a forensic alcohol analyst." See also Rodriguez.
- The § 353 lab report proffered by the DMV bears the signature of Charlotte Swain, who is identified by the title of "Senior Laboratory Technician," not the requisite "Forensic Alcohol Analyst." See Rodriguez. The "signature" of Daniel Gans, a "Forensic Alcohol Analyst," was executed by Swain.
- As a result, the § 353 lab report does not comply with the requirements of § 121 of the Code of Regulations. As in Rodriguez, "the public employee here was not authorized to perform the forensic alcohol analysis in the first place."
- Therefore, the DMV cannot establish the necessary foundation for the public-records exception to the hearsay rule with respect to the § 353 lab report.
- In addition, there is a question as to whether the § 353 lab report was prepared "at or near the time of the…event." Fr. Evid. Code § 1280.
  - In Schwartz, the lab test results were recorded over five weeks after the defendant's arrest and blood draw, and the DMV conceded that, as a result of the delay, the § 353 lab report did not satisfy the public-records exception to the hearsay rule.
  - Here, Ronald's blood sample was tested just two days after her arrest, and the § 353 lab report was completed and certified eight days later, on December 29, 2008, during a holiday week.
  - While much shorter than the five-week delay in Schwartz, an applicant could argue that the delay in preparing the report places it outside of the public-records exception.
  - Applicants who make this argument may receive some credit, but the delay should not be the sole focus of their public-records exception argument.
  - Rather, the fact that the alcohol analysis was performed by a laboratory technician and not a forensic alcohol analyst categorically precludes the report from satisfying the public-records exception. See Rodriguez.

To recap, the § 353 lab report would be inadmissible to support a finding in a judicial proceeding because it does not satisfy the requirements of the public-records exception to the hearsay rule. Although hearsay is admissible in administrative proceedings such as Ronald's, it is accorded limited weight; it cannot support a finding by itself, but may be used only to supplement or explain other evidence. See Fr. Admin. Proc. Act § 115.

C. In light of all the evidence, the DMV has not met its burden of proving that Ronald was driving with a prohibited blood-alcohol concentration.

- Assuming, arguendo, that there was reasonable suspicion for the traffic stop, the DMV still cannot meet its burden to prove by a preponderance of the evidence that Ronald had a blood-alcohol concentration of 0.08 percent or more.
- The only evidence in addition to the problematic § 353 lab report of Ronald's possible intoxication is found in the police incident report and Officer Thompson's testimony.
- Officer Thompson's report notes that he observed Ronald's vehicle "weaving back and forth in her lane." When he stopped her vehicle, he noted that "her eyes appeared bloodshot and watery," and that she told him that she had had two glasses of white wine. According to Officer Thompson, her gait was unsteady, she performed poorly on field sobriety tests, and she was distracted.
- Officer Thompson's incident report was undermined by the testimony of Thompson himself, who made admissions supporting Ronald's testimony.
  - At the hearing, he conceded that Ronald had not exceeded the speed limit and that he had been following her closely with his high beams on.
  - Furthermore, he agreed, upon questioning, that Highway 13 is a busy truck route, and that Ronald performed the balancing and coordination tests while wearing high heels and standing on the shoulder of a busy highway.
  - Most telling, he could not recall smelling alcohol on Ronald's breath, nor is there any mention of his smelling alcohol in his report.
- Ronald's counsel called Ronald herself, who testified as follows:
  - She had no more than two glasses of white wine at dinner.
  - She was not under the influence of alcohol, but was drained after working for 18 hours straight.
  - She weaved while she was driving because the police officer was following too closely and she became distracted and afraid.
  - She noted that when she performed the field sobriety tests she was wearing high heels, her arthritis was acting up, and "traffic was whizzing by the side of the road."
  - Finally, she averred that she was sure that she was not under the influence of alcohol because she had long worked in the hospitality business and knew how persons acted when they were under the influence.
- Without more, the circumstantial evidence proffered by the DMV (the police report and the testimony) is insufficient to show that it was more likely than not that Ronald was driving with a prohibited blood-alcohol concentration.
  - In Schwartz, the arresting officer testified that the driver, after being stopped for driving in an erratic manner, exhibited "slurred speech, bloodshot eyes, a strong odor of alcohol, and an unsteady gait," and then performed poorly on field sobriety tests. The court of appeal held that this circumstantial evidence of intoxication, when supplemented by a blood test (which, as is the case here, did not meet the public-records hearsay exception, and therefore could not by itself prove intoxication), provided adequate support for the ALJ's finding that the driver had a blood-alcohol level of 0.08 percent or more.
  - However, in Rodriguez, the court emphasized the danger of allowing the DMV to "rescue" testing by an unqualified person with unscientific testimony." Thus, where the DMV proffered "only cursory proof of the officer's observations" of the driver's intoxication, a § 353 lab report that did not meet the exception to the hearsay rule could not be used to bolster the scant circumstantial evidence of intoxication even though, under APA § 115, such a blood test could be used "for the purpose of supplementing or explaining other evidence."
- Applicants should argue that the case at hand is much closer to Rodriguez than to Schwartz, and therefore the § 353 lab report cannot sufficiently buttress Officer Thompson's testimony.
  - Unlike the facts in Schwartz, there is no evidence that Ronald slurred her words during her interchange with Officer Thompson, or that she gave off any odor of alcohol—two clear symptoms of intoxication.
  - Ronald explained that she was tired, having just finished working 18 hours straight. Under the circumstances, her alleged poor performance on the field sobriety tests is reasonably explained by the facts that she has arthritis, she was wearing high heels, and was forced to perform the tests next to a busy highway.
  - Such factors militating against intoxication were not present in Schwartz.
  - Moreover, the demeanor of the driver in Rodriguez was at least as suggestive of intoxication as Ronald's, but was nevertheless held insufficient.
- Even if, considered together, all of the evidence, including the flawed § 353 lab report, shows that it is *possible* that Ronald was driving with a blood-alcohol level of at least 0.08 percent, it fails to show that it is *more likely than not* that she was doing so.

Because the DMV has not carried its burden to prove by a preponderance of the evidence that Ronald was driving with a blood-alcohol level of at least 0.08 percent, the ALJ must vacate the suspension of her driver's license.

MPT Task 4F:
Phoenix Corporation v. Biogenesis, Inc.

FORBES, BURDICK & WASHINGTON LLP
777 Fifth Avenue
Lakewood City, Franklin 33905

MEMORANDUM

To: Applicant
From: Ann Buckner
Date: February 24, 2009
Subject: *Phoenix Corporation v. Biogenesis, Inc.*

Yesterday, we were retained by the law firm of Amberg & Lewis LLP to consult on a motion for disqualification filed against it.

Amberg & Lewis represents Biogenesis, Inc., in a breach-of-contract action brought by Phoenix Corporation seeking $80 million in damages. The lawsuit has been winding its way through state court for almost six years. Phoenix is represented by the Collins Law Firm. There have been extensive discovery, motion practice, and several interlocutory appeals over the years, but the matter is now set for jury trial in a month and is expected to last six weeks. Two weeks ago, however, Phoenix filed a disqualification motion after Amberg & Lewis obtained one of Phoenix's attorney-client privileged documents—a letter from Phoenix's former president to one of its attorneys. Yesterday, I interviewed Carole Ravel, an Amberg & Lewis partner. During the interview, I learned some background facts; I also obtained a copy of the letter and Phoenix's brief in support of its disqualification motion.

Please prepare a memorandum evaluating the merits of Phoenix's argument for Amberg & Lewis's disqualification, bringing to bear the applicable legal authorities and the relevant facts as described to me by Ms. Ravel. Do not draft a separate statement of facts, but instead use the facts as appropriate in conducting your evaluation.

TRANSCRIPT OF CLIENT INTERVIEW

February 23, 2009

Buckner: Good to see you, Carole.

Ravel: Good to see you too, Ann. Thanks for seeing me on such short notice.

Buckner: My pleasure. What's the problem?

Ravel: The problem is a motion for disqualification. Here's the supporting brief.

Buckner: Thanks. Let me take a quick look. I'm unacquainted with the science, but the law is familiar. How can I help?

Ravel: To be candid, we've made a few mistakes, and I thought it would be prudent to consult with someone like you with substantial experience in representing lawyers in professional liability and ethics matters.

Buckner: Tell me what happened.

Ravel: Sure. Six years ago, Phoenix Corporation sued Biogenesis for breach of contract in state court, seeking about $80 million in damages. Phoenix is a medical research company; the Collins Law Firm represents it. Our client Biogenesis is one of the largest biotechnology companies in the world. Phoenix claims that Biogenesis breached a contract they entered into in 1978. There's a lot about this case that's enormously complicated and technical—all that science that you said you're unacquainted with—but the dispute is fairly simple. Under the agreement, Phoenix granted a license to Biogenesis to use a process that Phoenix invented for genetically engineering human proteins. In exchange, Biogenesis was obliged to pay Phoenix royalties on sales of certain categories of pharmaceuticals that were made using the licensed engineering process. Here is the dispute: While Biogenesis has taken the position that its royalty obligation is limited to the categories of pharmaceuticals specified, Phoenix claims that it extends to other categories of pharmaceuticals as well. If the jury agrees with Phoenix, Biogenesis owes about $80 million beyond what it has already paid in royalties.

Ravel: Right. The factual background and procedural history set out in the brief are accurate—but of course we disagree with Phoenix's argument about Biogenesis's royalty obligation.

Buckner: Fine. But what about this Phoenix letter that's allegedly protected by the attorney-client privilege?

Ravel: Here it is, a letter to Peter Horvitz, a Collins partner, from Gordon Schetina, who was then Phoenix's president.

Buckner: Thanks. It certainly looks privileged.

Ravel: It is. I can't deny it. But it's important. Let me go back to the 1978 agreement. Discovery in Phoenix's breach-of-contract action has established to our satisfaction that, by their conduct from 1978 to 1998, Biogenesis and Phoenix revealed that they understood that Biogenesis's royalty obligation was limited to the categories of pharmaceuticals specified in the agreement. During that period, Biogenesis made a lot of money and paid Phoenix a great deal in royalties. It was only in 1998 that Phoenix began to claim that Biogenesis's royalty obligation extended to other categories of pharmaceuticals—when it saw how much more in royalties it could obtain and became greedy to get them.

Buckner: And the Schetina letter...

Ravel: And the Schetina letter amounts to an admission by Phoenix that Biogenesis was correct in its understanding of its limited royalty obligation.

Buckner: So how did you get it?

Ravel: Phoenix's lawyers assume that the Schetina letter was disclosed to us inadvertently during discovery, but they're wrong. The letter arrived on February 2, 2009, by itself, in an envelope with the Collins Law Firm's return address. My assistant opened the envelope and discovered the letter all by itself, with a note reading "From a 'friend' at the Collins Law Firm."

Buckner: Do you know who the "friend" was?

Ravel: No. But it's not hard to guess. Collins is in the process of laying off staff in an effort to increase profits. The letter was obviously sent by a disgruntled employee.

Buckner: That makes sense. But what happened next?

Ravel: When the letter arrived, my team and I were in full trial-preparation mode. Of course, I recognized that the letter appeared privileged on its face; it's a classic confidential communication from a client to an attorney. In our eyes, the letter was a smoking gun. It made our case and we wanted to use it.

Buckner: So what happened?

Ravel: We were pretty sure that we were within the ethical rules. But that same day, two of the associates on my team went out for lunch. As they were discussing the impact of the Schetina letter in what turned out to be too much detail, a man at a neighboring table asked whether they knew who he was. They said no, and the man said he was Peter Horvitz and stormed out. Horvitz called me within minutes, and he was furious. He demanded return of the letter and I refused. A few days later, he filed the disqualification motion.

Buckner: I see. And precisely what is it you'd like us to do for you?

Ravel: Ann, I'd like you to evaluate the merits of Phoenix's argument that we should be disqualified. Trial is only a month away, and Biogenesis would have to incur tremendous costs if it were forced to substitute new attorneys if we were disqualified. And let's be candid, we've been charged with a violation of an ethical obligation and might face some exposure as a consequence.

Buckner: I understand, Carole. Let me do some research, and I'll get back to you.

Ravel: Thanks so much.

PHOENIX CORPORATION
1500 Rosa Road
Lakewood City, Franklin 33905

January 2, 1998

CONFIDENTIAL

Peter Horvitz, Esq.
Collins Law Firm
9700 Laurel Boulevard
Lakewood City, Franklin 33905

Dear Peter:

I am writing with some questions I'd like you to consider before our meeting next Tuesday so that I can get your legal advice on a matter I think is important. I have always understood our agreement with Biogenesis to require it to pay royalties on specified categories of pharmaceuticals. I learned recently how much money Biogenesis is making from other categories of pharmaceuticals. Why can't we get a share of that? Can't we interpret the agreement to require Biogenesis to pay royalties on other categories, not only the specified ones? Let me know your thoughts when we meet.

Very truly yours,

Gordon Schetina

Gordon Schetina
President

IN THE DISTRICT COURT OF THE STATE OF FRANKLIN
FOR THE COUNTY OF LANCASTER

PHOENIX CORPORATION,)
          Plaintiff,)
    v.)
BIOGENESIS, INC.,)
          Defendant.)

No. Civ. 041033

PLAINTIFF'S BRIEF IN SUPPORT OF MOTION TO DISQUALIFY COUNSEL FOR DEFENDANT

I. Introduction

The rule governing this motion is plain: A trial court may—and, indeed, must—disqualify an attorney who has violated an ethical obligation by his or her handling of an opposing party's attorney-client privileged material and has thereby threatened that party with incurable prejudice. Just as plain is the result that the rule compels here: Defendant's attorneys obtained one of plaintiff's attorney-client privileged documents evidently by inadvertent disclosure. In violation of their ethical obligation, they chose to examine the document, failed to notify plaintiff's attorneys, and then refused to return the document at the latter's demand. By acting as they did, they have threatened plaintiff with incurable prejudice. Since this Court cannot otherwise prevent this prejudice, it must disqualify them to guarantee plaintiff a fair trial.

II. Factual Background and Procedural History

In 1977, Phoenix Corporation, a medical research company, invented a process for genetically engineering human proteins—a process essential to the development of entirely new categories of pharmaceuticals capable of managing or curing the most serious conditions and diseases afflicting human beings, including diabetes and cancer.

In 1978, Phoenix entered into an agreement with Biogenesis, Inc., one of the pioneers in the field of biotechnology: Phoenix licensed its invention to Biogenesis, and Biogenesis obligated itself to pay Phoenix royalties on its sales of various categories of pharmaceuticals.

Between 1979 and 1997, Biogenesis produced dozens of pharmaceuticals and generated billions of dollars in revenue as a result of their sale. To be sure, Biogenesis paid Phoenix substantial royalties—but, as it turns out, far less than it was obligated to.

In 1998, Phoenix learned that Biogenesis had not been paying royalties on its sales of all the categories of pharmaceuticals in question, but only categories specified in the 1978 agreement. For the first time, Biogenesis stated its position that the agreement so limited its obligation. Phoenix rejected any such limitation.

Between 1999 and 2002, Phoenix attempted to resolve its dispute with Biogenesis. Each and every one of its efforts, however, proved unsuccessful.

In 2003, Phoenix brought this action against Biogenesis for breach of the 1978 agreement, seeking $80 million in damages for royalties Biogenesis owed but failed to pay. Between 2003 and 2009, Phoenix and Biogenesis have been engaged in extensive discovery and motion practice and in several interlocutory appeals as they have prepared for a jury trial, set to begin on March 30, 2009, and expected to last six weeks.

On February 2, 2009, Phoenix learned, fortuitously, that Biogenesis's attorneys, Amberg & Lewis LLP, had obtained a document evidently through inadvertent disclosure by Phoenix's attorneys, the Collins Law Firm, in the course of discovery.

On its face, the document showed itself to be protected by the attorney-client privilege, reflecting a confidential communication from Phoenix, by its then president Gordon Schetina, to one of its attorneys, Peter Horvitz, seeking legal advice, and clearly the document was not intended for the Amberg firm. Nevertheless, the Amberg firm failed to notify Collins about its receipt of the Schetina letter. As soon as it learned what had transpired, Collins instructed the Amberg firm to return the letter, but the Amberg firm refused.

III. Argument

A. This Court Should Disqualify Amberg & Lewis from Representing Biogenesis Because It Has Violated an Ethical Obligation Threatening Phoenix with Incurable Prejudice in Its Handling of Phoenix's Attorney-Client Privileged Document.

The law applicable to Phoenix's motion to disqualify Amberg & Lewis from representing Biogenesis in this action is clear.

A trial court may, in the exercise of its inherent power, disqualify an attorney in the interests of justice. *Indigo v. Luna Motors Corp.* (Fr. Ct. App. 1998). The court may—and, indeed, must—disqualify an attorney who has violated an ethical obligation by his or her handling of an opposing party's attorney-client privileged material and has thereby threatened that party with incurable prejudice. Id. Although the party represented by the disqualified attorney may be said to enjoy an "important right" to representation by an attorney of its own choosing, any such "right" must yield to ethical considerations that affect the fundamental principles of our judicial process." Id. As the court said, "The paramount concern, however, must be to preserve public trust in the scrupulous administration of justice and the integrity of the bar." Id.

As will be demonstrated, the law compels the disqualification of Amberg & Lewis.

1. Phoenix's Document Is Protected by the Attorney-Client Privilege.

To begin with, the Schetina letter is protected by the attorney-client privilege. Under Franklin Evidence Code § 954, the "client...has a privilege to refuse to disclose, and to prevent another from disclosing, a confidential communication between client and attorney...." On its face, the Schetina letter reflects a confidential communication from Phoenix's then president, Schetina, to one of its attorneys, Horvitz, seeking legal advice.

2. Amberg & Lewis Has Violated an Ethical Obligation.

Next, Amberg & Lewis has violated an ethical obligation by handling the Schetina letter as it did. In the face of the inadvertent disclosure of attorney-client privileged material, such as evidently occurred in this case, the ethical obligation is plain under Franklin Rule of Professional Conduct 4.4: "An attorney who receives a document relating to the representation of the attorney's client and knows or reasonably should know that the document was inadvertently sent shall promptly notify the sender."

Because on its face the Schetina letter reflects a confidential communication from Phoenix's then president, Schetina, to its attorney, Horvitz, seeking legal advice, and is therefore protected by the attorney-client privilege, Amberg & Lewis should surely have known that the letter was not intended for it. The Amberg firm was at the very least obligated to notify Collins that it had received the letter. It should also have refrained from examining the letter, and should have abided by our instructions. On each point, the Amberg firm acted to the contrary, choosing to examine the letter, failing to notify Collins, and then refusing to return it at Collins's demand.

Even if it should turn out that Amberg & Lewis obtained the Schetina letter as a result of unauthorized disclosure as opposed to inadvertent disclosure, the outcome would be the same. In *Mead v. Conley Machinery Co.* (Fr. Ct. App. 1999) the Court of Appeal imposed an ethical obligation similar to that of Rule 4.4 to govern cases of unauthorized disclosure. It follows that the misconduct of the Amberg firm, as described above, would amount to an ethical violation if the letter's disclosure were unauthorized and not inadvertent.

3. Amberg & Lewis Has Threatened Phoenix with Incurable Prejudice.

Finally, by its unethical actions, Amberg & Lewis has threatened Phoenix with incurable prejudice. The Schetina letter could well prejudice the jury in the midst of a long and complex trial, especially if it were cleverly exploited by Biogenesis. Whether or not any *direct* harm could be prevented by the exclusion of the letter from evidence—which Phoenix intends to seek in the coming days—the *indirect* harm that might arise from its use in trial preparation cannot be dealt with so simply: The bell has been rung, and can hardly be unrung, except by disqualification of Amberg & Lewis—an action that is necessary in order to guarantee Phoenix a fair trial.

Even if it should turn out that Amberg & Lewis obtained the Schetina letter by *unauthorized* disclosure as opposed to *inadvertent* disclosure, the result would not change. It is true that in *Mead v. Conley Machinery Co.*, the Court of Appeal suggested in a footnote that, in cases of unauthorized disclosure, the "threat of 'incurable prejudice'...is neither a necessary nor a sufficient condition for disqualification." But that suggestion is mere dictum, inasmuch as Mead did not involve the threat of *any* prejudice, incurable or otherwise.

IV. Conclusion

For the reasons stated above, this Court should grant Phoenix's motion and disqualify Amberg & Lewis from representing Biogenesis in this action.

Respectfully submitted,

Kimberly Block

Kimberly Block
COLLINS LAW FIRM LLP
Attorneys for Plaintiff Phoenix Corporation

Date: February 9, 2009

LIBRARY

Rule 4.4 of the Franklin Rules of Professional Conduct

Rule 4.4. Inadvertent disclosure of attorney-client document

An attorney who receives a document relating to the representation of the attorney's client and knows or reasonably should know that the document was inadvertently sent shall promptly notify the sender.

HISTORY

Adopted by the Franklin Supreme Court, effective July 1, 2002.

COMMENT

[1] Rule 4.4, which was adopted by the Franklin Supreme Court in 2002 in response to *Indigo v. Luna Motors Corp.* (Fr. Ct. App. 1998), recognizes that attorneys sometimes receive documents that were mistakenly sent or produced by opposing parties or their attorneys. If an attorney knows or reasonably should know that such a document was sent inadvertently, then this rule requires the attorney, whether or not the document is protected by the attorney-client privilege, to promptly notify the sender in order to permit that person to take protective measures.

[2] Rule 4.4 provides that if an attorney receives a document the attorney should know was sent inadvertently, he or she must promptly notify the sender, but need do no more. *Indigo v. Luna Motors Corp.*, which predated this rule, concluded that the receiving attorney not only had to notify the sender (as this rule would later require), albeit only as to a document protected by the attorney-client privilege, but also had to resist the temptation to examine the document, and had to await the sender's instructions about what to do. In so concluding, *Indigo v. Luna Motors Corp.* conflicted with this rule and, ultimately, with the intent of the Franklin Supreme Court in adopting it.

[3] Rule 4.4 does not address an attorney's receipt of a document sent without authorization, as was the case in *Mead v. Conley Machinery Co.* (Fr. Ct. App. 1999). Neither does any other rule. *Mead v. Conley Machinery Co.*, which also predated this rule, concluded that the receiving attorney should review the document—there, an attorney-client privileged document—only to the extent necessary to determine how to proceed, notify the opposing attorney, and either abide by the opposing attorney's instructions or refrain from using the document until a court disposed of the matter. The Franklin Supreme Court, however, has declined to adopt a rule imposing any ethical obligation in cases of unauthorized disclosure.

Indigo v. Luna Motors Corp.

Franklin Court of Appeal (1998)

The issue in this permissible interlocutory appeal is whether the trial court abused its discretion by disqualifying plaintiff's attorney for improper use of attorney-client privileged documents disclosed to her inadvertently. We hold that it did not. Accordingly, we affirm.

I

Plaintiff Ferdinand Indigo sued Luna Motors Corporation for damages after he sustained serious injuries when his Luna sport utility vehicle rolled over as he was driving.

In the course of routine document production, Luna's attorney's paralegal inadvertently gave Joyce Corrigan, Indigo's attorney, a document drafted by Luna's attorney and memorializing a conference between the attorney and a high-ranking Luna executive, Raymond Fogel, stamped "attorney-client privileged," in which they discussed the strengths and weaknesses of Luna's technical evidence. As soon as Corrigan received the document, which is referred to as the "technical evidence document," she examined it closely; as a result, she knew that it had been given to her inadvertently. Notwithstanding her knowledge, she failed to notify Luna's attorney. She subsequently used the document for impeachment purposes during Fogel's deposition, eliciting damaging admissions. Luna's attorney objected to Corrigan's use of the document, accused her of invading the attorney-client privilege, and demanded the document's return, but Corrigan refused.

In response, Luna filed a motion to disqualify Corrigan. After a hearing, the trial court granted the motion. The court determined that the technical evidence document was protected by the attorney-client privilege, that Corrigan violated her ethical obligation by handling it as she did, and that disqualification was the appropriate remedy. Indigo appealed.

II

It has long been settled in Franklin that a trial court may, in the exercise of its inherent power, disqualify an attorney in the interests of justice. *See, e.g., In re Klein* (Fr. Ct. App. 1947). Ultimately, disqualification involves a conflict between a client's right to an attorney of his or her choice and the need to maintain ethical standards of professional responsibility. The paramount concern, however, must be to preserve public trust in the scrupulous administration of justice and the integrity of the bar. The important right to an attorney of one's choice must yield to ethical considerations that affect the fundamental principles of our judicial process.

Appellate courts review a trial court's ruling on disqualification for abuse of discretion. A court abuses its discretion when it acts arbitrarily or without reason. As will appear, we discern no arbitrary or unreasonable action here.

A

Indigo's first claim is that the trial court erred in determining that Corrigan violated an ethical obligation by handling the technical evidence document as she did.

From the Franklin Rules of Professional Conduct and related case law, we derive the following, albeit implicit, standard: An attorney who receives materials that on their face appear to be subject to the attorney-client privilege, under circumstances in which it is clear they were not intended for the receiving attorney, should refrain from examining the materials, notify the sending attorney, and await the instructions of the attorney who sent them.

Under this standard, Corrigan plainly violated an ethical obligation. She received the technical evidence document; the document appeared on its face to be subject to the attorney-client privilege, as it was stamped "attorney-client privileged"; the circumstances were clear that the document was not intended for her; nevertheless, she examined the document, failed to notify Luna's attorney, and refused to return it at the latter's demand.

B

Indigo's second claim is that the trial court erred in determining that disqualification of Corrigan was the appropriate remedy in light of her violation of her ethical obligation.

The trial court predicated Corrigan's disqualification on the threat of incurable prejudice to Luna. Such a threat has long been recognized as a sufficient basis for disqualification. *See, e.g., In re Klein.* We find it more than sufficient here. Corrigan used the technical evidence document during the deposition of Luna executive Fogel, eliciting damaging admissions. Even if Corrigan were prohibited from using the document at trial, she could not effectively be prevented from capitalizing on its contents in preparing for trial and perhaps obtaining evidence of similar force and effect.

III

The trial court concluded that disqualification was necessary to ensure a fair trial. It did not abuse its discretion in doing so.

Affirmed.

Mead v. Conley Machinery Co.
Franklin Court of Appeal (1999)

The issue in this permissible interlocutory appeal is whether the trial court abused its discretion by disqualifying plaintiff's attorney on the ground that the attorney improperly used attorney-client privileged documents disclosed to him without authorization. *Cf. Indigo v. Luna Motors Corp.* (Fr. Ct. App. 1998) (inadvertent disclosure). We hold that it did and reverse.

I

Dolores Mead, a former financial consultant for Conley Machinery Company, sued Conley for breach of contract. Without authorization, she obtained attorney-client privileged documents belonging to Conley and gave them to her attorney, William Masterson, who used them in deposing Conley's president over Conley's objection.

Conley immediately moved to disqualify Masterson. After an evidentiary hearing, the trial court granted the motion. Mead appealed.

II

In determining whether the trial court abused its discretion by disqualifying Masterson, we ask whether it acted arbitrarily or without reason. *Indigo.*

III

At the threshold, Mead argues that the trial court had no authority to disqualify Masterson because he did not violate any specific rule among the Franklin Rules of Professional Conduct. It is true that Masterson did not violate any specific rule—but it is *not* true that the court was without authority to disqualify him. With or without a violation of a specific rule, a court may, in the exercise of its inherent power, disqualify an attorney in the interests of justice, including where necessary to guarantee a fair trial. *Indigo.*

IV

Without doubt, there are situations in which an attorney who has been privy to his or her adversary's privileged documents without authorization must be disqualified, even though the attorney was not involved in obtaining the documents. By protecting attorney-client communications, the attorney-client privilege encourages parties to fully develop cases for trial, increasing the chances of an informed and correct resolution.

To safeguard the attorney-client privilege and the litigation process itself, we believe that the following standard must govern: An attorney who receives, on an unauthorized basis, materials of an adverse party that he or she knows to be attorney-client privileged should, upon recognizing the privileged nature of the materials, either refrain from reviewing such materials or review them only to the extent required to determine how to proceed; he or she should notify the adversary's attorney that he or she has such materials and should either follow instructions from the adversary's attorney with respect to the disposition of the materials or refrain from using the materials until a definitive resolution of the proper disposition of the materials is obtained from a court.

Violation of this standard, however, amounts to only one of the facts and circumstances that a trial court must consider in deciding whether to order disqualification. The court must also consider all of the other relevant facts and circumstances to determine whether the interests of justice require disqualification. Specifically, in the exercise of its discretion, a trial court should consider these factors: (1) the attorney's actual or constructive knowledge of the material's attorney-client privileged status; (2) the promptness with which the attorney notified the opposing side

THE MPT
MULTISTATE PERFORMANCE TEST

Phoenix Corporation v. Biogenesis, Inc.

POINT SHEET

Copyright ©2008 by the National Conference of Bar Examiners.
All rights reserved

The MPT point sheet, grading summary, and grading guidelines describe the factual and legal points encompassed within the lawyering task to be completed. They outline all the possible issues and points that might be addressed by an applicant. They are provided to the user jurisdictions for the sole purpose of assisting graders in grading the examination by identifying the issues and suggesting the resolution of the problem contemplated by the drafters. These are not official grading guides. Applicants can receive a range of passing grades, including excellent grades, without covering all the points discussed in these guides. The model answer is included as an illustration of a thorough and detailed response to the task, one that addresses all the legal and factual issues the drafters intended to raise in the problem. It is intended to serve only as an example. Applicants need not present their responses in the same way to receive good grades. User jurisdictions are free to modify these grading materials, including the suggested weights assigned to particular points. Grading the MPT is the exclusive responsibility of the jurisdiction using the MPT as part of its admissions process.

---

that he or she had received such material; (3) the extent to which the attorney reviewed the material; (4) the significance of the material, i.e., the extent to which its disclosure may prejudice the party moving for disqualification, and the extent to which its return or other measure may prevent or cure that prejudice; (5) the extent to which the party moving for disqualification may be at fault for the unauthorized disclosure; and (6) the extent to which the party opposing disqualification would suffer prejudice from the disqualification of his or her attorney.[1]

Some of these factors weigh in favor of Masterson's disqualification. For example, Masterson should have known after the most cursory review that the documents in question were protected by the attorney-client privilege. Nevertheless, he did not notify Conley upon receiving them. Also, it appears that he thoroughly reviewed them, as he directly referenced specific portions in his response to Conley's disqualification motion. Finally, Conley was not at fault, since Mead copied them covertly.

Other factors, however, weigh against Masterson's disqualification. The information in the documents in question would not significantly prejudice Conley, reflecting little more than a paraphrase of a handful of Mead's allegations. The court may exclude the documents from evidence and thereby prevent any prejudice to Conley—all without disqualifying Masterson. Exclusion would prevent ringing for the jury any bell that could not be unrung. To be sure, it would not erase the documents from Masterson's mind, but any harm arising from their presence in Masterson's memory would be minimal and, indeed, speculative. In contrast, Mead would suffer serious hardship if Masterson were disqualified at this time, after he has determined trial strategy, worked extensively on trial preparation, and readied the matter for trial. In these circumstances, disqualification may confer an enormous, and unmerited, strategic advantage upon Conley.

In conclusion, because the factors against Masterson's disqualification substantially outweigh those in its favor, the trial court abused its discretion in disqualifying him.

Reversed.

---

[1] In *Indigo v. Luna Motors Corp.*, we recently considered the issue of disqualification in the context of *inadvertent* disclosure of a document protected by the attorney-client privilege as opposed to *unauthorized* disclosure. The analysis set out in the text above renders explicit what was implicit in *Indigo*, and is generally applicable to disqualification for inadvertent disclosure as well as unauthorized disclosure. Although we found the threat of "incurable prejudice" decisive in *Indigo*, it is neither a necessary nor a sufficient condition for disqualification.

Phoenix Corporation v. Biogenesis, Inc.
Drafters' Point Sheet

About six years ago, Phoenix Corporation, a medical research company represented by the Collins Law Firm, brought a breach-of-contract action in state court seeking about $80 million in damages against Biogenesis, Inc., a biotechnology company represented by Amberg & Lewis LLP. A jury trial is set to begin in a month and is expected to last six weeks. Two weeks ago, however, Phoenix filed a motion to disqualify Amberg & Lewis as Biogenesis's attorneys. Phoenix claims that Amberg & Lewis violated an ethical obligation threatening incurable prejudice through its handling of one of Phoenix's attorney-client privileged documents, which Phoenix assumes was disclosed inadvertently.

Amberg & Lewis has retained applicants' law firm to consult on the motion for disqualification. Applicants' task is to prepare an objective memorandum evaluating the merits of Phoenix's argument to disqualify.

The File contains the following materials: a memorandum from the supervising attorney describing the assignment (task memo), the transcript of the client interview, the document that is the subject of the disqualification motion, and Phoenix's brief in support of its motion for disqualification. The Library contains Rule 4.4 of the Franklin Rules of Professional Conduct and two cases bearing on the subject.

The following discussion covers all of the points the drafters intended to raise in the problem. Applicants need not cover them all to receive passing or even excellent grades. Grading is left entirely to the discretion of the user jurisdictions.

I. Overview

Applicants are given a general call: "Please prepare a memorandum evaluating the merits of Phoenix's argument for Amberg & Lewis's disqualification...." To complete the assignment, applicants should identify and discuss two key issues: (1) whether Amberg & Lewis has violated the rules of professional conduct, and (2) whether disqualification is indeed the appropriate remedy on the facts as given.

There is no specific format for the assigned task. Applicants' work product should resemble a legal memorandum such as one an associate would draft for a supervising partner. Applicants may choose to follow the lead of Phoenix's motion to disqualify and organize their answer in response to each of the issues raised in Phoenix's supporting brief. However, it should be an objective memorandum; applicants who draft a memorandum that is persuasive in tone have not followed instructions (jurisdictions may want to consider whether points should be deducted from such papers). The task memorandum instructs applicants not to incorporate the relevant facts but to be sure to incorporate the relevant facts into their discussions.

Applicants should conclude that even if Amberg & Lewis has violated an ethical obligation (and it is not at all clear that it has), disqualification is not the appropriate remedy in this case.

II. Detailed Analysis

These are the key points that applicants should discuss, taking care to incorporate the relevant facts and explain and/or distinguish the applicable case law, in an objective memorandum evaluating the merits of Phoenix's argument to disqualify Amberg & Lewis:

As a preliminary matter, applicants should set forth the basis for why the Schetina letter may trigger disqualification under the Franklin Rules of Professional Conduct.

- Franklin Evidence Code § 954 provides that a client has a privilege to refuse to disclose, and to prevent another from disclosing, a confidential communication between client and attorney.
- It appears undisputed that the Schetina letter is protected by the attorney-client privilege under § 954.
- It is a communication, labeled "CONFIDENTIAL," from Phoenix's then president, Schetina, to one of its attorneys, Horvitz.
- Amberg & Lewis concedes that the letter is privileged.
- Even if the Schetina letter were not privileged, it relates "to the representation of the attorney's client," which is the standard used in Rule 4.4. In other words, a document does not have to be attorney-client privileged for its handling by opposing counsel to constitute a violation of the Rule.
- In *Indigo v. Luna Motors Corp.* (Fr. Ct. App. 1998), the court affirmed the granting of a motion for disqualification in a case where an attorney inadvertently received privileged materials and did not return them forthwith to opposing counsel.

A. Whether Amberg & Lewis violated its ethical obligation by its handling of the Schetina letter

Applicants should incorporate into their discussion of this issue the following facts surrounding Amberg & Lewis's receipt of the Schetina letter:

- On February 2, 2009, Amberg & Lewis obtained the Schetina letter as a result of the letter's unauthorized disclosure by some unidentified person at the Collins Law Firm, which represents Phoenix. (The letter arrived in an envelope bearing Collins's return address and was accompanied by a note reading "From a 'friend' at the Collins Law Firm.") The letter is dated January 2, 1998, and is labeled "CONFIDENTIAL."[2]
- Amberg & Lewis did not notify Collins of its receipt of the letter.
- Indeed, Amberg & Lewis would like to use the letter in its case against Phoenix—Schetina's statement is essentially an admission that Biogenesis's interpretation of the royalty agreement is the correct one.
- Also on February 2, 2009, Phoenix learned, by chance, that Amberg & Lewis had obtained the Schetina letter, but assumed, incorrectly, that it had done so as a result of inadvertent disclosure by Collins in the course of discovery. Collins instructed Amberg & Lewis to return the letter, but Amberg & Lewis refused.
- In response, Phoenix filed the present motion to disqualify Amberg & Lewis.

Phoenix's argument regarding Amberg & Lewis's handling of the Schetina letter

In its brief, Phoenix's first argument assumes that the Schetina letter's disclosure was inadvertent and cites Rule 4.4 in support of its position that, at a minimum, Amberg & Lewis was required to "promptly notify the sender" (i.e., the Collins Law Firm) after it received the Schetina letter.

---

[2] The letter states in its entirety: "I am writing with some questions I'd like you to consider before our meeting next Tuesday so that I can get your legal advice on a matter I think is important. I have always understood our agreement with Biogenesis to require it to pay royalties on specified categories of pharmaceuticals. I learned recently how much money Biogenesis is making from other categories of pharmaceuticals. Why can't we get a share of that? Can't we interpret the agreement to require Biogenesis to pay royalties on other categories, not only the specified ones? Let me know your thoughts when we meet."

- If the letter's disclosure was unauthorized, Phoenix contends that *Mead v. Comley Machinery Co.* (Fr. Ct. App. 1999) "imposed an ethical obligation similar to that of Rule 4.4 to govern cases of unauthorized disclosure."
- Contrary to both Rule 4.4 and *Indigo*, Amberg & Lewis chose to examine the Schetina letter, failed to notify Collins of its receipt, and then refused to return it at Collins's demand.
- So, either way, whether the disclosure was inadvertent or unauthorized, Phoenix argues that Amberg & Lewis has committed an ethical violation.

Application of Rule 4.4 and relevant case law

Applicants should realize that Phoenix's argument overstates its position and that it is not so clear that Amberg & Lewis has violated the Franklin Rules of Professional Conduct.

- Rule 4.4 provides in its entirety that "[a]n attorney who receives a document relating to the representation of the attorney's client and knows or reasonably should know that the document was inadvertently sent shall promptly notify the sender."
- Thus, under Rule 4.4, an attorney receiving a document disclosed inadvertently need do no more than notify the sender.
- On its face, the text of the rule pertains only to situations involving *inadvertent* disclosure. The comments to Rule 4.4 are very clear on this point. In short, Rule 4.4 does not address the ethical implications for cases of *unauthorized* disclosure of privileged communications.
- Accordingly, Amberg & Lewis's conduct is not forbidden by the plain language of Rule 4.4.

1. *Indigo v. Luna Motors Corp.* is not dispositive.

- In *Indigo*, the plaintiff's attorney received an attorney-client privileged document during document production as a result of inadvertent disclosure. The attorney closely examined the document, which discussed the opposing side's technical evidence, and then used the document at deposition to obtain damaging admissions from the opposing party. Plaintiff's attorney refused opposing counsel's demands to return the document. The court held that this conduct by plaintiff's attorney constituted a violation of an ethical obligation and was grounds for disqualification.
- The *Indigo* court then articulated the following standard for how attorneys should proceed in such situations:
  - An attorney who receives materials that on their face appear to be subject to the attorney-client privilege, under circumstances in which it is clear they were not intended for the receiving attorney, should refrain from examining the materials, notify the sending attorney, and await the instructions of the attorney who sent them.
- The facts of the present case distinguish it from *Indigo*. Here, an unknown Collins employee intentionally sent the Schetina letter to Amberg & Lewis. (Phoenix could not know this, because it is unaware of how Amberg & Lewis came into possession of the Schetina letter.)
- Presumably, someone at Amberg & Lewis kept the envelope and note that came with the Schetina letter ("From a 'friend' at the Collins Law Firm") and so it can easily prove that the disclosure was unauthorized, as opposed to inadvertent.
- More to the point, in adopting Rule 4.4, the Franklin Supreme Court expressly pulled back from the holding in *Indigo*. *See* Rule 4.4, Comment 2. The Comment explains that when there is an inadvertent disclosure, the attorney "must promptly notify the sender, but need do no more…. *Indigo v. Luna Motors Corp.* conflicted with this rule and, ultimately, with the intent of the Franklin Supreme Court in adopting it."
- Thus, to the extent that it concluded otherwise, *Indigo* conflicts with Rule 4.4 and, ultimately, with the intent of the Franklin Supreme Court in adopting it. Rule 4.4 does not apply to unauthorized disclosure. Notwithstanding *Mead* (discussed below), the Franklin Supreme Court has declined to adopt a rule imposing any ethical obligation in such cases.

2. Application of *Mead*

- In *Mead*, the Franklin Court of Appeal held that an attorney who received privileged documents belonging to an adverse party through an unauthorized disclosure should do the following: "upon recognizing the privileged nature of the materials, either refrain from reviewing such materials or review them only to the extent required to determine how to proceed; he or she should notify the adversary's attorney that he or she has such materials and should either follow instructions from the adversary's attorney with respect to the disposition of the materials, or refrain from using the materials until a definitive resolution of the proper disposition of the materials is obtained from a court."
- But the court goes on to state that violation of this standard, standing alone, does not warrant disqualification.
- So, while *Mead* appears to require Amberg & Lewis to notify the Collins firm that it received the Schetina letter, following the offended law firm's instructions on what to do with the letter is optional—instead, Amberg & Lewis can wait for the court to weigh in on the issue.
- But, under *Mead*, Amberg & Lewis must still refrain from using the materials until such court resolution is obtained.
- In addition, astute applicants will point out that, while Amberg & Lewis wanted to use the Schetina letter in its case against Phoenix, Phoenix found out that Amberg & Lewis had the Schetina letter the *same day* that Amberg & Lewis received it (when Peter Horvitz, Phoenix's attorney, overheard the associates talking about the letter at lunch). Arguably, Amberg & Lewis could have notified the Collins firm that it had received the letter, if not for the fact that Horvitz found out about it before Amberg & Lewis had a chance to tell him.
- Again, applicants should note that *Mead* was decided in 1999, before the Franklin Supreme Court enacted Rule 4.4 in 2002. It could be implied that, had the court intended that there be an ethical rule regarding the use of privileged documents that were disclosed without authorization, it could have created one.
- In fact, Comment 3 to Rule 4.4 mentions the *Mead* case and then notes that "[t]he Franklin Supreme Court…has declined to adopt a rule imposing any ethical obligation in cases of unauthorized disclosure."
- As a consequence, *Mead* may lack continuing vitality on the ground that it is inconsistent with the Franklin Supreme Court's presumed intent not to impose any ethical obligation.
- That being said, it is also arguable that Amberg & Lewis did indeed violate an ethical obligation. Although the Franklin Supreme Court declined to adopt a rule imposing any ethical obligation in cases of unauthorized disclosure, it may have done so because it was satisfied with *Mead*, which had already imposed such an ethical obligation.

3. Even if there was no ethical violation, a violation of a rule is not necessary for disqualification.

- Language in both *Indigo* and *Mead* suggests that a motion for disqualification may be granted by a court even if there has been no rule violation. "It has long been settled in Franklin that a trial court may, in the exercise of its inherent power, disqualify an attorney in the interests of justice." *Indigo*, citing *In re Klein* (Fr. Ct. App. 1947). *See also Mead* ("[w]ith or without a violation of a specific rule, a court may…disqualify an attorney…where necessary to guarantee a fair trial") citing *Indigo*.

4. Conclusion of Issue A

- Phoenix's argument that Amberg & Lewis violated an ethical obligation by its handling of the Schetina letter fails insofar as it incorrectly assumes that Amberg & Lewis obtained the letter as a result of inadvertent, rather than unauthorized, disclosure.

It appears that Amberg & Lewis would *not* have violated the ethical obligation imposed by *Indigo*. *Indigo* conflicts with Rule 4.4 and, ultimately, with the intent of the Franklin Supreme Court in adopting it, and therefore lacks continuing vitality.

By contrast, Phoenix's argument that Amberg & Lewis violated an ethical obligation may succeed insofar as it assumes in the alternative that Amberg & Lewis obtained the letter as a result of unauthorized disclosure, depending, as indicated above, on whether *Mead* is still good law in light of the comments to Rule 4.4.

Accordingly, there is a strong argument to be made that Amberg & Lewis has not violated the letter of the Professional Rules. Nevertheless, because the import of the *Mead* decision is uncertain, that does not end the inquiry and the court will still, most likely, go on to consider whether disqualification is required in the interests of justice.

B. Whether disqualification of Amberg & Lewis is the appropriate remedy

A trial court may, in the exercise of its inherent power, disqualify an attorney in the interests of justice. It must exercise that power, however, in light of the important right enjoyed by a party to representation by an attorney of its own choosing. Such a right must nevertheless yield to ethical considerations that affect the fundamental principles of the judicial process. *Indigo*.

Phoenix contends that Amberg & Lewis has threatened it with incurable prejudice and therefore disqualification must follow. In Phoenix's view, whether or not any *direct* harm could be prevented by exclusion of the Schetina letter from evidence, the *indirect* harm that might arise from its use in trial preparation cannot be dealt with so simply, inasmuch as "[t]he bell has been rung, and can hardly be unrung." (Pltf's br.)

- It is true that in *Mead* the court suggested in a footnote that, in cases of unauthorized disclosure, the "threat of 'incurable prejudice' . . . is neither a necessary nor a sufficient condition for disqualification." But that suggestion is mere dictum, inasmuch as *Mead* did not involve the threat of *any* prejudice, incurable or otherwise (in *Mead*, the court described the document at issue as "little more than a paraphrase of a handful of [the plaintiff's] allegations").

- Applicants should conclude that disqualification is not mandated in this case.

- Even if Amberg & Lewis violated an ethical obligation, it should not be disqualified.

- Under *Mead*, disqualification in all cases of disclosure, whether inadvertent or unauthorized, depends on a balancing of six factors: (1) the receiving attorney's actual or constructive knowledge of the material's attorney-client privileged status; (2) the promptness with which the receiving attorney notified the opposing side of receipt; (3) the extent to which the receiving attorney reviewed the material; (4) the material's significance, i.e., the extent to which its disclosure may prejudice the party moving for disqualification, and the extent to which its return or other measure may cure that prejudice; (5) the extent to which the party moving for disqualification may be at fault for the unauthorized disclosure; and (6) the extent to which the party opposing disqualification would suffer prejudice from disqualification.

- Contrary to any implication in *Indigo*, the threat of incurable prejudice is neither a necessary nor a sufficient condition for disqualification.

- The balance weighs *against* disqualification here.

- As in the *Mead* case, where the documents were covertly copied, Phoenix is not at fault (Factor 5)—the Schetina letter was passed on to Amberg & Lewis by a disgruntled Collins employee. This favors disqualification.

- Furthermore, Amberg & Lewis knew or should have known of the letter's attorney-client privileged status (Factor 1), did not notify Collins of its receipt (Factor 2), and reviewed it thoroughly—in part because of its brevity (Factor 3). Concededly, these factors favor disqualification.

- But that being said, the Schetina letter nonetheless proves to be of dubious significance (Factor 4). True, it amounts to an admission by Phoenix that Biogenesis was correct in its understanding of its royalty obligation under the 1978 agreement. But its exclusion from evidence would prevent any prejudice to Phoenix. (Contrary to the situations in *Indigo* and *Mead*, where the attorneys in each case made use of the disclosed materials at depositions, here Amberg & Lewis has not yet made any use of the letter.) Moreover, any harm arising from any conceivable non-evidentiary use of the letter would be at best speculative.

- By contrast, Biogenesis would suffer substantial prejudice from Amberg & Lewis's disqualification, inasmuch as it would have to incur appreciable costs if it were forced to attempt to substitute new attorneys for a trial set to begin in a month after six years of preparation. These factors (Factors 4 and 6) disfavor disqualification—and they appear to predominate.

- Biogenesis enjoys an "important right" to representation by Amberg & Lewis as its chosen attorneys. *Indigo*.

- And there appear to be no "ethical considerations" so affecting the "fundamental principles of our judicial process" as to require that "right" to "yield." *Id.*

- In sum, disqualification of Amberg & Lewis does not appear necessary to guarantee Phoenix a fair trial.

Contrary to Phoenix's argument, which relies on language that appears in *Indigo*,[3] disqualification of Amberg & Lewis does not depend solely on the threat of incurable prejudice. Although Phoenix attempts to dismiss the court's analysis in *Mead* as mere dictum, the *Mead* court intended its analysis at least to clarify, and at most to supersede, its earlier language in *Indigo* in order to make plain that disqualification depends on a balancing of factors not reducible to the threat of incurable prejudice alone. In any event, there is no threat of incurable prejudice here. As stated, the exclusion of the Schetina letter from evidence would avoid any prejudice, and any harm arising from its presence in the memory of Amberg & Lewis attorneys would be at best speculative.

---

[3] In *Indigo*, the court relied on the opinion in *In re Klein*, which held that the threat of incurable prejudice "has long been recognized as a sufficient basis for disqualification." *Indigo*, citing *In re Klein*.

MPT Task 4G:
In re Emily Dunn

FILE

Reilly, Ingersol & Powell, PC
Attorneys-at-Law
300 Willis Road
Jackson City, Franklin 33399
e-mail: rip@aol.com
(555) 999-4567
(555) 999-4555 (Fax)

MEMORANDUM

July 29, 1999

To: Applicant
From: Robert Reilly
Re: Emily Dunn

Yesterday I met with Emily Dunn, who was recently widowed. She has asked me to prepare a new will for her.

The transcript of the interview should give you a good overall sense of what Mrs. Dunn is trying to accomplish. Looking back over it, however, I see some potential holes in my understanding of her precise intentions. In particular, I'm concerned about how she wants to deal with the disposition of potential insurance proceeds, her gifts of stock, the equalization of gifts to her grandchildren, and the distribution of the residuary estate. These ambiguities are not surprising. There are always some unresolved details that we must review with a client at a subsequent meeting. At such meetings, however, I find it useful to have a draft of the will to help clients refine their choices. I'd like you to do the following:

1. Draft the introductory and all dispositive clauses for Mrs. Dunn's proposed new will. Please set them forth in separately numbered paragraphs and in an order consistent with our firm's Will Drafting Guidelines. Don't concern yourself with the definitional and boilerplate clauses.

2. In drafting the dispositive clauses regarding the four areas I've said I'm concerned about, you will have to fill in the gaps left in the interview by making some assumptions about exactly what Mrs. Dunn wants. Therefore, in drafting a dispositive clause that requires an assumption about the insurance, the stock, the grandchildren, or the residuary estate, following that clause write a short explanatory paragraph that does two things:
   a. Tells me what assumptions you've made about the facts and Mrs. Dunn's intentions;
   b. Tells me why, based on those assumptions, you drafted the particular clause the way you did.

Reilly, Ingersol & Powell, PC
Attorneys-at-Law
300 Willis Road
Jackson City, Franklin 33399
e-mail: rip@aol.com
(555) 999-4567
(555) 999-4555 (Fax)

May 27, 1999

Mrs. Emily Dunn
23 Ipswich Lane
Jackson City, Franklin 33399

Dear Emily:

It was quite a shock to learn of Chuck's sudden heart attack given how fit he had been all of his life. He was a wonderful friend, and he will be sorely missed.

I am enclosing the completed documents finalizing your gift to the Franklin Museum of Art of the Claude Monet painting that you inherited from your grandfather.

When we last talked, you asked me to review your files and see if other things require your attention. In light of Chuck's death, it is appropriate that you review your 1965 will to see what changes you might like to make. A copy of that will is enclosed.

Please call me for an appointment to talk about possible revisions to your will. When we meet, we can talk about your family and other people to whom you might want to leave your property.

I look forward to seeing you soon.

Sincerely,

Bob

Robert Reilly

/vins
Enclosure

Reilly, Ingersol & Powell, PC

MEMORANDUM

September 8, 1995

To: All Attorneys
From: Robert Reilly
Re: Will Drafting Guidelines

Over the years, this firm has used a variety of formats in drafting wills. Effective immediately, all wills drafted for this firm should follow this format:

Introduction:
A. Set forth the introductory clause with the name and domicile of the testator.
B. Include an appropriate clause regarding the revocation of prior testamentary instruments.
C. Include a clause describing the testator's immediate family (parents, sibling, spouse, children, and grandchildren).

Part ONE: Dispositive Clauses (to be set forth in separate subdivisions or subparagraphs by type of bequest or topic). Bequests should be set forth in the following order, as appropriate:
A. Specific bequests
 1. Real property
 2. Tangible personal property
 3. Other specific bequests
 4. Any other clauses stating conditions that might affect the disposition of the real and tangible personal property
B. General bequests
C. Demonstrative bequests
D. Residuary clauses

Part TWO: Definitional Clauses. Clauses relating to how words and phrases used in the will should be interpreted.

Part THREE: Boilerplate Clauses. These are clauses relating to the naming of fiduciaries and their administrative and management authority, tax clauses, attestation clauses, and self-proving will affidavits.

Last Will and Testament

I am Emily Dunn, a resident of Jackson City, Franklin. This is my Last Will, and I revoke all previous wills and codicils.

ONE:

A. I give all of my tangible personal property to my husband, Charles Dunn, if we are married to each other at the time of my death.

B. I give my family home located at 23 Ipswich Lane, Jackson City, Franklin to my husband, Charles Dunn, if we are married to each other at the time of my death.

C. At the present time my husband is Charles Dunn, and we have two children, Andrea and Jonathan.

D. I give 500 shares of Wilson Corporation stock to my cousin, Alice Dunn.

E. If Alice Dunn does not survive me, I give those 500 shares to her son, Drew Dunn.

F. I give the Claude Monet painting I inherited from my grandfather to the Franklin Museum of Art.

TWO:

The remainder of my estate shall be disposed of in the following manner:

A. I give the sum of $25,000 to Bea Willis who for many years was my governess and who now lives in Sarasota, Florida.

B. I give the sum of $50,000 to Thomas Hardman who for 25 years served my parents faithfully as a gardener, provided he is married at the time of my death.

C. The balance of my residuary estate I give to my husband, Charles Dunn, or if he does not survive me or if we are not married at the time of my death, I give the balance of my residuary estate equally to our two children if they survive me, or all thereof to the survivor, or if none of my children survives me, I give the balance of my residuary estate to the Franklin Museum of Art.

THREE:

A. I nominate First Federal Bank as Executor of my estate. I empower my Executor to exercise all administrative and management powers conferred on it as Executor by the laws of the State of Franklin. I direct that my Executor not be required to post a bond.

IN WITNESS WHEREOF, I, Emily Dunn, have signed this, my Last Will, on the 18th day of January, 1965.

Emily Dunn

Witnesses:

Margaret Carnegie

Judy Carter

EXCERPTS OF TRANSCRIPT OF INTERVIEW WITH EMILY DUNN

July 28, 1999

* * * *

Attorney: By the way, are you going to be OK financially?

Dunn: I'll be fine. Chuck insured everything we own and I should be able to get by on what he left me.

Attorney: Good. I know we could go on talking about Chuck for hours and that it's hard to go from talking about Chuck to talking about your own will, but we need to go over a number of facts so that I can revise the will you signed in 1965.

Dunn: I realize my will is really out of date. Both Bea Willis and Thomas Hardman are dead.

Attorney: Let me go over some basics. When and where were you born?

Dunn: 1928 in Jackson City, Franklin.

Attorney: When did you and Chuck marry?

Dunn: On June 15, 1947. He died on April 30, 1999.

Attorney: What are the names and ages of your children and their spouses?

Dunn: I have three children: Andrea Dunn Little, age 45; Jonathan Dunn, age 42; and Bertha Dunn, age 30. My daughter Andrea is married to Elliott Little. Jonathan and Bertha are single.

Attorney: What are the names and ages of your grandchildren?

Dunn: I have four grandchildren. Andrea's kids are Nelson Little, age 12; Becky Little, age 9; and Steven Little, age 5. Also, there is my grandson, Sidney Dunn, age 8, who is my daughter Bertha's only child.

Attorney: Let's talk about how you'd like to divide your property. Is there anyone to whom you would like to give cash?

Dunn: Yes, $20,000 to Helen Rossini, a good friend of mine whose husband, Harry, recently died. He left her his car. Apparently, it has been stolen and now there is some question about whether the insurance proceeds are payable to her or to her husband's children from his first marriage. She is very upset, as she should be. What a terrible thing. Wouldn't you think that she would get the insurance if she also got the car under his will?

Attorney: That must have been very hard for Helen, but that's a lesson to us about how careful we have to be when we're setting up our wills. How old is Helen?

Dunn: Oh, she's a little older than I am, about 75.

Attorney: What would you like to have happen with the $20,000 if Helen doesn't survive you?

Dunn: If Helen dies before me, I suppose I don't really care, although I'd like the money to stay in my family.

Attorney: What else do you have that you'd like to give away?

Dunn: Well, I have 10,000 shares of Wilson Corporation stock, and I want to give my grandchildren, Nelson, Becky, Steven, and Sidney, 500 shares each. Of course, if I have more grandchildren before I die, as I hope, I'd like each of them to receive 500 shares, too. Oh, and I'd like to give some stock to the children of my cousin, Alice Dunn. She's dead now, but she had three children, Drew, Bobby, and Marilyn, who is the child of her husband from his first marriage whom she adopted. While I haven't had much contact with any of them, I'd still like to leave her kids 600 shares of Wilson. After all, it is the family-owned company founded by our great-grandfather. The 600 shares should be divided equally among any of Alice's three children if they are still alive when I die.

Attorney: So you want to treat your grandchildren equally with respect to the gift of stock.

Dunn: Yes, I've always tried to treat them equally. After all, I love them all the same.

Attorney: Now, if your grandchildren die before you, you can make the gift to another person, including any of their children. What would you like to have happen with the stock if one of the grandchildren does not outlive you?

Dunn: If any of them die before me, I suppose the stock should go to their kids. I mean, I would want any children of a grandchild who might die before me to get what his or her parent would have gotten.

Attorney: What about other personal property?

Dunn: I want Andrea and Bertha to have my jewelry. They should split it up between them as they see fit.

Attorney: What if Andrea and Bertha can't agree on how to divide it?

Dunn: Then my executor will have to divide it up as equally as possible.

Attorney: What if one of them dies before you?

Dunn: In that case, let my executor divide it up and then sell the share of the one who died before me.

Attorney: Other than the jewelry, how would you like the rest of your property divided?

Dunn: Jonathan should get the things located in my home, as well as the house itself.

Attorney: What if Jonathan dies before you?

Dunn: If he dies before me, the house and the things in the house should be sold and the money from the sale should be distributed along with everything else I have left.

Attorney: OK. Then let's talk about how you would like the balance of your estate to be disposed of.

Dunn: Now that Chuck's gone, I want what's left of my estate to go equally to my kids, or their families, of course.

Attorney: When you say "family," do you mean to include spouses of your children?

Dunn: No. Just my kids.

Attorney: What if all your children and grandchildren outlive you?

Dunn: Then I would just want things divided up equally among the kids, not the grandchildren.

Attorney: What if one or two of your children die before you, leaving grandchildren? Would you still want the balance of your estate divided into three equal parts?

Dunn: Yes. But would that mean my grandchildren wouldn't be treated equally?

Attorney: It might, depending on whether any of your children dies before you.

Dunn: It's hard for me to think about that now. Let me tell you this. I want my estate divided equally among my three children whether or not they are alive when I die. Then, I want all the children of my deceased children to be treated equally.

Attorney: We may not be able to do that without setting up a trust because we don't know at this time whether any of your kids will die before you.

Dunn: No, I don't want a trust. I want my heirs to have the total freedom to do what they want with my property when I die.

Attorney: OK, I think I have a fairly clear picture of how you would like your estate handled. I'll have a revised will prepared for you within the next few weeks. I'll call you to set up an appointment so that we can go over it together and make sure it's what you want.

Dunn: Well, you won't be able to reach me for a few weeks. I always wanted to see the Great Wall of China, and Helen and I are leaving tomorrow for Beijing and beyond. I'll call you when I return. Attorney: Have a wonderful trip, Emily. We'll get together when you get back.

LIBRARY

In re Estate of Rich
Franklin Supreme Court (1996)

Harry Dawson, a legatee under the will of Michael Rich, and the Estate of Tom Rich appeal the judgment of the Franklin Probate Court approving the final accounting of the executor of the Estate of Michael Rich.

Decedent, Michael Rich, died on April 15, 1994, a domiciliary of Parklane, Franklin, leaving a Last Will dated February 4, 1991. Under the terms of this will, decedent bequeathed:

1. All of my household goods to my daughter, Sylvia Rich Yankow;
2. My summer home on Lake Forest, State of Franklin to my best friend, Harry Dawson;
3. 100 shares of New Pioneer, Inc. common stock to my aunt, Nancy Rich, if she survives me;
4. $50,000 to my friend, Ellen Gray, if she survives me; and
5. The residue of my estate to my daughter, Sylvia Rich Yankow, and my son, Tom Rich, in equal shares.

Other than his son, Tom Rich, who died during the Gulf War, all of decedent's named beneficiaries survived him.

Decedent died leaving an estate of over $1,000,000, including his summer home on Lake Forest. Two months following decedent's death, the summer home was totally destroyed by fire. Home Casualty Insurance Company, which had issued the fire insurance policy on this home, immediately paid $150,000, the value of the home, to the executor.

In the final accounting for the estate, the executor determined that the insurance proceeds and all of the other residuary assets of the estate should be paid to Sylvia Rich as the sole surviving residuary legatee under the will. Both Harry Dawson, the legatee of the summer home, and the Estate of Tom Rich appeal.

Harry Dawson claims that, as the specific legatee of the summer home, all insurance proceeds payable thereon as a result of its destruction following the decedent's death are payable to him rather than to the residuary legatee under the decedent's will. The Estate of Tom Rich claims that one-half of the residuary estate should have been distributed to it under the terms of the residuary clause in the will.

Walker on Wills, one of the country's leading treatises on wills, notes that all bequests under wills are classified as either (1) general, (2) specific, (3) demonstrative, or (4) residuary.

A general legacy (typically a gift of money) is defined as a "bequest payable out of general estate assets or to be purchased for a beneficiary out of general estate assets." Walker on Wills, § 501.

A specific legacy is defined as a "bequest of a specific asset." Id. at § 502(a).

A demonstrative legacy is a bequest of a "specific sum of money payable from a designated account. Such legacy is specific as to the funds available in the account to pay the bequested amount and general as to the balance." Id. at § 502(b).

Lastly, Walker states that a residuary bequest is a "bequest that is neither general, specific or demonstrative and includes bequests that purport to dispose of the whole estate." Id. at § 503.

The bequest to Harry Dawson is of specific property, the summer home of the testator. If the identical thing bequeathed is not in a decedent's probate estate, the legacy is "adeemed" and the legatee's rights are gone. Walker on Wills, § 600. In this case, the summer home was in existence at the time of the decedent's death, so the bequest to Harry Dawson did not adeem. On the other hand, it was totally destroyed by fire following the decedent's death. The question raised is whether the specific legatee is entitled to receive the casualty insurance proceeds payable as a result of the fire. In resolving this question, the court, as it does in construing wills generally, must consider the testator's intent. Here, testator's will is completely silent regarding who should receive the insurance proceeds under the facts as they occurred. Thus, we are unable to ascertain the testator's intent. As such, the insurance policy must be treated like any other estate asset that is not the subject of specific bequest.

While there are cases in other jurisdictions to the contrary, we believe that the insurance policy insuring the summer home is merely another asset of the decedent's estate and forms part of the residuary estate because it was not specifically bequeathed to any other legatee. Accordingly, the Franklin Probate Court correctly upheld the decision of the executor to distribute such proceeds as part of the residuary estate.

Having determined that the insurance proceeds were part of the residuary estate, we turn to the claim of the Estate of Tom Rich.

Section 331 of the Franklin Probate Code ("Lapse Statute") provides that: "If a legatee or devisee predeceases the testator, the bequest or devise that would have passed to the deceased legatee or devisee passes to his issue that survive the testator, unless the will otherwise provides." Cases in this jurisdiction have repeatedly held that unless a decedent's will expressly conditions a residuary or other bequest on survivorship, the bequest passes to the estate of a deceased legatee unless the legatee dies leaving issue who survive the testator.

Unlike the specific bequest of the stock and the general bequest of cash, decedent's will does not expressly condition the residuary bequests to Sylvia Rich Yankow and Tom Rich on survivorship, and Tom Rich predeceased the testator leaving no surviving issue. In light of the statute and relevant cases, the probate court erred in holding that the Estate of Tom Rich was not entitled to one-half of the decedent's residuary estate.

Order of the Franklin Probate Court affirmed in part and reversed in part.

In re Estate of Young
Franklin Supreme Court (1978)

Decedent, Harry Young, died on March 12, 1974, a resident of Jackson City, Franklin. Mr. Young was a successful businessman in Jackson City and by the time of his death had accumulated a substantial fortune.

Two provisions of Mr. Young's will were called into question by the residuary legatees under his will. The first reads: "I give 100 shares of Gemet Corporation stock to my nephew, Ron Winky." Gemet Corporation stock is publicly traded on the New York Stock Exchange. Mr. Young did not own any Gemet Corporation stock at the time of his death and there is no evidence whether he ever owned any such stock. Mr. Winky argues that the bequest of stock was a general bequest to be purchased for his benefit with assets of Mr. Young's estate. The residuary legatees argue it is a specific bequest that adeemed because no such stock was in the decedent's probate estate at the time of his death.

Generally, whether a gift of specific shares of stock is a specific or general bequest depends on the intent of the testator. Gifts of specific stock are presumptively specific. If the stock was not owned at the time the will was signed, the bequest is more likely general. See generally, Walker on Wills, § 10320. If the stock was owned by testator at the time the will was executed or was stock in a closely held corporation—or if there is language in the will evidencing such ownership at the time the will was signed, such as "mystock"—the bequest is specific and, if such stock is not in the estate when testator dies, the bequest adeems. In the absence of evidence to the contrary and given the presumption of classification as specific, we affirm the Probate Court's finding that the gift to Ron Winky adeemed.

The second contested provision of the will reads: "I give $100,000 to my friend, Phil Darby, or if Phil predeceases me, to his children." Phil Darby predeceased decedent. While none of Darby's children survived the decedent, he had two grandchildren who did. One of these grandchildren had been adopted by Mr. Darby's deceased child. The grandchildren claim to be entitled to the $100,000 as alternate beneficiaries under the will. The residuary legatees claim the bequest lapsed under § 331 of the Franklin Probate Code.

The question on appeal is what the decedent meant or intended when he used the word "children." Mr. Darby's grandchildren argue that, when Mr. Young signed his will, Mr. Darby's children had already been dead for five years and that his grandchildren who lived with him were known to the decedent. Thus, they argue, it is reasonable to believe that, when decedent referred to "Mr. Darby's children," he was thinking of these grandchildren. We find this argument persuasive and hold that, for purposes of this case, the word "children" means issue.

We hold that the $100,000 passes to the grandchildren of Mr. Darby and affirm the judgment of the Probate Court.

Walker on Wills

§ 11200: In construing wills, all courts adhere to the principle that testator's intent controls in the interpretation of the language in the will. For this reason, there is a very high premium on drafting wills in which the language is clear and unambiguous. Attorneys who draft wills also must be aware of governing rules of law that can affect how wills might be construed if the language is not clear.

For example, suppose a testator bequeaths "my 100 shares of X Corporation stock to B" but at the time of the testator's death, she owns 200 shares of X Corporation stock. Is B entitled to only 100 shares of the X Corporation stock or to the 200 shares of that stock that testator owns at death? The answer to this question often depends on how testator acquired the additional 100 shares of stock.

If the additional shares were acquired either as a stock split or stock (as distinguished from cash) dividend, most courts hold that they pass to the specific legatee because they represent the stated gift in its current form. However, since this matter is not always free of doubt, if a testator intends that result, a will construction proceeding to resolve the question could be avoided if, for example, the will had read: "I give my 100 shares of X Corporation stock to B, including any additional shares I receive between the date of the execution of this will and the date of my death as either a stock split or as a dividend paid to me by X Corporation in its own shares."

* * * *

§ 14920: There had been much confusion surrounding how property should be distributed among class members where the class gift is limited to persons potentially of different generational levels to the named ancestor, such as a gift to "issue." Fortunately, the matter has been universally resolved in all states by their adoption of the Uniform Act on Per Capita and Per Stirpes Distributions. This act provides that:

1. If property is distributed "per capita" to the "issue" or "descendants" of a named ancestor, each person who is an issue or descendant of the named ancestor takes an equal share.

2. If property is distributed "per stirpes" to the "issue" or "descendants" of a testator, the property is distributed among the issue or descendants most closely related to the testator. However, if there would have been other issue or descendants at the same generational level who, had they survived, would have participated in the gift, then their issue or descendants, if any, take the share these deceased persons would have taken. The following example illustrates distribution "per stirpes":

(1) Testator (T) had three children, A, B, and C.
- A dies before T and had 7 children.
- B dies before T and had 1 child.
- C survives T and has 1 child.

(2) A's children each take 1/7 of the 1/3 share A would have received had he lived.

(3) B's child gets the entire 1/3 share B would have received had he lived.

(4) C takes a 1/3 share and C's child takes nothing.

As can be seen, in a "per stirpes" distribution, grandchildren with dead parents get a proportionate share of what their parents would have gotten.

3. If property is distributed "per stirpes but per capita at each generation" to the "issue" or "descendants" of a testator, the outcome is quite different. The following example, using the same facts that were used to illustrate "per stirpes" distribution, illustrates distribution "per stirpes but per capita at each generation":

(1) Testator (T) had three children, A, B, and C.
- A dies before T and had 7 children.
- B dies before T and had 1 child.
- C survives T and has 1 child.

(2) A and B's children each take 1/8 of the 2/3 share A and B would have received had they lived.

(3) C takes a 1/3 share and C's child takes nothing.

As opposed to a pure "per stirpes" distribution, in this case the grandchildren with dead parents each get an equal share of what all the dead parents would have gotten.

In this example, B's child gets much less. Instead of a 1/3 share, B's child shares equally with all the grandchildren whose parents have died.

THE MPT
MULTISTATE PERFORMANCE TEST

In re Emily Dunn

POINT SHEET

The MPT point sheet, grading summary, and grading guidelines describe the factual and legal points encompassed within the lawyering task to be completed. They outline all the possible issues and points that might be addressed by an applicant. They are provided to the user jurisdictions for the sole purpose of assisting graders in grading the examination by identifying the issues and suggesting the resolution of the problem contemplated by the drafters. These are not official grading guides. Applicants can receive a range of passing grades, including excellent grades, without covering all the points discussed in these guides. The model answer is included as an illustration of a thorough and detailed response to the task, one that addresses all the legal and factual issues the drafters intended to raise in the problem. It is intended to serve only as an example. Applicants need not present their responses in the same way to receive good grades. User jurisdictions are free to modify these grading materials, including the suggested weights assigned to particular points. Grading the MPT is the exclusive responsibility of the jurisdiction using the MPT as part of its admissions process.

Copyright © 2008 by the National Conference of Bar Examiners.
All rights reserved

In Re Emily Dunn

Drafters' Point Sheet

The task for the applicants in this test item is to draft the introductory and dispositive clauses of a will for a client, Emily Dunn. The recent death of Mrs. Dunn's husband is the reason for rewriting her will. Most of the will is straightforward but there are special problems associated with the disposition of insurance policies and stock in the family company, equalizing gifts to the grandchildren, and the disposition of the residuary estate. In addition to drafting dispositive provisions dealing with these latter issues, the applicants are directed to write an explanation after each of the relevant clauses articulating the factual assumptions used in resolving the insurance, stock, grandchildren, and residuary clause issues and giving the reasons why they drafted the provisions the way they did.

The File contains the instructional memo from the supervising attorney, a transcript of an interview with Mrs. Dunn, an office memo prescribing the wills format used by the firm, and a copy of the client's old will. The client's wishes regarding the disposition of her property are to be gleaned from the transcript of the interview. There are some ambiguities and factual gaps in the wishes expressed by the client. These are intentional, and the applicants are expected to recognize and deal with them.

The Library consists of two decisions of the Franklin Supreme Court. One of them, Estate of Rich, deals with the treatment of insurance proceeds when a casualty loss occurs to bequeathed property, defines the different categories of bequests, and illustrates an application of the Franklin lapse statute. The other, Estate of Young, deals with gifts of corporate stock and a question of interpretation, i.e., whether the testator's use of the term "children" can be construed to mean "issue." These are all relevant to the resolution of the problems in the test item.

The other authority in the Library is an excerpt from Walker on Wills, the leading treatise in Franklin. It instructs the applicants on bequests of stock and, more importantly, provides the wherewithal for resolving the problem of distributing the residuary estate in a way that equalizes the gifts to the grandchildren if one or more of Mrs. Dunn's grandchildren predeceases her.

The following discussion covers all the points the authors of the item intended to incorporate, but applicants can certainly receive passing and even excellent grades without covering them all. That is left to the discretion of the user jurisdictions.

1. **Overview**: Applicants are expected to use the format set forth in the firm's will drafting guidelines. It is not merely a formality. In part, the format memo, by setting forth the order of bequests, tests whether applicants can classify the gifts properly as specific, general, demonstrative and residuary bequests. It also sets up a template for grading consistency.

No particular style of language is necessary, but Mrs. Dunn's old will should serve as guide to the kinds of words the applicants can use to express the dispositive wishes of the client. They have to be careful not to follow the form of that will blindly because, as suggested in the will drafting guidelines, the firm's preferred format has changed since 1965 when Mrs. Dunn's old will was drafted. The authors of the test item did this intentionally so that the task would not become merely an exercise in copying from the old will.

There is no particular format for the explanations regarding issues relating to the insurance, stock, equal gifts to the grandchildren, and gift of the residuary. However, it calls for them to do two things. First, they must articulate whatever factual assumptions they have to make to fill in the factual gaps in the File. For example, there is a suggestion, which is less than clear in the interview with Mrs. Dunn, that there is insurance on all her personal and real property, and the applicants will have to make the assumption that the insurance exists or at least account for the possibility that it might exist at the time of Mrs. Dunn's death.

Second, they must explain why they have drafted the will provisions in the particular way they have. For example, regarding Mrs. Dunn's wish to treat her grandchildren equally, they will have to explain why the language they have chosen adequately satisfies the "per stirpes but per capita at each generation" concept set forth in Walker on Wills.

2. The Introductory Clause: This is a fairly straightforward task. The office memo tells the applicants what it must include:

- Mrs. Dunn's name and domicile, Jackson City, Franklin;
- Revocation of "all prior wills and codicils";
- Recitation of Mrs. Dunn's immediate family, i.e., her three children and the grandchildren. In the old will, the immediate family recitation is incorporated into one of the bequest sections. In the new will, it should be in the introductory clause. The better applicants might recite that Mrs. Dunn is widowed.

3. Part One A—Specific Bequests: In this section, the applicants are expected to recognize which of Mrs. Dunn's bequests fall into the category of specific bequests, to set them forth in the order specified in the will drafting guidelines according to the kind of property being bequeathed and to express any conditions that might affect the disposition of the property.

- **Real Property—Bequest of her house and the contents to Jonathan**: This is a specific bequest because these are "specific assets." See Estate of Rich. Mrs. Dunn wants Jonathan to have the house and the contents ("the things in the house"), so the language should simply and plainly say that she gives these assets to him.

- A strict reading of the will drafting guidelines would seem to require that the gift of the house be set forth in one paragraph and the gift of the contents in another. It might be more efficient, and certainly acceptable, if an applicant makes in a single paragraph the gift of "my home and its contents that are not otherwise disposed of" to Jonathan.

- **Insurance**: There should be an expression in the language of this bequest that, in the event there are casualty losses affecting the house or the contents, Mrs. Dunn wants the insurance policies or proceeds to follow the assets and to go to Jonathan, not to the residue. See Estate of Young. This intention is clear from the concern she expressed during the interview.

- **Lapse Issue**: Mrs. Dunn says that, if Jonathan predeceases her, she wants the house and contents sold and added to the residue (i.e., "sold and distributed along with everything else I have left").

  - Although Jonathan has no issue right now, it is possible that he might have issue when Mrs. Dunn dies. In light of that possibility, the will should specifically condition this gift upon Jonathan's survival in order to avoid the effect of the lapse statute and comply with Mrs. Dunn's wish.

- **Points re insurance for the explanatory paragraph**: It is fair from the interview transcript to make the factual assumption that there is insurance on the house and the contents (i.e., "Chuck insured everything we own…") and that Mrs. Dunn wants the insurance policies to follow the assets. The explanation should make this assumption and explain how

the language in the dispositive clause complies with that wish.

- **Tangible Personal Property - Bequest of the jewelry to Andrea and Bertha**: Again, this is a gift of specific property and therefore a specific bequest. The language should state simply and plainly that Mrs. Dunn gives the jewelry to Andrea and Bertha to be divided between them as they see fit.

- The clause should also account for the contingencies that:
  - If they can't agree on how to divide the jewelry, the executor should divide it as equally as possible; and
  - If either predeceases Mrs. Dunn, the executor should divide the jewelry and "sell the share of the one who died before me."
  In this respect there is something of an ambiguity. Does Mrs. Dunn intend that the proceeds of the sale by the executor go to the issue of the deceased daughter or to the residue? Applicants should probably resolve it in favor of the residue in light of Mrs. Dunn's desire to treat all grandchildren equally, but it would be acceptable for them to allow the proceeds to go to the issue of the deceased daughter. Remaining silent on the point will allow the lapse statute to operate to pass the decedent's share to her issue. The better papers, however, will cover the point explicitly.

- **Insurance**: Here also, the clause should recite that the insurance policies and the proceeds follow the assets in case of casualty loss affecting the jewelry.

- **Points for the explanatory paragraph**: Again, it is a fair assumption that there is insurance to cover the jewelry ("Chuck insured everything we own…"). The same assumption and explanation should be made here as was made regarding the house and contents. Also, the applicants should state whatever assumption is made about the descent of the proceeds of a sale of a deceased daughter's

share of the jewelry and explain how the language of the bequest supports the assumption.

- **Intangible Personal Property—Bequests of Wilson Corporation stock**: There are two specific bequests of Wilson Corporation stock, which is intangible personal property, each requiring different treatment.

- **In General**: Mrs. Dunn currently owns 10,000 shares of Wilson stock. Wilson Corporation is apparently a closely held corporation and presumably not available on the open market. As suggested in Walker.

- The clause should make it clear that she is bequeathing "shares of my Wilson Corporation stock";

- It should also cover the possibility that the corporation might split the stock or pay stock dividends, which would increase the number of shares. Presumably, Mrs. Dunn would want the corresponding increase to accompany the bequests.

- **500 shares to each grandchild**: The clause should name the existing grandchildren and state clearly that each of them, Nelson Little, Becky Little, Stephen Little, and Sidney Dunn, are to receive 500 shares of "my Wilson Corporation stock" and adapt the language in Walker regarding share increases on account of stock splits or dividends.

- Mrs. Dunn has also expressed the desire that afterborn grandchildren also each receive 500 shares, so the clause should provide for it. The only condition she has expressed is that the grandchildren be born before she dies.

- Mrs. Dunn has also said she wants the shares bequeathed to any predeceased grandchild to pass to the "kids/children" of that grandchild. It is probably fair to assume that she means "issue," and the holding in Estate of Young can be brought to bear on that point.

- Likewise, it is possible that one or more individuals might become "grandchildren" by adoption. The disposition clause should provide for this contingency one way or another, but the fact that Mrs. Dunn is willing to include her cousin Alice's adopted child in the will (infra) is an indication that she would intend to include adopted grandchildren.

- The lapse statute will operate to pass the shares bequeathed to a predeceased grandchild to that decedent's issue if the will is silent on the point, but better applicants will make it explicit.

Points re this bequest of stock for the explanatory paragraph: One assumption the applicants need to make is that Mrs. Dunn intends that only shares she owns at her death shall be used to satisfy this bequest. Another is that she would not intend the increase on account of stock splits or dividends to go to the individual legatees. These assumptions are inferable from the fact that Wilson Corporation is a family company and that she has a desire to treat the grandchildren equally. The applicants should then explain why it is that the language they have used accomplishes these things. The assumption regarding who Mrs. Dunn intends to include among the afterborn grandchildren is disposed of by her statement that "more grandchildren" means those born before she dies. This should probably be expanded to include those who became grandchildren by adoption before she dies.

600 shares to the children of deceased cousin, Alice Dunn: This specific bequest is essentially a class gift to a closed class, i.e., there will be no more children of Alice Dunn because she is dead. The clause should name the three children, Drew Dunn, Bobby Dunn and Marilyn Dunn (the adopted child of Alice Dunn) and state that Mrs. Dunn wants to leave them 600 shares of "my Wilson Corporation shares."

- The shares are to be divided equally among those of Alice's children who survive Mrs. Dunn. The survival condition removes any question about the application of the lapse statute.

- Again, it can be presumed that Mrs. Dunn wants any increase on account of stock splits and dividends to follow the bequest.

- If the bequest specifically names the three children, the fact that Marilyn is an adopted child is moot because she is specifically named beneficiary. If, however, the words of the bequest refer only to "the children of my deceased cousin, Alice Dunn," the applicants should make it clear that Mrs. Dunn intended to include Marilyn in the class. See Estate of Young.

- **Points re this bequest of stock for the explanatory paragraph:** As with the bequest of stock to the grandchildren, the same assumptions can be made regarding the bequest being only of shares owned at her death and the disposition of splits and stock dividends. If Marilyn Dunn is not specifically mentioned as a beneficiary, the fact that she was adopted should be mentioned and the assumption made that Mrs. Dunn intended that Marilyn be treated as a "child" of Alice. In both cases, the applicants should explain why the language supports the assumptions.

4. **Part One B—General Bequest:** There is only one general bequest as that is defined in Estate of Rich: the gift of $20,000 to Helen Rossini. The clause should simply make the gift to Helen and make it clear it is conditioned on Helen's surviving Mrs. Dunn. Since Mrs. Dunn wants the money to stay in my family" if Helen does not survive, the applicants should state specifically that the money drops to the residue if Helen predeceases Mrs. Dunn.

5. **Part One D—Residuary Clauses:** Mrs. Dunn wants "what's left of my estate to go equally to my kids, or their families...", not including the spouses of her children.

More specifically, she wants the residue "divided equally among my three children, whether or not they are alive when I die. Then I want all the children of my deceased children to be treated equally." Walker on Wills furnishes the means of satisfying this intent.

Applicants can either try to craft language that expresses Mrs. Dunn's wish that each of her children should get one-third and that the shares of any of her children who predecease her are aggregated and divided equally among all the children of her deceased children or they can use the shorthand given in Walker; i.e., she wants the residue to be distributed "to my issue per stirpes but per capita at each generation."

- **Points re equal treatment of grandchildren in distribution of the residue for the explanatory paragraph:** Applicants should recognize that this is the closest they can come to insuring equal treatment of grandchildren because, unless both Andrea and Bertha predecease Mrs. Dunn, the grandchildren by the survivor of those two daughters will take nothing under the will. They must make the assumption that Mrs. Dunn will be satisfied with that result and explain how the language they have written accomplishes that result.

FILE

MPT Task 4H:
In re Franklin Construction Company

Axtell, Maynard & Sandrego
Attorneys at Law
One Central Post Plaza
Boyceville, Franklin 33321
(555) 521-7108

MEMORANDUM

To: Applicant
From: Max Sandrego
Date: February 26, 2002
Subject: Franklin Construction Company

Our new client, Franklin Construction Company (FCC), a joint venturer in the New Millennium Hotel Venture (the Venture), has asked for our advice regarding a demand letter it received from its co-venturer, Millman Developers, Inc. (MDI). I met yesterday with Ralph Dirksen, chief executive officer of FCC.

Please draft an opinion letter to Mr. Dirksen for my signature advising him on the following questions:

1. Is FCC obligated under either of its two contractual undertakings to pay either MDI or the Venture any part of the money demanded in the letter from MDI?
2. Is FCC obligated under the statutes and case law to pay either MDI or the Venture any part of the money demanded in the letter from MDI?
3. Does FCC have any obligation to undertake efforts to recover the money from the Boyceville Redevelopment Agency?

Follow the usual office format for opinion letters: (a) a short "Factual Statement"; (b) a "Short Answer" for each issue in which you state the essence of the opinion; and (c) an "Opinion" segment in which you state your conclusions and explain your reasoning, supported by the legal authorities. Mr. Dirksen is a sophisticated businessman but he is not a lawyer, so be sure to explain things fully and in language that a layperson can understand.

EXCERPT FROM TRANSCRIPT OF INTERVIEW WITH RALPH DIRKSEN

February 25, 2002

* * * *

Dirksen: I've got this letter from Art Millman—president of a company with which my company, Franklin Construction, had a joint venture. He wants us to pay back the $350,000 his company contributed. It was never represented to be a loan. I don't want to have anything to do with Millman or his company ever again.

Lawyer: Well, why don't you start from the beginning.

Dirksen: OK. Back in January of last year, we got interested in some property owned by the Boyceville Redevelopment Agency. You know, the block at Third and Market that was razed a couple years ago.

Lawyer: Yeah. I'd heard a new hotel is supposed to go in there.

Dirksen: That's right. It's a tremendously valuable property. I thought we were going to get it, but the Agency pulled the rug out from under us.

Lawyer: What happened?

Dirksen: Well, when I first heard the Agency was going to put that property on the market, I started lobbying for an exclusive right to negotiate with them. Frankly, I pulled some political strings and got the mayor to go to bat for me. Anyway, the Agency passed a resolution giving Franklin Construction the exclusive right to negotiate for six months.

Lawyer: To negotiate for what?

Dirksen: For acquisition and development of the property.

Lawyer: Oh, OK. What amount of money are we talking about?

Dirksen: Well, it was sort of a package deal. We were supposed to get the property and the development rights in return for our commitment to build a Class A hotel—685 rooms—for at least $35,000,000.

Lawyer: How does that compare to other projects you've had?

Dirksen: By far the biggest. And that's the problem. I guess I never thought getting the financing on such a valuable property would be as tough as it was.

Lawyer: What do you mean?

Dirksen: It's the most money I've ever had to dig up. That, coupled with the fact that one of our ongoing projects ran into trouble last year. I couldn't find any individuals or lending institutions to back us on this one. I was pretty frantic because this project is a hands-down winner. The successful bidder stands to make a ton of money.

Lawyer: Did you get the loan commitments?

Dirksen: Not exactly. I got in touch with Art Millman. He's the president of Millman Developers, a major land developer out of Allensburg. He's done some huge projects, and I thought with his clout maybe he could help me get the backing. He was enthusiastic because I'd gotten the Redevelopment Agency to give us the exclusive rights, so he offered to go into partnership with us—that is, his company and mine.

Lawyer: Was he able to get the loan commitments?

Dirksen: No, but I was able to convince the Agency that, with Millman's backing, we'd be able to wrap it up pretty soon. So the Agency OK'd my involving Millman and extended my exclusive negotiating right for 90 days. I thought that would give us plenty of time.

Lawyer: OK. Go on.

Dirksen: Millman's lawyers figured out that what we needed to do was for Franklin Construction and Millman Developers to set up a partnership or joint venture or whatever. The first thing, to give Millman a stake in the deal, was for Franklin Construction to assign all its rights to Millman. Then Millman would put up the front money.

Lawyer: Front money?

Dirksen: Yeah. To get the Agency to extend my negotiating rights, Franklin Construction had to agree to deposit with the Agency 1% of the project price—$350,000.

Lawyer: When you say "deposit," what do you mean? Was it refundable if the deal fell through, or what?

Dirksen: Well, now that things have fallen through, the Agency is claiming the money was forfeited and we're not entitled to get it back. Anyway, part of the assignment agreement was for Millman to put up the money, and, once the Agency OK'd Millman as our partner, we'd then set up the joint venture.

Lawyer: Did that ever happen?

Dirksen: Yeah. It's all spelled out in this stack of documents, and I'll just leave them with you. Millman's attorneys drafted the Assignment Agreement and the Joint Venture Agreement. I confess, I was pretty desperate to save the deal, so I just signed them. The long and short of it is that Millman would basically take over and run things.

Lawyer: What part would you play in the joint venture?

Dirksen: Not much, really. FCC's role was only to provide services. The deal was that I'd use my political connections to keep us in the race and maintain a relationship with city officials after the project got started. Basically, my company would stay in the joint venture to do whatever work Millman asked it to do, such as securing building permits and approvals once construction got underway, and we'd get 10% of the profits down the road.

Lawyer: Then what?

Dirksen: Well, we weren't making much progress in getting loan commitments. Other local developers began agitating at City Hall. Then, out of the blue, the Agency sends me a letter terminating our exclusive negotiating right. The next thing I know, I get Art Millman's letter telling me to go after the Agency and pay back the $350,000. Do I have to do those things?

Lawyer: I'll need to read the documents and do some research in order to answer your question. Then I'll give you a written opinion.

Assignment and Agreement

This ASSIGNMENT AGREEMENT ("Agreement") is between Franklin Construction Company ("FCC"), a Franklin corporation, and Millman Developers, Inc. ("MDI"), a Franklin corporation.

RECITALS

1. The Boyceville Redevelopment Agency ("Agency"), by Resolution No. 126-98, granted to FCC the exclusive right to negotiate for the acquisition and development of Redevelopment Parcel 2B at Third and Market Streets in Boyceville, Franklin (the "Property"). The Agency has, by Resolution No. 43-99, extended FCC's exclusive negotiating right until March 14, 2002.

2. FCC requires MDI's assistance in satisfying the requirements of the Agency Resolutions.

AGREEMENT

A. FCC transfers and assigns to MDI all right, title and interest conferred upon FCC by the Agency under the above-mentioned Resolutions, including without limitation the right of exclusive negotiation thereunder.

B. MDI accepts this assignment and agrees to transfer to FCC the sum of $350,000 to be deposited with the Agency as required in Resolution No. 43-99.

C. MDI agrees to pay FCC $60,000 in consideration of this assignment.

D. MDI and FCC agree to form a corporation, partnership, joint venture or other entity ("Entity"), the business purpose of which will be to acquire the Property and develop thereon a 685-room Class A hotel.

E. This Agreement is expressly conditioned on the following:
  (i) Execution by MDI and FCC of a definitive agreement regarding formation of the Entity within 30 days from the date hereof; and
  (ii) Agency acceptance of MDI as an authorized party to the acquisition and development of the Property.

In the event of the failure of either of the conditions set forth in (i) and (ii), above, this Agreement shall be null and void and FCC shall refund to MDI the $350,000 transferred hereunder.

F. MDI shall have the right to assign all rights acquired under this Agreement to any successor in interest, including without limitation the Entity

Date: November 30, 2001

Millman Developers, Inc.

By *Arthur D. Millman*
Arthur D. Millman
President

Franklin Construction Company

By *Ralph P. Dirksen*
Ralph P. Dirksen
Chief Executive Officer

Millman Developers, Inc.
Builders for the New Millennium
Millman Towers
Suite 4200
Allensburg, Franklin 33323
February 22, 2002

Ralph P. Dirksen
Chief Executive Officer
Franklin Construction Company
12543 Wrangel Road
Boyceville, FR 33324

Re: New Millennium Hotel Venture

Dear Mr. Dirksen:

As you know, we have done everything humanly possible to satisfy the Boyceville Redevelopment Agency ("Agency") that we are pursuing all avenues to obtain the acquisition and development funding commitments for the Third and Market Street property. Notwithstanding our efforts, the Agency has abruptly terminated the exclusive right granted to Franklin Construction Company to negotiate for acquisition of the property. This termination effectively destroys any chance that we will be able to acquire and develop the property.

Accordingly, Millman Developers, Inc., exercises its right under Section M of the New Millennium Hotel Venture Agreement to terminate the Venture. We hereby demand that Franklin Construction Company pursue the Agency to recover the $350,000 Millman Developers advanced to Franklin Construction under our Assignment Agreement. Regardless of whether you are successful, we demand that you repay that sum.

Sincerely yours,

Arthur D. Millman
Arthur D. Millman
President

Boyceville Redevelopment Agency

Resolution No. 43-99

WHEREAS, in Agency Resolution No. 126-98, the Boyceville Redevelopment Agency ("Agency") granted to Franklin Construction Company ("FCC") the exclusive right for six months to negotiate with the Agency for the acquisition and development of Redevelopment Parcel 2B (the "Property") at Third and Market Streets in Boyceville, Franklin, on condition that the Property be acquired for the purpose of developing a Class A hotel; and

WHEREAS, the six-month exclusive negotiating period expires on December 14, 2001; and

WHEREAS, the Agency is satisfied that FCC has been attempting diligently to obtain the necessary $35,000,000 acquisition and construction funding for development of the Property; and

WHEREAS, the Agency has approved the involvement of Millman Developers, Inc., in FCC's efforts to secure the financing;

NOW, THEREFORE, the Agency hereby grants to FCC an extension of the exclusive negotiating right on the following conditions:

1. Said extension shall be for 90 days, which shall begin on December 15, 2001, and expire on March 14, 2002, unless terminated sooner as provided in Paragraph 3, below.

2. Within 10 days of the date of this Resolution, FCC shall deposit $350,000 with the Agency. This deposit is 1% of the anticipated acquisition and development costs. The Agency shall apply this deposit to the overall cost of the project.

3. If, at any time within said 90-day extension period it appears that FCC is unlikely to obtain the necessary loan commitments by the end of the 90-day period, the Agency may in its sole discretion terminate FCC's exclusive negotiating rights and solicit other interested parties to participate in the bidding to develop the Property.

Date: November 20, 2001

Attest: This is a true and correct copy of Resolution No. 43-99 of the Board of Directors of the Boyceville Redevelopment Agency.

By *Royland Vernon*
Royland Vernon
Clerk of the Board

Joint Venture Agreement of New Millennium Hotel Venture

This JOINT VENTURE AGREEMENT is entered into by Millman Developers, Inc. ("MDI"), a Franklin corporation, and Franklin Construction Company ("FCC"), a Franklin corporation.

RECITALS

1. Pursuant to Resolutions Nos. 126-98 and 43-99 of the Boyceville Redevelopment Agency (the "Agency"), FCC acquired the exclusive right to enter into negotiations with the Agency for the acquisition and development of Redevelopment Parcel 2B at the corner of Third and Market Streets, Boyceville, Franklin (the "Property").

2. FCC has been unable to obtain the necessary loan commitments to satisfy the Agency and has therefore sought the assistance of MDI, which is a corporation with substantial experience in the development of commercial properties.

3. On November 20, 2001, the Agency recognized MDI as an authorized party to the negotiations for acquisition and development of the Property.

4. On November 30, 2001, FCC assigned to MDI all its right, title and interest in and to the exclusive right of negotiation under the Resolutions. A copy of the Assignment Agreement between MDI and FCC is attached as an exhibit and made a part of this Joint Venture Agreement.

5. The negotiations with the Agency contemplate the development of the Property as a 685-room Class A hotel.

6. MDI and FCC desire to undertake a joint venture to develop the Property as a hotel property and, in consideration of the foregoing and the following, hereby agree to do so.

AGREEMENT

A. <u>Purpose.</u> The joint venture shall be known as the NEW MILLENNIUM HOTEL VENTURE (the "Venture"). Its purpose is to pursue a development agreement with the Agency for the acquisition, development, construction, ownership, operation, sale, lease or other disposition of the Property as a 685-room Class A hotel at an overall cost of at least $35,000,000, all for the production of income and profit.

B. <u>Capital Contributions to the Venture.</u> MDI assigns to the Venture as its capital contribution all its right, title and interest to (i) the exclusive right of negotiation transferred by FCC to MDI and (ii) the $350,000 paid by MDI as the result of the attached Assignment Agreement. FCC's capital contribution to the Venture shall consist of its local expertise and such assistance and services as MDI may from time to time require of it during the construction phase of the project. The venturers agree that any and all rights and property hereafter acquired as a result of the negotiations with the Agency, including the Property and any financing commitments relating thereto, shall belong to the Venture.

C. <u>Management of the Venture.</u> The venturers agree that MDI shall be the Managing Venturer of the Venture. In its capacity as Managing Venturer, MDI shall have exclusive management and control of the Venture and shall make all decisions and be authorized to do anything and everything it deems necessary or beneficial in running the business of the Venture.

D. **Sharing in Distributions and Profits.** The venturers agree that they will share in distributions of the profits of the Venture (other than returns of capital), including distributions of operating cash flow, as follows:

Venturer	Percentage of Share
MDI	90%
FCC	10%

* * * *

M. **Term of the Venture.** The term of the Venture shall commence on the date of this Agreement and, unless sooner dissolved by agreement of the venturers, by operation of law, or by failure or impracticability of the purpose of the Venture, shall continue in existence until December 31, 2012; provided, however, that if, prior to acquisition of the Property by the Venture, the Agency terminates the exclusive right of negotiation, MDI shall have the right to declare the Venture terminated and to withdraw.

Date: December 26, 2001

Millman Developers, Inc.

By *Arthur D. Millman*
Arthur D. Millman
President

Franklin Construction Company

By *Ralph P. Dirksen*
Ralph P. Dirksen
Chief Executive Officer

BOYCEVILLE REDEVELOPMENT AGENCY

City of Boyceville
City Hall, Room 301
Boyceville, Franklin 33322

February 13, 2002

Ralph P. Dirksen
Chief Executive Officer
Franklin Construction Company
12543 Wrangel Road
Boyceville, FR 33324

Re: Redevelopment Parcel 2B
Agency Resolution No. 43-99

Dear Mr. Dirksen:

The Redevelopment Agency has determined that efforts being undertaken by Franklin Construction Company and its partner, Millman Developers, Inc., are unlikely to result in the receipt of meaningful loan commitments at any time in the near future. You are therefore notified that, pursuant to subparagraph 3 of Resolution No. 43-99, the Agency has terminated the exclusive negotiation rights granted in Agency Resolution No. 126-98 and extended in Resolution No. 43-99. All monies heretofore deposited with the Agency are deemed nonrefundable.

For the Board of Directors

Royland Vernon
Royland Vernon
Clerk of the Board

cc: Arthur D. Millman
Millman Developers, Inc.

LIBRARY

Franklin Business Associations Code
(Uniform Partnership Act)

§ 203. Property Acquired by Partnership

Property acquired by a partnership is property of the partnership and not of the individual partners.

§ 204. What Constitutes Partnership Property; Acquisition

* * * *

(b) Property is acquired in the name of the partnership by a transfer to either of the following:

(1) The partnership in its name.

(2) One or more partners in their capacity as partners in the partnership, if the name of the partnership is indicated in the instrument transferring title to the property.

* * * *

§ 306. Partner's Liability

(a) Except as otherwise provided in [this chapter] all partners are liable jointly and severally for all obligations of the partnership unless otherwise agreed by the claimant or provided by law.

§ 401. Partner's Rights and Duties

* * * *

(b) Each partner is entitled to an equal share of the partnership profits and, subject to § 306..., is chargeable with a share of the partnership losses in proportion to the partner's share of the profits.

(c) A partnership shall reimburse a partner for payments made and indemnify a partner for liabilities incurred by the partner in the ordinary course of the business of the partnership or for the preservation of its business or property.

(d) A partnership shall reimburse a partner for an advance to the partnership beyond the amount of capital the partner agreed to contribute.

(e) A payment or advance made by a partner that gives rise to a partnership obligation under subdivision (c)or (d) constitutes a loan to the partnership that accrues interest from the date of the payment or advance.

* * * *

§ 404. General Standards of Partner's Conduct

(a) The only fiduciary duties a partner owes to the partnership and the other partners are the duty of loyalty and the duty of care set forth in subdivisions (b) and (c).

(b) A partner's duty of loyalty to the partnership and the other partners is limited to the following:

(1) To account to the partnership and hold as trustee for it any property, profit, or benefit derived by the partner in the conduct and winding up of the partnership business or derived from a use by the partner of partnership property or information, including the appropriation of a partnership opportunity.

(2) To refrain from dealing with the partnership in the conduct or winding up of the partnership business as or on behalf of a party having an interest adverse to the partnership.

(3) To refrain from competing with the partnership in the conduct of the partnership business before the dissolution of the partnership.

(c) A partner's duty of care to the partnership and the other partners in the conduct and winding up of the partnership business is limited to refraining from engaging in grossly negligent or reckless conduct, intentional misconduct, or a knowing violation of law.

Stilwell v. Trutanich
Franklin Court of Appeal (1995)

Plaintiff, owner of a seafood company, sued defendants, the owner and the captain of a fishing vessel, for an accounting after breach of an alleged joint venture agreement. The trial court dismissed the suit on the motion of defendants, finding that there was no joint venture but, rather, that the arrangement was nothing more than a charter by plaintiff of defendants' vessel without captain or crew. Plaintiff appeals the dismissal.

A joint venture is an undertaking by two or more persons jointly to carry out a single enterprise for profit. It has been stated that a joint venture is a partnership formed for the accomplishment of a single project. Indeed, our supreme court has held that the relationships of joint venturers among themselves are governed by the partnership laws of the State of Franklin. *Mellor v. Brightman*, Franklin Supreme Court (1986).

The elements of a joint venture are: (a) a community of interest in the subject of the undertaking; (b) a sharing in profits and losses; (c) an equal right or a right in some measure to direct and control the conduct of each other and of the enterprise; and (d) a fiduciary relationship between and among the parties.

A community of interest may exist although the property forming the capital of the venture is not jointly owned by the parties and although one party has contributed money, another property, and another skill to the enterprise. Although it is usual to provide for an equal sharing of profits and losses, the parties may agree to an unequal distribution of the profits, or they may agree that all the parties shall participate in the profits and only certain of them in the losses. In addition, the omission of a provision for the sharing of losses in a joint venture is immaterial since, in the absence of agreement, the law implies a provision that the losses are to be shared among the parties in the same proportion as the profits were to have been divided.

The parties to a joint venture can agree to have unequal control of operations. While in the absence of a special agreement one joint venturer cannot bind the others, they may by agreement grant authority to one or more of the joint venturers, which would not be implied from the relationship alone.

Interpreted in light of these rules, the complaint in this case adequately establishes the existence of a joint venture. It pleads and incorporates a written joint venture agreement to which one of the defendants was an undisclosed principal. The agreement is denominated "Joint Venture Agreement" and refers to the business relationship between the parties. It contemplates the making of a single voyage into Mexican waters to catch, transport, and sell seafood products. It designates the percentage of the net profits each party shall receive.

The complaint further alleges that the voyage referred to in the agreement was completed, that the venture suffered losses, and that said losses were borne by plaintiff, who was not reimbursed therefor. Although the agreement is silent on the manner in which the losses of the venture are to be apportioned, the law implies an obligation on the part of the joint venturers to bear losses in the same proportion as they agreed to divide the profits.

The fact that the defendants had no right to direct their joint venturer in making the voyage, procuring the seafood, and selling the products does not negate the existence of a joint venture agreement because, by written agreement, they delegated their authority.

Reversed.

Kovacik v. Reed

Franklin Supreme Court (1996)

In this suit for dissolution of a joint venture and for an accounting, defendant Reed appeals from a judgment that plaintiff Kovacik recover one-half of the losses of the venture, plus prejudgment interest, and declaring that Reed was obligated to return one-half of the amount Kovacik had invested as capital in the joint venture.

Kovacik told Reed he (Kovacik) had the opportunity to do kitchen remodeling work for a builder who was refurbishing a number of low-income dwellings. He said he had about $10,000 to invest and that, if Reed would become his job superintendent and estimator, Kovacik would share the profits on the job with Reed on a 50-50 basis. Reed agreed and commenced the work on various projects. As the work proceeded, it became clear that it was unprofitable, and the builder for whom the work was being done fell seriously in arrears. At the end of the project, the Kovacik/Reed venture had suffered significant losses.

Reed's only contribution to the venture was his own labor. Kovacik provided all the venture's financing. The parties had never discussed apportionment of any losses that might accrue to the venture and, despite periodic requests by Kovacik that Reed "put up some money to get us out of the red," Reed had consistently refused to contribute any money.

Kovacik also claimed that, by failing to file mechanic's liens against the properties, Reed had breached a fiduciary duty of care as a joint venturer to preserve Kovacik's claims for the delinquent amounts, thereby eroding Kovacik's capital investment.

The trial court concluded as a matter of law that, as joint venturers, Kovacik and Reed were bound to share the losses in the same proportion as they had agreed to share the profits; that Kovacik was therefore entitled to recover from Reed one-half of the losses; and that Reed, having breached his duty of care to Kovacik, was liable to Kovacik for one-half of the amount advanced by Kovacik to the venture.

It is the general rule that in the absence of an agreement to the contrary the law presumes that partners or joint venturers intended to participate equally in the profits and losses of the common enterprise. This is true irrespective of any inequality in their contributions to the venture.

In cases in which the above stated general rule has been applied, each of the parties contributed capital consisting of either money or land or other tangible property, or else was to receive compensation for services rendered to the common undertaking, which was to be paid before computation of the profits or losses. Where, however, as in the present case, one partner or joint venturer contributes the money capital as against the other's skill and labor, all the cases hold that neither party is liable to the other for contribution for any loss sustained. Thus, upon loss of the money, the party who contributed it is not entitled to recover any part of it from the party who contributed only services.

The rationale is that where one party contributes money and the other contributes services, then in the event of a loss each would lose his own capital—the one his money and the other his labor. Another view of it would be that the parties, by their agreement to share equally in the profits, agreed that the value of their respective contributions of money and labor were equal. Accordingly, upon incurring the loss of both money and labor, the parties have shared equally in the loss.

We also find as a matter of law that Reed's failure, if any, to file mechanic's liens did not rise to the level of gross negligence or reckless misconduct such as would constitute a breach of a partner's duty of care. It appears that, as between the parties, Kovacik was charged with the management of the enterprise. If anything, it is the duty of the managing venturer to take action against debtors of the venture to preserve and recover assets of the joint venture. Moreover, in the absence of an agreement to do so, there is no obligation on the part of one joint venturer to protect the other from loss of investment, to take steps to assist the other to recover the investment, or to reimburse him personally for advances made in the conduct of the joint business.

Indeed, if the parties here were successful in recovering what the delinquent builder owed them, Kovacik would not have a superior claim to the entire amount. The money so recovered would belong to the joint venture. It would go into the coffers of the joint venture to be used first to pay the debts and obligations of the joint venture; then, if there were a resultant profit, 50% of the profit would be paid to Reed; and only the balance would go to Kovacik toward recoupment of his investment.

We reverse and remand for entry of judgment in accordance herewith.

THE MPT

MULTISTATE PERFORMANCE TEST

In re Franklin Construction Company

POINT SHEET

The MPT point sheet, grading summary, and grading guidelines describe the factual and legal points encompassed within the lawyering task to be completed. They outline all the possible issues and points that might be addressed by an applicant. They are provided to the user jurisdictions for the sole purpose of assisting graders in grading the examination by identifying the issues and suggesting the resolution of the problem contemplated by the drafters. These are not official grading guides. Applicants can receive a range of passing grades, including excellent grades, without covering all the points discussed in these guides. The model answer is included as an illustration of a thorough and detailed response to the task, one that addresses all the legal and factual issues the drafters intended to raise in the problem. It is intended to serve only as an example. Applicants need not present their responses in the same way to receive good grades. User jurisdictions are free to modify these grading materials, including the suggested weights assigned to particular points. Grading the MPT is the exclusive responsibility of the jurisdiction using the MPT as part of its admissions process.

Copyright ©2008 by the National Conference of Bar Examiners.
All rights reserved

In Re Franklin Construction Company

DRAFTERS' POINT SHEET

In this performance test item, the applicant's firm represents Franklin Construction Company (FCC), one of two corporate parties in a failed joint venture. The applicant is asked to write an opinion letter to FCC explaining whether it is required to pay back the money the other joint venturer contributed as capital or to take action to recover the other joint venturer's capital contribution.

FCC obtained a valuable exclusive right to negotiate with the local Redevelopment Agency (the Agency) for the acquisition and development of a parcel of land. The project called for the development of a large, class A hotel involving the ultimate expenditure of $35 million. The six-month exclusive negotiation period was about to expire, and FCC had not yet secured the necessary loan commitments. FCC enlisted the aid of Millman Developers, Inc. (MDI), a large developer who FCC believed could facilitate the loan arrangements, and convinced the Agency to grant a 90-day extension of the exclusive negotiation right.

The extension was granted on the condition that FCC deposit with the Agency $350,000—1% of the project price. MDI advanced the money in consideration of a written assignment by FCC of the exclusive negotiation right to MDI. FCC and MDI then formed a joint venture called the New Millennium Hotel Venture (the Venture) evidenced by a written agreement. MDI's capital contribution to the Venture consisted of the exclusive negotiation right and the $350,000 that had been deposited with the Agency. FCC's contribution consisted of its "local expertise" and future services, such as securing building permits and approvals during the construction phase. The Joint Venture Agreement specified that MDI would receive 90% of the profits and FCC, 10%. It was silent on how the losses would be shared.

FCC and MDI were not making satisfactory progress toward securing the necessary loan commitments, so the Agency, as it had the right to do, revoked the exclusive negotiation right. The Agency has not returned the $350,000, claiming it was a nonrefundable deposit. Pursuant to an escape clause in the Joint Venture Agreement, MDI served notice on FCC that it was terminating the agreement and, in addition, has demanded that FCC take action against the Agency to recover the $350,000 and pay back that sum.

FCC seeks the advice of the applicant's firm on what its obligations are.

The following discussion covers all the points the drafters intended to raise in the problem. Applicants need not cover them all to receive passing or even excellent grades. The grading decisions are within the discretion of the graders in the user jurisdictions.

I. Overview. The assignment here is to write an opinion letter. The format is suggested in the memo from the partner, and the applicant is instructed to use the relevant authorities, explain his or her reasoning, and write the letter in language that a non-lawyer can understand. Graders should take into account how well applicants follow these instructions.

The problem breaks down into three major parts:

- Whether FCC has any contractual obligation to pay the money to either MDI or the Venture.
- Whether the statutes or case law impose any obligation on FCC to pay the money to either MDI or the Venture.
- Whether FCC has any obligation to undertake efforts to recover the money from the Redevelopment Agency.

No particular order of discussion is required, but the applicant is expected to present a well-organized letter. The analysis proceeds as follows:

II. Whether FCC has any contractual obligation to refund the money. The applicant is expected to analyze the Assignment Agreement and the Joint Venture Agreement, both of which are in the File, and to conclude that neither of those contracts requires FCC to refund the $350,000.

- **The Assignment Agreement**. It is under this agreement that the money was advanced to FCC. The advance of $350,000 was expressly conditioned on the occurrence of two things:
  - The execution by FCC and MDI within 30 days of a definitive agreement leading to the formation of an "entity" through which they would carry out the acquisition and development of the property.
    - This event occurred 26 days later when they entered into the Joint Venture Agreement.
  - Agency acceptance of MDI as a party entitled to engage in the acquisition and development of the property.
    - This event had occurred 10 days earlier when the Agency, in Resolution No. 43-99, "approved the involvement of Millman Developers, Inc., in FCC's efforts to secure the financing."
    - Although this language does not specifically say that MDI is an "authorized party to the acquisition and development of the Property," it is clear enough and was obviously construed by the parties as being the equivalent.
  - Both conditions were fulfilled. Accordingly, there was no obligation under the Assignment Agreement to refund the money.

- **The Joint Venture Agreement**. There is no real question about whether the arrangement between MDI and FCC is a joint venture. It clearly fits within the rules articulated in *Stilwell v. Trutanich*.

The only mention of the $350,000 in the capital contribution section of the Joint Venture Agreement is that "MDI assigns to the Venture...all its right, title and interest to...the $350,000 paid by MDI as the result of the attached Assignment Agreement."

- By this language, MDI is clearly making a capital contribution of whatever rights it had in the money.
- There is no express mention in the agreement about any obligation to refund the money to MDI or to the Venture on the occurrence of any event, and there appears to be nothing that gives rise to an implied obligation.
  - The closest the agreement comes is in Section M, where it provides for termination of the Venture in the event of a revocation of the exclusive negotiation right. But it would be a stretch to infer from that language an obligation on the part of FCC to refund the money.

III. Whether the law imposes any obligation on FCC to refund the money either to the Venture or to MDI. The letter from MDI demands that FCC "repay that sum." It is intentionally vague as to whether MDI is demanding that the money be refunded to it or to the Venture. The memo from the partner instructs the applicant to explain whether there is an obligation to pay the money to "*either* MDI or the Venture." This is a clue to the applicants that they should discuss the demand from both angles.

- **Applicable statutory law**. The applicants should acknowledge somewhere in their answers that, as indicated in *Stilwell v. Trutanich*, "the relationships of joint venturers among themselves are governed by the partnership laws of the State of Franklin" and that the applicable statutory law is the Uniform Partnership Act found in the Franklin Business Associations Code.

- **Obligation to pay MDI**. In the Joint Venture Agreement, MDI assigned its "right, title and interest in the $350,000" to the Venture as a capital contribution. That transfer made all rights in the money the property of the Venture.
  - Sections 203 and 204 of the Franklin Business Associations Code make it clear that property acquired by the partnership is partnership property. Therefore, the rights in the $350,000, whatever they may be, belong to the Venture.
  - Even if there were a "payback" of the $350,000, or any part of it, the repayment would have to be for the benefit of the Venture, and, under Franklin Business Associations Code § 404, MDI would have a fiduciary duty to hold it for the benefit of the Venture.
  - Accordingly, FCC has no obligation to pay the money to MDI because MDI has no present rights in it.
  - Franklin Business Associations Code §§ 401(c) and (d) are distractors.
    - Those subsections deal with the obligation of the *partnership* to reimburse a partner who makes payments on behalf of or *advances* to the partnership over and above the partner's capital contribution. The $350,000 was a capital contribution. Thus, these subsections do not apply.

- **Obligation to pay the Venture**. If FCC did not have an obligation to pay any of the money, it would be, as indicated above, an obligation to the Venture. To determine whether there is any such obligation and, if so, the extent of it, one must look to the agreement between the parties. And where, as here, the partnership/joint venture agreement is silent as to sharing of the losses, the issue is how does the law allocate the losses?
  - The general rule is stated in Franklin Business Associations Code § 401(b) and in *Stilwell v. Trutanich*. Partners or venturers are chargeable with a share of the losses in proportion to their respective shares of the profits. "[T]he law implies an obligation on the part of the joint venturers to bear losses in the same proportion as they agreed to divide the profits."

- If that rule prevailed here, FCC would be liable to the Venture for $35,000, (10% of $350,000) because, under the agreement, FCC was allocated 10% of the profits.
- However, § 401(b) incorporates § 306(a), which specifically states that "all partners are liable...for all obligations of the partnership unless otherwise...*provided by law.*"
- The rule stated in *Kovacic v. Reed* provides otherwise: "Where...one partner or joint venturer contributes the money capital as against the other's skill or labor, all the cases hold that neither party is liable to the other...for any loss sustained.... The rationale is that where one party contributes money and the other contributes services, then in the event of a loss each would lose his own capital—the one his money and the other his labor."
- In the present case, FCC contributed only "its local expertise and such assistance and services as MDI may from time to time require of it during the construction phase of the project."
- Having contributed only its services, FCC is not liable for any of the lost capital and, therefore, has no obligation to refund any of the $350,000 to the Venture.

IV. Whether FCC has any obligation to undertake efforts to recover the money from the Redevelopment Agency. Section 404 of the Franklin Business Associations Code spells out the fiduciary duties among partners or, as in this case, joint venturers. There is nothing in § 404 that imposes any duty on FCC to pursue the Redevelopment Agency. The fiduciary duty of care requires only that a partner/venturer refrain from "engaging in grossly negligent or reckless conduct, intentional misconduct, or a knowing violation of law." There is nothing here to implicate FCC in such conduct.

- Under the Joint Venture Agreement, MDI is the managing partner and, if any party has the obligation to go after the Agency, it would be MDI.
- But, FCC, which is not a managing partner of the joint venture, has no such obligation.
- As the court held in *Kovacik v. Reed*, "If anything, it is the duty of the managing venturer to take action against debtors of the venture to preserve and recover assets of the joint venture. Moreover, in the absence of an agreement to do so, there is no obligation on the part of one joint venturer to protect the other from loss of investment, [or] to take steps to assist the other to recover the investment.

MPT Task 4I:
In re Gardenton Board of Education

FILE

ALLEN, EISNER & THOMAS
Attorneys at Law
1427 Marsden Place
Gardenton, Franklin 33301
(434) 277-8901

MEMORANDUM

TO: Applicant
FROM: Frank Eisner
DATE: February 24, 1998
SUBJECT: Gardenton Board of Education—Proposed Communications Code for Gardenton High School

Dr. Edwina Kantor, the President of the Gardenton Board of Education, came to see me a few days ago about a new code to regulate the content of student communications at our public high school, Gardenton High. At its next meeting, the Board wants to present for public comment the most restrictive communications code permissible, one that gives the school the greatest flexibility to prevent the publication of offensive material. Dr. Kantor wants me to meet with and advise the Board in advance of that meeting and to be prepared to respond to comments from members of the public who have signed up to speak pro and con about the code.

Over the last few months, parents and civic groups have objected to what they consider to be intemperate, irresponsible reporting, profanity, and sexually charged material of questionable taste appearing in the various student media.

I've included in the file a transcript of my conversation with Dr. Kantor so you can get a better idea of what the issues are and how she'd like to have this matter resolved.

Please prepare a memorandum in which you evaluate the preamble and each of the guideline provisions in the draft of the communications code that Dr. Kantor left with me. Identify the legal issues that can give rise to constitutional challenges to each of the provisions and analyze whether each such provision is likely to be found legally permissible. Make suggestions for deleting, modifying, or adding any items in order to help the Board achieve its goal. Be sure to state your reasons for concluding that each guideline provision is legally permissible or impermissible, as well as the reasons for any suggestions you make. Support your reasons with appropriate discussion of the facts and law.

TRANSCRIPT OF DISCUSSION WITH DR. EDWINA KANTOR

Lawyer: Thanks for allowing me to record this discussion, Dr. Kantor. It'll make it easier to reconstruct it later on.

Kantor: That's fine. This problem is becoming a real headache.

Lawyer: Tell me what the situation is.

Kantor: With increasing frequency, we've been getting complaints from local residents, some city leaders, parents, and various church and civic groups about the degenerating quality of the subject matter being reported in The Weekly Cougar and the language being used by students in their student theatrical and video productions. In fact, we've come pretty close to being sued for defamation by a number of really irate citizens who've read or seen things published about themselves or their families.

Lawyer: The Weekly Cougar—that's the student newspaper, right?

Kantor: That's right. It's published by the students in the senior journalism class. Students in drama and theatrical arts classes also publish plays. The performances are produced a couple of times a year. Sometimes there are live performances and sometimes the plays are filmed or videotaped by the students in the cinematography department and then shown in the auditorium or in classrooms in lieu of live plays.

Lawyer: Is the Cougar circulated beyond the student body? Who is invited to attend the student theatrical productions?

Kantor: Well, we don't consciously circulate the Cougar off campus. It's intended to be an educational vehicle for training students, but there's nothing to prevent anyone who's interested from getting copies. In order to finance the costs, the students solicit advertisements from local merchants and business operators. But it's not a newspaper of general circulation. As far as the theatrical productions are concerned, the regular annual live performances are made up mostly of students and their friends and relatives. Some of the smaller productions—I mean videos and films—are just for student consumption. We've never tried to open either the live plays or the smaller productions to the public at large.

Lawyer: What's the problem?

Kantor: Well, the student reporters for the Cougar have reported stories about individuals, relying on rumor and innuendo, without verifying the facts, without exercising mature judgment, and generally exceeding the boundaries of responsible journalism. They have used some profanity in their stories. They just don't have the experience to know better. As a result, there have been some pretty defamatory and tasteless things published. The plays and theatrical productions have sometimes bordered on being obscene. They frequently deal with sexually charged and morally questionable subject matter that parents, community leaders, and civic groups have found offensive. And, I've got to tell you that I agree with them.

Lawyer: Haven't the school administrators and classroom teachers been able to control the contents sufficiently to avoid these problems?

K Kantor: Not really. It's not that they don't want to. It's just that they haven't had any guidelines, and they've been unsure how far they can go to squelch what some people say is free speech The Board has worked up some guidelines as part of a communications code that we'd like to implement. I'll just leave this copy with you.

Lawyer: All right. Where would you like to end up with this thing?

Kantor: Well, in the best of worlds, we'd like to be able to implement each and every one of the controls we've listed in the draft. It was supposed to be a working draft and was supposed to be kept secret until we were ready to go public with it. Somehow it got out, and the next thing we know the opposition groups are coming out of the woodwork, and we're being threatened with litigation from both sides. The Union for Freedom of Speech is threatening to sue us if we promulgate any code at all, and the Gardenton Civic League is threatening to sue us if we don't. We really want to go as far as the law will allow us in controlling what the kids can publish and in giving the school district and the high school administration something they can enforce without being tied up in litigation. We have to satisfy the parents and the community that we're doing something to curb the problem and, at the same time, convince the students and free speech activists that what we're doing is within the law.

Lawyer: What, specifically, can I do to help?

Kantor: The next public meeting of the Board is scheduled for a week from Friday. The public session begins at 8:00 p.m. We already know from the sign-up list that there are going to be a lot of speakers on both sides of the issue. We are particularly concerned about the Union for Freedom of Speech, which we believe is champing at the bit to sue us. They've told us they'll sue to enjoin us. I think they believe that publication of any code would be a violation of the students' constitutional right of free speech.

We'd like you to meet with us before the meeting to advise us on whether or not the draft of the guidelines is something we can lawfully implement. If not, tell us why not, and tell us what we can do. We're not wedded to all the items in the draft. The main thing is that we be able to censor unacceptable language and morally questionable subject matter that runs counter to our educational goals, especially things that open us up to suits for libel and slander and invasion of privacy.

Lawyer: What about procedures for implementing the guidelines?

Kantor: One step at a time. First, let's get agreement on these substantive guidelines at the Board meeting. Then we can turn our attention to the procedures for applying them. Later on, we'll draft some procedures and ask you to look at them.

Lawyer: OK, Dr. Kantor. Let me get to work. I'll see you at the Board meeting at 6:00 p.m. 4 April 26, 2001

LIBRARY

The Constitution of the United States: Amendment 1

Congress shall make no law respecting an establishment of religion, or prohibiting the free exercise thereof; or abridging the freedom of speech, or of the press; or the right of the people peaceably to assemble, and to petition the Government for a redress of grievances.

Constitution of the State of Franklin: Article I

Section 2. Every person may freely speak, write, or publish his or her sentiments on all subjects, being responsible for the abuse of this right. A law may not restrain or abridge liberty of speech or press.

Franklin Education Act: Section 48. Student Exercise of Freedom of Speech or Press

Students of public schools shall have the right to exercise freedom of speech and of the press including, but not limited to, the use of bulletin boards, the distribution of printed materials or petitions, the wearing of buttons, badges, and other insignia, and the right of expression in official publications, whether or not such publications or other means of expression are supported financially by the school or by use of school facilities, except that expression is prohibited which is obscene, libelous, or slanderous. Also prohibited shall be material which so incites students as to create a clear and present danger of the commission of unlawful acts on school premises or the violation of lawful school regulations, or the substantial disruption of the orderly operation of the school.

Student editors of official school publications shall be responsible for assigning and editing the news, editorial, and feature content of their publications subject to the limitations of this section. However, it shall be the responsibility of journalism advisers or advisers of student publications within each school to supervise the production of the student staff, to maintain professional standards of English and journalism, and to maintain the provisions of this section.

"Official school publications" refers to material produced by students in the journalism, newspaper, yearbook, or writing classes and distributed to the student body either free or for a fee.

STUDENT COMMUNICATIONS CODE FOR GARDENTON HIGH SCHOOL

Preamble:

This Communications Code shall apply to all student publications and media representations produced either as a result of course work or intramural extracurricular activities that are published, distributed, or otherwise disseminated on or off campus. This code shall apply to school newspapers, yearbooks, plays and other literary publications, films, movies, videos, signs, posters, and other photographic productions and graphic displays.

Guidelines for Student Publications and Productions:

1. All student publications and productions shall maintain professional standards of English language and journalistic style.
2. All student publications and productions shall avoid language and depictions that are not in good taste, having regard for the age, experience, and maturity of the general student population.
3. No stories or reports of events shall be published unless the accuracy of the facts and any quotations from individuals have first been verified to the satisfaction of the teacher supervising the publication.
4. No person shall be quoted or photographically depicted in any student publication or production without that person's prior permission and, in the case of a minor, the permission of the minor's parent or guardian, except that persons posing for group photographs shall be deemed to have given their implied consent.
5. No publication, literary piece, play, film, video, or other student production shall include material that:
   a. is libelous or slanderous or violates any person's right of privacy;
   b. contains profanity, which means language that would not customarily be used in local newspapers, to wit: The Gardenton Times or The Morning Herald;
   c. criticizes or demeans any public official, including officials, administrators, and teachers of the school; or
   d. is deemed by the principal not to be in the school's best interest.
6. Material must receive the prior approval of the principal before it is published, distributed or otherwise disseminated.

Procedures for Implementation: [to come later.]

Hazelwood School District v. Kuhlmeier

United States Supreme Court (1988)

Respondents contend that school district officials violated their First Amendment rights by deleting two pages of articles from the May 13, 1983 issue of *Spectrum*, the Hazelwood High School student newspaper. Written and edited by the Journalism II class at Hazelwood High, the newspaper was distributed to students, school personnel, and members of the community.

The practice at Hazelwood was for the journalism teacher, Robert Mackinac, to submit each *Spectrum* issue to Eugene Reynolds, the school principal, for his review prior to publication. On May 10, Reynolds objected to two of the articles scheduled to appear in the May 13 edition. One of the stories described three Hazelwood students' experiences with pregnancy; the other discussed the impact of divorce on students at the school, quoting a student's remarks about the cause of her parents' divorce. Reynolds directed Mackinac to withhold the two stories from publication.

The district court found that Principal Reynolds' concern that the pregnant students' anonymity would be lost and their privacy invaded was "legitimate and reasonable," given "the small number of pregnant students at Hazelwood and several identifying characteristics that were disclosed in the article." The deletion of the article on divorce was seen by the court as a reasonable response to the invasion of privacy concerns raised by the named student's remarks. Because the student's parents had not been offered an opportunity to respond, there was cause for "serious doubt that the article complied with the rules of fairness which are standard in the field of journalism and were covered in the textbook used in the Journalism II class."

The Court of Appeals for the Eighth Circuit reversed. We granted certiorari, and we now reverse the decision of the Eighth Circuit and affirm the district court.

The First Amendment rights of students in the public schools are not automatically coextensive with the rights of adults in other settings and must be applied in the special circumstances of the school environment. A school need not tolerate student speech that is inconsistent with its basic educational mission, even though the government could not censor similar speech outside the school.

Accordingly, we have held that a school could discipline a student for having delivered a speech that was "sexually explicit" but not legally obscene at an official school assembly, because the school was entitled to disassociate itself from the speech in a manner that would demonstrate to others that such vulgarity is wholly inconsistent with the fundamental values of public school education. The determination of what manner of speech in the classroom or in school assembly is inappropriate properly rests with the school board, rather than with the federal courts. It is in this context that respondents' First Amendment claims must be considered.

We deal first with the question of whether *Spectrum* may appropriately be characterized as a forum for public expression. The public schools do not possess all the attributes of streets, parks, and other traditional forums that have been used for purposes of assembly and discussion of public questions. Hence, school facilities may be deemed to be public forums only if school authorities have by policy or practice opened those facilities for indiscriminate use by the general public or by some segment of the public, such as student organizations. The government does not create a public forum by inaction or by permitting limited discourse, but only by intentionally opening a nontraditional forum for public discourse.

Educators have authority over school-sponsored publications, theatrical productions, and other expressive activities that students, parents, and members of the public might reasonably perceive to bear the imprimatur of the school. These activities may fairly be characterized as part of the school curriculum so long as they are supervised by faculty members and designed to impart particular knowledge or skills to student participants and audiences.

Educators are entitled to exercise greater control over this form of student expression to assure that participants learn whatever lessons the activity is designed to teach, that readers or listeners are not exposed to material that may be inappropriate for their level of maturity, and that the views of the individual speaker are not erroneously attributed to the school. Hence, a school may in its capacity as publisher of a school newspaper or producer of a school play disassociate itself not only from speech that would substantially interfere with its work or impinge upon the rights of other students, but also from speech that is, for example, ungrammatical, poorly written, inadequately researched, biased or prejudiced, vulgar or profane, or unsuitable for immature audiences. A school must be able to set standards that may be higher than those demanded in the "real" world.

In addition, on potentially sensitive topics, a school must be able to take into account the emotional maturity of the intended audience. Sensitive topics *might* range from the existence of Santa Claus in an elementary school setting to the particulars of teenage sexual activity in a high school setting. A school must also retain the authority to refuse to associate the school with any position other than neutrality on matters of political controversy. It is only when the decision to censor a school-sponsored publication, theatrical production, or other vehicle of student expression has no valid educational purpose that the First Amendment is so directly and sharply implicated as to require judicial intervention to protect students' constitutional rights.

We cannot reject as unreasonable Principal Reynolds' conclusion that the students who wrote these articles had not sufficiently mastered those portions of the Journalism II curriculum that pertained to the treatment of controversial issues and personal attacks, the need to protect the privacy of individuals whose most intimate concerns are to be revealed in the newspaper, and the legal, moral, and ethical restrictions imposed upon journalists within a school community that includes adolescent subjects and readers. Accordingly, no violation of the First Amendment occurred.

Lopez v. Union High School District

Franklin Supreme Court (1994)

The issue presented is whether a school district is precluded by Section 48 of the Education Act and Article I, Section 2, of the Franklin Constitution from requiring, on the ground of educational suitability, that a film arts class instructor have his students delete the profanity in a student-produced film. We hold that school authorities may restrain such expression because it violates the "professional standards of English and journalism" provision of Section 48.

Plaintiffs, students at Union High School, wrote and produced a film entitled *Melancholianne* in a film arts class. The film addresses the problems faced by teenaged parents. The film dialogue contains profanity and references to sexual activity that the students believed made the film characters more realistic and "real world." The school principal, upon review of the draft of the script, found the language highly offensive and educationally unsuitable. After public hearings, the school board held that "sound educational policy," as well as a district administrative regulation required that the profanity be deleted.[1] Plaintiffs sued for declaratory and injunctive relief challenging the censorship of the videotape script.[2]

We need not decide whether the legislature intended to include the profanity at issue within the term "obscene expression." Legislative history demonstrates the legislature intended to preclude the students' use of "four-letter words" under the auspices of the "professional standards of English and journalism" provision of Section 48. The words of the statute permit prior restraint of material prepared for official school publications when the material "violates" the statute. Further, the legislative history of Section 48 indicates the legislature did not intend to protect student expression that constitutes profanity, especially when the expression is aimed at minors rather than adults. The school authorities have a substantial interest in protecting the student audience from expression that could be embarrassing or detrimental to their stage of development. Censorship of "four-letter words" does not unduly hinder the students' ability to express their ideas or opinions on any subject. It enjoins only the indecent manner in which an idea is expressed.

Having concluded that Section 48 permits prior restraint of profane student expression in official student publications, we must consider whether such restraint is constitutional under the federal or state constitutions. The question is easily answered under the First Amendment. Teaching students to avoid vulgar and profane language is obviously a legitimate pedagogical concern and proper under the First Amendment. *Hazelwood School District v. Kuhlmeier* (U.S. Supreme Court, 1988).

The answer is the same under the Franklin Constitution. This court has adopted a forum analysis to determine when the government's interest in limiting the use of its property to its intended purpose outweighs the interest of those wishing to use the property for other purposes. We have divided public property into three categories: public, nonpublic, and limited.

A public forum is the traditional soapbox in a town square; no one can be denied access, and prior restraints are rarely permissible. A nonpublic forum is public property that is not a public forum by tradition or design, such as a military base or a jail or a "house organ" school bulletin for dissemination of educational or administrative information to students or faculty, over which school officials retain full power to regulate access and content.

The so-called limited forum is property the state has opened for expressive activity by part or all of the public. "Official school publications" in Franklin fall into the limited forum category. *Melancholianne* is conceptually no different from a school yearbook or newspaper produced in a journalism class. While the primary purpose for producing the videotape is to teach the students writing and film-making skills, the film also serves as an avenue of student expression. Thus, *Melancholianne* is a limited public forum.

When a school publication is deemed to be a limited public forum, school officials must demonstrate that the particular regulation of student expression advances a compelling state interest. Here, the compelling state interests advanced by the board are to maintain an environment where the educational process may occur without disruption, to teach students the boundaries of socially appropriate behavior, to promote "moral improvement," and to teach students to refrain from the use of profane and vulgar language.

School officials must also show that the speech regulations are narrowly drawn to achieve the compelling interest and sufficiently precise to avoid a challenge on grounds that they are void for vagueness. The board has done so here. The board has not censored the students' expression of ideas; rather, the board has prohibited their expression of those ideas by the use of profane language. The board's directive cannot be construed as the type of censorship we have deemed unconstitutional—censorship based on a disagreement with the views presented or censorship designed to avoid discussion of controversial issues. Rather, the board's directive was content neutral and served a valid pedagogical purpose.

Accordingly, the judgment is affirmed.

---

[1] The administrative regulation in question is a "Student Publications Code" that, among other things, confers upon school authorities the power to require that school-sponsored publications maintain "professional standards of English grammar and journalistic writing style" and to prohibit the publication of "obscene" or "profane" material, defining those terms to mean language that would not ordinarily be used in certain specified local newspapers of general circulation.

[2] The parties have not raised or briefed the issue of whether the video is an "official school publication" within the meaning of Section 48. Nevertheless, we see no policy reason for distinguishing between student expression in school-sponsored activities solely on the basis of the medium by which the expression is conveyed.

Leeb v. DeLong
Franklin Court of Appeal (1999)

David Leeb was the student editor of the Rancho High School newspaper. On March 29, 1994, Leeb submitted for the school principal's approval, as required by the school district's communication code, the April Fool's edition. An article appeared under the headline "Nude Photos: Girls of Rancho." According to the article, the July issue of Playboy magazine would carry nude photographs of Rancho students, and those interested in posing should sign up at the school darkroom. The article was accompanied by a photograph of five fully clothed female students standing in line with their school books, purportedly with applications in hand. Principal DeLong recognized each of them.

Mr. DeLong formed the opinion that "the article and photograph taken together are damaging to the reputation of each of the girls in the photograph." He was also of the view that the reputation of the school and the school district would be injured by the publication of the material. On March 30, he prohibited distribution of the newspaper. Leeb sued for declaratory and injunctive relief, and the court below granted summary judgment in favor of the school district.

Section 48 of the Education Act and Franklin decisional authority clearly confer editorial control of official student publications on the student editors alone, with very limited exceptions. The broad power to censor in school-sponsored publications for pedagogical purposes recognized by the U.S. Supreme Court in *Hazelwood School District v. Kuhlmeier* (1988) is not available to this state's educators. Student free speech rights under Section 48 are broader than rights arising under the First Amendment.

Under Education Act Section 48, a school district may constitutionally censor expression from official school publications which it reasonably believes to contain an actionable defamation. A school district may not, however, censor defamatory material that is not actionable because it is privileged or deals with a public figure without malice. *New York Times v. Sullivan* (U.S. Supreme Court, 1964). For example, an article suggesting that a public official is wrong, illogical, or was a poor choice for office could never lead to a recovery in tort, and could for that reason not be suppressed. But the girls in the photograph in this case are not public figures, and the principal's concerns were justifiable. The censorship in this case was not, therefore, precluded either by the federal or state constitutions or by Section 48.

To the extent that the school district's communication code suggests that an article such as one mentioned above about a public official could be censored, the code should be amended. The code should also be amended to require that any decision to delete an item thought to be defamatory should, insofar as it is possible, be limited to the offending material itself.

Judgment affirmed.

THE MPT
MULTISTATE PERFORMANCE TEST

In re Gardenton Board of Education

POINT SHEET

The MPT point sheet, grading summary, and grading guidelines describe the factual and legal points encompassed within the lawyering task to be completed. They outline all the possible issues and points that might be addressed by an applicant. They are provided to the user jurisdictions for the sole purpose of assisting graders in grading the examination by identifying the issues and suggesting the resolution of the problem contemplated by the drafters. These are not official grading guides. Applicants can receive a range of passing grades, including excellent grades, without covering all the points discussed in these guides. The model answer is included as an illustration of a thorough and detailed response to the task, one that addresses all the legal and factual issues the drafters intended to raise in the problem. It is intended to serve only as an example. Applicants need not present their responses in the same way to receive good grades. User jurisdictions are free to modify these grading materials, including the suggested weights assigned to particular points. Grading the MPT is the exclusive responsibility of the jurisdiction using the MPT as part of its admissions process.

Copyright ©2008 by the National Conference of Bar Examiners.
All rights reserved

In re Gardenton Board of Education

DRAFTERS' POINT SHEET

This performance test deals principally with constitutional law and prior restraints, i.e., the First Amendment rights of high school students in the context of school-sponsored publications. It requires applicants to make a factual and legal analysis of a proposed Communications Code (the "Code") in light of state and federal constitutional provisions as modified by statutes and case law. The task for the applicants is to prepare a memorandum to a partner of the law firm telling the partner how the proposed Code complies with or departs from the law and to make suggestions for improvement of the Code. The memorandum should be written as if it were a communication to a layperson, as opposed to a communication to a lawyer. Thus, one should expect to see the use of legal terms and citations to statutes and case law. We expect the applicants to follow the directions contained in the file memo from the partner:

- Explore the law in the library, draw conclusions as to how far the school board can push the envelope, and give reasons for those conclusions; and
- Go through each item in the draft Code, state whether it is legally permissible, if need be suggest changes to make it legally permissible, and give reasons for the suggested changes.

Following are the points that emerge from the problem and that should be recognized by the applicants:

1. Legal Analysis:

- There is a tension between the free speech rights that arise under the state and federal constitutions on the one hand, and Section 48 on the other. Section 48 confers upon the students' broader free speech rights than do the constitutional provisions as interpreted by the cases in the library. It also purports to give them editorial control, with certain specified exceptions.
- The "professional standards of English and journalistic style" provision of Section 48 is the board's best argument why it has the power to "clean up" the student publications. Using that as the rationale avoids disputes over whether something is obscene or actionable.
- Ostensibly, Section 48 allows prior restraints only in cases of actionable libel and slander, obscenity, clear and present danger, and situations that would result in violation of the statute. There is language in the case law that suggests that the "professional standards" provisions of the statute allow prior restraint in other circumstances as well. Applicants should be able to reconcile these apparent differences.
- The level of court scrutiny will be determined by whether and to what extent the school-sponsored student publications are "public forums." The case law suggests that a student newspaper is a "limited public forum" and that, therefore, a high level of scrutiny is warranted. The facts suggest that perhaps the public performances of school plays might be "public forums" and subject to yet a higher level of scrutiny. Perceptive applicants will pick up on this nuance.
- There is an issue, resolved by the case law, of whether plays, videos, films, etc. are even covered by the statute or whether it only applies to the "print media" and the publications specifically mentioned in Section 48.
- To what extent do the educational goals of the school and its obligation to inculcate values in the students expand its power to exercise prior restraint? There is language in the cases that deals with this point and with which applicants must deal.
- There are references in the Code to "good taste," "having regard for age, experience, and maturity of the general student population," and the like. Applicants should raise questions about whether such terms are too vague to withstand legal scrutiny.
- To the extent that the Code (in the Preamble) purports to regulate off-campus speech, it is probably too broad, although there is language in the cases to suggest that if the speaker attempts to link it to school-sponsored activity, the school has the right to disassociate itself by taking action to demonstrate to the community that the school does not approve. Is that justification for off-campus regulation? Probably not.
- Overall, the promulgation of a Code is permissible, but the proposed Code needs to be modified in several respects. *Leeb v. DeLong* is a source for ideas about such modifications.

2. Evaluation of the Proposed Code:

- The scope of the Code as stated in the Preamble (i.e., applying to "all student publications and media representations") is all right. The case law supports a broad interpretation of the statute on this point. Restricting the off-campus distribution of unapproved materials is problematic. The argument in favor of it is that the school has a right to "disassociate" itself, and any case law to deal with is sui generis. In *Leeb*, however, the court notes that the broad powers which Hazelwood ascribes under the First Amendment are not available here because Section 48 confers upon the students broader speech rights than does the First Amendment. Applicants should recognize this point and might suggest that the off-campus provision should be stricken and troublesome situations handled ad hoc.
- Item 1: Measuring the "professional standards" against local newspapers is the statutory standard (see Section 48) and has the apparent approval of the courts.
- Item 2: The "good taste" language used here is probably too vague to be enforceable and should be modified to be measured against something like local newspapers. The "age, experience, and maturity" provision has received case law approval.
- Item 3: The requirement that facts and quotations be checked for accuracy before publication is probably all right. The case law and the statute suggest that it is part of teaching a high school course in journalism to encourage accurate reporting. Applicants should note, however, that this conflicts to some degree with the provision of Section 48, which confers editorial control on the students, and that it might, nevertheless, be an impermissible prior restraint.
- Item 4: The requirement for obtaining prior permission for quotes and photographs is probably all right. It is supported by Section 48 and the cases.
- Item 5a: Prohibiting libel, slander, and invasion of privacy by prior restraint is all right, both under the Education Act and the case law.
- Item 5b: Measuring "profanity" against local newspapers is approved by the case law, and regulating profanity by prior restraint is all right. Nevertheless, any publication using local newspapers as the standard of measurement is susceptible of a "void for vagueness" argument.
- Item 5c: The prohibition against criticizing public officials is patently unlawful. Because of *New York Times v. Sullivan*, it is highly unlikely that any such criticism would be actionable defamation. This item should probably be stricken.
- Item 5d: The power to determine what is "not in the school's best interest" is probably too broad and vague to withstand scrutiny. Unless some very restrictive limitations are imposed, this provision should be stricken.
- Item 6: There is nothing wrong in principle with requiring prior approval from the principal. It appears to be supported by the case law.

MPT Task 4J:
In re Steven Wallace

Piper, Morales & Singh
Attorneys at Law
One Dalton Place
West Keystone, Franklin 33322

MEMORANDUM

To: Applicant
From: Eva Morales
Date: July 27, 1999
Subject: Steven Wallace—Painting Titled "Hare Castle"

Steven Wallace, a long-time friend of mine, recently retired as Chair of the English Department at the University of Franklin to pursue full time what has until now been his avocation as an artist. He came in yesterday to get my advice and brought the documents I've included in the file. On reviewing the file, I can see that there are other facts we need in order to advise him properly.

About a year ago, Steven left one of his paintings, a canvas he had titled "Hare Castle," with Lottie Zelinka, an art dealer friend of his, with the understanding that she would try to sell it for him. Ms. Zelinka is the owner of Artists' Exchange, an art gallery here in West Keystone. Ten days or so ago, Ms. Zelinka returned the painting to Steven. A few days ago, he received a letter from Martin Feldner, a bankruptcy practitioner here in town. Mr. Feldner represents Charles Sims, the court-appointed Trustee in Bankruptcy. The letter advises Steven that Ms. Zelinka has filed for bankruptcy and demands that Steven turn "Hare Castle" over to the Trustee in Bankruptcy. Naturally, Steven is upset by this turn of events and wants to know how to respond.

Please draft for me a two-part memorandum:

- First, analyze the legal and factual bases of the trustee's claim that the painting is an asset of the bankruptcy estate under the Bankruptcy Act and the Franklin Commercial Code (FCC).
- Second, for each of the four defenses under FCC § 2-326(3), discuss how the facts we already know support the defense, identify additional facts that might be helpful to us, state why they would be helpful, and indicate from what sources we might be able to obtain them.

NOTES OF JULY 26, 1999 MEETING WITH STEVEN WALLACE

- Steven can't believe this letter he got (copy attached) two days ago—a bankruptcy attorney is demanding that Steven turn over one of his best paintings ("Hare Castle") to a Trustee.
- A friend of his, Lottie Zelinka, has an art gallery in West Keystone—the gallery is called Artists' Exchange. She operates it as a sole proprietorship.
- Lottie has a sizeable inventory of paintings and sculptures—Steven thinks (but isn't sure) that most of the art in the gallery is on consignment from artists and that Lottie doesn't really own it. That's how Steven and every other artist he knows deal with the galleries in town—i.e., by consignment. He's pretty sure that's how galleries work everywhere. Maybe Lottie owns some of the art, but, mainly, she shows the art, sells it for the artists, and makes her money on the sales commissions.
- Steven thinks (but is not sure) Lottie had placed a sign in the window at the front of the gallery that said something like, "All offers will be considered and forwarded to the artists."
- About a year ago, Lottie was at Steven's house for dinner with Steven and Ella, his wife. Lottie saw "Hare Castle" (oil on canvas—about 2' x 3') hanging on the dining room wall. She admired it and said she thought she could sell it for "a lot of money," maybe as much as $25,000 (some of Steven's recent paintings have been fetching pretty good prices, but he'd never thought about trying to sell "Hare Castle"—it was one of his favorite paintings and had been hanging in his dining room since he finished it a couple of years ago). Lottie told Steven, if he's interested, to bring it to her gallery and she'd put it up for sale.
- Steven and Ella talked it over and, although they had recently purchased a new rug for their dining room that coordinated with the colors in the painting, $25,000 sounded like a lot of money, so they decided to see if Lottie was right. Steven took "Hare Castle" to Lottie's gallery, they did some paperwork (copies attached), and Steven left the painting with Lottie. He had put a label (about 2" x 3") on the back of the painting that said: "Hare Castle—Property of Steven Wallace (+ his address and phone number)."
- From time to time, Lottie called Steven to tell him about offers for the canvas—three offers all told—the highest one for $6,000. Steven rejected them—not enough money.
- Maybe 10 days ago, Lottie called Steven at about 10 p.m.—told him she was going to come right over and leave "Hare Castle" at his house—she didn't think she could sell it and she needed the space in the gallery. He thought it was strange, but he didn't ask any questions and Lottie didn't let on that anything was unusual. Now he realizes she tried to do him a favor by returning the painting—apparently, she filed for bankruptcy.
- Steven is now into painting full time—retired from Univ. of Franklin at the end of the last school year. His paintings seem to have caught on, and he's been selling more and more of them (in fact, he has offered to buy back for $750 paintings he originally sold for $500—says he can probably sell them now for $2,500).
- He now has a studio in a loft on Parker St.—up until now, he's been working out of a spare room at home.
- Steven can't believe he jeopardizes his paintings every time he puts them up for sale in a gallery!

Artist's Exchange
West Keystone's Premier Gallery
9 Wharf Alley
West Keystone, Franklin 33322
(555) 942-5060

Inventory Receipt

Date: August 15, 1998
Artist: Steven Wallace
Agent: none
Address: 749 Galewood Circle
West Keystone, Franklin 33322
Phone: (555) 942-3342

Medium	Inventory Number	Size	Title	Artist's Net
Oil/Canvas	C 6076	2' x 3'	Hare Castle	Sale price minus 40% commission to Gallery

General Conditions:

The item(s) of artwork listed above is (are) being placed by the Artist or his/her agent, as consignor, on consignment with Artists' Exchange (Gallery), as consignee, to be sold by Gallery for the account of Artist. Artist retains title to the artwork until sold by Gallery. Gallery makes no representations regarding its ability to sell any or all of said artwork or the sales price thereof. Gallery may return artwork to Artist at any time if not sold. All offers shall be communicated to Artist by Gallery, and Artist shall have the right to accept or reject any offers. Artist shall have the right to determine price of sale, except that if an offer exceeds the appraised value of the artwork plus the amount of Gallery's commission, Artist shall be required to accept the offer. Risk of loss over and above amount of Gallery's liability and hazard insurance shall be borne by Artist. Artist's Net shall be paid to Artist upon payment in full of sale price by buyer.

Lottie Zelinka
Artists' Exchange
By: Lottie Zelinka

Steven Wallace
Artist or Agent

Martin R. Feldner
Attorney at Law
2298 West Arden Boulevard
West Keystone, Franklin 33322
(555) 942-4324

July 23, 1999

Mr. Steven Wallace
749 Galewood Circle
West Keystone, Franklin 33322

Re: In the Matter of Lottie Zelinka dba
Artists' Exchange
Bkpcy No. 980-7 (99)

Dear Mr. Wallace:

I represent Charles A. Sims, Trustee in Bankruptcy in the Chapter 7 bankruptcy case of *Lottie Zelinka dba Artists' Exchange* ("Debtor"). The Debtor filed a petition for bankruptcy under Chapter 11 of the Bankruptcy Act on May 25, 1999. She converted the case to a liquidation under Chapter 7 on July 19, 1999, on which date Mr. Sims was appointed trustee.

The Debtor has recently provided us with an accounting and business records detailing certain actions taken by her after the filing of the petition. According to Ms. Zelinka, she transferred a piece of artwork titled "Hare Castle" to you on July 20, 1999. The transfer was improper under Franklin Commercial Code § 2-326 and § 544 of the Bankruptcy Act.

The Trustee has elected to exercise his power under § 549 of the Bankruptcy Act to avoid improper transfers made during the pendency of a bankruptcy case. Accordingly, demand is hereby made that you forthwith return to the Trustee the artwork titled "Hare Castle" or all proceeds from the sale thereof. If you fail to do so within 15 days of the date of this letter, the Trustee will commence legal action to recover the artwork or the proceeds.

Very truly yours,

Martin R. Feldner

Martin R. Feldner

APPRAISAL

APPRAISAL OF ARTWORK

Date: August 15, 1998

Title: "Hare Castle"

Artist: Steven Wallace

Medium: Original Oil on Canvas

Value: $25,000.00

Owner: Steven Wallace

THE ABOVE INFORMATION IS TRUE AND CORRECT
TO THE BEST OF OUR KNOWLEDGE.

Signed: *Lottie Zelinka*
Lottie Zelinka

Title: Owner
ARTISTS' EXCHANGE

LIBRARY

Walker On Bankruptcy (3d. Ed. 1995)
A Short Course for the Non-Bankruptcy Lawyer

* * *

§ 4 – Definitions:

§ 4.07 – Chapter 11: A petition for a Chapter 11 "reorganization" commences a proceeding in which the insolvent debtor continues to operate as an ongoing business with certain restrictions. The business operates by the direction of the Bankruptcy Court under the management either of a court-appointed trustee or the debtor (debtor-in-possession). The Bankruptcy Act provides for an automatic stay of legal and self-help proceedings against the debtor pending the preparation and execution of a "plan of arrangement" pursuant to which the debtor "works out" its obligations to its creditors over an extended period of time.

§ 4.08 – Chapter 7: Often, Chapter 11 proceedings that fail are converted to Chapter 7 cases. A petition for bankruptcy under Chapter 7 commences a proceeding for liquidation of the debtor's assets for the benefit of its creditors. A court-appointed trustee takes possession of the business, including all items in inventory, which thereafter come under the exclusive control of the trustee. The trustee is vested with all the rights possessed by the creditors of the bankrupt debtor prior to the filing of the petition. The trustee's principal function is to marshal and, subject to the rights of secured creditors, sell the assets and distribute the proceeds proportionately to the creditors in accordance with their interests. Under § 549 of the Bankruptcy Act, "the trustee may avoid a transfer of property of the estate…that occurs after commencement of the case…."

* * *

§ 4.27 – Schedules of Assets, Debts, and Creditors: It is incumbent on the debtor in any bankruptcy proceeding to file with the court schedules of its assets, debts and creditors. All property, including goods delivered on consignment and accounts receivable, in which the debtor has any interest must be described and its location shown on the schedule of assets. Likewise, the amount of each debt and the name and address of the creditor to whom each debt is owed are required to be listed on the schedules of debts and creditors, with designations in each case as to whether the particular creditor is secured or unsecured. The schedules of secured creditors must describe with particularity the property of the debtor in which the creditor has a security interest.

Franklin Commercial Code

* * *

§ 2-326. Sale on Approval and Sale or Return; Consignment Sales and Rights of Creditors.

(1) Unless otherwise agreed, if delivered goods may be returned by the buyer even though they conform to the contract, the transaction is

    (a) a "sale on approval" if the goods are delivered primarily for use, and

    (b) a "sale or return" if the goods are delivered primarily for resale.

(2) Except as provided in subsection (3), goods held on approval are not subject to claims of the buyer's creditors until acceptance; goods held on sale or return are subject to such claims while in the buyer's possession.

(3) Where goods are delivered to a person for sale and such person maintains a place of business at which he deals in goods of the kind involved, under a name other than the name of the person making the delivery, then, with respect to claims of creditors of the person conducting the business, the goods are deemed to be on sale or return. The provisions of this subsection are applicable even though an agreement purports to reserve title to the person making delivery until payment or resale or uses such words as "on consignment" or "on memorandum." However, this subsection is not applicable if the person making the delivery

    (a) complies with an applicable law providing for a consignor's interest or the like to be evidenced by a sign, or

    (b) establishes that the person conducting the business is generally known by his creditors to be substantially engaged in selling goods of others, or

    (c) complies with the filing of provisions of the Article on Secured Transactions (Article 9), or

    (d) delivers goods which the person making delivery used or bought for personal, family, or household purposes.

Franklin Civil Code

§ 3533 - Sign Law.

If a person transacts business and identifies his place of business by a sign and fails by another sign or signs in letters easy to read and posted conspicuously in his place of business to state that he is dealing in property in which others have an interest and identifying such property, then all the property, stock of goods, money, and choses in action used or acquired in such business shall, as to the creditors of such person, be liable for his debts and be in all respects treated in favor of his creditors as his property unless the provisions of Franklin Commercial Code § 2-326(3)(b) through (d) are applicable.

First National Bank v. Marigold Farms, Inc.

Franklin Court of Appeal

In this case, we determine the priority of the claims of First National Bank (the Bank) and Marigold Farms, Inc. (Marigold) to $139,000 in a bank account (the Fund) of Pacific Wholesalers (Pacific). The trial court held that the Bank was entitled to the Fund. Marigold appeals.

The Bank had loaned $600,000 to Pacific and Pacific, in turn, had executed a security agreement granting the Bank a security interest in certain assets of Pacific. The Bank had perfected its security interest by filing a financing statement with the Secretary of State. Pacific defaulted on the loan and the Bank sued. Pacific and the Bank negotiated a settlement pursuant to which cash received by Pacific in the conduct of its business would be delivered to the Bank and applied to the balance of the loan. Marigold asserted claims to the same cash and also asserted that its claims had priority over any claim of the Bank. The court approved the settlement subject to resolution of the competing claims of Marigold and the Bank and ordered $139,000 of Pacific's cash receipts held in a "blocked" account (i.e., the Fund).

The facts of the relationship between Marigold and Pacific are undisputed. Marigold was a grower of flowers. Pacific was a flower wholesaler. They had a longstanding relationship under which Marigold would deliver flowers to Pacific and obtain a delivery receipt. Pacific would mark the flowers with Marigold's name, package them, and attempt to sell them to retail florists at prices determined by Pacific. If the flowers were sold and Pacific received payment, Pacific would remit to Marigold 75% of the sale price, retaining 25% as its commission. If the flowers were not sold, Pacific would with Marigold's approval discard them, and Marigold would receive nothing for those flowers. It is also undisputed that the Bank had no actual knowledge of the nature of the commercial arrangement between Marigold and Pacific.

The Bank's financing statement and the security agreement between Pacific and the Bank describe the collateral as: "All inventory used in Pacific's business now owned or hereafter acquired; and all accounts and rights to payment of every kind now or hereafter arising in favor of Pacific out of Pacific's business, including all proceeds from the sale of inventory."

Under the Franklin Commercial Code, it is clear that, upon delivery of Marigold's flowers to Pacific, the flowers became part of Pacific's "inventory" because they were held by Pacific for sale. The Fund consists of "proceeds" of this inventory.

Marigold contends that its sale of flowers to Pacific was a "consignment sale," that Pacific never had title to the flowers and that, therefore, Pacific never owned the collateral (inventory) to which the Bank's security interest could attach. Marigold also asserts, *First National Bank v. Marigold Farms, Inc.*, Franklin Court of Appeal (1997), that Franklin Commercial Code § 2-326(3) is inapplicable in this case.

A consignment sale is one in which the merchant takes possession of goods and holds them for sale with the obligation to pay the owner of the goods from the proceeds of the sale. If the merchant does not sell the goods, the merchant may return them to the owner (or, as in this case of perishable flowers, discard them) without obligation. In a consignment sale transaction, title to the goods generally remains with the original owner. The arrangement between Marigold and Pacific was a consignment sale arrangement; Marigold was the consignor and Pacific was the consignee. Under FCC § 2-326(3), which clearly governs this transaction, the retention of title by Marigold is irrelevant to the ability of the Bank to obtain a security interest in the collateral.

Marigold does not contend that it complied with the filing requirement under the secured transactions division of the FCC as provided for in § 2-326(3)(c). Nor does Marigold claim that it complied with an applicable "sign law" under § 2-326(3)(a) or that it had delivered goods it had "used or bought for personal, family, or household purposes" as provided for in § 2-326(3)(d).[1] Rather, Marigold claims that, as provided for in § 2-326(3)(b), Pacific was generally known by its creditors "to be substantially engaged in selling goods of others."

At the evidentiary hearing, Bank officials testified unequivocally that the Bank was unaware that Pacific was selling the goods of others. Three flower growers who also consigned flowers to Pacific testified that Pacific was "well-known as a commission selling agent" and that other flower growers knew it as well. Although it is true that consignors, all of whom are necessarily also creditors, might know that Pacific deals in the goods of others, such knowledge cannot be extrapolated into a fact "generally known by its creditors." The purpose of § 2-326(3) is to protect general creditors of the consignee from claims of consignors who have undisclosed arrangements with the consignee. To impute as a matter of law the self-interested knowledge of the consignors/creditors to the general creditors does not give general creditors the opportunity to protect themselves from the undisclosed interests of the consignors.[2]

A consignor asserting that the consignee is "generally known by his creditors to be substantially engaged in selling the goods of others" must establish such general knowledge by proof other than that a few other consignors know that fact. He must establish that non-consignor creditors possess the requisite knowledge. Marigold failed to meet that burden of proof.

---

[1] The obvious reason for the exception for goods "used or bought for personal, family, or household purposes" is to avoid the situation where one who is not a merchant, and who should not therefore be deemed to know of the intricacies by which merchants protect their interests under the commercial code, unwittingly loses his right to property. If a householder occasionally delivers an item of property to a dealer to see if the dealer can sell it for him, the FCC protects that item from claims of the dealer's creditors. On the other hand, if the deliverer is one who deals in goods of the kind sold by the person to whom he delivers the goods, he should be held to the rules in the FCC that bind merchants. There are hybrid situations such as, for example, where one collects gemstones for his personal use and enjoyment but also regularly places the gems on consignment with jewelers to test the market and sell if the price is right. At some point the casual collector crosses over the line from being the householder, whom the personal goods exception is designed to protect, to being a merchant or dealer, who is bound by the filing or other protective provisions of § 2-326. In this case, Marigold is clearly at the extreme end of the merchant spectrum.

[2] The result might be different if all or most of Pacific's creditors were flower consignors but the fact does not appear from the evidence in this case. If all or most of the creditors were consignors, then one might be able to conclude that the creditors did have such "general knowledge."

THE MPT
MULTISTATE PERFORMANCE TEST

In re Steven Wallace

POINT SHEET

The MPT point sheet, grading summary, and grading guidelines describe the factual and legal points encompassed within the lawyering task to be completed. They outline all the possible issues and points that might be addressed by an applicant. They are provided to the user jurisdictions for the sole purpose of assisting graders in grading the examination by identifying the issues and suggesting the resolution of the problem contemplated by the drafters. These are not official grading guides. Applicants can receive a range of passing grades, including excellent grades, without covering all the points discussed in these guides. The model answer is included as an illustration of a thorough and detailed response to the task, one that addresses all the legal and factual issues the drafters intended to raise in the problem. It is intended to serve only as an example. Applicants need not present their responses in the same way to receive good grades. User jurisdictions are free to modify these grading materials, including the suggested weights assigned to particular points. Grading the MPT is the exclusive responsibility of the jurisdiction using the MPT as part of its admissions process.

Copyright ©2008 by the National Conference of Bar Examiners.
All rights reserved

In re Levy
United States District Court, E.D. Pennsylvania (1993)
Bankruptcy No. 29054

In December 1992, Bernard Levy, owner of a retail shoe store in Reading, Pennsylvania, filed a voluntary petition in bankruptcy. One of his suppliers, Acme Shoe Co. (Acme), had delivered a stock of shoes to Levy for resale in his store under the terms of a written agreement in which Levy, the bankrupt, acknowledged that the shoes were "on consignment" and could be returned to the consignor at any time.

Acme has filed a reclamation petition to recover the shoes it delivered to the bankrupt. The trustee resists the petition on the ground that the transaction was one of "sale or return," and, since there had been no compliance with § 2-326(3) of the Pennsylvania Uniform Commercial Code, the stock of shoes in Levy's possession was subject to the claims of Levy's creditors.

Acme concedes that it had not filed any financing statements in the public records offices. Acme did, however, produce evidence that small cards had been placed upon certain sections of shelving in Levy's store where Acme's shoes were stored and displayed, identifying the shoes placed on those sections of the shelving as shoes manufactured by Acme.

Under § 2-326 of the UCC, if goods are delivered to a consignor primarily for resale with the understanding that they may be returned by the consignor, the transaction is one of "sale or return" and such goods are subject to the claims of the buyer's creditors while in the buyer's possession even though the consignee has retained title. The consignee may avoid the consequences of having the goods subjected to the claims of the consignor's creditors by doing one or more of three things: (a) complying with "an applicable law" evidencing a consignor's interest or the like by a sign to that effect, or (b) establishing that the consignor is generally known by his creditors to be substantially engaged in selling the goods of others, or (c) complying with the provisions for filing financing statements and other notice documents under UCC Article 9 having to do with secured transactions.

There was no filing under Article 9. There was an effort by Acme to protect its goods by posting signs on the sections of shelving where its shoes were kept, but Acme has failed to show that there is in Pennsylvania "an applicable [sign] law" as that term is used in § 2-326(3)(a). The phrase "an applicable law" means a statute, and there is no such statute in Pennsylvania. Absent such a statute or an Article 9 filing, Acme is left with the burden of proving that Levy was generally known by his creditors to be substantially engaged in selling the goods of others.

Acme argues that, although the absence of a sign law might mean that the cards Acme caused to be placed on the shelves did not invoke the "sign law" subsection of § 2-326, the cards nonetheless served to impart knowledge that Levy was selling the goods of others. That argument might have had some merit if Acme could have shown that the cards did in fact impart such knowledge to Levy's creditors to such an extent that it was "generally known" by the creditors and that the cards also suggested that Levy was "substantially engaged" in selling goods not owned by him. On the record before the United States District Court, E. D. Pennsylvania (1993) court, however, the most that can be said is that the cards were designed to impart to Levy's customers, not his creditors, the knowledge that the shoes were Acme's. Thus, Acme's proof fell short.

Under § 544 of the Bankruptcy Act, the trustee is vested with the rights that the creditors had prior to the filing of the petition in bankruptcy. Section 2-326(2) of the UCC expressly makes goods held on sale or return subject to the claims of the debtor's creditors. That is the situation in this case.

Acme's petition for reclamation is denied.

In Re Steven Wallace

DRAFTERS' POINT SHEET

In this performance test item, Steven Wallace, an artist, delivers a painting to Lottie Zelinka, an art dealer, on consignment. Lottie files bankruptcy under Chapter 11 and later converts it to a straight Chapter 7 case. Thereafter, she returns the painting to Steven, and the trustee demands that Steven return the painting to the bankrupt estate. Steven consults Eva Morales, the supervising attorney in this case.

The task for the applicant is to draft a two-part memo in which he/she: first, analyzes the facts and the law regarding the bankruptcy trustee's claim that the painting is an estate asset; second, identifies what UCC defenses are available to Steven, explains how the facts currently known support the defenses, and suggests what additional facts might be developed to support the defenses.

The File consists of the assignment memo from Ms. Morales to the applicant, notes of the interview with Steven, and some documents Steven left with Ms. Morales. The Library contains excerpts from a basic bankruptcy treatise, § 2-326 of the Franklin Commercial Code (FCC), a section of the Franklin Civil Code, and two cases. All of the materials the applicants will need to work their way through the problem are contained in the test item.

The following points that might be discussed by an applicant are suggested by the problem. Grades will be assigned depending on the degree of thoroughness, and an applicant can get an excellent grade without covering all of these points.

1. Based on the facts as they appear in the file, does the bankruptcy trustee have a legitimate claim to the painting?

- The facts make it clear that the painting was redelivered to Steven by Lottie after the bankruptcy proceeding began. Thus, she made a "post-petition transfer" of property that was in the possession of the bankruptcy estate.
- Drawing on the excerpts from Walker on Bankruptcy and In re Levy, the applicants should conclude that the trustee has the right to "avoid a transfer of property of the estate...that occurs after the commencement of the case." *Walker on Bankruptcy* § 4.08.
- The real question then becomes whether the painting was "property of the estate." That calls for an in-depth analysis of the FCC provision on consignments—§ 2-326.
- The interview notes and the Inventory Receipt show clearly that Steven (consignor) delivered the painting to Lottie (consignee) on a true consignment; i.e., he delivered it to her to see if she could sell it for him, he retained title, she would get a commission if she could sell it, and she could return it without obligation if she couldn't sell it. Thus, it was a "sale or return" transaction under FCC § 2-326.
- Unless one or more of the exceptions provided for in § 2-326(3) applies, the FCC makes it clear that "goods held on sale or return are subject to [claims of the consignee's creditors] while in the [consignee's] possession," irrespective of whether the consignor (Steven) retained title. This point is fully discussed in the *First National Bank* and *Levy* cases, and the applicants should have no problem understanding the concept.
- Thus, on the face of it, the trustee, standing as he does in the shoes of a lien creditor of Artists' Exchange, has a legitimate claim to the painting.

2. The defenses and the current and additional facts that might support them.

- **Known facts**: The applicants should discuss each of the defenses under § 2-326(3) exceptions and whatever known facts there are to support them; and, if there are no supporting facts, simply say so and move on.
- The "sign law" exception (§ 2-326(3)(a)) probably doesn't apply on the known facts. Although Steven put a 2" x 3" label on the back of the painting identifying himself as the owner, it is not likely that it was "posted conspicuously" within the meaning of Franklin Civil Code § 3533. See, also, the discussion in *Levy* as to whether the label was calculated to inform creditors or just possible customers. Whether there was a sign posted by Lottie in the front window (as Steven seems to "think" there was) is not known at this point.
- There is no basis, on the facts currently known, to conclude that it was "generally known to [Lottie's] creditors" that she was "substantially engaged in selling goods of others." It is arguable that Artists' Exchange, communicates such a notion and that the sign Steven "thinks" he saw in the window (i.e., "All offers will be considered and forwarded to the artists") does too, but there are not enough facts currently known. Thus, the § 2-326(3)(b) exception doesn't help at this stage.
- There is no current information that Steven filed a UCC financing statement, so there is no basis for invoking the § 2-326(3)(c) exception.
- The strongest defense based on the known facts is that the painting, before Steven delivered it to Lottie, was "used...for personal, family, or household purposes," and that the exception in § 2-326(3)(d) applies.[1] The interview notes are ambiguous on that point. On the one hand, they show that Steven had the painting hanging in his dining room and hadn't thought about selling it until Lottie suggested it. It is also helpful that Steven and his wife had purchased a new rug with colors that complemented the colors in the painting; this is evidence that they intended to keep the painting for personal use. On the other hand, it is clear enough that Steven did regularly sell his paintings. More facts are needed on what their intentions were.

- **Additional facts, sources, and why the additional facts are important**: The notion in this part of the test item is to require the applicants to scour materials for facts that are hinted at in the File and Library, focusing on facts that would help invoke the protective exceptions listed in § 2-326(3).

- Whether Steven filed a UCC financing statement.
  - **Why important**: Although it is not probable that he did file a financing statement, it does not appear affirmatively from the facts that Ms. Morales even asked the question. It would help if he had because it would invoke the protective exception of § 2-326(3)(c) and might get him home free.
  - **Sources**: Ask Steven himself or make a search with the Secretary of State's office or other public filing offices.

- Whether the painting can persuasively be characterized as "goods... used...for personal, family or household purposes."
  - **Why important**: If that can be shown, it will, without more, invoke

---

[1] This exception, found in the library version of § 2-326, is not part of the official version of the UCC. It is part of the California UCC and is included here because it makes a good test issue.

the protective exception of § 2-326(3)(d) and establish Steven's right to keep the painting. The footnote in *First National Bank* suggests the inquiry, and it is possible that, as to this painting, Steven might still be a "casual collector." After all, he has only recently retired to go into painting full time.

- **Sources:** Get the facts from Steven and Ella, his wife. The interview notes suggest that, even though Steven regularly sold some of his paintings, perhaps there are some he painted and intended to keep for his own personal use. Check whatever records he maintains because they may help to show that some of his paintings (e.g., the ones he hangs in his home) are intended for "personal, family or household purposes." Ascertain what discussions they had about keeping the painting when they purchased the rug to complement the colors in the painting. Identify what other paintings, if any, they intended to keep for themselves as opposed to selling.

- **Whether Lottie dba Artists' Exchange was in fact substantially engaged in selling goods of others.**

  - **Why important:** The threshold question (as opposed to the ensuing question whether Lottie's general creditors had such knowledge) is whether Lottie's business was in fact predominantly a business. If so, then the applicant can proceed to the inquiry regarding whether the general creditors knew it sufficiently to invoke the protective exception. This inquiry is prompted by Steven's suggestion during the interview that most of the art at Artists' Exchange was on consignment and that most artists he knows of deal with galleries on a consignment basis.

  - **Sources:** Lottie herself is probably the best source of this information. The property schedules filed with the court will at least identify the inventory of art and maybe even whether a particular item was on consignment or owned by Lottie. The consignors are also creditors (see, First National Bank), so they will have to be listed on the bankruptcy schedules as well. The schedules will furnish their names and addresses in case it becomes necessary to contact them directly. The question whether art galleries in general do business predominantly on a consignment basis may be a subject for expert testimony, so a suggestion that an expert be consulted as a source for this information would be in order.

- **Whether the general creditors of Lottie dba Artists' Exchange knew that the gallery sold predominantly the goods of others.**

  - **Why important:** Proof of such "general knowledge" is essential to the invocation of the protective exception of § 2-326(3)(b). See, *First National Bank* and *Levy*. If it can be shown, it will get Steven home free.

  - **Sources:** The bankruptcy schedules will disclose the names and addresses of all the creditors. It may be necessary to contact the bulk of them to find out what they knew when they extended credit. Perceptive applicants might distinguish *First National Bank*. There, the court found that the knowledge of other consignors was irrelevant to the knowledge of "general" creditors. Here, if it can be shown that almost all of Lottie's creditors were consignors, as is suggested in the footnote in *First National Bank*, then their knowledge is perforce relevant to establish general knowledge.

  Ask Lottie and check correspondence and other records of communication between Lottie and her creditors for the possibility that the extent of her dealing in the goods of others was disclosed to her creditors.

  Steven said during the interview that he thinks there was a sign posted in the front window of the gallery to the effect that, "All offers will be considered and forwarded to the artists." If so, that could be evidence of notice to creditors that Lottie was selling the goods of others.

  The very name of the gallery, Artists' Exchange, is another source of the knowledge of the creditors. It suggests that Lottie is dealing in the goods of others and that the creditors must therefore have known it. Finally, expert testimony might help establish that creditors of art galleries were on constructive notice because almost all galleries do business on a consignment basis.

- **Whether there was a sign such as Steven thinks he saw in the front window of the gallery.**

  - **Why important:** It can serve two purposes: (1) to establish that the general creditors knew that Lottie was dealing predominantly in the goods of others, thus bringing into play § 2-326(3)(b), and (2) as evidence of compliance with the "sign law" (Franklin Civil Code § 3533). Either one will get Steven home free.

  - **Sources:** Perhaps a visit to the gallery will show that the sign is still there. Lottie herself can be asked about it. Inquiry can be made of the "general" creditors, including other consignors whose names and addresses can be obtained from the bankruptcy schedules. Photographs, if any, of the front of the gallery might be a source. If the sign was purchased by Lottie, perhaps the vendor can be ascertained and asked about it.

- **Whether other consignors of art filed UCC financing statements.**

  - **Why important:** If any significant number of the other consignors filed financing statements, it could be argued that the public nature of such filings served at least constructive notice of the fact that some substantial portion of Lottie's business was dealing in the goods of others. This, too, would help invoke the protective exception of § 2-326(3)(b).

  - **Sources:** The other consignors and secured creditors, whose names and addresses can be obtained from the bankruptcy schedules, can be asked directly or a search can be made of the filings at the Secretary of State's office. This will help establish the breadth of constructive knowledge imputable to other creditors.

- **Whether any of the other consignors of art complied with the "sign law."**

  - **Why important:** If enough of them did so effectively, it would be evidence that there was at least a form of public notice that the goods of others were in Lottie's gallery. And, if it were widespread enough, it could be argued that it imparted knowledge to the general creditors. It would, however, have to be shown that the signs were intended to impart knowledge to others than the customers of the gallery. C.f., *Levy* (small cards kept with the shoes satisfied neither the sign law nor the general knowledge requirements).

  - **Sources:** Again, the other consignors would be the best source of this information. Their identities can be obtained from the bankruptcy schedules. Lottie might also be able to provide information on this point.

FILE

MPT Task 4K: *Kantor v. Bellows*

Crystal, Hughes & Bernstein
Attorneys at Law
47 Bridge Street
Oakton, Franklin 33311

MEMORANDUM

July 27, 1999

To: Applicant
From: Pat Moore
Re: Linda Kantor

Linda Kantor has asked us to represent her in her divorce from her husband, Bill Bellows. The only contested issue is whether the enhanced earning capacity created by Bill's law degree will be treated as property, subject to division between the parties. Franklin has an equitable distribution statute as part of its divorce law, but two divisions of our Court of Appeal are in conflict on the issue of how to treat spousal contributions to professional degrees. The Franklin Supreme Court has not ruled on this issue.

I want to persuade Bill's lawyer, Shawn Martin, that we have a good chance of convincing a court that the enhanced earning capacity created by Bill's law degree and license to practice law is property subject to equitable distribution. As the law now stands in Franklin, there are two conflicting policy views. It won't do us any good to simply distinguish the two cases. Our job is to convince the other side that the Supreme Court will most likely end up adopting the view that favors us.

As the first step in the negotiation process, I want to send a letter to Shawn Martin that:

- argues that Linda is entitled to a share of Bill's enhanced earning capacity;
- addresses counter-arguments that would deny or diminish her share; and
- includes a specific dollar demand that is justified in light of these arguments.

Please draft such a letter for my signature. Be sure to discuss both the legal principles and the facts of our case in making the arguments. Shawn is a thoroughly competent family law practitioner and a straight-shooter. I have no hesitancy in honestly laying out my entire case.

Crystal, Hughes & Bernstein
Attorneys at Law
47 Bridge Street
Oakton, Franklin 33311

MEMORANDUM   June 1, 1999

To: File
From: Pat Moore
Re: Linda Kantor—Interview Notes

Linda Kantor, who is 29, has been married to William Bellows, also 29, for seven years. They have one child, Jason, who is three. They have agreed that they want to be divorced, and Linda believes that they are in agreement as to most issues. The only issue about which there seems to be dispute is how William's law degree will be treated in the divorce.

The parties married soon after they both graduated from the University of Franklin in June 1992. Linda began work as a programmer for Computech, a computer consulting firm specializing in the development of software, and Bill as a legislative aide in the office of Andy Pepper, a state assemblyman from Oakton. Three years later, Bill entered law school at the University of Franklin Law Center, which is in Oakton. Linda was also interested in attending law school, but the parties decided that Bill would attend first, with Linda attending after Bill graduated. They both wanted to have children soon and thought it would be easier to stagger their law school careers. Jason was born just as Bill began law school in the fall of 1995. Linda got a three-month, paid parental leave from Computech, after which she returned to work full time. Linda arranged to share with another couple who have a child Jason's age the cost of hiring a child care worker to care for the two children from 8:30 a.m. to 5:30 p.m. While Bill was in law school, Linda did most of the housework and child care. (She estimates that she did more than 75% of each.) She usually did Jason's morning routine with him, picked him up from the child care worker at 5:30 p.m., gave him dinner and a bath, and played with him in the evening. Bill participated in these activities, but usually in a secondary kind of role. Because of flexible policies at Computech, Linda was able to take time off work when Jason was sick.

Linda has continued at Computech to the present, where she has advanced steadily, gaining an increasingly important role in the development of specialized software programs for small- to medium-sized institutions. The company is committed to personnel development, devoting significant resources to those employees it sees as promising. Although Linda has been identified as one of the "stars," she has not been able to take full advantage of all the educational opportunities they offer because of her many responsibilities at home. She has been able to attend only one extended, out-of-town workshop in software design each year, but could have gone to as many as three each year at the company's expense if her circumstances had permitted it. In addition, the company pays for employees to take up to four graduate-level courses in computer science each year at the university, but Linda has been able to take advantage of this opportunity only one semester in which she took one course. Linda has contributed all of her earnings to the family. When she first started at Computech, her salary was $16,000. She has received steady raises as her responsibilities have increased, and she currently earns $35,000 per year.

Bill was successful in law school, graduating in June of 1998 magna cum laude, with a special award for the high quality of his performance in the clinical program. During the three years Bill was attending law school, Linda contributed her entire pay of $85,000 to support the family. Bill's tuition averaged approximately $12,000 per year; he obtained loans amounting to $25,000, and his parents gave him another $10,000. For two of the six semesters, he worked ten hours per week, earning a total of $3,000 from this employment. Last summer, he took and passed the Franklin bar exam. He obtained a position in the prestigious Honors Program at the Franklin State Attorney General's Office, which he began in September 1998. In that program, he rotates for a year through the different divisions in the A.G.'s office and at the end of the year can choose a permanent position among any of the positions available, if he wishes. His salary for the first year of the program is $35,000, but it will go up to $40,000 the following year if he decides to work there on a permanent basis. Because of his excellent law school record and the prestige of the Honors Program, he would have no trouble getting a job with a major law firm in Oakton, or anywhere else in the state, where a beginning salary could be as high as $61,000.

Linda and Bill have accumulated almost no assets during their marriage. Before Bill entered law school, they purchased two cars, one in the first year of their marriage and the other in the third year, both of which they continue to drive. They rent the modest two-bedroom house they live in. They accumulated savings of approximately $3,000 when they were both working, but that money was spent after Jason was born and Bill began law school. All of their money has gone into paying living expenses, raising a child, and putting Bill through school.

Linda feels very strongly that, as part of the divorce, she should be able to share in the benefits from Bill's law degree. They decided together that he would go to law school first, and she worked very hard to make that possible. Now it's supposed to be her turn. She also is anxious to get on with her own education, although she has decided that she would like to pursue full-time graduate studies in computer science rather than go to law school. Although Computech has been a good place for her, she has become interested in the more theoretical aspects of computer science. After all her sacrifices, Linda feels that she should be able to share in the benefits of Bill's law degree.

Although Linda and Bill have been able on their own to agree that they will share joint legal and physical custody of Jason and that Bill will pay child support, they have not been able to agree on how to treat Bill's law degree. I discussed with Linda litigation of this issue, including the uncertain state of the law. She is not averse to trial on the issue, if necessary, but she would prefer to resolve the matter through negotiation because she would like to avoid the expense of a trial and maintain a cordial relationship with Bill.

LIBRARY

Franklin State University
Bentonville, Franklin 33312

Millicent Elstein, Ph.D.
Professor of Economics

July 20, 1999

Patricia Moore
Crystal, Hughes & Bernstein
Attorneys at Law
47 Bridge Street
Oakton, Franklin 33311

Dear Ms. Moore:

Please excuse the delay in responding to your inquiry. As requested, I provide the following summary of my analysis of the value of the law degree held by Bill Bellows.

In arriving at the present value, I began by comparing the projected life earnings of an average college graduate to the projected earnings of two types of lawyers: a lawyer engaged in private practice in a large law firm and a lawyer employed in government service. I used the time between Mr. Bellows' admission to practice and his 65th birthday in making these projections. I then considered the impact of taxes, inflation, and interest rates. From all this, I calculated the present value of these projected earnings.

Based on these calculations, it is my opinion that the present value of Mr. Bellows' law degree is $520,000 should he choose to remain in government service and $820,000 should he enter the private practice of law.

A complete report will follow under separate cover. If I can be of any additional assistance, please let me know.

Sincerely,

Millicent Elstein

Millicent Elstein, Ph.D.

Franklin Domestic Relations Law

Section 3—The term "marital property" shall mean all property acquired by either or both spouses during the marriage. Marital property shall not include separate property as hereinafter defined.

Section 4—The term "separate property" shall mean

A. property acquired before marriage or property acquired by bequest, devise, or descent, or gift from a party other than the spouse;

B. compensation for personal injuries;

C. property acquired in exchange for or the increase in value of separate property as defined in subpart (A) of this section, except when the increase is attributable to the direct or indirect contribution by the party not having title;

D. property described as separate property by valid written agreement of the parties.

Section 5—Disposition of property in divorce actions.

A. The court, in an action for divorce, shall determine the respective rights of the parties in their separate or marital property.

B. Separate property shall remain such.

C. Marital property shall be distributed equitably between the parties, considering the circumstances of the case and the respective parties.

D. In determining an equitable disposition of property under paragraph C, the court shall consider

(1) the income and property of each party at the time of marriage and at the time of the commencement of the action;

(2) the duration of the marriage and the age and health of both parties;

(3) any equitable claim to, interest in, or direct or indirect contribution made to the acquisition of such marital property by the party not having title, including joint efforts or expenditures and contributions and services as a spouse, parent, wage earner and homemaker, and to the career or career potential of the other party;

(4) the liquid or non-liquid character of all marital property;

(5) the probable future financial circumstances of each party;

(6) the impossibility or difficulty of evaluating any component asset or any interest in a business, corporation or profession, and the economic desirability of retaining such asset or interest intact and free from any claim or interference by the other party.

E. In any action in which the court determines that an equitable distribution is appropriate but would be impractical or burdensome or where the distribution of an interest in a business, corporation or profession would be contrary to law, the court, in lieu of equitable distribution, shall make a distributive award in order to achieve equity between the parties.

Section 6—Maintenance.

A. Except where the parties have entered into an agreement, in any divorce action the court may order temporary maintenance or maintenance in such amount as justice requires, having regard for the standard of living of the parties established during the marriage, whether the party in whose favor maintenance is granted lacks sufficient property and income to provide for his or her

reduced or lost lifetime earning capacity of the party seeking maintenance as a result of having foregone or delayed education, training, employment, or career opportunities during the marriage;

reasonable needs, whether the other party has sufficient property or income to provide for the reasonable needs of the other, and the circumstances of the case and the respective parties. In determining the amount and duration of maintenance, the court shall consider

(1) the income and property of the respective parties, including marital property distributed pursuant to Section 5.

(2) the duration of the marriage and the age and health of both parties;

(3) the present and future earning capacity of both parties;

(4) the ability of the party seeking maintenance to become self-supporting and, if applicable, the period of time and training necessary therefor;

(5) reduced or lost lifetime earning capacity of the party seeking maintenance as a result of having foregone or delayed education, training, employment, or career opportunities during the marriage;

(6) the presence of children of the marriage in the respective homes of the parties;

(7) contributions and services of the party seeking maintenance as a spouse, parent, wage earner and homemaker, and to the career or career potential of the other party.

B. The court may award permanent maintenance, but an award of maintenance shall terminate upon the death of either party or upon the recipient's valid or invalid marriage.

Reginald Morgan v. Victoria Morgan

Franklin Court of Appeal, Second Appellate Division (1998)

The question in this case is whether the defendant, Victoria Morgan, has the right to share the value of a professional business (MBA) degree earned by her former husband, Reginald Morgan, during their marriage. The court must decide whether the plaintiff's degree is "property" for purposes of Franklin Domestic Relations Law Section 3. If the MBA degree is not property, we must still decide whether Victoria can nonetheless recover the money she contributed to her husband's support while he pursued his professional education. We hold that Reginald's professional degree is not property and therefore not subject to equitable distribution but that Victoria may be reimbursed for her financial contributions to Reginald's professional training.

When the parties married in 1984, Reginald had an engineering degree and Victoria had a bachelor of science degree. From that time until the parties separated in October 1991, they generally shared all household expenses. The sole exception was the period between September 1988 and January 1990, when the plaintiff attended the Wharton School of the University of Pennsylvania and received an MBA degree.

During the 16-month period in which Reginald attended school, Victoria contributed $26,000 to cover household expenses plus another $10,000 for Reginald's tuition. Reginald made no financial contribution while he was a student. After receiving his degree, Reginald went to work as a commercial lending officer for Franklin National Bank. Meanwhile, in 1989 Victoria began a part-time graduate program at Franklin State University, paid for by her employer, that led to a master's degree in microbiology one year after the parties had separated. Victoria worked full time throughout the course of her graduate schooling.

The trial court granted a divorce. At the time of trial, Reginald's annual income was $48,200 and Victoria's income was $40,000. No claim for maintenance was made. The parties owned no real property and they divided the small amount of their personal property by agreement. The only issue at trial was Victoria's claim for an equitable share of the present value of the enhanced future earning capacity of plaintiff attributable to the MBA degree.

The trial court did not attempt to determine the value of Reginald's MBA degree. Instead, the court held that the education and degree obtained by Reginald constituted a property right and reimbursed Victoria for the contribution she made to acquiring the degree. The court awarded her the $10,000 she contributed to Reginald's tuition and 50% of her $26,000 contribution to household expenses during the educational period.

This court must decide whether the legislature intended an MBA degree to be "property" so that, if acquired by either spouse during a marriage, its value must be equitably distributed upon divorce. Since there is no legislative history on the meaning of the word "property" and the statute itself offers no guidance, statutory construction in this case means little more than an inquiry into the extent to which professional degrees and licenses share the qualities of other things that the legislature and courts have treated as property.

Franklin courts have subjected a broad range of assets and interests to equitable distribution, including vested but unmatured private pensions, military retirement pay and disability benefits, and personal injury claims. This court, however, has never subjected to equitable distribution an asset whose future monetary value is as uncertain and unquantifiable as a professional degree or license. A professional license or degree cannot be sold and its value cannot readily be determined. It represents the opportunity to obtain an amount of money only upon the occurrence of highly uncertain future events. The value of a professional degree is nothing more than the possibility of enhanced earnings that the particular academic credential will provide, income that the degree holder might never acquire. Moreover, any assets resulting from future income for professional services would be property acquired after the marriage; the statute restricts equitable distribution to property acquired during the marriage.

Valuing a professional degree in the hands of any particular individual at the start of his or her career would involve a gamut of calculations that reduces to little more than guesswork. Even if such estimates could be made, however, there would remain a world of unforeseen events that could affect the earning potential—not to mention the actual earnings—of any particular degree holder. A person qualified by education for a given profession may choose not to practice it, may fail at it, or may practice in a specialty, location, or manner which generates less than the average income enjoyed by fellow professionals. The potential for inequity in the result is at once apparent; his or her spouse will have been awarded a share of something which never existed in any real sense.

Valuing educational assets, even if they were marital property, in terms of the cost to the supporting spouse of obtaining the degree would be an erroneous application of equitable distribution law. The cost of a professional degree has little to do with any real value of the degree and fails to consider at all the nonfinancial efforts made by the degree holder in completing his course of study. The cost of a spouse's financial contributions has no logical connection to the value of that degree. The cost approach is not conceptually predicated on a property theory at all but rather represents a general notion of how to do equity. Equitable distribution in these cases derives from the proposition that the supporting spouse should be reimbursed for contribution to the marital unit that, because of the divorce, did not bear its expected fruit for the supporting spouse. Although the trial court found that the degree was distributable property, it actually reimbursed the defendant without attempting to give her part of the value of the degree. This court does not support reimbursement between former spouses in maintenance proceedings as a general principle. Marriage is not a business arrangement in which the parties keep track of debits and credits, their accounts to be settled upon divorce. Rather, marriage is a shared enterprise, a joint undertaking in many ways akin to a partnership. It is improper for a court to treat a marriage as an arm's-length transaction by allowing a spouse to come into court after the fact and make legal arguments regarding unjust enrichment. Courts should assume, in the absence of contrary proof, that the decision to obtain a professional degree was mutual and took into account what sacrifices the husband and wife needed to make in furtherance of that decision. But every joint undertaking has its bounds of fairness. Where a partner to marriage takes the benefits of his or her spouse's support in obtaining a professional degree or license with the understanding that future benefits will accrue and inure to both of them, and the marriage is then terminated without the supported spouse giving anything in return, an unfairness has occurred that calls for a remedy.

In this case, the supporting spouse made financial contributions towards her husband's professional education with the expectation that both parties would enjoy material benefits flowing from the professional license or degree. It is therefore patently unfair that the supporting spouse be denied the mutually anticipated benefit while the supported spouse keeps not only the degree, but also all of the financial and material rewards flowing from it. Furthermore, in this case a supporting spouse has contributed more than mere earnings to her husband with the mutual expectation that both of them will realize and enjoy material improvements. Also, the wife has presumably made personal financial sacrifices, resulting in a reduced or lowered standard of living. She has postponed present consumption and a higher standard of living for the future prospect of greater support and material benefits. If the parties had remained married long enough after the husband had completed his postgraduate education so that they could have accumulated substantial property, the court would have determined how much of the marital property to allocate to the wife, taking into account her contributions to her husband's earning capacity. In this sense, an award that is referable to the spouse's monetary contributions to her partner's education significantly implicates basic considerations of marital support and standard of living.

Although not explicitly provided for in Section 6 of our Domestic Relations Law, to provide a fair and effective means of compensating a supporting spouse, we now introduce the concept of reimbursement maintenance into divorce proceedings. Regardless of the appropriateness of permanent maintenance or the presence or absence of marital property to be equitably distributed, there will be circumstances where a supporting spouse should be reimbursed for the financial contributions he or she made to the spouse's successful professional training. Such reimbursement maintenance should cover all financial contributions towards the former spouse's education, including household expenses, educational costs, school travel expenses and any other contributions used by the supported spouse in obtaining his or her degree or license. Although courts may not make any permanent distribution of the value of professional degrees and licenses, whether based upon estimated worth or cost, where a spouse has received financial contributions used in obtaining a professional degree or license with the expectation of deriving material benefits for both, that spouse may be called upon to reimburse the supporting spouse for the amount of contributions received.

We do not hold that every spouse who contributes toward his or her partner's education or professional training is entitled to reimbursement maintenance. Only monetary contributions made with the mutual and shared expectation that both parties to the marriage will derive increased income and material benefits should be a basis for such an award. For example, it is unlikely that a spouse who has been married to a financially successful executive and returns to school after many years of homemaking would upon divorce be required to reimburse her husband for his contributions toward her degree.

We remand the case so the trial court can determine whether reimbursement maintenance should be awarded and, if so, what amount is appropriate.

Michael Sooke v. Loretta Sooke

Franklin Court of Appeal, Fourth Appellate Division (1999)

In this divorce action, the parties' only asset of any consequence is the husband's medical degree. The principal issue is whether that degree, acquired during their marriage, is marital property. The trial court held that it was and made a distributive award in the wife's favor. It also granted her expert witness fees.

Michael and Loretta Sooke married in 1982. Both were employed as teachers. Loretta had a bachelor's degree and a temporary teaching certificate but required 18 months of postgraduate classes at an approximate cost of $3,000, excluding living expenses, to obtain permanent certification in Franklin. She relinquished the opportunity to obtain permanent certification while Michael pursued his education. In 1984 the parties moved to Guadalajara, Mexico, where Michael became a full-time medical student. Loretta taught and contributed her earnings to their joint expenses. The parties returned to Franklin in 1987 so that Michael could complete the last two semesters of medical school and internship training here. Loretta resumed her former teaching position, where she remained at the time this action was commenced. Michael was licensed to practice medicine in 1991 and filed for divorce two months later. At the time of trial, he was a resident in general surgery. During the marriage, both parties contributed to paying the living and educational expenses. In addition to performing household work and managing the family finances, Loretta contributed 76% of the parties' income exclusive of a $10,000 student loan obtained by Michael.

Loretta presented expert testimony that the present value of Michael's medical degree was $950,000. Her expert testified that he arrived at this figure by comparing the average income of a college graduate and that of a general surgeon between 1996, when Michael's residency would end, and 2023, when he would reach age 65. Taking into account taxes, inflation, and interest rates, he gave his opinion that the present value of Loretta's contribution to Michael's medical education was $210,000. Michael offered no expert testimony on the subject.

The court made a distributive award to Loretta of $380,000, representing 40% of the value of the degree, and ordered it paid in 11 annual installments. The court also ordered Michael to pay Loretta's counsel fees of $20,000 and her expert witness fee of $5,000. We affirm.

Our statutes contemplate only two classes of property: marital and separate. The former, which is subject to equitable distribution, is defined broadly as "all property acquired by either or both spouses during the marriage." Michael does not contend that his license is separate property, but rather, relying on Morgan v. Morgan (Franklin Court of Appeal, 1998), he claims that it is not property at all.

We disagree with the decision of the Second Appellate Division in that case.

The Franklin Domestic Relations Law recognizes that spouses have an equitable claim to things of value arising out of the marital relationship and classifies them as subject to distribution by focusing on the marital status of the parties at the time of acquisition. Those things acquired during marriage and subject to distribution have been classified as marital property, although they hardly fall within traditional property concepts because there is no common-law property interest remotely resembling marital property.

Having classified the property subject to distribution, the legislature did not define it but left it to the courts to determine what interests come within its terms.

Section 5 provides that in making an equitable distribution of marital property, the court shall consider "any equitable claim to, interest in, or direct or indirect contribution made to the acquisition of such marital property by the party not having title, including joint efforts or expenditures and contributions and services as a spouse, parent, wage earner and homemaker, and to the career or career potential of the other party [and] ... the impossibility or difficulty of evaluating any component asset or any interest in a business, corporation or profession...." Where such difficulty exists, the court shall make a distributive award in lieu of an actual distribution of property. The words mean exactly what they say: an interest in a profession or professional career potential is marital property which may be represented by direct or indirect contributions of the nontitleholding spouse, including financial contributions and nonfinancial contributions made by caring for the home and family.

Few undertakings better qualify as the type of joint effort that the statute's implicit economic partnership theory is intended to address than contributions toward one spouse's acquisition of a professional degree. The legislature has decided, by its explicit reference in the statute to the contributions of one spouse to the other's profession or career, that these contributions represent investments in the economic partnership of the marriage and that the product of the parties' joint efforts should be considered marital property. It does not matter whether the spouse has established a practice or whether he or she has yet to do so. An established practice merely represents the exercise of the privileges conferred upon the professional spouse by the degree, and the income flowing from that practice represents the receipt of the enhanced earning capacity that a professional degree allows.

Michael contends that alternative remedies should be employed, such as reimbursement for direct financial contributions. Limiting a working spouse to a maintenance award not only is contrary to the economic partnership concept underlying the statute but also retains the uncertain and inequitable economic ties of dependence that the legislature sought to extinguish by equitable distribution. Maintenance is subject to termination upon the recipient's remarriage, and a working spouse may never receive adequate consideration for his or her contribution and may even be penalized for the decision to remarry. When a marriage ends, each of the spouses, based on the totality of the contributions made to it, has a stake in and right to a share of the marital assets accumulated while it endured, not because that share is needed, but because those assets represent the capital product of what was essentially a partnership entity.

Turning to the question of valuation, it has been suggested that even if a professional degree is considered marital property, the working spouse is entitled only to reimbursement of his or her direct financial contributions. Such a result is completely at odds with the statute's requirement that the court give full consideration to both direct and indirect contributions. If the degree is marital property, then the working spouse is entitled to an equitable portion of it, not merely a return of funds advanced. Its value is the enhanced earning capacity it affords the holder and, although fixing the present value of that enhanced earning capacity may present problems, the problems are not insurmountable. Certainly they are no more difficult than computing tort damages for wrongful death or diminished earning capacity resulting from injury, and they differ only in degree from valuing a professional practice, which courts routinely do. The trial court retains the flexibility and discretion to structure the distributive award equitably, taking into consideration factors such as the working spouse's need for immediate payment and the current ability of the spouse with the degree to pay. Once it has received evidence of the present value of the degree and the working spouse's contributions toward its acquisition, it may then make an appropriate distribution of the marital property, including a distributive award for the professional degree. For these reasons, we affirm.

DISSENT by Meyer, J.

Michael Sooke's principal argument is that a professional degree is not marital property because it does not fit within the traditional view of property as something which has an exchange value on the open market and is capable of sale, assignment or transfer. I agree. An educational degree is simply not encompassed even by the broad views of the concept of "property." It does not have an exchange value or any objective transferable value on an open market. It is personal to the holder. It terminates on death of the holder and is not inheritable. It cannot be assigned, sold, transferred, conveyed or pledged. An advanced degree is a cumulative product of many years of previous education, combined with diligence and hard work. It may not be acquired by the mere expenditure of money. It is simply an intellectual achievement that may potentially assist in the future acquisition of property. In my view, it has none of the attributes of property in the usual sense of that term. My interpretation is in accord with the Second Appellate Division of this court. I would reverse.

THE MPT
MULTISTATE PERFORMANCE TEST

Kantor v. Bellows

POINT SHEET

The MPT point sheet, grading summary, and grading guidelines describe the factual and legal points encompassed within the lawyering task to be completed. They outline all the possible issues and points that might be addressed by an applicant. They are provided to the user jurisdictions for the sole purpose of assisting graders in grading the examination by identifying the issues and suggesting the resolution of the problem contemplated by the drafters. These are not official grading guides. Applicants can receive a range of passing grades, including excellent grades, without covering all the points discussed in these guides. The model answer is included as an illustration of a thorough and detailed response to the task, one that addresses all the legal and factual issues the drafters intended to raise in the problem. It is intended to serve only as an example. User jurisdictions are free to modify these responses in the same way to receive good grades. User jurisdictions are free to modify these grading materials, including the suggested weights assigned to particular points. Grading the MPT is the exclusive responsibility of the jurisdiction using the MPT as part of its admissions process.

Copyright ©2008 by the National Conference of Bar Examiners.
All rights reserved

Kantor v. Bellows

DRAFTERS' POINT SHEET

This performance test asks the applicant to write a persuasive letter to an opposing attorney proposing a settlement as a prelude to negotiations in a divorce case. It is set in the context of an impending divorce in which the only open issue is the treatment as divisible property of the husband's law degree and license, which were acquired during the marriage. The applicant works for the firm representing the wife. The question is whether the enhanced earning capacity attributable to the law degree and license constitutes "property" and is subject to division as marital property. The intermediate appellate courts of the jurisdiction (Franklin) are split, and the Franklin Supreme Court has not ruled on the issue.

The instructional memorandum to the applicant from the partner, the partner's interview notes, and an opinion letter from an expert contain the necessary factual materials. The Library contains the jurisdiction's Domestic Relations Law and the two divergent decisions of the Franklin Court of Appeal.

The applicant is told to draft a letter to the husband's attorney, arguing persuasively that the wife is entitled to a share of the enhanced earning capacity created by the husband's law degree, taking into account as much as possible the arguments that cut against the wife, and making a settlement demand in a specific amount.

The following points were intended by the drafters to be covered in varying degrees of depth by the applicants and to affect the grading of the test item:

1. **Overview:** The applicants are expected to observe the specific instructions set forth in the memo from the partner and to exhibit a good deal of judgment in what the communication to the other attorney says and how it says it:

- The answers should be in the form of a letter to opposing counsel, using fairly formal language, but not relying on legal jargon.
- Applicants must "discuss" the facts and legal principles in formulating their arguments. This instruction from the partner (i.e., to "discuss") is intended to require the applicants to integrate the facts and the law, not merely recite them.
- Similarly, the instruction to conclude the letter with a dollar demand is intended to require the applicants to work with the numbers in the file and to calculate a demand using the principles stated in the statutes and the cases.
- Better answers will emphasize the facts and law that favor the wife but will avoid the use of hyperbole (particularly in the framing of legal arguments that cannot be sustained by the case law) and inflammatory language, recognizing that the letter is the first step in a series of negotiations that will require some give and take.
- Better answers will also frankly recognize the conflicting authorities and formulate the settlement demand accordingly. An answer that makes an extreme monetary demand will not be as persuasive as one that makes a reasoned reduction taking into account the effect of the conflicting authorities.
- A good answer will present principled justifications of the dollar amount chosen, rooted in the law and the facts of the case.

2. **The Statutes and Cases:** The following points, which the applicants should extract and use in formulating their arguments and demand, emerge from the Domestic Relations Law (DRL) and the cases:

- There is nothing in the DRL itself that limits the meaning of the term "property." It is wide open for interpretation, as, indeed, is exemplified by the divergent views of the court in *Morgan* and *Sooke*.

- *Morgan*, a 1998 case, adopts a somewhat wooden view and holds that the law degree is not property because it is not physically subject to equitable division and because the ultimate fruits of the degree have an element of futurity, i.e., the income, of which Linda seeks a share, will have been earned after the dissolution of the marriage and is therefore not "property acquired during marriage."

- *Sooke*, a slightly more recent case (1999), takes a more flexible view, holding that, absent any statutory proscription, it is up to the courts to define what is property. This division of the Court of Appeal finds language in the DRL that aids in the characterization of the law license as property, i.e., Section 5 talks about "evaluating . . . any interest in a . . . profession." That language, says the court, means that "an interest in a profession or professional career potential is marital property. . . ." The applicants, however, must deal with the dissent in *Sooke*, which takes much the same position as does the court in *Morgan*.

- Both divisions of the court, however, recognize that Linda made a contribution to the acquisition of Bill's degree and license for which she is entitled to compensation. Both courts acknowledge the "economic partnership" theory in determining the financial interests of a spouse in the assets of the marriage, differing in how they characterize the asset (property vs. joint undertaking) and how they calculate the amount of the compensation. One point to be extracted by the applicants is that, under either holding, Linda is going to receive some measure of compensation.

- The *Morgan* court would use the concept of "reimbursement maintenance" to compensate Linda. On that basis, Linda would be entitled to a return of the amount of her investment in the partnership, i.e., the actual amount that she contributed during the marriage to allow Bill to acquire his degree. The underlying notion is that, in traditional partnership terms, Linda would not have made the investment had she not expected it to generate future benefits; upon the dissolution of the partnership, she is entitled to get her investment back to the extent that the asset (i.e., the degree) exists at the time of dissolution.

- The *Sooke* court also applies the partnership theory and considers the contribution by Linda to have been an investment in the partnership, but parts company with the *Morgan* court on the amount to which Linda is entitled. The *Sooke* court holds that Linda is entitled not just to reimbursement of her actual investment, but to the fruits of her investment. In this case, her investment in the law license contributed to the creation of an "enhanced earning capacity," of which she is entitled to a share.

- The *Sooke* court also differs with the *Morgan* court on the question whether a value can rationally be placed on the degree or license. The *Morgan* court says a value cannot be placed on the degree because of the inherent uncertainties relating to career choices of the degree holder, whereas the *Sooke* court says that valuing the license is no different from valuing professional practices and damages in other types of actions. Accordingly, the *Sooke* court would allow expert testimony on the present value of the enhanced earning capacity resulting from the law license and would make a "distributive award" (see Section 6(e) of the DRL), payable over time, based on the wife's contribution measured by the factors enumerated in Section 5(d) of the DRL. The *Sooke* court would also allow Linda to recover her expert witness fees and attorneys fees.

- Both courts reject an award of traditional maintenance under Section 6 of the DRL as a substitute for division of the degree as property. Such an award, say the courts, would perpetuate economic dependence of the wife on the husband long after the termination of the marriage. Moreover, a maintenance award under Section 6 would be subject to termination, a circumstance that might deprive the wife of the benefit of her investment and confer a windfall on the husband.

A minor difference between the two cases is that *Morgan* addresses a professional degree and *Sooke* deals with a professional license. For the purposes of this case, the difference is of no consequence as Linda contributed to both Bill's degree and license. The real issue is the enhanced earning capacity resulting from the degree and/or license.

3. Application of the Facts: Having in mind Linda's goal of attempting to reach a negotiated settlement, the applicants should compose a letter designed to make Bill's attorney appreciate the benefits of engaging in settlement talks and the risks of not resolving the matter out of court:

- First, Linda is intent on realizing the benefit of her contribution to Bill's enhanced earning capacity. She considers it property acquired during the marriage, and she claims an equitable share of it.

- Linda is willing to negotiate a settlement, but her willingness should not be taken as a sign that she is unprepared to litigate the matter to a conclusion. In view of the split in the Franklin courts, this case, if litigated, will almost certainly go to the Franklin Supreme Court for final resolution. Litigation will be an expensive proposition for both parties, and, since Linda views her chances of success to be better than even, the ultimate cost of the litigation will probably be borne by Bill.

- Linda is entitled to an award under either the Morgan or the Sooke view. The only question is how much.

- The facts are all in her favor on the issue of whether she made a cognizable contribution to the acquisition of Bill's enhanced earning capacity: she put off her own schooling in favor of allowing Bill to go to law school; she worked to support the family; she had a child and did most (75%) of the child-rearing and housework; she contributed all her earnings ($85,000) to the support of the family.

- While it is true that Bill essentially financed his own tuition ($25,000 in loans plus $10,000 from his family), he earned only $3,000 that could possibly have been used for family support, plus one-half of the $3,000 savings he and Linda had accumulated.

- Had it not been for Linda's earnings, which supported the family, Bill would not have been able to get his degree.

- Linda gave up opportunities for her own professional advancement (workshops, courses).

- Even if Linda's claim were limited to the "reimbursement maintenance" amount favored by the Morgan court, she would receive at least 50% of the $85,000 she contributed, and probably more, in light of her 75% non-monetary contributions in the form of child-rearing and housework.

- At the other extreme, if the Sooke view is adopted, Linda could get an award of up to 50% and maybe more of the $820,000 estimated by the expert to be the present value of the high end of Bill's earning capacity, plus costs and fees.

- The applicants should use as the framework for these arguments the factors enumerated in DRL Section 5(d), which the court would use in determining the equitable division of the property.

- The fact that Linda is earning an amount equal to 50% of Bill's earnings (i.e., $35,000) should not militate against Linda. The issue, at least under Sooke, is whether she is entitled to a share of Bill's earning power, "…not because that share is needed, but because those assets represent the capital product of what was essentially a partnership entity."

- There are facts that support the uncertainty concern of the Morgan court, and should not be ignored. Bill does not know what his career choice will be. Linda herself has had a change of heart, wanting to move from law to computer science. Why should Bill be denied this same flexibility to planning his life?

- Bill's economic prospects are particularly good because of his own intellectual achievements. He graduated with high honors and got the clinic award. Should Linda be entitled to compensation for these aspects of his enhanced earning capacity?

- Although Linda gets compensation under either Morgan or Sooke, her recovery under Sooke is far greater and, therefore, the facts supporting the future benefit Linda anticipated should be identified, i.e., they planned for each to attend graduate school, going one at a time in order to have a child soon and realize the benefits from their advanced training while having children at the same time.

- Applicants should address the short duration of the marriage and the likelihood that Linda will be able to benefit from the enhanced earning capacity she will have in getting an advanced degree herself.

4. The Demand: It is important for the applicants to realize that they are making an opening demand. It must not be so high as to be deemed by Bill to be outrageous, but it must be high enough so that it leaves Linda room to negotiate. It must be based on a rational construct, justified by the law and the facts of the case. Something along the following lines would show that the applicant has taken into account the strengths and weaknesses of the relative positions and the sensitive points of the situation:

- The parameters are already set: under the Morgan view, a minimum of 50% of the $85,000 Linda actually contributed; under the Sooke view, a maximum of something more than 50% of the high end of the expert's present value calculation of $820,000, plus fees and costs.

- For openers, the applicants could, and perhaps should, argue that, because of Bill's academic record, it is more likely that Bill will pursue the more promising career as a major law firm lawyer. This puts in issue the $820,000 figure.

- It would be reasonable to suggest that the base figure for a settlement would be $670,000, the average of the high and low present value figures (because of the uncertainty about Bill's choice), and to concede that Linda's demand would be limited to 50%, notwithstanding Linda's greater-than-50% contribution. This would put the demand at $335,000.

- Propose that Linda is willing to accept payment over time (i.e., as a "distributive award" under Sooke), but that she requires a substantial up-front payment to cover her immediate needs. A satisfactory up-front payment would be $42,500, being the amount she would almost certainly receive as a lump-sum award under the Morgan view (i.e., one-half of her actual contribution of $85,000). The balance could be paid in escalating quarterly installments over, say, a 10-year period, the amounts of the quarterly payments increasing in proportion to increases in Bill's income.

- Suggest that, if a settlement is reached, Linda would be willing to bear her own fees and costs.

- The letter should suggest a willingness to negotiate and expressly invite a response. Perhaps it should even set a deadline for the response, suggesting that Linda has authorized the commencement of litigation if no timely, meaningful response is received.

MPT Task 4L:
Franklin Asbestos Handling Regulations

FILE

INSTRUCTION FROM THE ATTORNEY GENERAL

Office of the Attorney General
State of Franklin
Environmental Protection Division

Candace G. Meyer, Attorney General

To: Applicant
From: Colin Dillard, Deputy Attorney General
Re: Regulations Implementing the Asbestos Handling Act
Date: July 27, 2000

Six months ago, the Franklin Legislature enacted the Asbestos Handling Act (AHA), which, among other things, requires the Franklin Department of Environmental Protection (DEP) to implement health and safety programs to train and certify workers who handle asbestos. DEP has asked us to review the proposed regulations it has drafted.

I anticipate the AHA statutory and regulatory scheme will be challenged on the ground that it is preempted by the federal Occupational Safety and Health Act (OSH Act) and the implementing federal regulations. Franklin has not adopted a State Plan under the OSH Act and has no intention of doing so.

Please prepare a memorandum for me that:

1) States the best case for why, in light of the absence of a State Plan, the statutory and regulatory scheme is not preempted in its entirety; and

2) Discusses whether each provision of Section 8 of the draft regulations can survive a preemption challenge.

ASBESTOS HANDLING ACT

Franklin Environmental Protection Code
Title 6 - Asbestos Control
Chapter 15. Asbestos Handling Act

Section 1. Findings and Purpose. The legislature of the State of Franklin finds that the predominant cause of asbestos becoming airborne is the performance of building renovation and demolition without adequate adherence to appropriate procedures for safeguarding the general public by persons who have not received adequate training in the handling of materials containing asbestos. The purposes of this subtitle are: 1) to safeguard the public health by requiring that renovation or demolition projects that disturb asbestos be conducted in accordance with procedures established pursuant to the provisions of this law; and 2) to ensure that workers who handle materials containing asbestos receive appropriate training designed to protect the public health.

* * *

Section 3. Unlawful Activities.

(a) It shall be unlawful for any person to perform a renovation or demolition project involving asbestos unless that person has received approval from the Franklin Department of Environmental Protection of a written plan specifying all steps that will be taken to protect the public, including monitoring air quality in the area surrounding the renovation or demolition site and restricting access to the site by anyone other than certified workers.

(b) It shall be unlawful to employ any person to handle asbestos material in the course of performing work for compensation on an asbestos project unless such person is a holder of a current, valid asbestos handling certificate.

* * *

Section 5. Fees and Assessments. The Franklin Department of Environmental Protection shall set reasonable fees and assessments to be used for the safe elimination of asbestos from buildings.

Section 6. Permits. No town or municipality shall issue a permit for a renovation or demolition project involving asbestos unless the applicant has established a plan pursuant to Section 3(a) and can show that each person working on the project holds a valid asbestos handling certificate pursuant to Section 3(b).

Section 7. Regulations to be Issued by the Secretary of the Franklin Department of Environmental Protection. In order to safeguard the health and safety of the public, including all persons who work at a renovation or demolition project involving asbestos, the Secretary of the Franklin Department of Environmental Protection shall establish criteria for: 1) certifying persons as eligible to receive an asbestos handling certificate; 2) certifying programs as approved safety and health programs; and 3) controlling asbestos during renovation or demolition projects. The Department shall implement an assessment procedure for funding the certification and training.

* * *

PROPOSED REGULATIONS

Department of Environmental Protection
Chapter 4 - Regulations Regarding Asbestos Control
Proposed Regulations Implementing Asbestos Handling Act
May 26, 2000

DRAFT

SUMMARY: These Proposed Regulations implement the Asbestos Handling Act, codified in Chapter 15 of Title 6 of the Franklin Environmental Protection Code. The Proposed Regulations govern procedures for conducting renovation and demolition projects that disturb asbestos and for training and certification of asbestos handlers, asbestos supervisors and asbestos investigators.

BACKGROUND: See attached Report of the Research and Investigation Unit of the Department of Environmental Protection (DEP) on *The Dangers of Airborne Asbestos Created by Construction Work in the State of Franklin.*

* * *

Section 8. Training and Certification of Asbestos Handlers.

(a) Any employee seeking an asbestos handling certificate must complete a five-day, DEP-approved training course and pass a two-hour written examination.

(b) An approved DEP training course for asbestos handlers must cover the following specific topics:

(1) the physical characteristics, including hazards and effects, of asbestos
(2) worker protective equipment
(3) state-of-the-art practices for asbestos abatement and remediation
(4) procedures for collecting asbestos samples to minimize airborne fibers
(5) personal hygiene pertaining to asbestos handling

(c) Any employee having an asbestos handling certificate must complete a one-day, DEP-approved biennial review course to renew the handler certificate.

(d) Upon receiving proof of completion of a DEP-approved training or review course for asbestos handlers and payment of $100, DEP shall issue an asbestos handler's certificate.

(e) Each employer performing work on a project in which any employee must handle asbestos must provide to the DEP the names of all employees possessing an asbestos handler's certificate, along with an assessment of $600 per year for each such employee.

* * *

RESEARCH PAPER

Department of Environmental Protection
State of Franklin

The Dangers of Airborne Asbestos Created by Construction Work in the State of Franklin

John P. Ripka, Chief, Research and Investigation Unit

Asbestos, a family of inorganic fibrous mineral substances once thought to be "wonder materials," has been identified in recent years as a formidable health threat. Much attention has been given to workplace hazards created by asbestos, but only recently has the focus been broadened to encompass the public health hazards presented by the widespread presence of friable asbestos.

Asbestos is the name given to a group of minerals that occur naturally as masses of strong, flexible fibers that can be separated into thin threads and woven. Asbestos tends to break easily into a dust composed of tiny particles that can float in the air and stick to clothes. The fibers of this so-called "friable" asbestos may be easily inhaled or swallowed and can cause serious health problems.

Exposure to airborne asbestos fibers may induce several serious diseases: asbestosis, a nonmalignant scarring of the lungs that causes extreme shortness of breath and often death; lung cancer, gastrointestinal cancer; and mesothelioma, a cancer of the lung lining or abdomen lining that develops 30 years after the first exposure to asbestos and that, once developed, invariably and rapidly causes death.

Widespread public concern about the hazards of asbestos has resulted in a significant annual decline in U.S. use of asbestos. In 1972, Franklin completely banned asbestos spraying in construction. Before the deadly hazards of asbestos were understood, however, more than half of the high-rise commercial buildings built in the state between 1958 and 1972 used asbestos as fireproofing material and, moreover, virtually every boiler room used the material as a thermal insulator. Franklin buildings contain an estimated 3.5 million tons of asbestos.

Since the early 1940s, millions of American workers have been exposed to asbestos dust. Health effects have been recognized in workers exposed in many trades and occupations. Even workers who have not worked directly with asbestos but whose jobs were located near contaminated areas have developed diseases associated with asbestos exposure.

Family members of workers heavily exposed to asbestos face an increased risk of developing asbestos-related diseases. This risk is thought to result from exposure to asbestos dust brought into the home on the shoes, clothing, skin, and hair of workers. Asbestos is so widely used that the entire population has been exposed to some degree. To protect all citizens, proper safety precautions should always be taken by people working with asbestos.

Both the federal government and the state of Franklin have recognized that safety lies in speedy action, which each has taken. The federal Occupational Safety and Health Administration has promulgated regulations to minimize the threat to construction workers from asbestos exposure. To minimize the threat to the general public from asbestos removal, Franklin and its Department of Environmental Protection have established a program to ensure the safe elimination of asbestos from buildings for workers who handle asbestos.

LIBRARY

United States Code

OCCUPATIONAL SAFETY AND HEALTH ACT

29 U.S.C. § 652 Definitions

* * * *

(8) The term "occupational safety and health standard" means a standard which requires conditions, or the adoption or use of one or more practices, means, methods, operations, or processes reasonably necessary or appropriate to provide safe or healthful employment and places of employment.

* * * *

29 U.S.C. § 667 State jurisdiction and plans

(a) **Assertion of State standards in absence of applicable Federal standards.** Nothing in this chapter shall prevent any State agency or court from asserting jurisdiction under State law over any occupational safety or health issue with respect to which no Federal standard is in effect.

(b) **Submission of State plan for development and enforcement of State standards to preempt applicable Federal standards.** Any State which, at any time, desires to assume responsibility for development and enforcement therein of occupational safety and health standards relating to any occupational safety or health issue with respect to which a Federal standard has been promulgated shall submit a State plan for the development of such standards and their enforcement.

* * * *

OSHA STANDARDS

Code of Federal Regulations

CHAPTER XVII—OCCUPATIONAL SAFETY AND HEALTH ADMINISTRATION
U.S. DEPARTMENT OF LABOR
PART 1910—OCCUPATIONAL SAFETY AND HEALTH STANDARDS
SUBPART Z—TOXIC AND HAZARDOUS SUBSTANCES

29 C.F.R. § 1926 Asbestos.

* * * *

(f) Exposure limit. The employer shall ensure that no employee is exposed to an airborne concentration of asbestos in excess of 1.0 fiber per cubic centimeter of air (1 f/cc) as averaged over a sampling period of thirty (30) minutes.

(g) All employers of employees exposed to asbestos hazards shall comply with applicable protective provisions to protect their employees.

(h) Each employer who has a workplace or work operation where exposure monitoring is required shall perform monitoring to determine accurately the airborne concentrations of asbestos to which employees may be exposed.

(i) The employer shall notify affected employees of the monitoring results that represent that employee's exposure as soon as possible following receipt of monitoring results.

(j) When a building owner or employer identifies previously installed asbestos-containing material, labels or signs shall be affixed or posted so that employees will be notified of the presence of asbestos-containing materials.

(k) Where vacuuming methods are used, filtered vacuuming equipment must be used. The equipment shall be used and emptied in a manner that minimizes the reentry of asbestos into the workplace.

(l) All employees performing work covered by this paragraph shall be trained in a training program that meets the requirements of this section.

(m) Employee Information and Training.

    (i) The employer shall, at no cost to the employee, institute a training program for all employees who are likely to be exposed to asbestos and ensure their participation in the program.

    (ii) Training shall be provided prior to or at the time of initial assignment and at least annually thereafter.

(iii) Training shall include "hands-on" training and shall take at least eight (8) hours.

(iv) The training program shall be conducted in a manner that the employee is able to understand. The employer shall ensure that each such employee is informed of the following:

(A) Methods of recognizing asbestos;

(B) The health effects associated with asbestos exposure;

(C) The relationship between smoking and asbestos in producing lung cancer;

(D) The nature of operations that could result in exposure to asbestos, the importance of necessary protective controls to minimize exposure, including, as applicable, engineering controls, work practices, respirators, housekeeping procedures, hygiene facilities, protective clothing, decontamination procedures, emergency procedures, and waste disposal procedures, and any necessary instruction in the use of these controls and procedures;

(E) The purpose, proper use, fitting instructions, and limitations of respirators;

(F) The appropriate work practices for performing the asbestos job;

* * * *

Gade v. National Solid Wastes Management Association
United States Supreme Court (1992)

In 1988, the Illinois General Assembly enacted the Hazardous Waste Crane Operators Licensing Act. The purpose of the act is both to promote job safety and to protect life, limb and property. We consider whether such a dual impact statute, which protects both workers and the general public, is preempted by the federal Occupational Safety and Health Act of 1970 (OSH Act) and the standards promulgated thereunder.

The OSH Act authorizes the Secretary of Labor to promulgate occupational safety and health regulations. In the Superfund Amendments and Reauthorization Act of 1986, Congress directed the Secretary of Labor to promulgate regulations for the health and safety protection of employees engaged in hazardous waste operations, including routine training.

The Occupational Safety and Health Administration (OSHA) promulgated the required regulations, including detailed regulations on worker training requirements. Those who have satisfied the eight-hour training requirement receive a written certification; uncertified workers are prohibited from engaging in hazardous waste operations.

The Illinois licensing act at issue here is designated as an act "in relation to environmental protection," and its stated aim is to protect both employees and the general public. The licensing act requires a license applicant to provide a certified record of at least 40 hours of training under an approved program conducted within Illinois, to pass a written examination, and to complete an annual refresher course. Employees who work without the proper license and employers who knowingly permit an unlicensed employee to work are subject to fines.

National Solid Wastes Management Association (Association) is a national trade association of businesses that dispose of waste material, including hazardous waste. The Association's members are subject to the OSH Act and OSHA regulations. For hazardous waste operations conducted in Illinois, certain of the workers employed by the Association's members are also required to obtain state licenses. Thus, for example, some of the Association's members must ensure that their employees receive not only the eight hours of field experience required for certification under the OSHA regulations, but also the 40 hours of training required for licensing under the state statutes.

The Association brought a declaratory judgment action against Mary Gade, the Director of the Illinois Environmental Protection Agency (IEPA), and sought to enjoin IEPA from enforcing the Illinois act, claiming that the act was preempted by the OSH Act and OSHA regulations. While finding that some provisions of the Illinois law were preempted by the OSH Act, the district court held that state laws that attempt to regulate workplace safety and health while regulating other areas are not necessarily preempted. The United States Court of Appeals for the Seventh Circuit affirmed in part and reversed in part. We granted certiorari.

Before addressing the scope of the OSH Act's preemption of dual impact state regulations, we consider the threshold question of whether the Act preempts nonconflicting state regulations at all. Whether a state action is preempted by federal law is a question of congressional intent. In the OSH Act, Congress endeavored "to assure so far as possible every working man and woman in the nation safe and healthful working conditions." Congress authorized the Secretary of Labor to set mandatory occupational safety and health standards applicable to all businesses affecting interstate commerce and thereby brought the federal government into a field that traditionally had been occupied by the states. Federal regulation of the workplace was not intended to be all encompassing, however. The Act does not prevent state regulation of any occupational safety or health issue "with respect to which no Federal standard is in effect." 29 U.S.C. § 667(a). In addition to reserving areas for state regulation, the Act gave the states the option of entirely assuming regulation in an area. 29 U.S.C. § 667(b). Illinois has not sought or received the Secretary's approval for its own state plan. 29 U.S.C. § 667(b) preempts any state law or regulation that establishes an occupational health and safety standard on an issue for which OSHA has already promulgated a standard, unless the State has obtained approval for its own plan.

Absent explicit preemptive language, we have recognized at least two types of implied preemption: *field preemption*, where the scheme of federal regulation is so pervasive as to make reasonable the inference that Congress left no room for the states to supplement it, and *conflict preemption*, where compliance with both federal and state regulations is a physical impossibility or where state law stands as an obstacle to the accomplishment and execution of the full purposes and objectives of Congress.

We hold that nonapproved state regulation of occupational safety and health issues for which a federal standard is in effect is impliedly preempted as in conflict with the full purposes and objectives of the OSH Act. Congress intended to subject employers and employees to only one set of regulations, be it federal or state, and the only way a state may regulate an OSHA-regulated occupational safety and health issue is through an approved state plan. The OSH Act as a whole evidences Congress' intent to avoid subjecting workers and employers to duplicative regulation; a state may develop an occupational safety and health program, but only if it displaces applicable federal regulations with an approved state plan.

Also, 29 U.S.C. § 667(a), which saves from preemption any state law regulating an occupational safety and health issue with respect to which no federal standard is in effect, implies that state laws regulating the same issue as federal laws are not saved, even if they merely supplement federal law.

In determining whether state law stands as an obstacle to the full implementation of a federal law, it is not enough to say that the ultimate goal of both federal and state law is the same. A state law is preempted if it interferes with the methods by which the federal statute was designed to reach that goal.

We now consider whether a state law that addresses public safety as well as occupational safety, a dual impact law, can be an "occupational safety and health standard" subject to preemption under the Act. The OSH Act does not lose its preemptive force merely because the state legislature articulates a purpose other than (or in addition to) workplace health and safety. In assessing the impact of a state law on the federal scheme, we have refused to rely solely on the legislature's professed purpose and have looked as well to the effects of the law. Any state legislation that frustrates the full effectiveness of federal law is rendered invalid by the Supremacy Clause.

The key question is at what point the state regulation sufficiently interferes with federal regulation that it should be deemed preempted. In the absence of an approved state plan, the OSH Act preempts all state law that constitutes, in a direct, clear and substantial way, regulation of worker health and safety. State laws of general applicability that do not conflict with OSHA standards and that regulate the conduct of workers and nonworkers alike would generally not be preempted. Although some laws of general applicability may have a direct and substantial effect on worker safety, they cannot fairly be character-ized as occupational standards because they regulate workers as members of the general public. A law directed at workplace safety, however, is not saved from preemption simply because it has effects outside of the workplace.

Because the provisions of Illinois law have a direct and substantial effect on the federal scheme for regulation of hazardous waste, they are preempted. Affirmed.

Chamber of Commerce v. Noter, Secretary of Franklin Department of Labor, et al.

United States Court of Appeals for the Fifteenth Circuit (1995)

This is an appeal from a summary judgment in consolidated actions challenging the constitutionality of the Franklin Worker and Community Right-to-Know Act (Know Act), which requires the disclosure of substances that may pose workplace and environmental hazards. The district court held that some of the sections of the Know Act are preempted by the federal Occupational Safety and Health Act (OSH Act) and OSHA's Hazard Communication Regulations. All parties appeal. We affirm in part and reverse in part.

The legislative findings and declaration of purpose, included in the Know Act, provide that

The proliferation of hazardous substances in the environment poses a threat to the public health. Individuals have a right to know the risks they face so that they can make reasoned decisions and take informed action concerning their employment and their living conditions. Local health, fire, police, safety and other government officials require detailed information about the identity of hazardous substances in order to adequately plan for, and respond to, emergencies. It is in the public interest to establish a comprehensive program for the disclosure of information about hazardous substances in the workplace and the community and to provide a procedure for residents to gain access to this information.

The Know Act directs the Franklin Department of Environmental Protection (DEP) to develop an environmental hazardous substance list, which must contain

substances used, manufactured, stored, packaged, repackaged, or disposed of or released into the environment of the state which, in the department's determination, may be linked to the incidence of cancer and other diseases.

Whether a state law or regulation is preempted by a federal statute is a question of congressional intent. *Gade v. National Solid Wastes Management Association* (U.S. Supreme Court, 1992).

The Chamber of Commerce contends that 29 U.S.C. § 667 (a) and (b) should be read expansively to preempt all state statutes that relate to a safety or health issue for which a standard has been promulgated. It further contends that, since all provisions of the Know Act relate to issues that are regulated by the OSHA Hazard Communication Regulations, the Franklin statute is preempted in its entirety. We reject this broad reading.

The Supreme Court in *Gade (supra)* has acknowledged that a state law or regulation that has a "dual purpose" may escape complete preemption even though it might have an incidental effect upon the scheme of federal regulations. For example, a law or regulation the principal purpose of which is to train employees in safety-affecting measures aimed at protecting the public from dangers arising from processes or materials handled in the workplace may escape complete preemption even though it has incidental effects on workplace safety. Thus, it may be necessary to parse the components of the state regulation into its preempted and non-preempted provisions.

Consideration of whether a state provision violates the Supremacy Clause starts with the basic assumption that Congress did not intend to displace state law. A section is preempted only to the extent that congressional intent can be found expressly or by implication. The mere fact that a state law provision increases the regulatory burden on employers does not make the state law provision contrary to congressional intent. Portions of the Know Act, however, are preempted.

The first part of the Know Act directs the Franklin DEP and Department of Health to develop environmental and workplace hazardous substance lists. In these provisions, Franklin has opted for a different hazard identification procedure than that adopted in the federal Hazard Communication Regulations. The federal procedure depends primarily upon identification and communication of hazards by the original manufacturer or importer of the substance.

Franklin's development of its own list of hazardous substances through governmental agencies in all sectors of the economy will in no way inhibit the implementation of the federal standard. The state lists are not an obstacle to the full implementation of the federal law because they do not "interfere with the methods" used in the Hazard Communication Regulations to achieve the goal of worker health and safety.

In addition, where, as here, a state statute has a dual purpose of promoting both the health and safety of the worker and the health and safety of the general population, the statute is preempted only if it has a "direct and substantial" effect on the federal system of regulation. Therefore, the sections of the Know Act regarding the development of lists by the agencies of the Franklin government are not preempted.

The second part of the Know Act requires employers to complete both environmental and workplace hazard surveys and to furnish the workplace surveys to state agencies concerned with the protection of employees and to state and local agencies concerned with the protection of the public at large. The requirement that they be furnished to both kinds of agencies suggests that these sections of the Act may have a broader purpose than the federal Hazard Communication Regulations. However, any hazardous substance listed as a workplace hazard and not listed as an environmental hazard is deemed to be a specific threat to workers. The sections of the surveys about workplace hazards have a direct and substantial effect on the promotion of occupational health and safety through hazard communication. The federal Hazard Communication Regulations preempt these sections because they are in conflict with the methods chosen by the federal government to promote hazard communication. Similarly, the obligation of employers to keep a central file of workplace surveys is also preempted.

However, since the sections requiring reporting of environmental hazards (as opposed to workplace hazards) to agencies concerned with public health and safety are not a matter governed by the OSH Act and OSHA regulations, they are not preempted. Neither are the sections requiring employers to keep and make available environmental surveys. OSHA regulations govern occupational safety and health issues; they do not preempt state laws that regulate other concerns. OSHA regulations cannot have a preemptive effect beyond that field.

The Know Act provides that the governmental activity will be funded by assessments against all Franklin employers. The Chamber of Commerce argues that since this financing mechanism indicates that the Act is aimed solely at occupational safety and health, rather than at community health and safety in general, all provisions of the Act should be preempted. That contention is without merit. The funding provision is a logical means for accomplishing a broad community health and safety purpose. It does not interfere with compliance with the OSH Act or impose obstacles to the accomplishment of the OSH Act's purposes. *John Saint, Secretary of the Franklin Department of Labor v. Port Orey Co.* (15th Cir. 1994).

The judgment is affirmed in part, reversed in part, and the case remanded for proceedings consistent with this opinion.

THE MPT
MULTISTATE PERFORMANCE TEST

Franklin Asbestos Handling Regulations

POINT SHEET

The MPT point sheet, grading summary, and grading guidelines describe the factual and legal points encompassed within the lawyering task to be completed. They outline all the possible issues and points that might be addressed by an applicant. They are provided to the user jurisdictions for the sole purpose of assisting graders in grading the examination by identifying the issues and suggesting the resolution of the problem contemplated by the drafters. These are not official grading guides. Applicants can receive a range of passing grades, including excellent grades, without covering all the points discussed in these guides. The model answer is included as an illustration of a thorough and detailed response to the task, one that addresses all the legal and factual issues the drafters intended to raise in the problem. It is intended to serve only as an example. Applicants need not present their responses in the same way to receive good grades. User jurisdictions are free to modify these grading materials, including the suggested weights assigned to particular points. Grading the MPT is the exclusive responsibility of the jurisdiction using the MPT as part of its admissions process.

Copyright ©2008 by the National Conference of Bar Examiners.
All rights reserved

Franklin Asbestos Handling Regulations

DRAFTERS' POINT SHEET

In this performance test item, the applicant is cast in the role of a lawyer in the Office of the Attorney General. The Franklin Department of Environmental Protection (DEP) has asked the Attorney General to opine whether the Franklin Asbestos Handling Act (AHA) and the proposed regulations implementing the AHA are preempted by the federal Occupational Safety and Health Act (OSH Act).

The File contains the relevant provisions of the AHA, a draft of the proposed regulations, and a recent report of the DEP on the dangers of airborne asbestos. The Library contains excerpts from the OSH Act and the federal OSHA regulations, and two cases dealing with the subject.

The task is for the applicant to prepare a two-part memorandum: 1) arguing that the AHA and the proposed DEP regulations as a whole are not preempted; and 2) discussing whether each of the particular provisions of the proposed regulations can survive a preemption challenge. The contending principles are whether the DEP regulations intrude upon the OSH Act's domain of workplace safety regulations or whether they can be justified in whole or in part as regulations aimed at non-workplace, public safety measures.

1. **Overview:** The applicants are not required to follow any particular format, except that the work product ought to end up looking like an office memorandum. It should consist of two separate parts, the first part dealing with the overall preemption issue and the second with the individual provisions of the proposed regulations, testing each provision against the preemption principles articulated in the cases. Applicants need not cover them all to receive "passing" or even very good scores.

2. **Overall Preemption:** Here, the applicants should set out the general grounds of federal preemption and examine the AHA and the proposed DEP regulations in light of the "dual impact" holding of the *Gade* case.

- In *Gade*, the Supreme Court states that, unless Congress has explicitly preempted state activity in a particular area of legislation, a state may act unless the two types of implied preemption preclude it: field preemption and conflict preemption.
- Congress did not explicitly preempt all state activity in the area of safety and health regulation.
- Congress did, however, intend to preempt *occupational* safety and health regulation insofar as it pertains to employee workplace safety, unless:
  - The state regulation purports to establish a protective measure as to which there is no federal "standard" and the state regulation does not burden commerce; or
  - The state has chosen to retain jurisdiction by submitting and obtaining approval of its own "state plan."
    - It is clear from the facts that Franklin does not have or intend to submit a state plan.
- In matters relating to employee workplace safety and health, there is no "field" preemption but there will be "conflict" preemption when a state attempts to regulate employee workplace safety and health in a way that conflicts with or even purports to supplement an existing federal standard. See *Gade*.

However, it is possible to avoid total preemption if the state action under scrutiny has a "dual impact," e.g., is aimed both at workplace regulation and public safety.

- The preamble to the AHA states that, "The purposes of this subtitle are: 1) to safeguard the public health by requiring that renovation or demolition projects that disturb asbestos be conducted in accordance with procedures established pursuant to this law; and 2) to ensure that workers who handle materials containing asbestos receive appropriate training designed to protect the public health."
  - This section contains something of an ambiguity in that it says that one of the two purposes is "to ensure that . . . *workers* . . . receive appropriate training," thus giving it a "dual impact" character.
- The "Background" section of the proposed regulations refers to the DEP's investigative report as the impetus for the regulations. The focus of that report is on the public health hazards associated with the handling of friable asbestos (i.e., asbestos-containing materials that, when dry, can be crumbled by hand) and the need for training of workers who handle the materials.
- Again, the proposed regulations partake of a "dual impact" because they involve both workers (the subject of the federal OSH Act regulations) and public health (not covered by the OSH Act).

- In the final analysis, the AHA probably avoids complete preemption because of its dual impact character.
  - As the *Gade* court says, the key question is at what point the state regulation sufficiently interferes with the federal regulation that it should be preempted.
    - Merely labeling a statute as having a dual impact will not avoid preemption.
      - The AHA and the proposed regulations are arguably preempted because they deal with an area where the federal OSH Act and the OSHA regulations have established a "standard," i.e., asbestos handling in the workplace.
      - But, according to *Gade*, a statute of general application will not be preempted, even though it has a direct effect on worker safety, if the focus is on workers as members of the general public rather than as employees working in a regulated workplace.
  - The conclusion the applicants should reach is that the AHA and the proposed regulations are not completely preempted because they are not aimed principally at protecting workers but, rather, at training and certifying them in work methods designed to protect the public.

3. **Whether each of the particular provisions of the proposed regulations can survive a preemption challenge:** Having concluded that the proposed regulations are not completely preempted, the applicants must turn to the teaching of the *Noter* case: that certain parts might be preempted if they have a "direct and substantial effect on the federal system of regulation."
   - The task here is to test each of the provisions of the proposed regulations against the guidelines articulated in *Noter*, i.e.:
     - Whether the particular provision is preempted because it interferes with the federal regulations or the methods chosen by the federal regulations to implement the OSH Act;
     - Whether any particular provision relates so much to a workplace safety standard that it *per se* falls within the ambit of the OSHA regulations and is therefore preempted; or
     - Whether it is not at all a workplace safety measure within the ambit of the OSH Act and is, for that reason, not preempted.

The Individual Provisions:

- The DEP requirement for employee certification: The purpose of the DEP regulations is to implement the requirement of the AHA that persons employed to work in occupations involving the handling of friable asbestos in asbestos-containing renovation and demolition projects be certified in asbestos handling technology.
  - The OSHA regulations do not require certification of employees handling asbestos in the workplace. Arguably, therefore, because OSHA has established a "standard" that does not require certification, the OSHA regulations preempt the DEP regulations.
  - However, the threshold certification requirement under the AHA is designed basically to ensure public health and safety as opposed to employee workplace safety.
    - As such, it deals with an area not within the ambit of the OSH Act.
  - Resolution: Because of the disparate purpose of the AHA certification requirement, it is not preempted by the OSH Act. As the court said in *Gade*, even though this dual impact law might have a direct effect on worker safety, it is not preempted as an occupational standard because it regulates workers as members of the general public.
- DEP Reg. § 8(a)—Five-day training course and two-hour exam: Both the proposed DEP regulations and the existing OSHA regulations require *employees* to undergo asbestos training. Under the OSHA regulations, it is the employer's responsibility to "institute a training program . . . and ensure [employee] participation." Under the DEP regulations, it is the employee's obligation to "complete a five-day, DEP-approved training course."
  - Both sets of regulations are aimed at *employees* who handle asbestos in their occupations and places of employment.
    - It is a distinction without a difference that, under the OSHA regulations, the employer must initiate the program while, under the DEP regulations, it is the employee's responsibility to take the course.

The DEP regulations require each employee to take a five-day training course and to pass a two-hour written exam.

- By way of contrast, the OSHA regulations provide for a course of "at least eight (8) hours" and do not require passage of an exam.
- Resolution: It is probable that this part of the DEP regulation is preempted to the extent that it requires a five-day course and a two-hour test, i.e.:
  - Although its ultimate aim is to train employees in methods of protecting the public, it is nonetheless a workplace regulation in an area where the federal OSHA regulations have an existing standard and the two are in conflict. It can be argued that DEP's five-day requirement is not in conflict because the OSHA regulations say "at least" eight hours, but the disparity is so great that the two cannot be reconciled.
  - See *Gade*, which holds that a state regulation is preempted if it tries to regulate the same "issue" as the federal regulation, even if it purports only to supplement the federal issue.
  - Thus, this requirement is preempted either because it is inextricably related to a workplace regulation and is therefore in the sole domain of federal OSHA or because it interferes with the method chosen by the federal regulation to implement the OSH Act.

DEP Reg. § 8 (b)—Required content of the training course: Both sets of regulations specify the areas in which the employees shall be trained. The corresponding provisions regarding *worker* protection, as to which federal OSHA has exclusive jurisdiction (e.g., respiratory protection, personal protective equipment, hazards and effects of asbestos), are largely identical. There appears to be no conflict and no reason to assert preemption.

- To the extent that the DEP regulations impose additional requirements, those additional requirements appear to be aimed at protection of the *public* (e.g., asbestos abatement and remediation, collection of samples) and are not within the ambit of the OSH Act.
- However, it can be argued that if the five-day training course is preempted (as argued *supra*), then all components of it, including the course content, are also preempted.
- Resolution: On balance, however, this part of the DEP regulations would probably not be preempted.
  - See *Notes*, where it holds that preemption only occurs in a dual purpose statute where there is a direct and substantial effect on the federal system of regulation.

DEP Reg. § 8 (c)—Periodic review course: Both sets of regulations require that employees undergo a periodic review course. The DEP regulations require a one-day *biennial* review course. The OSHA regulations require it annually and, by implication, for eight hours (the equivalent of one day).

- Although there is no apparent conflict, the OSHA regulation prevails because it has established a standard relating to a workplace activity, over which the OSH Act has exclusive jurisdiction.
- It can be argued, however, that as to the additional, non-workplace training requirements (*supra*), federal OSHA has no jurisdiction and, therefore, the DEP biennial review requirement is not preempted.

Resolution: This part of the DEP regulations is probably preempted as to the mutually required training topics because they are workplace issues and federal OSHA regulations have established a standard. As to the training topics related to public safety issues, however, the biennial review requirements are not preempted.

DEP Reg. § 8(d)—The requirement for payment of $100 upon completion of the training course: Here, there is a direct conflict. The DEP regulations require payment of $100 for issuance of an asbestos handler's certificate. The OSHA regulations require that the training be at no cost to the employee.

- It is unclear from the DEP regulations whether the employer or the

handling occupation, the burden falls on the employee.

- Resolution: This provision of the DEP regulations is almost certainly preempted because it is in direct conflict with the OSHA regulation and interferes with the method chosen by federal OSHA to implement the OSH Act.

• DEP Reg. § 8 (e)—The employer's reporting requirement and the $600 assessment: The OSHA regulations are silent on this subject. Because the DEP requirements for employee certification are designed to implement a public safety measure and not to advance workplace safety, the annual assessment does not intrude upon an area where federal OSHA has jurisdiction. As the court observed in *Noter*, "The funding requirement is a logical means for accomplishing a broad community health and safety purpose. It does not interfere with compliance with the OSH Act or impose obstacles to the accomplishment of the OSH Act's purposes."

- Resolution: This part of the DEP regulation is probably not preempted.

Perform Your Best™ Materials
for MPT Task 4A:
In re Lisa Peel

Perform Your Best on the Multistate Performance Test

Note to the Reader: Your MPT-Matrix™ will have only page numbers, not words. The words in this MPT Matrix™ simply show you the information you will be indexing and cross-referencing. Do not attempt to write words in your own MPT-Matrix™.

MPT-Matrix™ *In re Lisa Peel*, MPT, February 2008

FRSA	A. Lisa Peel Interview	B. Blog Post	C. *America Today*	D. Dictionary	E. *In re Bellows* (Franklin Ct. App. 2005)	F. *Lane v. Tichenor* (Franklin Sup. Ct. 2003)
"Reporter" Any person "regularly engaged in collecting...."	**P-2.** Lisa Peel attends the meeting of several public bodies. **P-2.** Lisa Peel collects and posts agendas, minutes. **P-2.** Against Peel: She is retired, has no training.			[Dictionary definition not relevant, because statute defines term.]	**P-9.** Sole issue is whether appellant is a "reporter" under FRSA. Key is intent at inception of news-gathering.	
					P-9. Examples of reporters: freelance writer; author of medical journal article. Not covered: paid ads; defamatory messages on bulletin board.	
writing or editing news	**P-2.** Peel writes commentary. **P-2.** Peel decides what to post.					

MPT-Matrix™ *In re Lisa Peel*, MPT, February 2008, *cont'd*

FRSA	A. Lisa Peel Interview	B. Blog Post	C. *America Today*	D. Dictionary	E. *In re Bellows* (Franklin Ct. App. 2005)	F. *Lane v. Tichenor* (Franklin Sup. Ct. 2003)
	Against Peel: "writer" and "editor" refer to traditional media. Against Peel: **P-2.** She includes pet photos and family news.					
"For publication through a news medium" "Any newspaper,…"		Lisa Peel's blog post reads like a news story. Posting is like printing. Against Peel: Blog not a newspaper or magazine.	**P-6.** Some bloggers have press credentials. Blogs are alternative media.	**P-8.** "Publication" is communication of information to the public.		**P-11.** Burden is on the party claiming the reporter's privilege, so court may look to external aids. **P-11.** To determine whether hayriding is included in "other similar activities," the court must give effect to the intent of the legislature. **P-11.** General words after particular words mean things of the same kind.

Perform Your Best on the Multistate Performance Test

MPT-Matrix™ *In re Lisa Peel*, MPT, February 2008, *cont'd*

FRSA	A. Lisa Peel Interview	B. Blog Post	C. America Today	D. Dictionary	E. *In re Bellows* (Franklin Ct. App. 2005)	F. *Lane v. Tichenor* (Franklin Sup. Ct. 2003)
"issued at regular intervals"	**P-2.** Lisa Peel blogs every weekend, normally but not always on Friday. Against Peel: less regular than newspaper.				**P-9.** In *Haush*, defamatory posts were neither "news" nor posted at regular intervals.	
"Having a general circulation"	**P-2.** Ms. Peel's blog has 3500 registrants in town of 38,000 people, plus numerous non-registered viewers.			**P-8.** "Circulation."		
This act "is intended to promote the free flow of information to the public by prohibiting courts from compelling reporters to disclose unpublished news sources or information received from such sources." "Source" is the person from whom or the means through which the information was obtained.	**P-3.** Peel talks to people on the inside, promises confidentiality. **P-3.** Peel says that because of the limits on subject matter in the local newspaper, her blog is the "only avenue for real news" in the county.				**P-10.** Principal rule of statutory construction is to ascertain and give effect to the legislature's intent. Court must give legislative language "its plain and ordinary meaning and construe the statute as a whole. . . ." **P-9.** The burden is on the party claiming the reporter's privilege under the Act. **P-10.** Extending FRSA to photographers "consistent with the purposes of the act."	

203

Perform Your Best on the Bar Exam Performance Test (MPT)

Perform Your Best™ Sample Answer for *In re Lisa Peel*

Black, Fernandez & Hanson LLP

Attorneys at Law
Suite 215
396 West Main Street
Greenville, Franklin 33755

MEMORANDUM

To: Henry Black

From: Bar Candidate

Re: Peel subpoena

Date: _____

INTRODUCTION

You have asked me to prepare an objective memorandum examining both sides of the question whether our client Lisa Peel qualifies under the Franklin Reporter Shield Act (FRSA) to resist a subpoena ordering her to appear before a grand jury and produce notes regarding persons she interviewed for a post on her blog. I conclude that Lisa Peel is a "reporter" under the FRSA, and that she qualifies for its protection. The court will probably grant her motion to quash the subpoena.

DISCUSSION

I. Lisa Peel qualifies as a "reporter" under the Franklin Reporter Shield Act (FRSA), if her blog is a "news medium."

The Franklin Reporter Shield Act (FRSA) gives reporters a privilege not to "disclose the source of any information or any unpublished material" except as the Act provides. FRSA sec. 902. For the Franklin Reporter Shield Act to apply to blogger Lisa Peel she must be a "reporter." The burden is on Peel to show that she qualifies. *In re Bellows* (Franklin Sup. Ct. 2002).

The principal rule of statutory construction is to ascertain and give effect to the legislature's intent. *In re Bellows*. The primary purpose of the FRSA is to "safeguard the media's ability to gather news," promoting the free flow of information by prohibiting courts from "compelling reporters to disclose unpublished news sources or information received from such sources."

Section 901(a) of the FRSA defines "reporter" as follows:

"[R]eporter" means any person regularly engaged in collecting, writing, or editing news for publication through a news medium.

In *Bellows*, where the court held that a photographer is a reporter under the FRSA, the court said that the key is the person's intent at the inception of news-gathering. Here, like the photographer in *Bellows*, Lisa Peel does all her news-gathering with the intent of publishing it.

Peel is also like a freelance writer and like the author of a medical journal article, both of them held to be reporters in cases cited in *Bellows*. Peel's blog is arguably distinguishable from the venues where the court found that writers were not reporters: paid ads or defamatory messages on sports bulletin boards.

On the other hand, Peel may appear not to qualify as a reporter because she has no training as a reporter, she does not get paid, and she includes pet pictures, family news, and other matter lacking newsworthiness on her blog. In light of her performing the work of a reporter, however, these arguments are not compelling.

Collecting news. Lisa Peel does the work of a reporter collecting news. She attends meetings and collects and posts agendas and minutes of local government agencies, and she makes calls and does interviews. Peel Interview. Writing news. Ms. Peel writes news and commentary about the news. Peel Interview. Editing news. Ms. Peel edits what goes into the blog. She decides which stories to pursue and what to post.

II. Posts on Lisa Peel's blog are "publication" through a "news medium" within the meaning of the Franklin Reporter Shield Act, and her source for information about Assistant Superintendent Frank Peterson's retaining equipment belonging to the Greenville School District qualifies as a "source" within the meaning of the FRSA.

Publication through a news medium. The FRSA protects work done "for publication through a news medium," but it does not define "publication." Thus, the court may look to external aids. *Lane*. According to the *American Heritage Dictionary* (4th ed., 2000), "publication" is "communication of information to the public." Lisa Peel's blog is definitely communication of information to the public.

News medium. "News medium" under Section 901(b) of the Franklin Reporter Shield Act (FRSA) means any "newspaper, magazine, or other similar medium issued at regular intervals and having a general circulation: a radio station; a television station; a community antenna television service . . . ."

For the following reasons, I conclude that Lisa Peel's blog is likely to be held a "news medium" within the meaning of the FRSA. While the blog is neither a newspaper nor a magazine, the blog post in issue here ("$10,000 in School Equipment Diverted from Schools to Home of Assistant Superintendent") reads like a news story in a newspaper. And Ms. Peel's posting on the internet is arguably like a newspaper's printing and distributing its stories. In addition, blogs are replacing newspapers. According to *America Today*, some 30 per cent of Americans "read one or more blogs regularly." *America Today* says that blogs are even replacing news web sites. They provide "more means of sharing news." Even traditional newspapers are now publishing blogs. *America Today*, July 5, 2007.

Other similar medium. Although the blog is not a newspaper or magazine, the FRSA also includes the language "other similar medium," and it gives a list: "a radio station; a television station; a community antenna television service . . . ." The court in *Lane v. Tichenor*, says that where the legislature provides a list and says "other similar activities," the court must inquire into legislative intent. Where the intent is not clear and enumeration is neither exclusive nor exhaustive, courts may use external aids, e.g., a dictionary. *Lane*.

According to *America Today*, today some 30 per cent of Americans "read one or more blogs regularly." *America Today*, July 5, 2007. While blogs did not exist when the FRSA was enacted in 1948, the fact that the legislature included examples of media that were relatively new in 1948, arguably indicates legislative intent to include new media.

"Issued at regular intervals." Ms. Peel blogs every week-end, normally on Friday. Thus, on the one hand, her schedule is regular, unlike the internet bulletin board in *Haush*. On the other hand, her blog does not always appear on the same day of the week, so it is not totally regular.

"Having a general circulation." *The American Heritage Dictionary* defines "circulation" as "the passing of something, such as money or news, from place to place or person to person . . . distribution . . . ." Ms. Peel can argue that her blog has a general circulation. It has 3,500 registrants in a town of 38,000 people, or almost 10 per cent of the population, and there have been more than 15,000 visitors. Peel Interview.

Source. The final question is whether the person whose identity Lisa Peel wishes to keep confidential is a "source" within the meaning of the FRSA. The statute says that a "source" is "the person from whom or the means through which the information was obtained." Ms. Peel's source is the person from whom she obtained the information in her blog post.

III. Lisa Peel meets her burden under the Franklin Reporter Shield Act of showing that protecting her against the subpoena compelling her to reveal the source of her story about Frank Peterson fulfills the intent of the statute.

The intent of the FRSA is "to safeguard the media's ability to gather news." It serves the purpose of "promoting the free flow of information to the public." FRSA sec. 900.

If, as Lisa Peel says, the publisher of the only newspaper in Montgomery County discourages reporters from doing stories and investigations that might portray the communities in a bad light, then her blog is necessary to provide the public in Montgomery County with information. Peel Interview. To afford the protections of the FRSA to her blog is to promote the "free flow of information to the public."

Examination of the plain and ordinary meaning of the FRSA and construction of the statute as a whole, above, yields the conclusion that Peel is a "reporter" within the meaning of the FRSA, and that she is entitled to its protections.

CONCLUSION

Having examined both sides of the question, I conclude that our client Lisa Peel can meet her burden of showing that she is a "reporter" within the meaning of the Franklin Reporter Shield Act (FRSA), and that protecting Peel's sources is consistent with the purposes of the FRSA. If so, the court cannot compel Peel to reveal the identity of the source for her blog post about Frank Peterson, and the court is likely to grant her motion to quash the subpoena.

Perform Your Best™
Note on Analyzing *In re Lisa Peel*

Objective Memorandum
Context: Litigation
Structure: Statutory Analysis

The Partner Memo for *In re Lisa Peel* tells the bar candidate to write a memorandum analyzing whether the firm can use the Franklin Reporter Shield Act (FRSA) to quash a subpoena against client Lisa Peel, compelling her to divulge the source for one of her blog posts. Since this entails looking at both sides of the question, your memorandum will be an objective memorandum. Your memorandum will state explicitly that it is an objective memorandum. The sample memo in this book begins:

> You have asked me to prepare an objective memorandum examining both sides of the question whether our client Lisa Peel qualifies under the Franklin Reporter Shield Act (FRSA) to resist a subpoena ordering her to appear before a grand jury and produce notes regarding persons she interviewed for a post on her blog.

How to Read the Partner Memo to Make Your Outline in the MPT-Matrix™. Following the instructions in the Partner Memo is always the key to success on the MPT. With the *Perform Your Best*™ MPT System, the instructions in the Partner Memo, also called the task memorandum, are the starting point for the outline in the MPT-Matrix™. The Partner Memo for *In re Lisa Peel* asks the bar candidate to write an objective memorandum, that is, a memorandum that argues both sides of the assigned question.

You must normally divide each instruction in the Partner Memo into its smallest parts. But the instruction in the Partner Memo for *In re Lisa Peel* asks a simple Yes-No question, whether the firm's client Lisa Peel can use the Franklin Reporter Shield Act (FRSA) to quash a subpoena demanding her sources for a post she published on her blog. Thus, that statute is what you will divide into its smallest parts. The Partner Memo says:

> Please draft an objective memorandum for me analyzing whether we can use the FRSA to move to quash Peel's subpoena.

The first line of your outline in the MPT-Matrix™ cannot be just the Yes-No question "Does the FRSA apply to Lisa Peel?" Nor can it be just "Is Lisa Peel a reporter under the FRSA?" Bar candidates who do not read the instructions in the Partner Memo carefully enough will run into trouble.

Second Document to Use in the Outline in the MPT-Matrix™: The Statute. To do a lawyerlike job on *Lisa Peel*, you must pull apart Section 901 of the FRSA, which defines "reporter" as any person regularly engaged in *collecting, writing*, or *editing* news for publication through a *news medium*." (Italics added.)

Under Section 901, as used in the FRSA:

(a) "reporter" means any person regularly engaged in collecting, writing, or editing news for publication through a news medium.

(b) "news medium" means any newspaper, magazine, or other similar medium issued at regular intervals and having a general circulation; a radio station; a television station; a community antenna television service; or any person or corporation engaged in the making of newsreels or other motion picture news for public showing.

(c) "source" means the person from whom or the means through which the information was obtained.

Your outline on the MPT-Matrix™ will have a separate row for each applicable key term in the FRSA. The assignment is to write an objective memorandum, so in each row, you will put the page numbers from the File and Library where you find material that cuts either for or against Lisa Peel. Does Peel *collect* news? Does she *write* news? Does she *edit* news? And so on. Since she must be a reporter for a *news medium* to be covered by the FRSA, analyzing whether Peel can quash the subpoena also requires analyzing whether her blog qualifies as a *news medium* under the FRSA. That means pulling *news medium* apart. Is her blog a *newspaper* or one of the other types of publications enumerated in the statute? Or do the cases suggest that the statute may cover kinds of media that are not enumerated? Is the blog *issued at regular intervals*? Does it have a *general circulation*? And so on.

The sample answer in this book provides the following analysis of the application of the statutory terms *issued at regular intervals* and *having a general circulation*. This is typical of statutory analysis.

"Issued at regular intervals." Ms. Peel blogs every week-end, normally on Friday. Thus, on the one hand, her schedule is regular, unlike the internet bulletin board in *Haush*. On the other hand, her blog does not always appear on the same day of the week, so it is not totally regular.

"Having a general circulation." The *American Heritage Dictionary* defines "circulation" as "the passing of something, such as money or news, from place to place or person to person . . . distribution . . . ." Ms. Peel can argue that her blog has a general circulation. It has 3,500 registrants in a town of 38,000 people, or almost 10 per cent of the population, and there have been more than 15,000 visitors. Interview.

Since the Partner Memo calls for an objective memorandum, you must point out that some facts cut against Lisa Peel's qualifying as a "reporter," for example, the fact that she posts not only news but pictures of animals. The weight of the facts, however, is in her favor.

Finally, under *Bellows*, the burden is on Peel to show that to bring her blog under the FRSA fulfills the intent of the legislature. According to the Preamble of the Franklin Reporter Shield Act:

The primary purpose of this Act is to safeguard the media's ability to gather news. It is intended to promote the free flow of information to the public by prohibiting courts from compelling reporters to disclose unpublished news sources or information received from such sources.

Again, in the third row of your MPT-Matrix™ you will put down the page numbers in the File and the Library where you find material that cuts either for or against Peel.

How to Apply the Rule of Three. You may choose to divide the Discussion part of the memorandum for *In re Lisa Peel in* to either two or three sections. The sample answer in this book applies the Rule of Three and divides the memo into three sections. The section headings in the sample answer conform to the strong, persuasive, style the National Conference of Bar Examiners prefers. Note that each section heading in the sample memorandum argues both law and facts:

I. Lisa Peel qualifies as a "reporter" under the Franklin Reporter Shield Act (FRSA), if her blog is a "news medium."
II. Posts on Lisa Peel's blog are "publication" through a "news medium" within the meaning of the Franklin Reporter Shield Act, and her source for information about Assistant Superintendent Frank Peterson's retaining equipment belonging to the Greenville School District qualifies as a "source" within the meaning of the FRSA.
III. Lisa Peel meets her burden under the FRSA of showing that protecting her against the subpoena compelling her to reveal the source of her story about Frank Peterson will fulfill the intent of the legislature.

The primary question, since the FRSA protects only reporters, is whether Lisa Peel is a "reporter" under the FRSA. If analysis of the facts in the light of the statute and the case law reveals that a court is more likely to decide that Lisa Peel is a "reporter," then the statute will protect her, and the court will probably grant her motion to quash the subpoena.

The final issue is, what are the purposes of the FRSA, and is protecting Lisa Peel consistent with those purposes? The intent of the legislature is discussed in *Bellows*, which states that the burden is on the party seeking protection under the FRSA. According to the Preamble of the Franklin Reporter Shield Act:

> The primary purpose of this Act is to safeguard the media's ability to gather news. It is intended to promote the free flow of information to the public by prohibiting courts from compelling reporters to disclose unpublished news sources or information received from such sources.

Franklin Reporter Shield Act, Section 900. The purpose of the Franklin Reporter Shield Act is to promote the "free flow of information."

Lisa Peel's blog arguably fills an important gap in providing news in her community. If the FRSA keeps courts from compelling her to disclose her sources, this promotes the "free flow of information."

Thus, a bar candidate might write a Conclusion like the following for *In re Lisa Peel*:

CONCLUSION

Having examined both sides of the question, I conclude that our client Lisa Peel can meet her burden of showing that she is a "reporter" within the meaning of the Franklin Reporter Shield Act (FRSA), and that protecting Peel's sources is consistent with the purposes of the FRSA. If so, the court cannot compel Peel to reveal the identity of the source for her blog post about Frank Peterson, and the court is likely to grant her motion to quash the subpoena.

Perform Your Best™ Materials
for MPT Task 4B:
In re Velocity Park

Perform Your Best on the Multistate Performance Test

Note to the Reader: Your MPT-Matrix™ will have only page numbers, not words. The words in this MPT Matrix™ simply show you the information you will be indexing and cross-referencing. Do not attempt to write words in your own MPT-Matrix™.

MPT-Matrix™ *In re Velocity Park*, MPT, February 2008

	A. Interview with client Zeke Oliver	B. *The Banford Courier*, Newspaper Article 2/2/08	C. Franklin Civil Code sec. 41	D. *Lund v. Swim World* (Franklin Sup. Ct. 2005)	E. *Holum v. Bruges Soccer Club, Inc.* (Columbia Sup. Ct. 1999)
1. Whether proposed waiver will protect Velocity Park from liability for injuries.	**P-2.** Usual injuries are scrapes, bruises, and occasional sprained wrist. **P-2.** Signs will state that skateboarders must wear helmets. **P-3.** Usefulness of Velocity Park to Branford. Better to have kids skateboarding in park than on streets, which city council doesn't like. Eventually client would like to "partner with the city of Branford to operate the park and make it free." **P-2.** "suppose some kids may not read it closely, especially if they're anxious to get in and skateboard . . . ."	**P-6.** Injuries to skateboarders often result from flaws in the surface. **P-6.** The most common injuries are wrist sprains and fractures; possibility of serious head injuries or even death. **P-6.** Injuries can result from carelessness of other skaters.		**P-9.** Three factors for an enforceable exculpatory clause: (i) whether the language is overly broad and ambiguous as to types of injuries contemplated and types of actions covered. The language cannot be overbroad, including even reckless or intentional conduct, or failing to make clear what types of acts the words encompass. Exculpatory agreements "will bar only those claims that the parties contemplated . . . ."	

211

Perform Your Best on the Multistate Performance Test

MPT-Matrix™ *In re Velocity Park*, MPT, February 2008, *cont'd*

	A. Interview with client Zeke Oliver	B. *The Banford Courier*, Newspaper Article 2/2/08	C. Franklin Civil Code sec. 41	D. *Lund v. Swim World* (Franklin Sup. Ct. 2005)	E. *Holum v. Bruges Soccer Club, Inc.* (Columbia Sup. Ct. 1999)
2. Design and layout of waiver.				**P-10.** (ii) whether the waiver is conspicuous. The liability waiver must "alert the signer to the nature and significance of what is being signed." Lund was not alerted to the waiver, had too little time to read it, had no opportunity for clarification or negotiation.	
				P-10. (iii) [not dispositive] whether there is a substantial disparity in bargaining power between the parties.	
3. Enforceability of waiver signed only by a minor.			**P-7.** Except as to contracts for necessaries, contract signed only by a minor is voidable by the minor.		**P-11.** An adult's waiver of liability for negligent acts during recreational activities on his own behalf is enforceable. **P-12.** There is a public policy basis for finding waiver enforceable where signed by parent on behalf of minor where activity is volunteer-staffed non-profit.

212

Perform Your Best™ Sample Answer for *In re Velocity Park*

Hall & Gray, LLP
Attorneys at Law
730 Amsterdam Avenue
Banford, Franklin 33701

DRAFT

MEMORANDUM

To: Deanna Hall

From: Bar Candidate

Re: Liability Waiver for Velocity Park

Date: _____

INTRODUCTION

Our client Zeke Oliver will soon open an outdoor skateboarding park ("skate park") called Velocity Park. You have asked me to analyze whether the waiver form that he proposes using will protect Velocity Park from liability for injuries; to suggest specific revisions to the waiver, including replacement language and changes to design and layout; and to discuss whether any waiver will be enforceable if signed only by a minor. I conclude that Velocity Park must revise the language and the layout of the waiver. Velocity Park must require an adult to sign the form. There is no law in Franklin as yet, however, on whether this will relieve Velocity Park of liability.

DISCUSSION

I. A waiver may protect Velocity Park from liability for injuries, but Velocity Park must modify the form and require a parent to sign it.

In *Lund v. Swim World, Inc.* (2005), relying on *Schmidt v. Tyrol Mountain* (Franklin Sup. Ct. 1996), the Franklin Supreme Court stated the requirements for an enforceable waiver of liability. First, the language of the waiver cannot be overbroad, but "must clearly, unambiguously, and unmistakably inform the signer of what is being waived." In *Lund*, the waiver aimed to absolve the defendant of fault, but it did not make clear "what type of acts the word 'fault' encompassed." Indeed, the word "fault" was broad enough to cover a reckless or an intentional act. A waiver of liability for an intentional act, however, would clearly violate public policy.

A well-drafted waiver, by contrast, will not be overbroad but will bar "only those claims that the parties contemplated when they executed the contract." Exculpatory clauses will be strictly construed against "serious injury and/or death."

Velocity Park must therefore substitute new language for this overbroad language:

> any and all legal liability, including but not limited to all causes of action, claims, damages in law, or remedies in equity of whatever kind I have or which hereafter accrue to me, whether such injuries and/or claims arise from equipment failure, conditions in the park, or any actions of Velocity Park, its employees, third parties, or other skateboarders.

Velocity Park must specify the most frequent types of injuries suffered by skateboarders and clearly inform the user of the types of risks he is assuming. According to our client and according to the *Banford Courier*, wrist injuries are the most common, either sprains or fractures. The form must say so.

Velocity Park should also use the word "negligence," to remove doubt about the type of conduct as to which users will waive claims. Because of the risk of injury caused by the aggressive behavior of other users, the waiver should clearly absolve Velocity Park of liability for negligent supervision.

Accordingly, I suggest the following language:

> I hereby release Velocity Park from all liability for negligent injury, including injuries resulting from the negligence of Velocity Park or its employees or of third parties, including other users of the Park. I understand that the most frequent injuries are wrist injuries, whether sprains or fractures.

Although waivers of liability may sometimes be vulnerable where there is a "substantial disparity in bargaining power" between the parties, the *Lund* court stated emphatically that a disparity in bargaining power, by itself, would not automatically render an exculpatory clause void under public policy.

Here, as in *Lund*, there might be pressure on young people waiting in line to sign the form quickly so as not to hold up the other patrons waiting to get in. The waiver portion might not be pointed out to patrons, nor might the terms be explained to them.

Accordingly, Velocity Park may wish to institute procedures for explaining the form to all skateboarders and for making sure that everyone entering the Park has ample time to read and understand the form.

Under *Lund*, in addition, the effort to extend the waiver of liability to third parties may be unenforceable. Finally, our client should be aware that new or unexpected types of injuries may occur, and even the best waiver form will not protect them.

II. Velocity Park must revise the waiver's design and layout so as to "alert the signer to the nature and significance of what is being signed."

The form itself must "alert the signer to the nature and significance of what is being signed." The waiver in *Lund* was invalidated in part because "the exculpatory language appeared to be part of, or a requirement for, a larger registration form." It was all on one page, and there was only one place to sign the form.

Velocity Park must, therefore, change the format of the form, which currently places the waiver on the same page with general information about the Park, including hours of operation and admission fees. If everything is in the same font and the same size, it will leave users confused about whether being admitted to Velocity Park is the same as or different from waiving liability.

Accordingly, I suggest that the waiver be placed on a separate form with a label reading "Waiver of Liability" conspicuously at the top and a place for a signature conspicuously at the bottom. Above the signature should be a line saying: "I have read and understood this waiver, and I understand what rights I am waiving."

III. Velocity Park must require a parent to sign on behalf of every minor who uses the Park, since in Franklin, no waiver signed only by a minor will be enforceable. Indeed, the Franklin courts have not yet decided whether a waiver signed by the parent is enforceable.

Under Franklin law, an adult's release from liability for injuries he suffers owing to negligent acts during recreational activities is enforceable. *Lund v. Swim World, Inc.* A recent Columbia case concludes that parents may release their own claims arising out of injury to their minor children. *Holum v. Bruges Soccer Club, Inc.* Under Franklin Law of Civil Actions, Section 41(b)(1), however, except for contracts for necessaries, in Franklin, contracts of minors are voidable by the minor. While *Holum* presents persuasive public policy arguments for permitting parents to sign waivers on behalf of their minor children when they participate in sports activities of nonprofit associations staffed by volunteers, Franklin courts appear not to have decided whether an adult parent may waive liability, especially against a for-profit business, on behalf of a minor child.

Accordingly, Velocity Park must require a parent to sign the waiver of liability on behalf of every minor who uses the Club and on his own behalf. The waiver will be effective as to the adult's causes of action. The Franklin courts have not decided whether the releases will be effective against a for-profit business like Velocity Park with regard to minors' injuries. As to the adults' causes of action, however, the waiver will be effective.

Should the issue arise, Velocity Park has plausible public policy arguments, along the lines of those in *Holum*, for recognizing the right of parents to waive liability on behalf of their children, and for acknowledging the fact that Velocity Park provides a type of recreational facility that is much needed but not available elsewhere in Franklin. Velocity Park can argue that it is performing a public service and should be treated as though it were a non-profit.

Note, incidentally, that, even where the Club does not believe a waiver will in fact be enforceable, there is a good reason for requiring one, since signing may make it less likely that lawsuits will be brought.

CONCLUSION

I have examined the waiver form our client Zeke Oliver proposes for Velocity Park. I conclude that to protect Velocity Park from liability, Velocity Park must include language specifying the types of injuries anticipated and the kind of conduct referred to. Velocity Park must change the design and layout to distinguish the waiver from other printed material. We must also emphasize to the client that although a parent may waive his own rights growing out of his child's injuries, the courts of Franklin have not decided whether a parent may waive the rights of a minor taking part in recreational activities sponsored by a for-profit business.

Perform Your Best™ Note on Analyzing *In re Velocity Park*

Objective Memorandum
Document Analysis
Purpose: Advice to Client

The Partner Memorandum for *In re Velocity Park* states that the firm's client, Zeke Oliver, is about to open an outdoor skateboarding park, to be called "Velocity Park." He has brought to the partner a sample form that he would like to use to ask patrons to waive liability for injuries. To help him advise the client, the partner asks the bar candidate to write an objective memorandum. An objective memorandum argues both sides of the question. This is a common type of MPT task.

How to Outline the Instructions in the Partner Memorandum. The first question for the assigned memorandum is "whether the proposed waiver will protect Velocity Park from liability for injuries occurring at the skate park." That question, which does not contain parts that must be pulled apart, must occupy the first row in the outline down the leftmost column of the MPT-Matrix™. When you find material in the File or the Library that is relevant to this question, you will put the page numbers into that first row. One of the cases in the Library, *Lund v. Swim World*, turns out to set out the standard in Franklin for enforceable exculpatory clauses. You will look at the interview with the client in the File for the information about typical injuries that the waiver form must specify and supplement that information with a report in the Library from the *Banford Courier* on injuries to skateboarders.

The second task is to suggest "specific revisions to the proposed waiver, including replacement language as well as any changes in the waiver's design and layout," but without redrafting the whole thing. You will reserve the second row of the MPT-Matrix™ for your analysis of the proposed waiver. This requires document analysis. Document analysis is common on the MPT. It is normally straightforward, even where, as here, analyzing a document section-by-section is coupled with making suggestions for re-drafting. In document analysis, you take the key sections of the document one at a time and examine available facts and case law and, as necessary, other sources, to decide whether each section of the document in turn is satisfactory as it reads, or whether it needs to be eliminated or re-drafted. Finally, you will consider the design of the waiver in the light of *Lund*.

The third task is to discuss whether any waiver will be enforceable if signed only by a minor. That is the third row of the MPT-Matrix™. Phrased another way, the question is whether a parent can waive liability on behalf of a child. It turns out that since Velocity Park is a for-profit business, albeit one serving a civic purpose, rather than a non-profit, there is no case law answering that question in Franklin. You must be careful to note that the case in the Library called *Holum v. Bruges Soccer Club, Inc.*, is not a Franklin case, but a Columbia case. It provides public policy arguments for finding a waiver enforceable where it is signed by a parent on behalf of a minor, but only where the activity is volunteer-staffed and non-profit. Not only is the case not controlling, it does not apply on the facts.

How to Use the Rule of Three. *In re Velocity Park* makes it easy to use the Rule of Three. The Partner Memo gives the bar candidate three instructions. The Discussion section of your memorandum will have three sections.

Perform Your Best™ *Note on Analyzing In re Velocity Park*

The sample memorandum in this book reaches the following conclusion:

CONCLUSION

I have examined the waiver form our client Zeke Oliver proposes for Velocity Park. I conclude that to protect Velocity Park from liability, Velocity Park must include language specifying the types of injuries anticipated and the kind of conduct referred to. Velocity Park must also change the design and layout to distinguish the waiver from other printed material. We must also caution the client that the courts of Franklin have not decided whether parents can waive the rights of minors taking part in recreational activities sponsored by a for-profit business.

Perform Your Best™ Materials
for MPT Task 4C:
Vargas v. Monte

Perform Your Best on the Multistate Performance Test

Note to the Reader: Your MPT-Matrix™ will have only page numbers, not words. The words in this MPT Matrix™ simply show you the information you will be indexing and cross-referencing. Do not attempt to write words in your own MPT-Matrix™.

MPT-Matrix™ *Vargas v. Monte*, MPT July 2003

	A. Stipulated Facts	B. Testimony of Les Vargas	C. Testimony of Stan Linhart	D. Testimony of Carla Monte	E. Letter from A. Vargas to B. Monte 4/18/1906 [Defendant's Exhibit A]	F. Letter to Ms. Monte from BLM, U.S. Dep't. of the Interior 5/27/00	G. Franklin Civil Code sec. 3346	H. Anderson v. Flush (Franklin Ct. App. 1953)	I. Hardaway Lumber v. Thompson (Franklin Ct. App. 1971)	J. Blackjack Lumber Co. v. Pearlman (Franklin Ct. App. 1986)
1. Timber Trespass	**P-3.** (1, 2) Plaintiff and defendant own adjoining properties. (3) Prior to 1880, parcels were both owned by U.S. gov't. (4) USGLO conducted first survey 1879. (5) In 1880 USGLO transferred respective parcels to parties' ancestors. (6, 7) As part of 1879 survey, boundary was established and marked with section corners and blazed trees. (8) BLM survey in 2000–2002 is only licensed survey since 1879. (9) Between March 2000 and January 2002 defendant cut and removed approximately 700 trees from land along shared boundary.	**P-3.** (Plaintiff's direct: Conflicting blaze marks; families gave up trying to figure out boundary. **P-4.** BLM surveyor Stan Linhart called plaintiff in fall of 2001. Plaintiff went out and saw dozens of trees along boundary had been chopped down. Left messages for defendant; posted "No Trespassing." A month later discovered that even more trees had been cut down. Decided on legal action. Defendant had no permission. **P-4.** Defendant's cross: Regarding 1906 letter.	**P-5.** Plaintiff's direct: Lead surveyor for BLM survey. Fall 2001 saw defendant cutting down trees 100 feet into Vargas property, had already cut down about 300 trees. Defendant alleged grandfathers agreed re boundary; said unfair to change line. Linhart warned her the boundary markers were not accurate, cautioned not to continue to log until end of survey. Later he saw defendant had logged more on Vargas property. Deteriorated boundary markings are common in county.	**P-6.** Defendant's direct: Defendant says followed existing blaze marks. Cites Exhibit A, letter, to prove agreement. **P-7.** She and plaintiff had discussions on boundary. **P-7.** Plaintiff's cross: Knew BLM survey imminent. Could have logged elsewhere. Says based on everything she knew, those were her trees.	**P-8.** Letter: Last summer we talked about arbitrarily setting boundary and agreeing. Describes boundary "more or less decided on," adds map drawn to show. "So, as far as I'm concerned, let's agree on that. Okay? If I don't hear back from you, I'll assume it's okay with you."	**P-9.** BLM will be conducting a land survey. If necessary to enter your lands, Stan Linhart will attempt to contact you for permission.	**P-10.** For wrongful injuries to timber, trees, or underwood upon the land of another, or removal thereof, the measure of damages is three times such sum as would compensate for the actual detriment, except			**P-13.** Doctrine of agreed boundary applies where: (1) uncertainty about true boundary; (2) agreement between landowners as to boundary; (3) identifiable agreed boundary; (4) acceptance and acquiescence as long as limitations period. In *Blackjack*, predecessors made informal line; later parties accepted; clearly marked. Elements of agreed boundary have been satisfied.

219

MPT-Matrix™ *Vargas v. Monte*, MPT July 2003, *cont'd*

	A. Stipulated Facts	B. Testimony of Les Vargas	C. Testimony of Stan Linhart	D. Testimony of Carla Monte	E. Letter from A. Vargas to B. Monte 4/18/1906 [Defendant's Exhibit A]	F. Letter to Ms. Monte from BLM, U.S. Dep't. of the Interior 5/27/00	G. Franklin Civil Code sec. 3346	H. *Anderson v. Flush* (Franklin Ct. App. 1953)	I. *Hardway Lumber v. Thompson* (Franklin Ct. App. 1971)	J. *Blackjack Lumber Co. v. Pearlman* (Franklin Ct. App. 1986)
2. Treble Damages	**P-3.** Between March 2000 and January 2002 defendant removed about 700 trees from land along shared boundary. After seeing trees cut in 2001, plaintiff left "No Trespassing." messages; posted A month later discovered even more trees gone.		**P-5.** In 2001, Linhart warned defendant that boundary markers were not accurate, cautioned not to continue to log in area until end of survey. Later he saw defendant had logged more on Vargas property.				**P-10.** Under section 3346(a) "the measure of damages is three times such sum as would compensate for the actual detriment, except . . . ."	**P-11.** Section 3346(a): "for willful and malicious trespass, the court may impose treble damages . . . ." "Because treble damages are punitive, the defendant must have acted willfully and maliciously." Not applicable where D tried to minimize damage.	**P-12.** In *Guernsey v. Wheeler* (Franklin Ct. App. 1966), treble damages are appropriate where defendant was warned . . . , committed trespass "with a reckless disregard of . . . the rights of the owner," in bad faith, to "vex, harass, annoy, or injure."	
3. Double Damages							Section 3346(a) provides for double damages where the trespass was "casual or involuntary," or where the defendant had probable cause to believe" the land was his.	Under 3346(a) the court must impose at least double damages. "Double damages must be awarded whether the trespass be willful and malicious or casual and involuntary."	*Hardway* defendant acted in good faith reliance on earlier agreement, attempted to harvest what he thought was his own timber. Double damages lie.	
4. Single Damages							Section 3346(b): single damages for trespass in reliance on survey by licensed surveyor.			

220

Perform Your Best™
Sample Answer for *Vargas v. Monte*

FRANKLIN DISTRICT COURT

Vargas v. Monte

Les Vargas,	)	
Plaintiff,	)	
	)	Case Number 03-CV-7272
v.	)	**Trial Brief**
	)	
Carla Monte,	)	
Defendant.	)	
_____	)	

PLAINTIFF'S TRIAL BRIEF IN SUPPORT OF LIABILITY AND TREBLE DAMAGES

Plaintiff seeks judgment in his favor for timber trespass under Franklin Civil Code §3346. He seeks treble damages for all of the trees removed from his land or, in the alternative, treble damages for some of the trees removed and double damages for the rest.

STATEMENT OF FACTS

During the period March 2000 to January 2002, defendant removed a total of 700 trees without permission from defendant's property, in an area close to the boundary of her own land. She removed trees both before and after being notified by the Department of the Interior that her logging was illegal. The history of the parties' titles and of the surveys conducted, together with the relevant facts, is set out in the Stipulated Facts and discussed below.

ARGUMENT

I. LIABILITY

A. <u>Defendant's Removal of Trees From Plaintiff's Land Constituted Trespass to Timber Under Franklin Civil Code §3346.</u>

Under section Franklin Civil Code §3346, a person is liable for trespass to timber who wrongfully injures or removes trees, timber, or undergrowth from the land of another. Here, it is undisputed that defendant removed trees from land within the plaintiff's boundaries as defined by the surveys of 1879 and 2000–2002. Therefore, defendant's actions constituted trespass to timber.

B. The Lack of Either Clear Agreement or Boundary Marks Precludes the Defense of "Agreed Boundaries."

According to *Blackjack Lumber Company v. Pearlman*, under the judicially-created doctrine of "agreed boundaries," the courts will favor boundary agreements made between parties where the official boundaries are uncertain, the parties have reached a clear agreement, the agreed boundary is marked and identifiable, and the parties have acquiesced in this unofficial boundary for at least as long as the statute of limitations.

Here, however, both parties testify that not only was the official boundary unclear but later boundary markers between their properties had also become obscure. Neither party claims adverse possession. The defendant presents as evidence of a long-standing agreement a letter dated 1906 and allegedly from the plaintiff's grandfather to the defendant's grandfather, proposing a boundary marked by Bella Creek, the boundary that the defendant claims she was respecting when she took plaintiff's trees.

Blackjack, however, requires clear boundary marks, and here there were none. The 1906 letter from plaintiff's grandfather says that the creek moves. In any event, neither party offers evidence of a reply by defendant's grandfather, and silence as assent falls short of the clarity of agreement *Blackjack* requires.

Therefore, the defense of agreed boundaries fails.

II. DAMAGES

A. Plaintiff Is Entitled To Treble Damages Because Defendant's Failure to Respect Any Boundary Line Made Her Taking of the Trees Deliberate and Malicious.

Under §3346(a), as interpreted by *Anderson v. Flush*, treble damages are optional when the trespass to timber is wrongful and deliberate; double damages are mandatory when the taking is merely involuntary or casual.

Here, Defendant began logging on plaintiff's property only when she knew a survey was imminent that would settle the boundary; the letter from Cecilia Chen of the Department of Interior shows that defendant knew as early as May 27, 2000, that the government survey was under way. Then, in the fall of 2000, the surveyor actually informed defendant of the boundary error. Testimony of Linhart. But she kept on logging anyway, ignoring not only Mr. Linhart's warning but the "No Trespassing" signs that plaintiff posted. Testimony of Vargas. By then, according to the surveyor, defendant had logged about 300 trees from the plaintiff's property. Even if those 300 trees were taken in innocent error, the trees taken after notice from the Department of the Interior were taken over the plaintiff's protests. Therefore, although this Court should find that all the trees taken were taken in bad faith and merit treble damages, those taken after the surveyor's visit clearly merit treble damages.

Defendant might argue that under *Anderson*, a trespass is not "deliberate and malicious" within the meaning of §3346(a), where the defendant took reasonable precautions to minimize damage. Defendant in *Anderson*, however, trimmed tree branches to prevent more serious damage to orchard tree limbs when a house was being moved. Here, the defendant's taking was not involuntary or casual. Therefore, treble damages apply.

Defendant might argue that she should be liable only for double damages because she acted in good faith on the basis of an earlier agreement regarding the boundary between the parties or their predecessors in interest. Under *Hardway Lumber v. Thompson*, where there had been an agreement to take timber but the plaintiff later revoked it, the court held that there had been constructive notice via filing with the Recorder of Deeds but no actual notice, and that the defendant had acted in good faith.

Here, however, notice cuts the other way. Both parties testified that they had discussed the disputed boundary, but not reached an agreement. Testimony of Vargas. Testimony of Monte. It is in any event not clear that the plaintiff had the power to authorize the taking of these trees, since they were possibly federally-protected as old-growth forest.

The *Hardway* court might seem to set a high standard for bad faith, when it says that the defendant there had not intended to "vex, harass, or annoy" the plaintiff. Bad faith, however, can also arise from purely economic motives, without personal animosity, as demonstrated in *Guernsey v. Wheeler*, cited in *Hardway*.

The parties have stipulated to 700 as the number of trees taken from the boundary area. Stipulated Facts. Plaintiff defers to the specificity of the surveyor's testimony: the defendant does not dispute it, and it would be against her interest to minimize it, since that could expand her liability for treble damages.

B. Because the Defendant Did Not Rely on a Survey by a Licensed Surveyor, Plaintiff's Recovery Cannot Be Limited to Actual Damages.

Under §3346(b), damages for trespass to timber are limited to actual damages if the trespasser acted in reliance on a survey by a licensed surveyor. Here, however, while there have been two such surveys, from 1879 and 2000–2002, defendant does not claim to have relied on either survey. Therefore, the limitation to actual damages does not apply.

CONCLUSION

For the foregoing reasons, this Court should hold the defendant liable for trespass to plaintiff's trees. The Court should impose punitive treble damages for the taking of all the trees or, at the least, double damages for the earlier trees and treble damages for the trees defendant took after the Department of the Interior warned her that her conduct was illegal.

Respectfully Submitted,

Jane Norman
Attorney for Plaintiff
Norman & Longfellow
405 East Gray, Suite 100
Lakeview, Franklin 33071

Perform Your Best™
Note on Analyzing *Vargas v. Monte*

Type of Task: Trial Brief
Type of Organizing Principle: Statutory and Case Law Analysis and Application
Purpose: Litigation

The Partner Memorandum in *Vargas v. Monte* states that the parties have presented their evidence in this timber trespass case at trial, and the judge has now requested briefs on several issues. The partner directs the associate to draft the trial brief for plaintiff Vargas. Since this is a persuasive brief, it will argue only one side of the case. The Partner Memo says:

> Our client, Les Vargas, brought this action against adjoining landowner Carla Monte for wrongfully cutting and removing trees from his property. He is seeking an award of statutory treble damages. The parties have presented their evidence at trial, and the judge has now requested briefs on the issues of whether, based on the evidence adduced at trial, (1) defendant Monte is liable for timber trespass and, if so, (2) whether single, double, or treble damages, or some combination thereof, should be assessed against her.
>
> Please draft a persuasive brief to the court addressing the liability and damages issues outlined above. Our goals are to persuade the judge to hold Monte liable for timber trespass and award Vargas the maximum damages allowable by law based on the evidence, explaining why any lower measure of damages is inappropriate.
>
> Prepare the brief in accordance with the guidelines set forth in the attached office memorandum.

How to Outline the Instructions in the Partner Memo. Notice that the Partner Memo poses two main questions, not just one, and that the second question must be pulled apart into several different topics. The first question goes to liability, whether "defendant Monte is liable for timber trespass." Accordingly, the first row of your *MPT-Matrix*™ will analyze liability. In this row, you will note the page numbers of materials in the File and Library bearing on defendant's liability. In reading the File, you will quickly discover that Monte says she has a defense to liability, namely, the defense of agreed boundaries. Accordingly, your first row will note page numbers for materials bearing not just for or against liability in general, but also for or against that defense.

The second question is whether, based on the evidence at trial, "single, double, or treble damages, or some combination thereof," should be assessed against Monte. At least the second and third rows of your *MPT-Matrix*™ will analyze damages, one row for treble damages, and one row for double damages. You may choose to add a third row for single damages, although single damages are appropriate only where defendant relied on a surveyor's report, and here there is no report defendant could rely on. You may include either two or three sections in the second main part of your brief.

How to Use the Second Document in the File: Persuasive Briefs. The Partner Memo tells you that your work product must follow the requirements in the office memorandum regarding Persuasive Briefs. See Part 2 of this book for guidance on formatting briefs. Pay particular attention to the need for powerful persuasive subject headings.

How to Apply the Rule of Three. The Argument part of your brief will have two main sections, and the second main section will have two or three parts. In all, therefore, your brief will have two main sections and three or four parts. The first main section will deal with liability, the second with damages.

The Franklin statute applicable here is Franklin Civil Code §3346. Drafting the brief will require using statutory analysis. But this statute is not logically an easy one, and therefore much trouble can be avoided by taking extra time to read and analyze the statute before attempting to apply it.

Under Section 3346, a person is liable for trespass to timber who "wrongfully injures or removes trees, timber, or undergrowth from the land of another." In the first section of the brief, Vargas will argue that it is undisputed that Monte removed trees from Vargas's land, and that she did so without permission, thus coming under Section 3346.

The brief must also address somewhere Monte's argument based on the defense of "agreed boundary." *Blackjack Lumber Co. v. Pearlman*. That defense goes to the basic issue of trespass, so it belongs in the first section of the brief. You will note the page numbers in the File and the Library of materials that show that Monte's defense of agreed boundary fails. It fails chiefly because for the defense of agreed boundary to apply, there must be clear boundaries, and here everyone concedes that the boundaries are unclear. It also fails because, while defendant Monte presents as evidence of an agreement a letter from plaintiff's grandfather that invited a response from her own grandfather, she presents no evidence that her grandfather replied.

The second main section of the Argument concerns damages. Section 3346(a) permits the court to award treble damages as follows:

> For wrongful injuries to timber, trees, or underwood upon the land of another, or removal thereof, the measure of damages is three times such sum as would compensate for the actual detriment, except . . . .

But then the statute reverses course and limits the applicability of punitive treble damages, excluding cases where "the trespass was casual or involuntary, or where the defendant had probable cause to believe that the land on which the trespass was committed was his own . . . ." Those will be among Monte's defenses. Thus, the task is to argue that the facts bring Monte's conduct within the treble damages provisions of Section 3346(a), because her conduct was wrongful and deliberate. Then to distinguish the cases permitting double damages and to argue that Monte's trespass was not "casual or involuntary," and she had no cause to believe the land was her own.

What remedy should the plaintiff seek? Monte took trees from Vargas's land both before and after the Department of the Interior notified her that her conduct was illegal. Accordingly, Vargas can ask for alternative remedies. Either the court can order treble damages as to all the trees Monte took, both before and after being notified, or the court can order treble damages for the trees Monte took after the Department of the Interior notified her that her conduct was illegal, and double damages for those she took earlier.

In the third and final section of the Argument, Vargas must confront Monte's possible argument that his recovery should be limited to actual damages because Monte relied on a survey by a licensed surveyor. Section 3346(b). Here, Vargas can argue conclusively from the facts, pointing out that while there have been two surveys by licensed surveyors, Monte does not claim, and cannot claim, to have relied on either one.

The Conclusion in our sample brief reads as follows:

> For the foregoing reasons, this Court should hold the defendant liable for trespass to plaintiff's trees. The Court should impose punitive treble damages for the taking of all the trees or, at the least, double damages for the earlier trees and treble damages for the trees defendant took after the Department of the Interior warned her that her conduct was illegal.

Perform Your Best™ Materials
for MPT Task 4D:
Arden Industries v. Freight Forwarders

Perform Your Best on the Multistate Performance Test

Note to the Reader: Your MPT-Matrix™ will have only page numbers, not words. The words in this MPT Matrix™ simply show you the information you will be indexing and cross-referencing. Do not attempt to write words in your own MPT-Matrix™.

MPT-Matrix™ *Arden Industries v. Freight Forwarders*, MPT February 2003

	A. Letter from Defendant's Attorney 2/25/02	B. Stipulated Statement of Facts	C. Franklin Commercial Code Article 1	D. Franklin Commercial Code Article 7	E. Franklin Commercial Code Article 9	F. *Freight Forwarders v. Wendover Mfg.* (D. Olympia 1997)	G. *Data Systems v. Link Assocs.* (Franklin Sup. Ct. 1998)	H. *Shellac's Drayage v. Pavel's Hardware Supply* (Franklin Ct. App. 1996)
1. Security Interest	**P.3.** Arden is in arrears on five invoices totaling $122,725. The printing press in FFI's possession has a value of $200,000. If Arden does not bring its account current within 10 days, FFI will sell the printing press and apply the proceeds to the arrearages.	**P.4.** (5.) Starting in 1998, Arden began using FFI's services. (6) Shipments arranged by telephone. **P.5.** (9) No negotiations regarding terms of shipment. (10) No writings other than FFI's invoices. (11) In the first year, Arden declined written contract.	**P.7.** 1-201 Agreement is bargain of the parties, indicated by language, course of dealing, usage, course of performance. 1-205(1) Sequence of previous conduct establishes a common basis of understanding. (3) "A course of dealing gives particular meaning to and supplements or qualifies terms of an agreement."		**P.8.** Section 9-102 creates or provides for security interest. 9-203(b) Security interest is enforceable only if (1) value given; (2) debtor has rights in the collateral; ... (3)(B) secured party possesses the property. 9-310 Filing is required to perfect a security interest unless property is in secured party's possession under Section 9-313.	Federal Bankruptcy case applying State of Olympia UCC. **P-10.** Section 15 of FFI invoice suffices as a security agreement, reinforced by course of dealing. There is evidence such terms and conditions are standard in the industry.	**P-12.** Box-top language on all boxes is merely desired terms. Mere repetition does not make it part of the contract. **P-12.** Under 1-205(3), course of dealing can supplement agreement, not create one.	

227

MPT-Matrix™ *Arden Industries v. Freight Forwarders*, MPT February 2003, *cont'd*

	A. Letter from Defendant's Attorney 2/25/02	B. Stipulated Statement of Facts	C. Franklin Commercial Code Article 1	D. Franklin Commercial Code Article 7	E. Franklin Commercial Code Article 9	F. *Freight Forwarders v. Wendover Mfg.* (D. Olympia 1997)	G. *Data Systems v. Link Assocs.* (Franklin Sup. Ct. 1998)	H. *Shellac's Drayage v. Patel's Hardware Supply* (Franklin Ct. App. 1996)
I. Security Interest (cont'd)	**P-3.** FFI's security interest arises from Section 15 on the back of the FFI invoices, and from course of dealing.	**P-5.** (13) Sec. 15 re "General Lien" on every invoice. (14) FFI intended to create a security interest. (15) Arden never intended to grant a security interest. (16, 17) There were no signed security agreements or filings with the Secretary of State. (18) Arden had constructive knowledge of Section 15.					**P-12.** Mere repetition [of language] does not make language part of contract. This is majority view. "Course of conduct is ordinarily a factual issue. But we hold as a matter of law that the . . . actions of LA in repeatedly sending a writing cannot by itself establish a course of dealing between the parties."	

MPT-Matrix™ *Arden Industries v. Freight Forwarders*, MPT February 2003, *cont'd*

	A. Letter from Defendant's Attorney 2/25/02	B. Stipulated Statement of Facts	C. Franklin Commercial Code Article 1	D. Franklin Commercial Code Article 7	E. Franklin Commercial Code Article 9	F. *Freight Forwarders v. Wendover Mfg.* (D. Olympia 1997)	G. *Data Systems v. Link Assocs.* (Franklin Sup. Ct. 1998)	H. *Shellac's Drayage v. Pavel's Hardware Supply* (Franklin Ct. App. 1996)
2. Carrier's Lien	**P-3.** FFI has a carrier's lien that arises under UCC 7-307. FFI has litigated this matter successfully before. *Freight Forwarders v. Wendover*.	**P-5.** (23) Arden shipped Model Z printing press Nov. 18, 2002. (18) Arden had constructive knowledge of Section 15. (22) Arden owes arrearages on five earlier shipments, in an amount totaling $122,725. (25) The earlier goods covered have already been delivered in the ordinary course of business and are no longer in FFI's possession.		**P-7.** Section 7-307(1). Carrier has a lien on goods covered by a bill of lading; (3) lien lost on voluntary delivery or unjustifiable refusal to deliver. Comment: No general lien; not common practice.				**P-13.** Under FCC 7-307, carrier loses lien on goods voluntarily delivered. No general lien for earlier shipments.

229

Perform Your Best™ Sample Answer for *Arden Industries v. Freight Forwarders*

FRANKLIN DISTRICT COURT
Arden Industries, Inc. v. Freight Forwarders, Inc.

Arden Industries, Inc.,	)	
	)	
Plaintiff,	)	
	)	Case Number 02-CV-4081
v.	)	
	)	MEMORANDUM IN SUPPORT
Freight Forwarders, Inc.,	)	OF PLAINTIFF'S MOTION
	)	FOR SUMMARY JUDGMENT
Defendant.	)	

SUMMARY OF THE CASE

In this motion for summary judgment, the plaintiff, Arden Industries, seeks a declaration of its rights and injunctive relief against the defendant, Freight Forwarders. At issue is the disposition of a Model Z printing press manufactured by plaintiff and shipped through the defendant, but which the defendant presently holds. The defendant intends to sell the printing press, valued at about $200,000, to pay five overdue invoices for past shipments totaling $122,725. The parties have stipulated to the jurisdiction of the court and the material facts of the dispute. The court has issued an injunction to prevent the sale while the action proceeds.

ARGUMENT

I. This Court Should Grant Summary Judgment for Plaintiff Because as a Matter of Law the Parties Had Neither an Explicit Security Agreement Nor an Implicit Agreement by Course of Dealing.

As a matter of law, the parties have neither explicitly nor implicitly agreed that the defendant would hold a general security interest in all of the plaintiff's goods. This Court should accordingly grant summary judgment for the plaintiff.

Under Franklin Commercial Code (FCC) sec. 1-201 (1), an "agreement" may be created, *inter alia*, by language or course of dealing. Sec. 9-102 defines a "security agreement" simply as an agreement that creates or defines a security interest. Under FCC sec. 9-203(3)(B), a security interest is enforceable when, *inter alia*, the collateral is in the possession of the secured party. Under FCC sec. 1-205 (1), a "course of dealing" may create an agreement by a sequence of previous conduct fairly to be regarded as a common basis for interpreting the parties' expressions and other conduct. Under FCC sec. 1-205 (3), a course of dealing gives particular meaning to and supplements or qualifies an agreement.

The parties here have stipulated that there are no agreements other than defendant's invoices. Stipulated Fact No. 10. There is thus no signed security agreement. Defendant nonetheless argues that the parties created a security agreement by course of dealing.

In *Data Systems v. Link Associates* (Supreme Court of Franklin, 1998), the Supreme Court of Franklin interpreted sec. 1-205 with respect to the creation of an agreement by course of dealing. The court held as a matter of law that the mere repetition of language cannot create an "agreement." A course of conduct can merely interpret or qualify an agreement, but it cannot create one.

The language at issue in *Data Systems* was a liability disclaimer clause in a box-top license on boxes used to ship about 142 disks in batches of 20 disks each. The court held it did not, by course of dealing under Section 1-205, create an agreement to insulate the software publisher from indemnification of the plaintiff for consequential losses. The terms of the license could not be said to have been part of a consistent course of conduct, since the issue never arose between the parties before the litigation. The very fact that the seller did not negotiate the license terms suggests that they were not part of the transaction. The Court held that a course of conduct can merely interpret or qualify an agreement between the parties, but it cannot create one.

Here, the defendant relies heavily on the language in Section 15 of its invoices, a small-print clause on the back of the 137 shipping invoices that the defendant sent the plaintiff during their five-year business relationship. Section 15 purports to create a general lien on the plaintiff's goods in transit for any unpaid charges on any of the plaintiff's shipments through the defendant. As in *Data Systems*, however, the language of the clause was never negotiated between the parties. Indeed, it is stipulated that, in the first year of their relationship, the defendant tried and failed to persuade the plaintiff to agree to a long-term shipping contract creating a general lien. Stipulated Fact No. 11. Under *Data Systems*, and by the equitable canons of interpretation, the invoices should in any event be construed against the drafter, Freight Forwarders.

The defendant's letter relies on *Freight Forwarders v. Wendover Mfg.* (D. Olympia 1997). But as a federal district court decision in a bankruptcy matter interpreting the law of another state, that case is not controlling. *Wendover*, too, involved Freight Forwarders. Again, the invoices contained language regarding a general lien (apparently the same language as here), and Freight Forwarders sought to sell some of the shipper's goods in transit to offset unpaid charges for earlier shipments. *Wendover* held that the repeated opportunity of a shipper to review this language sufficed as a course of dealing constituting acceptance, and creating a security interest. The *Wendover* court suggested that a general lien of this type might be industry practice. However, the Franklin court in *Data Systems* specifically rejected the *Wendover* rule. And the Comment to FCC sec. 7-307, observing that carriers generally do not claim a carrier's lien for charges for other goods, contradicts *Wendover's* suggestion about industry practice.

Therefore, neither explicitly nor by course of dealing did Arden Industries ever extend a general security interest in its printing press to defendant Freight Forwarders.

II. <u>The Court Should Grant the Plaintiff Summary Judgment Because the Defendant Has No Carrier's Lien, Having Already Delivered the Goods For Which It Claims Charges.</u>

Under FCC sec. 7-307(1), a carrier holds a lien on goods covered by the bill of lading for charges arising from their shipment, preservation, and sale. However, under sec. 7-307(3), this lien is lost if the goods are voluntarily delivered or the shipper unjustifiably refuses delivery. The Comment observes that this section does not create a general lien on collateral.

The Franklin Court of Appeal interpreted this code section in *Shellac's Drayage v. Pavel's Hardware Supply* (Franklin Court of Appeal 1996), a case in which the shipper's regular carrier claimed a lien on the shipper's goods that it was holding because payments for already-delivered shipments were delinquent. Charges for the shipment the shipper claimed as collateral had been prepaid and were not delinquent. The Court held that the shipper had no lien in the shipment it was currently holding.

Here, as in *Shellac's Drayage*, the defendant seeks to assert a lien in plaintiff's current shipment solely because payments for shipments that have already been delivered are delinquent. No charge is claimed for the shipment defendant actually holds.

Therefore, defendant here cannot recover charges for already-delivered goods by selling the shipment it now holds.

CONCLUSION

For the foregoing reasons, the plaintiff asks the Court to grant summary judgment. There are no issues of fact. As a matter of law, the parties have neither an explicit security agreement nor a security agreement by course of dealing. Nor does the law permit defendant to claim a carrier's lien for charges for already-delivered goods.

Respectfully submitted,

Lara Chanturia
Attorney for Plaintiff
Swann, Rubin & Chanturia LLP
One Belden Place
Taverly, Franklin 33056
(555) 965-3100

Perform Your Best™
Note on Analyzing *Arden Industries v. Freight Forwarders*

Type of Task: Memorandum (Brief) in support of a motion for summary judgment
Type of Structure: Statutory and contract analysis, applying terms to facts
Type of Situation: Litigation

Plaintiff Arden Industries seeks a declaration of its rights and injunctive relief against the defendant, Freight Forwarders ("FFI").

The parties have stipulated to the jurisdiction of the court and the material facts of the dispute. The issue is the disposition of a Model Z printing press manufactured by plaintiff and shipped through the defendant, but which the defendant presently holds. The defendant intends to sell the printing press, valued at about $200,000, to pay five overdue invoices totaling $122,725 on previous shipments made by the plaintiff. The court has issued an injunction to prevent the sale while this action proceeds. Arden argues that FFI has neither a security interest nor a carrier's lien in the printing press. It cannot, therefore, sell the printing press to pay past-due shipping charges, and the court should grant summary judgment for the plaintiff.

The standard for granting a motion for summary judgment is that there is no triable issue of fact, and the case can be decided entirely as a question of law. Here, the parties have stipulated to the facts, so there cannot possibly be triable issues of fact. Your job is to write a persuasive memo to the court (brief) that makes persuasive arguments of law.

How to Outline the Instructions in the Partner Memo. The Partner Memo says, "I would like you to draft our brief in support of Arden's position that FFI has neither a security interest nor a carrier's lien on the printing press." In addition to making the affirmative arguments, the bar candidates should be sure to "refute the points made in the November 25, 2002 letter from FFI's attorneys." So in the first row of your *MPT-Matrix*™ you will note page numbers in the File and the Library of material that cuts for or against the argument that FFI has a security interest. The second row will note page numbers where material bears on the argument that FFI has a carrier's lien. The third row will analyze the argument, on which the November 25, 2002 letter from FFI's attorneys relies, that the present issue has already been litigated and decided in FFI's favor, in *Wendover*.

How to Use the Rule of Three. There are two ways to apply the Rule of Three in your Argument here. In the first alternative, the opening section of the Argument starts by citing the applicable sections of the Franklin Commercial Code ("FCC"), and applying its rules and the case law to the stipulated facts. The first sub-part of this section demonstrates that as a matter of law, there is no explicit agreement giving defendant a security interest in plaintiff's printing press. The second sub-part demonstrates that defendant has no security interest by course of dealing. Alternatively, the opening section of the Argument can be one unitary presentation, covering both explicit agreement and course of dealing.

The second main section of the Argument then addresses defendant's contention that Section 15 of its invoices gives it a carrier's lien on plaintiff's printing press. The facts having been stipulated, this section of the brief argues by applying the relevant sections of the Franklin code to the facts. As a matter of good legal scholarship, incidentally, you will not normally rest an argument on a Comment. Here, however, the Comment simply supports an argument that is already complete:

Under FCC Section 7-307(1), a carrier holds a lien on goods covered by the bill of lading for charges arising from their shipment, preservation, and sale. However, under Section 7-307(3), this lien is lost if the goods are voluntarily delivered or the shipper unjustifiably refuses delivery. The Comment observes that this section does not create a general lien on collateral.

The third part of the Argument can refute FFI's attorneys' claim that *Wendover* is dispositive. *Wendover* is a bankruptcy case in a federal court in another state. It is therefore not controlling.

Thus, the sample brief in this book concludes:

For the foregoing reasons, the plaintiff asks the Court to grant summary judgment. As a matter of law, the parties have neither an explicit security agreement nor a security agreement by course of dealing. Nor does the law permit defendant to claim a carrier's lien for charges for already-delivered goods.

Perform Your Best™ Materials for MPT Task 4E:
Ronald v. Department of Motor Vehicles

Perform Your Best on the Multistate Performance Test

Note to the Reader: Your MPT-Matrix™ will have only page numbers, not words. The words in this MPT Matrix™ simply show you the information you will be indexing and cross-referencing. Do not attempt to write words in your own MPT-Matrix™.

MPT-Matrix™ *Ronald v. Department of Motor Vehicles*, MPT, February 2009

	A. Franklin Vehicle Code secs. 352, 353	B. Franklin Evidence Code secs. 1278, 1280, Franklin A.P.A. sec. 115, Franklin Code of Regulations sec. 121	C. Transcript of Administrative Hearing 2/23/09	D. Police Incident Report 12/19/08	E. Crime Lab Test Report 12/29/08	F. *Pratt v. DMV* (Franklin Ct. App. 2006)	G. *Schwartz v. DMV* (Franklin Ct. App. 1994)	H. *Rodriguez v. DMV* (Franklin Ct. App. 1994)
1. Officer had no reasonable suspicion to stop.	**P-6.** Sec. 352, unlawful to drive with prohibited blood-alcohol percentage: at or greater than 0.08 per cent. Sec. 353 (a) Immediate suspension of license on receipt of laboratory test report at or above 0.08. (b) Petition for hearing before ALJ. (c) Party aggrieved by ALJ decision may petition district court.		**P-2.** Incident occurred December 19, 2008. Driver's license suspended January 9, 2009. Ms. Ronald explained her conduct. **P-3.** Officer did not claim petitioner violated traffic laws. She left restaurant at bar time and wove in own lane. He did not smell alcohol.			**P-8.** The DMV has the burden of showing investigative stop rests on reasonable suspicion. *Taylor v. DMV.* In *Pratt*, defendant wove 10 feet from right to left, drove his car in parking lane, etc. **P-8, P-9.** In *Kessler*, defendant accelerated from slow to high rate of speed, etc. **P-9.** The test of reasonable suspicion is the totality of the circumstances.		

236

Perform Your Best on the Multistate Performance Test

MPT-Matrix™ *Ronald v. Department of Motor Vehicles*, MPT, February 2009, *cont'd*

	A.	B.	C.	D.	E.	F.	G.	H.
	Franklin Vehicle Code secs. 352, 353	Franklin Evidence Code secs. 1278, 1280, Franklin A.P.A. sec. 115, Franklin Code of Regulations sec. 121	Transcript of Administrative Hearing 2/23/09	Police Incident Report 12/19/08	Crime Lab Test Report 12/29/08	*Pratt v. DMV* (Franklin Ct. App. 2006)	*Schwartz v. DMV* (Franklin Ct. App. 1994)	*Rodriguez v. DMV* (Franklin Ct. App. 1994)
2. DMV cannot rely on lab test report.		**P-7.** Under FEC Sec. 1278, hearsay... Under FAPA sec. 115, hearsay evidence is admissible at administrative hearing if an exception to the hearsay rule. Sec. 1280 is public records exception. **P-6.** Under FCR sec. 121 forensic alcohol analysis must be performed by a forensic alcohol analyst....	**P-2.** Law firm challenges sufficiency of test results as inadmissible hearsay.		**P-5.** Test performed December 21, 2008. Report signed by Charlotte Swain, Senior Laboratory Technician.		**P-10.** Lab test results recorded more than five weeks after the arrest held inadmissible. **P-11.** But they may be used to supplement or explain other evidence.	

237

MPT-Matrix™ *Ronald v. Department of Motor Vehicles*, MPT, February 2009, cont'd

	A. Franklin Vehicle Code secs. 352, 353	B. Franklin Evidence Code secs. 1278, 1280, Franklin A.P.A. sec. 115, Franklin Code of Regulations sec. 121	C. Transcript of Administrative Hearing 2/23/09	D. Police Incident Report 12/19/08	E. Crime Lab Test Report 12/29/08	F. *Pratt v. DMV* (Franklin Ct. App. 2006)	G. *Schwartz v. DMV* (Franklin Ct. App. 1994)	H. *Rodriguez v. DMV* (Franklin Ct. App. 1994)
3. DMV has failed to meet its burden of proving Ms. Ronald was driving with a prohibited blood-alcohol level.	**P-6.** Under sec. 353(B), DMV has burden of proving by a preponderance of the evidence that the person operated a motor vehicle with 0.08 per cent or more of alcohol in his or her blood.		**P-2.** Petitioner has explanations for apparently poor performance on field sobriety tests. **P-3.** Officer could not recall smelling alcohol on petitioner's breath. Officer does not contradict petitioner's account	**P-4.** Officer reports that petitioner performed poorly on field sobriety tests. Officer does not contradict petitioner's account			**P-10.** ALJ must uphold suspension if he finds by a preponderance of the evidence that petitioner was driving with a blood alcohol concentration of 0.08 or more. **P-11.** In *Schwartz*, testimony of arresting officer, in addition to the blood test, supported finding of impermissible blood alcohol level.	**P-13.** Doubtful lab report cannot rescue other, insufficient evidence. If officer's testimony is inconclusive, test cannot "supplement or explain" it.

238

Perform Your Best™ Sample Answer for *Ronald v. Department of Motor Vehicles*

FRANKLIN DEPARTMENT OF MOTOR VEHICLES
In the Matter of Barbara Ronald

Barbara Ronald,   )
)
  Petitioner,   )
)
  v.   )
)
Department of Motor Vehicles,)
)
  Respondant.   )
_____   )
	MEMORANDUM IN SUPPORT OF MOTION
	TO VACATE SUSPENSION
	OF PETITIONER'S DRIVER'S LICENSE

INTRODUCTION

Petitioner Barbara Ronald asks this tribunal to vacate the suspension of her driver's license by the Department of Motor Vehicles ("DMV," "the Department") based on her allegedly driving with a blood-alcohol level of 0.08 per cent or more in violation of Section 352 of the Franklin Vehicle Code. The Department does not meet its burden of proving its case by a preponderance of the evidence. The officer did not have a reasonable suspicion that justified his stopping petitioner's car, and the lab test offered cannot support the DMV's case.

ARGUMENT

I. The totality of the circumstances fails to provide a reasonable suspicion justifying the officer's stop of petitioner's vehicle.

The police may stop a vehicle where they have a reasonable suspicion that a law has been broken, that is, less than probable cause but more than a hunch. *Terry v. Ohio.* The Department of Motor Vehicles has the burden of establishing that an investigative stop rests on reasonable suspicion. *Pratt v. Department of Motor Vehicles*, citing *Taylor v. Department of Motor Vehicles.* The test is the totality of the circumstances. *Pratt.*

Weaving in one's own lane does not suffice for reasonable suspicion. Ms. Ronald's case is distinguishable from *Pratt.* Pratt drove his car in the parking lane, and then he moved several times back and forth between the center line and the curb, so the totality of the circumstances supported a reasonable suspicion. *State v. Kessler*, cited in *Pratt*, is also distinguishable. The officer also had a reasonable suspicion justifying a stop because the defendant first traveled slowly, then "accelerated at a high rate of speed," then pulled into a parking lot and poured out a "mixture of liquid and ice" from a cup.

Here, by contrast, as the officer conceded, petitioner violated no traffic laws. She left a restaurant where alcohol was served at 1 A.M., "bar time," and as she drove along afterwards, she wove in her own lane and, as the officer conceded, she did not go over the line into the next lane. Weaving in her own lane, however, does not prove she was driving with an impermissible blood-alcohol level. There is insufficient support for a reasonable suspicion.

Therefore, the totality of the circumstances failed to support a reasonable suspicion that Petitioner Ronald was driving with a blood alcohol level in excess of 0.08 per cent.

II. The blood test report does not satisfy the public records exception to the hearsay rule, and it cannot, by itself, support a finding of driving with a prohibited blood-alcohol level.

Under Franklin Evidence Code Section 1278, hearsay is a statement, other than one made by the declarant while testifying at a judicial proceeding, offered in evidence to prove the truth of the matter asserted. Under Section 115 of the Franklin Administrative Procedure Act, evidence that would come in under an exception to the hearsay rule under the Franklin Evidence Code is admissible at an administrative hearing. Even if it is not admissible, it may be used to supplement or explain other evidence.

Franklin Evidence Code section 1280, the public records exception, provides an exception to the hearsay rule where a writing was made (a) "by and within the scope of duty of a public employee" and (b) "at or near the time of the act, condition or event," and (c) "the sources of information and method and time of preparation were such as to indicate its trustworthiness." However, under Section 121 of the Franklin Code of Regulations, forensic alcohol analysis may be performed only by a "forensic alcohol analyst who has been trained in accordance with the requirements of the Franklin Bureau of Investigation."

Here, the report of the Hawkins Falls Police Department Crime Laboratory certifying to the analysis of the blood-alcohol concentration of 0.08 per cent in the blood of Barbara Ronald is an out-of-court statement offered in evidence to prove the truth of the matter asserted. It is therefore hearsay. The DMV cannot establish the necessary foundation for the public records exception to the hearsay rule, however, since it was not made "by and within the scope of duty of a public employee." The report was not signed, as the law would require, by a Forensic Alcohol Analyst, but rather by Senior Laboratory Technician Charlotte Swain.

Nor can the lab report be used "for the purpose of supplementing or explaining other evidence," as Section 115 of the Franklin Administrative Procedure Act might otherwise permit. Section 1280 requires that the writing to be admitted under the public records exception must have been made "at or near the time of the act, condition, or event." Here, however, petitioner was arrested on December 19, 2008, but petitioner's blood sample was not tested until December 21, 2008, two days later. Moreover, the report was not prepared until December 29, 2008, which was 10 days after petitioner's arrest and eight days after the test was performed.

Therefore, the Crime Laboratory report is not admissible in evidence. Nor can it supplement or explain other evidence to support the conclusion that petitioner had a blood-alcohol level of 0.08 per cent or more.

III. The Department of Motor Vehicles has not met its burden of proving by a preponderance of the evidence that petitioner was driving with a prohibited blood-alcohol concentration.

Neither the police report nor testimonial evidence supports the DMV's burden of proving by a preponderance of the evidence that petitioner had a blood alcohol level of 0.08 or more.

According to the Hawkins Falls Police Department Incident report filed by Officer Barry Thompson, the field sobriety tests he administered included having petitioner walk a straight line and then stand on one foot. But she "performed poorly, lost her balance, and was distracted."

Officer Thompson administered this test to petitioner, however, when, as he conceded in testimony, she was wearing high heels and standing on the shoulder of a busy highway. Together with petitioner's testimony that she had been working 18 hours straight, was distracted by the heavy traffic on Highway 13, and was suffering from arthritis, accounts for her poor performance.

In addition, there were excellent explanations for all of the officer's observations at the scene, without reaching the conclusion that petitioner was driving under the influence of alcohol. Petitioner herself said that she was weaving because the police officer was following too closely. Her eyes were bloodshot because she had been working 18 hours straight.

The officer does not contradict petitioner's account. He could not recall smelling alcohol on petitioner's breath. There are sufficient other explanations for the facts.

This case is therefore less like *Schwartz* than like *Rodriguez*. In *Schwartz*, the arresting officer testified that the driver had "slurred speech, bloodshot eyes, a strong odor of alcohol, and an unsteady gait," and performed poorly on field sobriety tests. Together with the blood test, this supported the finding that the driver had a blood alcohol level of 0.08 per cent or more. The *Rodriguez* court, however, emphasized that where the officer's testimony is inconclusive, the police lab report cannot not be used to "supplement or explain," or rescues, that evidence.

Accordingly, the Department of Motor Vehicles has failed to meet its burden of proving its case against Ms. Ronald by a preponderance of the evidence.

CONCLUSION

For the foregoing reasons, petitioner asks the Court to vacate the suspension of her driver's license. The Department has failed to meet its burden of proving by a preponderance of the evidence that petitioner drove with an impermissible blood-alcohol level. The officer lacked reasonable suspicion to stop petitioner's car. The blood-alcohol test is inadmissible in evidence and suspect. Testimonial evidence, meanwhile, supports petitioner's account, while the officer's own testimony is compatible with hers.

Respectfully submitted,

Marvin Anders
Law Offices of Marvin Anders
1100 Larchmont Avenue
Hawkins Falls, Franklin 33311

Perform Your Best on the Bar Exam Performance Test (MPT)

Perform Your Best™ Note on Analyzing *Ronald v. Department of Motor Vehicles*

Type of Task: Memorandum (Brief) for the administrative agency in support of a motion to vacate suspension of a driver's license
Context: Litigation in an administrative tribunal
Structure: Statutory and case analysis, applying terms to facts

The Partner Memorandum in *Ronald v. Department of Motor Vehicles* asks the associate to draft a persuasive memorandum for the administrative agency, that is, a brief, in support of a motion to vacate suspension of the driver's license of the firm's client, Barbara Ronald. The evidentiary portion of the hearing before the administrative law judge occurred the previous day. Since this is a persuasive memorandum, you will argue only one side of the case.

The Partner Memo asks for argument that:

1. The police officer did not have reasonable suspicion to stop Ms. Ronald;
2. The administrative law judge cannot rely solely on the blood test report to find that Ms. Ronald was driving with a prohibited blood-alcohol concentration; and
3. In light of all the evidence, the DMV has not met its burden of proving by a preponderance of the evidence that Ms. Ronald was driving with a prohibited blood-alcohol concentration.

This task is a typical brief-writing task, in that the three instructions require application of two different types of law, criminal procedure and evidence. It calls for a written argument applying law to facts. You must pay the closest attention to the instructions in the Partner Memo, and also to the facts in relation to the burden of proof. This **is a straightforward task.** Once you have made the outline in the MPT-Matrix™, you will, as always, start by reading the applicable statutes. The basic statute here is Section 353 of the Franklin Vehicle Code.

How to Read the Instructions and Create the Outline in the MPT-Matrix™. To outline the instructions in the Partner Memo down the leftmost column of the MPT-Matrix™ it is normally necessary to pull each instruction in the Partner Memo apart into its smallest components. In *Ronald v. DMV*, the principal term in the first instruction is "reasonable suspicion." Noting that term is probably as far as you can go towards tearing the first instruction apart. But that does not mean you are finished. Your next job is to find the standard. What is the standard for reasonable suspicion? What facts meet that standard? As you read the task materials, you be looking in the File for factual evidence, and in the Library for law, that will help you interpret and apply "reasonable suspicion." You will note the page numbers for that material under the appropriate columns of the MPT-Matrix™.

The second instruction in the Partner Memo asks for arguments that, "The administrative law judge cannot rely solely on the blood test report to find that Ms. Ronald was driving with a prohibited blood-alcohol concentration." The blood test report will occupy the second row in your outline of the instructions. Why can't the ALJ rely solely on that report? That word "solely" should catch your eye. While you cannot tear the word "solely" out of the second instruction, you can be on the lookout for facts and evidence that will make the lab test report insufficient as proof.

Perform Your Best™ Note on Analyzing Ronald v. Department of Motor Vehicles

The third instruction tells you to argue that the DMV has not met its burden of proof. As usual, your first task must be to find and state the applicable standard. Here, the instructions in the Partner Memo tell you that the standard is "preponderance of the evidence." So you will be looking in the Library for statutory and case law establishing that standard, and then in the facts for evidence that the DMV has failed to meet it.

How to Choose a Format. The Partner Memo does not specify a format for this persuasive memorandum. A brief format is more appropriate than any other format when you are submitting work to a court or administrative tribunal, so the brief format will look more professional here. On the other hand, because the task is to write a memorandum, the memorandum format will also look professional. Remember, we are not talking here about a particular format's being required on this MPT task. We are talking about your work's making the best possible visual impression on the graders.

How to Use the Rule of Three. The Partner Memo asks for three arguments, and those three arguments become the three sections of the brief, making for a straightforward application of what this book calls the Rule of Three. As so often on the MPT, the task memo instructs the associate not to write a separate statement of facts, but to use the law and the facts to make the strongest case possible on each issue.

You will set out the rule for reasonable suspicion in *Terry v. Ohio* in the first section of the brief. The sample brief cites Franklin case law for the proposition that the Department of Motor Vehicles has the burden of establishing that an investigative stop rests on reasonable suspicion. *Pratt v. Department of Motor Vehicles*, citing *Taylor v. Department of Motor Vehicles*. The test is the totality of the circumstances. *Pratt*. The facts support your argument that the totality of the circumstances here did not support a reasonable suspicion.

In the second section of the brief, regarding the blood test report, the sample brief starts with the hearsay rule, citing the Franklin Rules of Evidence. Section 115 of the Franklin Administrative Procedure Act establishes that hearsay evidence is admissible at an administrative hearing if it would come under an exception to the hearsay rule under the Franklin Evidence Code. This second section of the sample brief then proves that in this case: the Crime Laboratory blood test does not qualify for admission under Section 115 of the Franklin Administrative Procedure Act. Nor can it "supplement or explain" other evidence.

Finally, the third section of the brief argues that the Department of Motor Vehicles has failed to meet its burden of proving that petitioner was driving with a prohibited blood-alcohol concentration. Note that this is a civil case, and the Department of Motor Vehicles must prove its case by a civil standard, the preponderance of the evidence. Franklin Vehicle Code sec. 353(b); *Schwartz v. Dept. of Motor Vehicles* (Franklin Ct. App. 1994).

Here, the brief finally attacks the Hawkins Falls Police Department Incident Report filed by Officer Barry Thompson. The field sobriety tests he administered included having Ms. Ronald walk a straight line and then stand on one foot. Ms. Ronald has entirely reasonable explanations for her failure to pass those tests, and the officer concedes that Ms. Ronald did not smell of alcohol. Therefore, the Department of Motor Vehicles has not met its burden of proof.

The conclusion of the sample brief in this book reads as follows:

> For the foregoing reasons, petitioner asks the Court to vacate the suspension of her driver's license. The Department has failed to meet its burden of proving its case that petitioner drove with an impermissible blood-alcohol level by a preponderance of the evidence. The officer did not have a reasonable suspicion justifying his stopping petitioner's car. The blood-alcohol test on which the DMV relies is inadmissible in evidence and suspect. Testimonial evidence before this tribunal supports petitioner's account of events, while the officer's own account is compatible with hers.

Perform Your Best™ Materials
for MPT Task 4F:
Phoenix Corporation v. Biogenesis, Inc.

Perform Your Best on the Multistate Performance Test

Note to the Reader: Your MPT-Matrix™ will have only page numbers, not words. The words in this MPT Matrix™ simply show you the information you will be indexing and cross-referencing. Do not attempt to write words in your own MPT-Matrix™.

MPT-Matrix™ *Phoenix Corporation v. Biogenesis, Inc.*, MPT, February 2009

	A. Interview with Carol Ravel 2/23/09	B. Schetina Letter 1/2/98	C. Rule 4.4 Franklin Rules of Professional Conduct 7/1/02	D. *Indigo v. Luna Motors* (Franklin Ct. App. 1998)	E. *Mead v. Conley Machinery* (Franklin Ct. App. 1999)
Phoenix Brief for Disqualification February 9, 2009 1. Document on its face is confidential Lawyer-Client communication. Argument. Amberg has violated ethical obligations in a case of inadvertent disclosure and threatens Phoenix with incurable prejudice.	**P-2.** Amberg concedes document is privileged	**P-4.** Document marked "confidential," sent by president of corporation to attorney for plaintiff corporation. Asks: "Can't we interpret the agreement to require Biogenesis to pay royalties on other categories, not only the specified ones?"			

245

MPT-Matrix™ *Phoenix Corporation v. Biogenesis, Inc.* (MPT February 2009), cont'd

A. Phoenix Brief for Disqualification February 9, 2009	B. Interview with Carol Ravel February 23, 2009	C. Schetina Letter January 2, 1998	D. Rule 4.4 Franklin Rules of Professional Conduct July 1, 2002	E. *Indigo v. Luna Motors* (Franklin Ct. App. 1998)	F. *Mead v. Conley Machinery* (Franklin Ct. App. 1999)
Argument: Rule 4.4 requires prompt notification. Says attorney must not just notify sender, but must refrain from examining document and must await sender's instructions. I.e., *Indigo v. Luna* rule.			**P-8.** Where document "relevant to representation" is inadvertently sent, receiving attorney must promptly notify sender. Comment: Rule 4.4 expressly supersedes *Indigo v. Luna*, attorney receiving document inadvertently sent may examine it, need not follow instructions of sender. Comment: Rule 4.4 does not treat unauthorized disclosure.	**P-9.** If document is Attorney-Client privileged and received inadvertently, attorney must promptly notify adversary's attorney; must not examine; must await instructions from sender.	
Argument. In violation of their ethical obligation, the attorneys did not notify the sender, examined the document, and refused to return it.	**P-3.** Amberg wants to use the letter. **P-3.** Amberg did not notify sender. Did examine, refused to return.				

246

Perform Your Best on the Multistate Performance Test

MPT-Matrix™ *Phoenix Corporation v. Biogenesis, Inc.* (MPT February 2009), *cont'd*

	A. Interview with Carol Ravel 2/23/09	B. Schetina Letter 1/2/98	C. Rule 4.4 Franklin Rules of Professional Conduct 7/1/02	D. *Indigo v. Luna Motors* (Franklin Ct. App. 1998)	E. *Mead v. Conley Machinery* (Franklin Ct. App. 1999)
Phoenix Brief for Disqualification February 9, 2009					
2. Argument. The same rule would apply if the letter had been sent without authorization.				**P-9.** In *Indigo*, disclosure is inadvertent.	**P-11.** Held. Trial court abused its discretion by disqualifying plaintiff's attorney. **P-11.** If document is Attorney-Client privileged and disclosed without authorization, receiving attorney must notify adversary's attorney; refrain from examining; either await instructions or submit to the court for instructions. Violation is only one of the facts the court must consider.
3. Argument. Failure to disqualify Amberg will cause "incurable prejudice."		**P-4.** Letter asks: "Can't we interpret the agreement to require Biogenesis to pay royalties on other categories, not only the specified ones?"		**P-10.** Disqualify where threat of incurable prejudice.	**P-11, P-12.** Counter-indications to disqualification: information did not significantly prejudice other side; can exclude documents from evidence; whether disqualification causes hardship.

247

Perform Your Best on the Bar Exam Performance Test (MPT)

Perform Your Best™ Sample Answer for *Phoenix Corporation v. Biogenesis, Inc.*

Forbes, Burdick & Washington, LLP
777 Fifth Avenue
Lakewood City, Franklin 33905

MEMORANDUM

To: Ann Buckner
From: Bar Candidate
Re: Phoenix Corporation v. Biogenesis, Inc.
Date: _____

INTRODUCTION

Amberg & Lewis ("Amberg") represents the defendant Biogenesis, Inc., in a breach of contract action brought by Phoenix Corporation. Amberg has sought our advice because Phoenix, which is represented by the Collins Law Firm, has moved to disqualify Amberg, alleging inadvertent receipt and possible prejudicial use of a confidential attorney-client document. You have asked me to evaluate the merits of Phoenix's arguments for disqualification. I conclude that Amberg has not violated any ethical rule and that Amberg has strong arguments why the court should in any event not disqualify it.

DISCUSSION

<u>I. Amberg has not violated Rule 4.4 of the Franklin Rules of Professional Conduct, which appears to be the only applicable rule.</u>

The Franklin Court of Appeal has affirmed the power of the courts to disqualify counsel for improper use of privileged documents. The leading case, *Indigo v. Luna Motors*, decided in 1998, made that clear. It concerned inadvertent, not unauthorized, disclosure. *Luna* required the attorney who received a privileged document inadvertently (i) to notify the sender, (ii) to resist the temptation to examine the document, and (iii) to await the sender's instructions about what to do.

Phoenix argues that *Indigo v. Luna* applies here, and that Amberg has violated the applicable ethical rules by not acting in conformity with the *Indigo* requirements. I conclude, on the contrary, that *Indigo* does not apply. Even if it did, Amberg should not be disqualified.

Amberg concedes that the letter at issue here, the Schetina letter, is subject to the attorney-client privilege. It is labeled "Confidential," and it is from the president of Phoenix, Gordon Schetina, to one of the corporation's attorneys, Peter Horvitz. Amberg has nonetheless not violated any ethical rule.

When Amberg received the document on February 2, 2009, receipt was not inadvertent. The document came without authorization from some undisclosed person in the Collins Law Firm. Amberg did not, contrary to the first *Indigo v. Luna* requirement, promptly notify the Collins Law Firm. Rather, although the Collins Law Firm almost immediately found out, it was only because a member of the Collins firm accidentally overheard two Amberg associates talking about the letter that same day. Amberg can argue that it simply did not have enough time to notify Collins. Amberg plainly failed to follow the second and third *Indigo v. Luna* requirements, however, since it examined the document and did not await the sender's instructions. Indeed, when Collins asked Amberg to return the letter, Amberg refused. Further, Amberg wishes to use the letter at trial.

The conclusion does not follow, however, that *Indigo v. Luna* applies and disqualifies Amberg. Rule 4.4 of the Franklin Rules of Professional Conduct was adopted by the Franklin Supreme Court in 2002. According to the Comment, Rule 4.4 expressly supersedes *Indigo v. Luna*. Rule 4.4 requires the attorney who inadvertently receives a privileged document only to notify the sender promptly. He or she need do no more.

Rule 4.4 states in its entirety:

> An attorney who receives a document relating to the representation of the attorney's client and knows or reasonably should know that the document was inadvertently sent shall promptly notify the sender.

The Comment to Rule 4.4 says that Rule 4.4 applies only to inadvertent disclosure and that neither Rule 4.4 nor any other rule applies to unauthorized disclosure. Therefore, since the document Amberg received was an unauthorized disclosure, Phoenix misapplies it, and Amberg has not violated the plain language of Rule 4.4.

The open question is whether *Mead v. Conley Machinery Co.*, dealing with unauthorized disclosure, and requiring the receiving law firm to await the court's instructions, remains good law in light of Rule 4.4. Dating from 1999, *Mead* predates Rule 4.4, and it states much the same three requirements as *Indigo v. Luna*. Under *Mead*, moreover, a firm in Amberg's position need not await the sender's instructions but may wait for the court to decide what it should do. Violation of this standard, however, is only one of the facts that *Mead* says the court should consider.

II. <u>The court should in any event not disqualify Amberg, since Amberg's use of the Schetina letter does not threaten Phoenix with incurable prejudice, while disqualification of Amberg would cause serious hardship to Biogenesis.</u>

While the court may disqualify Amberg even if Amberg has not violated any explicit ethical rule, *Mead v. Conley Machinery Co.*, it should not do so here. Phoenix suggests that failure to disqualify Amberg will result in incurable prejudice. *Mead*, however, said that the court must balance a number of factors in deciding whether or not to disqualify counsel who have received a privileged document:

(1) the attorney's actual or constructive knowledge of the material's attorney-client privileged status;
(2) the promptness with which the attorney notified the opposing side that he or she had received such material;
(3) the extent to which the attorney reviewed the material;
(4) the significance of the material, i.e., the extent to which its disclosure may prejudice the party moving for disqualification, and the extent to which its return or other measure may prevent or cure that prejudice;
(5) the extent to which the party moving for disqualification may be at fault for the unauthorized disclosure; and
(6) the extent to which the party opposing disqualification would suffer prejudice from the disqualification of his or her attorney.

As the length of this list of factors suggests, *Mead* does not consider disqualification of counsel an open-and-shut question. Indeed, the footnote to *Mead* says that even the threat of "incurable prejudice," as in *Indigo*, "is neither a necessary nor a sufficient condition for disqualification."

Amberg can argue, moreover, that the Schetina letter will not create incurable prejudice because it is not conclusive evidence on any point in issue in the case. While it is arguably an admission by Phoenix that it did not have a contractual right to the damages it seeks, it is not dispositive on that point. The fact that Phoenix had not sought the licensing fees earlier does not mean that a closer and entirely proper reading of the Phoenix-Biogenesis contract would not have disclosed such an entitlement.

An additional important consideration weighing against disqualification is that Biogenesis would suffer serious hardship were Amberg to be disqualified. The case has been going on for six years, and now it is finally only a month away from trial. To require Biogenesis to start over with new counsel would not serve the interests of justice.

CONCLUSION

Amberg has not violated any ethical rule, since Rule 4.4 supersedes *Indigo v. Luna* and in any event does not apply to use of documents obtained in unauthorized ways rather than inadvertently. Unless *Mead v. Conley Machinery Co.*, despite Rule 4.4, has continuing vitality as to unauthorized disclosures, no other ethical constraints apply. The court should not, in any event, disqualify Amberg, since the Schetina letter does not have conclusive evidentiary weight on any point in issue, and requiring Biogenesis to start over with new counsel would impose a serious hardship.

Perform Your Best™ Note on Analyzing *Phoenix Corporation v. Biogenesis, Inc.*

Type of Task: Objective memorandum
Context: Litigation
Structure: Statutory and case law analysis and application

The Partner Memorandum in *Phoenix Corporation v. Biogenesis, Inc.*, asks the associate to write a memorandum "evaluating the merits of Phoenix's argument for Amberg & Lewis's disqualification." The firm's client is Amberg & Lewis ("Amberg"), the law firm that represents the defendant Biogenesis in the litigation. Amberg has received a damaging attorney-client document without authorization, a letter from the president of plaintiff Phoenix to the company's attorney. Perhaps a disgruntled employee of Phoenix's law firm sent it to Amberg. Since the partner asks for an objective memorandum, the associate must examine both sides of the question, whether Phoenix is justified in demanding Amberg's disqualification. Other MPT tasks may raise points of attorney ethics in an incidental way. This MPT task is entirely about attorney ethics.

How to Read and Outline the Instructions in the MPT-Matrix™ Using a Second Document, Phoenix's Brief. The Partner Memo's instruction to the bar candidate is to "evaluate the merits of Phoenix's argument." You cannot tear this simple instruction apart to make your outline. Accordingly, the starting point for the outline in the MPT-Matrix™ must be the document the instruction refers to, Phoenix's brief in support of its motion to disqualify Amberg. Each of the three parts of the Phoenix brief will be a line in the outline in the MPT-Matrix™. In each of those three lines you will note the page numbers in the File and the Library of materials that cut for and against each of Phoenix's points.

How to Apply the Rule of Three. Following the instructions in the Partner Memo, the bar candidate's work product may simply present arguments for and against each of the three points in the Phoenix brief.

The Phoenix brief has three parts:

1. Phoenix's Document is Protected by the Attorney-Client Privilege;
2. Amberg & Lewis Has Violated an Ethical Obligation;
3. Amberg & Lewis Has Threatened Phoenix with Incurable Prejudice.

The bar candidate's work product may therefore have the following parts:

1. Amberg & Lewis concedes that Phoenix's document is protected by the attorney-client privilege;
2. Amberg & Lewis has not violated its ethical obligations;.
3. Amberg & Lewis does not threaten Phoenix with incurable prejudice, but disqualification on the eve of trial would result in severe prejudice to Biogenesis.

The Partner Memo instructs the bar candidate to "bring to bear" both the applicable legal authorities and the relevant facts as described by Ms. Ravel, a partner in the Amberg firm. As so often on the MPT, the Partner Memo tells the bar candidate not to draft a separate statement of facts.

Perform Your Best on the Bar Exam Performance Test (MPT)

Amberg's argument is clear, but to see it you must first distinguish between *inadvertent* and *unauthorized* receipt of a privileged document. The fact that Amberg's receipt of the document in issue here was unauthorized, not inadvertent, is key. You must also note the dates of the two cases and one rule in the File. Phoenix relies on *Indigo v. Luna Motors* (1998), which deals with inadvertent receipt of a privileged document. The *Indigo* rule required the attorney who receives a privileged document inadvertently not to examine it and to await instructions from the sender. Rule 4.4 of the Franklin Rules of Professional Conduct, however, superseded *Indigo* in 2002. In contravention of *Indigo*, the Comment to Rule 4.4 expressly states that the attorney may examine a privileged document he receives inadvertently, and need not await or follow instructions from the sender. The same analysis would arguably apply where, as here, the receipt of the privileged document is unauthorized rather than inadvertent. The Comment tells us, however, that Rule 4.4. does not include unauthorized transmission. *Mead v. Conley Machinery,* another decision of the Franklin Court of Appeals, dates from 1999, after *Indigo*, and it fulfills two functions in this MPT task. First, although, unlike *Indigo v. Luna Motors*, it applies to unauthorized receipt of a privileged document, it states much the same strict rules as *Indigo* for the attorney who receives the document. *Mead* concluded that the receiving attorney should review the document—there, an attorney-client privileged document—only to the extent necessary to determine how to proceed, notify the opposing attorney, and either abide by the opposing attorney's instructions or refrain from using the document until a court disposed of the matter. These are rules Amberg has not followed. Thus, as of the date of researching the issue here, the question is open whether *Mead* applies to this case of unauthorized transmission.

But *Mead* has a second function. It provides an escape route for Amberg. *Mead* says that even an attorney's violation of the rules is not dispositive as to disqualification. *Mead* lists counterindications to disqualification. These include the information's not significantly prejudicing the other side; the possibility of excluding the documents from evidence; and disqualification's causing hardship. Thus, even if *Mead* applies much the same strict requirements as *Indigo*, despite its having violated those rules, Amberg can argue that all three of *Mead's* counterindications cut against the court's disqualifying it.

In particular, the bar candidate can point out that to disqualify Amberg on the eve of trial would result in severe hardship to Amberg's client Biogenesis.

The sample brief in this book concludes as follows:

CONCLUSION

Amberg has not violated any ethical rule, since Rule 4.4 supersedes *Indigo v. Luna* and in any event does not apply to use of documents obtained in unauthorized ways rather than inadvertently. Unless *Mead v. Conley Machinery Co.*, despite Rule 4.4, has continuing vitality as to unauthorized disclosures, no other ethical constraints apply. The court should not, in any event, disqualify Amberg, since the Schetina letter does not have conclusive evidentiary weight on any point in issue, and requiring Biogenesis to start over with new counsel would impose a serious hardship.

Perform Your Best™ Materials for MPT Task 4G:
In re Emily Dunn

Perform Your Best on the Bar Exam Performance Test (MPT)

Note to the Reader: Your MPT-Matrix™ will have only page numbers, not words. The words in this MPT-Matrix™ simply show you the information you will be indexing and cross-referencing. Do not attempt to write words in your own MPT-Matrix™.

MPT-Matrix™ *In re Emily Dunn*, MPT, July 1999						
	A. Letter to Mrs. Dunn	B. Previous Will	C. Interview with Client	D. *In re Estate of Rich* (Franklin Sup. Ct. 1996)	E. *In re Estate of Young* (Franklin Sup. Ct. 1978)	F. *Walker on Wills*
Will Drafting Guidelines—Order:						
1. Introductory clauses A. Name and domicile of testator						
B. Revocation of prior testamentary instruments	*Legal formality. No authority needed.*					
C. Description of testator's immediate family						
I. Dispositive Clauses. A. Specific bequests 1. Real property.			**P-6.** House to Jonathan: if he predeceases T, proceeds to residuary estate.	**P-7.** Specific legacy is a "bequest of a specific asset." **P-8.** Lapse statute [avoided].		
Insurance on real property			**P-5.** *Testator: Insurance proceeds to follow the bequest.*	**P-8.** If testator does not specify otherwise, insurance is part of residuary estate.		
2. Tangible personal property			**P-6.** Things in the house to Jonathan: If he predeceases T, contents to residuary estate	**P-7.** Specific legacy. . . . **P-8.** Lapse statute [avoided].		

254

	A. Letter to Mrs. Dunn	B. Previous Will	C. Interview with Client	D. *In re Estate of Rich* (Franklin Sup. Ct. 1996)	E. *In re Estate of Young* (Franklin Sup. Ct. 1978)	F. *Walker on Wills*
			P-6. Jewelry to A. and B.: If one predeceases T, sell share and proceeds to residuary estate.	**P-8.** Lapse statute [avoided].		
Insurance on all tangible personal property			**P-5.** *Testator: Insurance proceeds to follow the bequest.*	**P-8.** If testator does not specify otherwise, insurance is part of residuary estate.		
3. Other specific bequests			**P-6.** Stock: To grandchildren, plus those born before T dies, include add'l shares [*Walker*].		**P-9.** Gift of stock is presumed to be specific, not general.	**P-10.** The will can specify that gift includes stock split or stock dividend.
			P-6. Stock: Residuary "to go equally to my kids, or their families, of course."			**P-10, P-11.** Per stirpes but per capita at each generation: grandchildren/ dead parents all share equally.
			P-5. Shares of Stock: Bequest to surviving children of Alice Dunn, include add'l shares. [*Walker*]		**P-9.** Gift of stock is presumed to be specific, not general. Here, "children" means issue, including adopted child.	**P-10.** The will can specify that gift includes stock split or stock dividend.

MPT-Matrix™ *In re Emily Dunn*, MPT, July 1999 *cont'd*						
	A. Letter to Mrs. Dunn	B. Previous Will	C. Interview with Client	D. *In re Estate of Rich* (Franklin Sup. Ct. 1996)	E. *In re Estate of Young* (Franklin Sup. Ct. 1978)	F. *Walker on Wills*
4. Any other clauses stating conditions			**P-5.** *Testator: Insurance proceeds to follow the bequest.*	**P-8.** If testator does not specify otherwise, insurance is part of residuary estate.		
B. General bequests			**P-5.** $20,000 to Helen Rossini: In the event she predeceases T, gift to residuary.	**P-7.** General bequest payable from general estate assets. **P-8.** Lapse statute [avoided].		
C. Demonstrative bequests	*Defined in In re Estate of Rich. Not applicable here.*					
D. Residuary clauses			**P-6.** *Residuary "to go equally to my kids, or their families, of course."*	**P-7.** "Includes bequests that purport to dispose of the whole estate."		**P-10, P-11.** Per stirpes but per capita at each generation: grandchildren/dead parents all share equally.

Perform Your Best™ Sample Answer for *In re Emily Dunn*

MEMORANDUM

Date: _____

To: Robert Reilly
From: Applicant
Re: Emily Dunn

Following is the draft will you asked me to prepare for our client Emily Dunn. As you requested, I have provided an explanation for each dispositive clause suggesting how Ms. Dunn may want to deal with the disposition of potential insurance proceeds, her gifts of stock, the equalization of gifts to her grandchildren, and the distribution of the residuary estate.

WILL

Introduction:

A. Set forth the introductory clause with the name and domicile of the testator.
   1. I am Emily Dunn, a resident of Jackson City, Franklin.
B. Include an appropriate clause regarding the revocation of prior testamentary instruments.
   2. This is my Last Will, and I revoke all previous wills and codicils.
C. Include a clause describing the testator's immediate family (parents, sibling, spouse, children, and grandchildren).
   3. My husband, Charles Dunn, died April 30, 1999. I have three children, Andrea Dunn Little; Jonathan Dunn; and Bertha Dunn. I have four grandchildren. Nelson Little, Becky Little, and Steven Little, are the children of Andrea Dunn Little. Sidney Dunn is the son of Bertha Dunn.

PART ONE: Dispositive Clauses (to be set forth in separate subdivisions or subparagraphs by type of bequest or topic), in the following order.

A. Specific bequests [Walker, in *Rich*] "A bequest of a specific asset."
   1. *Real property.*
      4. I leave my house to my son Jonathan, if he survives me. If he dies before me, the house should go into my residuary estate. The proceeds of insurance should follow the bequest.
   2. *Tangible personal property. Jewelry.*
      5. I give my jewelry to my daughters Andrea and Bertha, to be divided between them as they see fit. In the event that they cannot agree, I direct my executor to divide it as equally as possible.
      6. Should one of my daughters die before me, I direct my executor to divide the jewelry and sell the share of the one who died. I direct that the proceeds of the sale should go into my residuary estate. The proceeds of casualty insurance on the jewelry should follow the bequest.

EXPLANATION. This avoids application of the lapse statute, and it assures that everything in the estate not otherwise disposed of will go to the children and grandchildren. The distribution of potential insurance proceeds is consistent with Ms. Dunn's apparent wish that certain of her assets pass to her children if she predeceases them, but otherwise are divided equally among her grandchildren. I am assuming that there is insurance on all of Mrs. Dunn's property.

Tangible personal property. Contents of the home.
7. I give the contents of the family home to my son Jonathan, if he survives me.
8. If he dies before me, the contents of the house should go into my residuary estate.
   The proceeds of insurance on the contents of the family home should follow the bequest.

EXPLANATION. By making the property go into the residuary estate in the event that Jonathan predeceases Ms. Dunn, I have complied with Ms. Dunn's expressed wishes.

3. *Other specific bequests. Shares of stock.*
   9. I give 500 shares of the Wilson Corporation stock that I have at the time of my death to each of my grandchildren who survives me. I leave 500 shares to any grandchild born or adopted before I die who survives me. This bequest includes any additional shares I receive between the date of the execution of this will and the date of my death as either a stock split or as a dividend paid to me by Wilson Corporation in its own shares [Walker on Wills, sec. 11200, Library at 44].
   10. In the event a grandchild dies before me, I would like the stock to go to their issue.

EXPLANATION. *Estate of Young* explains my use of "issue." Ms. Dunn's acceptance of Alice's adopted child indicated that she would want an adopted child included. The lapse statute will apply.

11. I give 600 shares of Wilson Corporation stock to the children of my cousin Alice Dunn, including any additional shares I receive between the date of the execution of this will and the date of my death as either a stock split or as a dividend paid to me by Wilson Corporation in its own shares.
12. The 600 shares should be divided equally among any of Alice's three children if they are still alive when I die.
13. In the event that none of Alice's children survives me, the stock should go into my residuary estate.

EXPLANATION. Ms. Wilson wants her family members, including Alice's children—and adopted child—to have the stock. For that reason, I have directed that the stock should go to the issue of a beneficiary who predeceases Ms. Dunn. In addition, since Ms. Dunn's primary concern in distributing her estate is for her family, I have drafted the appropriate clauses to include stock splits or dividends in stock, rather than having that stock re-distributed through the residuary clause.

4. *Any other clauses stating conditions that might affect the disposition of the real and personal property.*
   14. I direct that the proceeds of insurance on any of my real or personal property should be distributed in accordance with my directions for distribution of that property.

EXPLANATION. I drafted this clause to have the insurance proceeds follow the gift of property because of Ms. Dunn's comments about how her friend Helen's inheriting the insurance proceeds on a car was being disputed.

B. General bequests: [Walker, cited in *In re Estate of Rich*:] Typically a gift of money; "a gift payable out of general estate assets or to be purchased for a beneficiary out of general estate assets."

    15. I give the sum of $20,000 to my friend Helen Rossini. In the event that she does not survive me, the money should go into my residuary estate.

C. Demonstrative bequests [Walker in Rich:] A bequest of a "specific sum of money payable from a designated account. Such legacy is specific as to the funds available in the account to pay the bequested amount and general as to the balance."

D. Residuary clauses [Walker in Rich:] A "bequest that is neither general, specific or demonstrative and includes bequests that purport to dispose of the whole estate."

    16. I leave the rest of my estate to my three children, per stirpes, but per capita in each generation. **The grandchildren.**

EXPLANATION. I have used the "per stirpes but per capita in each generation" language because Ms. Dunn said, "I want my estate divided equally among my three children whether or not they are alive when I die. Then, I want all the children of my deceased children to be treated equally." Though this creates the possibility that some grandchildren might take nothing, we must assume that Ms. Dunn preferred that her assets would come under the control of her living adult children.

I believe that this draft adequately reflects Ms Dunn's wishes, to the extent that they can be reconciled, and it reflects the firm's standards for the composition of wills. If there are any questions, please do not hesitate to contact me.

— The End —

Perform Your Best™ Note on Analyzing *In re Emily Dunn*

Task: Will
Context: Will drafting
Purpose: Draft will for partner, with explanations, for use in meeting with client who wishes to update her will
Structure: Definitional and case law analysis and application

First Document to Read and Outline in the MPT-Matrix™: Partner Memo. The Partner Memo in *In re Emily Dunn* demands especially careful reading, and rereading, along with the documents it refers to. The Partner Memo contains a number of separate instructions for the associate. The firm's client in this case is a recent widow, Emily Dunn, whose husband has died and who therefore needs a new will. The partner has interviewed the client, and he wants the associate to prepare a draft will so that he can have a new draft will in hand when he meets with the client again. The instructions say:

Draft the introductory and all dispositive clauses for Mrs. Dunn's proposed new will.

As usual, you must take apart the instructions in order to prepare the outline in the MPT-Matrix™. The introductory clauses might be one line in the MPT-Matrix™ But what does the instruction mean when it refers to "all dispositive clauses?"

Second Document to Read and Outline in the MPT-Matrix™: Will Drafting Guidelines. The Partner Memo tells the associate that in drafting the introductory and all dispositive clauses, the associate should follow the firm's Will Drafting Guidelines, which are in the MPT File. "Please set [the introductory and all dispositive clauses] forth in separately numbered paragraphs and in an order consistent with our firm's Will Drafting Guidelines." As often on the MPT, this second document shows the bar candidate how to format the work product.

The Will Drafting Guidelines also dictate the order of the sections of the will: specific bequests, general bequests, and so on. You must note that the order of the sections in this firm's wills has changed since Mrs. Dunn's first will was drafted. The Guidelines contain a number of terms of art with which you may not be familiar, for example, "general legacy" and "specific legacy." As you go through the library, you will discover that you can look to *In re Estate of Rich* to find the definitions of those terms. *In re Estate of Rich* quotes the definitions from the hornbook *Walker on Wills*.

The challenge does not end there. In addition to telling the associate to draft the entire will in accordance with the Will Drafting Guidelines, the Partner Memo asks the associate to resolve four issues. In looking back over his interview with Mrs. Dunn, he finds that there are some points on which he is unclear. Here is what the partner writes in the Partner Memo, with those four issues underlined and numbered:

In particular, I'm concerned about how she wants to deal with (i) the disposition of <u>potential insurance proceeds</u>, (ii) her <u>gifts of stock</u>, (iii) the <u>equalization of gifts to her grandchildren</u>, and (iv) <u>the distribution of the residuary estate</u>.

As to the clauses dealing with each of those four points, the partner asks the associate to answer two questions. The associate should state what <u>assumptions</u> he has made about the <u>facts</u> and about the client's <u>intentions</u>, and also <u>explain why he chose to draft those clauses as he did</u>.

Should each of these points, and each of these questions, be a separate line in the MPT-Matrix™? You have a choice. You can choose to make a separate line in the MPT-Matrix™ for each one. On the other hand, since these points and questions apply repeatedly, you may prefer to write your list of points and questions on a separate piece of paper and keep it on your desk, ready to be used, as appropriate, with the appropriate clauses in Mrs. Dunn's will.

In drafting the whole will, you will follow the format in the Will Drafting Guidelines in the File. But, again, this task does not require just a will, it requires both a will and explanations. Thus, in choosing a way to present the will-with-explanations, you have further choices. The sample answer in this book places the text of the proposed draft will inside the Discussion section of a memorandum addressed to the partner, and then it provides the explanations and answers the partner asks for inside the memo, along with the clauses being explained. This is an acceptable presentation, but it is not the only one. It would be entirely appropriate simply to draft Mrs. Dunn's will and answer the partner's secondary questions in parentheticals or else in footnotes to will. Alternatively, again, you could paste the draft will into one part of the Discussion section of a memorandum to the partner, providing the requested explanations in another section of the Discussion.

Once the instructions in the Partner Memo and the definitions are untangled, this task is straightforward. Format is key. The task requires using the format in the Will Drafting Guidelines as a framework, applying the definitions from *Walker on Wills*, plugging in the parts of Mrs. Dunn's will, and answering the partner's secondary questions.

Perform Your Best™ Materials
for MPT Task 4H:
In re Franklin Construction Company

Perform Your Best™ MPT-Matrix™ In re Franklin Construction Company

Note to the Reader: Your MPT-Matrix™ will have only page numbers, not words. The words in this MPT Matrix™ simply show you the information you will be indexing and cross-referencing. Do not attempt to write words in your own MPT-Matrix™.

MPT Matrix™ *Franklin Construction Company*, MPT, February 2002							
	A. Interview with Ralph Dirkson 2/25/02	B. Assignment Agreement 11/30/01	C. Joint Venture Agreement 12/26/01	D. Franklin Business Associations Code (UPA)	E. *Stilwell v. Trutanich* (Franklin Ct. App. 1995)	F. *Kovacik v. Reed* (Franklin Sup. Ct. 1996)	
1A. Obligations under Assignment Agreement	**P-3.** (i) Joint venture agreement was signed. (ii) BRA accepted MDI as FCC's partner.	**P-5.** FCC to transfer right of negotiation to MDI. MDI to transfer $350,000 to FCC to be deposited with BRA. FCC shall refund the $350,000 on the **failure** of either of two conditions, either: (i) execution of a joint venture agreement within 30 days; (ii) BRA acceptance of MDI as party.					
1B. Obligations under Joint Venture Agreement			**P-7.** MDI assigns to joint venture right of negotiation and the $350,000 MDI paid. FCC to contribute local expertise/ construction assistance and services.				
			P-7. "MDI shall be Managing Venturer of the Venture . . ." with "exclusive management and control . . . ." **P-8.** Profits: 90% to MDI and 10% to FCC.				

263

	MPT Matrix™ *Franklin Construction Company*, MPT, February 2002, *cont'd*						
	A. Interview with Ralph Dirkson 2/25/02	B. Assignment Agreement 11/30/01	C. Joint Venture Agreement 12/26/01	D. Franklin Business Associations Code (UPA)	E. *Stilwell v. Trutanich* (Franklin Ct. App. 1995)	F. *Kovacik v. Reed* (Franklin Sup. Ct. 1996)
			P-8. MDI has right to terminate and w/draw if BRA terminates right to negotiate prior to acquisition of the property.			
2. Obligations under statutes and case law				**P-10.** Sec. 401. Partner to share "in partnership losses in proportion to the partner's share of the profits."	**P-11.** "Joint venture is partnership . . . for a single project." Partnership law applies. In the absence of agreement, losses in same proportion as profits.	**P-12.** Irrespective of inequality in contributions to venture, in the absence of agreement, law presumes that joint venturers intend to share equally in both profits and losses.
				P-10. Secs. 203, 204: property acquired by partnership is partnership property. Sec. 404: Duty of care includes refraining from engaging in "grossly negligent or reckless conduct, intentional misconduct, or a knowing violation of law."		**P-12.** If "one partner . . . contributes the money capital as against the other's skill and labor, . . . neither party is liable to the other for contribution for any loss . . . ."

	A. Interview with Ralph Dirkson 2/25/02	B. Assignment Agreement 11/30/01	C. Joint Venture Agreement 12/26/01	D. Franklin Business Associations Code (UPA)	E. *Stilwell v. Trutanich* (Franklin Ct. App. 1995)	F. *Kovacik v. Reed* (Franklin Sup. Ct. 1996)
3. Obligation to make efforts to recover the money from BRA						**P-12.** Duty of managing venturer to take action against debtors of the joint venture.
						P-13. In the absence of agreement, no obligation to protect other joint venturer against loss of investment, or assist the other to recover the investment, nor to reimburse personally.

Perform Your Best™ Sample Answer for *In re Franklin Construction Company*

Axtell, Maynard & Sandrego
Attorneys at Law
One Central Post Plaza
Boyceville, Franklin 33321
(555) 521-7108

Ralph P. Dirksen
Chief Executive Officer
Franklin Construction Company
12543 Wrangel Road
Boyceville, FR 33324

Dear Ralph Dirksen:

Your company, Franklin Construction Company ("FCC," "you") has received a letter from Millman Developers, Inc. ("MDI"), your partner in an unsuccessful joint venture, demanding that you return to MDI its capital contribution to the venture, $350,000.00, or that you recover the $350,000.00 from the Boyceville Redevelopmment Agency ("BRA").

I know that MDI's demand must have come as a shock. I am happy to report that after careful review of the matter, I conclude that FCC is under no contractual or other legal obligation to return the $350,000.00 to MDI or to the Venture. Indeed, if either partner is obliged to recoup the money from the BRA, it is MDI, not FCC.

Factual Statement

In early 2001, FCC received from the BRA the exclusive right to negotiate for development of a project valued at $35,000,000.00. When you formed a joint venture with MDI, the Agency extended your exclusive negotiating right for 90 days. Under an Assignment Agreement dated November 30, 2001, MDI transferred to your company $350,000.00, the sum the BRA required as deposit. You agreed to form a joint venture with MDI, to transfer to MDI your exclusive right to negotiate, and to transfer the deposit to the Agency.

Under the Joint Venture Agreement of New Millennium Hotel Venture, signed by FCC and MDI, dated December 26, 2001, MDI assigned to the Venture as its capital contribution all its right, title and interest to (i) the exclusive right to negotiate; and (ii) the $350,000.00 paid under the Assignment Agreement. FCC's capital contribution to the Venture was "its local expertise and such assistance and services as MDI may from time to time require of it during the construction phase of the project." MDI was to be the Managing Venturer and receive 90 per cent of the profit, FCC, 10 per cent. The agreement was silent on apportionment of losses. When the Venture still could not obtain financing, the BRA revoked your right to negotiate, calling the $350,000 deposit nonrefundable.

Perform Your Best™ Sample Answer for In re Franklin Construction Company

On February 22, 2002, the president of MDI, Arthur D. Millman, wrote to you demanding that you recover its contribution or in any event return $350,000.00 to MDI.

Short Answers

1. FCC has no obligation to return the MDI contribution under either the Assignment Agreement or the Joint Venture Agreement, neither of which imposes on FCC any such obligation.
2. FCC has no obligation to return the MDI contribution under either the Franklin Business Associations Code, which imposes no obligation on one partner to return the capital contribution of another in the event of failure, nor under applicable case law, since FCC contributed "skill and labor," and so is not liable to MDI for loss of capital.
3. FCC has no obligation to try to recover the MDI contribution from the Boyceville Redevelopment Agency, since that obligation belongs to MDI, the managing venturer.

Opinion

I. FCC has no obligation to return the money to MDI under either the Assignment Agreement or the Joint Venture Agreement, neither of which imposes on FCC any such obligation.

IA. The Assignment Agreement. Under the Assignment Agreement dated November 30, 2001, and signed by Arthur D. Millman for MDI and by you, Ralph P. Dirkson, for Franklin Construction Company, MDI advanced $350,000.00, to FCC for submission to the BRA on behalf of the joint venture the two companies expected to form. The Assignment Agreement states only two situations where FCC agrees to refund the $350,000.00, namely, upon: (i) failure of the parties to execute a joint venture agreement within 30 days; (ii) failure of BRA to accept MDI as party. In the event of the failure of either condition, "this Agreement shall be null and void and FCC shall refund to MDI the $350,000 transferred hereunder." There is no other condition.

However, in fact neither condition applies. First, the parties executed a joint venture agreement within 26 days, on December 26, 2001. Second, BRA had already accepted MDI as a party, by its Resolution 43-99, dated November 20, 2001.

Therefore, the Assignment Agreement imposes on FCC no obligation to return the $350,000.00 to MDI.

IB. The Joint Venture Agreement. Under the Joint Venture Agreement, MDI assigns to the joint venture the right of negotiation and the $350,000 it has paid under the Assignment Agreement, which is clearly a capital contribution to the Venture. FCC is to contribute its local expertise and construction assistance and services. The Joint Venture Agreement provides that MDI has the right to terminate the agreement and withdraw if BRA terminates the right to negotiate. The Joint Venture Agreement is silent as to any circumstance under which MDI might recoup the money, nor does it impose on FCC or the Venture an obligation to return the money. Therefore, FCC has no obligation under the Joint Venture Agreement.

II. FCC has no obligation to return the money under either the Franklin Business Associations Code, which imposes no obligation on one partner to return the capital contribution of another in the event of failure, nor under applicable case law, since FCC contributed "skill and labor," and so is not liable to MDI for loss of capital.

Perform Your Best on the Bar Exam Performance Test (MPT)

IIA. Franklin Business Associations Code. Under the Franklin Business Associations Code, property a partnership acquires is partnership property. As the Franklin Court of Appeal said in a case called *Stilwell*, a joint venture is a partnership for a single project. Under the Franklin Business Associations Code, a partner's share "in partnership losses [is] in proportion to the partner's share of the profits." The statute does not, however, impose an obligation on either partner, or on the joint venture, to return the capital contribution of the other partner upon failure of the venture. Even assuming, for the sake of argument, that FCC made a payback of part or all of the $350,000.00 to MDI, the money would still belong to the Venture; MDI under Section 404 would simply be holding it as a fiduciary of Venture. Therefore, absent some other claim, FCC has no obligation to return the money to MDI.

IIB. Case Law. Two recent cases in Franklin are relevant. I conclude, however, that neither case imposes any obligation on FCC to repay the money.

According to the first of those cases, a joint venture is a partnership formed for a single project. In the absence of an agreement, the losses are apportioned in same proportion as profits. According to the other, where "one partner . . . contributes the money capital as against the other's skill and labor, . . . neither party is liable to the other for contribution for any loss . . . ."

In your matter, MDI contributed money capital, while FCC contributed "its local expertise and such assistance and services as MDI may from time to time require of it during the construction phase of the project," that is, its "skill and labor."

Accordingly, FCC is not liable for any of MDI and the Venture's lost capital. Therefore, FCC has no obligation to refund the $350,000 to MDI or the Venture.

III. FCC has no obligation to try to recover the money from the Boyceville Redevelopment Agency, since that obligation belongs to MDI, the managing venturer.

Under the Franklin Business Associations Code, every partner or joint venturer has a duty to refrain from "engaging in grossly negligent or reckless conduct, intentional misconduct, or a knowing violation of law." FCC has not engaged in such conduct. Therefore, FCC has not violated that duty.

It is the duty of the managing venturer to take action against debtors of the joint venture, like the Boyceville Redevelopment Agency here. It appears from your Joint Venture Agreement that MDI is the managing partner. If any partner is obliged to pursue the Redevelopment Agency, accordingly, it is MDI. In the absence of agreement, moreover, no venturer has an obligation to protect another joint venturer against loss of investment, nor to assist the other to recover the investment, nor to reimburse the other venturer personally. In sum, FCC need not pursue the BRA for return of the money that MDI contributed to the venture.

In conclusion, you can breathe more easily. You are not liable to MDI, nor need you seek return of the funds from the BRA.

Yours very truly,

Max Sandrego

Perform Your Best™ Note on Analyzing *In re Franklin Construction Company*

Type of task: Opinion Letter to a Client
Context: Contract dispute
Structure: Contract, statutory and case law analysis and application

A tangled web of facts makes *In re Franklin Construction Company* an interesting case. The firm's client, Franklin Construction Company ("FCC"), has brought in a larger joint venturer, Millman Development Inc. ("MDI"), as lead partner, so that both can have a chance at winning a large development project. MDI has assigned $350,000 to the venture, that is, the amount the public agency demands to allow the venture to be considered for participation. But the joint venture's attempt to get the job has been unsuccessful. So MDI's now seeks return of its $350,000. Is it FCC's legal obligation to return the money to MDI? Or does FCC perhaps have a responsibility to try to recoup the money from the development agency? The answer turns out to be neither of the above.

The opinion letter to the client that the Partner Memo asks the associate to draft must advise him, first, on whether either his company's contractual obligations or the statutes or case law compel the client to pay either MDI or the venture any of the money demanded. Second, whether the client has any obligation to try to recover the money from the Boyceville Redevelopment Agency. This is to be a persuasive letter, not an objective letter.

Choosing the appropriate tone and degree of formality is always important in drafting a letter. The instruction from the partner in *Franklin Construction* says that the associate should be sure to "explain things fully and in language that a layperson can understand." This applies to any letter in which a lawyer addresses a layperson. Here, the partner reminds the associate that the client is "a sophisticated businessman, but he is not a lawyer." Accordingly, the sample answer in this book does not cite case names or section numbers of statutes, and it avoids most technical legal language. It expresses sympathy for the unpleasant situation in which the client finds himself and satisfaction at finding that the client does not wind up having to restore $350,000.00 to MDI.

The Partner Memo says:

> Please draft an opinion letter to Mr. Dirksen for my signature advising him on the following questions:
>
> 1. Is FCC obligated under either of its two contractual undertakings to pay either MDI or the Venture any part of the money demanded in the letter from MDI?
> 2. Is FCC obligated under the statutes and case law to pay either MDI or the Venture any part of the money demanded in the letter from MDI?
> 3. Does FCC have any obligation to undertake efforts to recover the money from the Boyceville Redevelopment Agency?

<u>How to Read and Outline the Instructions for the MPT-Matrix</u>™. This case presents a classical instance of instructions in a Partner Memo that you must pull apart into their smallest components in order to outline them in the MPT-Matrix™. The Partner's first question must

Perform Your Best on the Bar Exam Performance Test (MPT)

be pulled apart into two questions, one for FCC's possible obligations under the Assignment Agreement and the other for its possible obligations under the Joint Venture Agreement. The first row of your MPT-Matrix™ will be for the Assignment Agreement, and the second row will be for the Joint Venture Agreement. As you read through the File and the Library you will be noting the page numbers where material appears bearing on liabilities under those two agreements. The second question in the Partner Memo must also be divided into two questions, and so it, too, will occupy two lines on your MPT-Matrix™, one regarding FCC's obligations under the Business Associations Code and the other regarding its obligations under the applicable case law. You will place page numbers in those rows when you find applicable material in the File and the Library. You will find that there are in fact two applicable cases, *Stillwell v. Trutanich* (Franklin Ct. App. 1995) and *Kovacik v. Reed* (Franklin Sup. Ct. 1996). The partner's third question will take up one row in your MPT-Matrix™. Reading the statute and the case law, you will have abundant material in the Library with which to argue that FCC has no obligation to attempt to recoup the $350,000.00 from the Boyceville Redevelopment Agency, but in fact that obligation belongs to MDI itself, as managing venturer.

How to Use the Firm's Format for Opinion Letters. The Partner Memo for this MPT task provides a format for opinion letters. The Partner Memo says:

> Follow the usual office format for opinion letters:
> (a) a short "Factual Statement";
> (b) a "Short Answer" for each issue in which you state the essence of the opinion; and
> (c) an "Opinion" segment in which you state your conclusions and explain your reasoning, supported by the legal authorities.

Keeping a Factual Statement short is often a challenge. In this case, the sample answer in this book reduces the facts, but it does not reduce them as much as possible. By omitting dates and other specifics, the Factual Statement might have been reduced still further. The Short Answers section in the sample letter gives answers in the same words used in the persuasive topic headings in the three parts of the central Opinion part of the letter. They include both law and facts. The Opinion segment states the legal reasoning leading to the answers.

How to Apply the Rule of Three. Like a memorandum, a business letter usually has three sections, (i) an opening section setting out the issue, (ii) a discussion section, and (iii) a conclusion, often with a call to action. If the discussion section has three parts, the bar candidate may give each part a powerful heading, as in a memorandum. Here are three possibilities this book uses in the sample letter:

1. FCC has no obligation to return the MDI contribution under either the Assignment Agreement or the Joint Venture Agreement, neither of which imposes on FCC any such obligation.
2. FCC has no obligation to return the MDI contribution under either the Franklin Business Associations Code, which imposes no obligation on one partner to return the capital contribution of another in the event of failure, nor under applicable case law, since FCC contributed "skill and labor," and so is not liable to MDI for loss of capital.
3. FCC has no obligation to try to recover the MDI contribution from the Boyceville Redevelopment Agency, since that obligation belongs to MDI, the managing venturer.

Completing Part I of the task requires contract analysis, while Parts II and III require combined statutory and case analysis. As always, one must start with the statute. To do the statutory analysis, the associate must apply the law to two contractual documents in the File, the Assignment Agreement and the Joint Venture Agreement. It turns out that under neither one does FCC have any obligation to return the money to MDI.

For Part 2, the associate must examine the Franklin Business Associations Code, in particular the Uniform Partnership Act, and the case law. Careful reading of the statute discloses that upon failure of a joint venture, the law imposes no obligation either (a) on one of the partners, or (b) on the joint venture, to return the capital contribution of another partner. According to the *Kovacik* case, in addition, if "one partner . . . contributes the money capital as against the other's skill and labor . . . neither party is liable to the other for contribution for any loss . . . ." This is good news for the firm's client, since the client, FCC, contributed skill and labor, while MDI contributed the money capital. Therefore, under *Kovacik*, FCC is not liable to MDI for the loss.

With regard to whether FCC must seek to recover the money from the BRA, our sample answer for this task concludes:

> As the *Kovacik* court affirmed, it is the duty of the managing venturer to take action against debtors of the joint venture, like the Boyceville Redevelopment Agency here. It appears from the Joint Venture Agreement here that MDI is the managing partner. If any partner is obliged to pursue the Redevelopment Agency, accordingly, it is MDI. In the absence of agreement, moreover, no venturer has an obligation to protect another joint venturer against loss of investment, nor to assist the other to recover the investment, nor to reimburse the other venturer personally. In sum, FCC need not pursue the BRA for return of the money that MDI contributed to the venture.

As always, in the Conclusion of the letter the associate will restate the questions, state that he or she has completed the analysis, and state the general conclusions. Here, the sample answer concludes as follows:

> In conclusion, you can breathe more easily. You are not liable to MDI, nor need you seek return of the funds from the BRA.

Perform Your Best™ Materials
for MPT Task 4I:
In re Gardenton Board of Education

Perform Your Best™ MPT-Matrix™ In re Gardenton Board of Education

Note to the Reader: Your MPT-Matrix™ will have only page numbers, not words. The words in this MPT Matrix™ simply show you the information you will be indexing and cross-referencing. Do not attempt to write words in your own MPT-Matrix™.

MPT-Matrix™ *In re Gardenton Board of Education*, MPT, February 1998							
Proposed Code	A. U.S. Constitution	B. Franklin Constitution	C. Sec. 48 Franklin Education Act	D. *Hazelwood* (U.S. 1988)	E. *Lopez v. Union High School District* (Franklin Sup. Ct. 1994)	F. *Leeb v. DeLong* (Franklin Ct. App. 1995)
Preamble	**P-5.** Congress shall make no law "abridging the freedom of speech, or of the press . . . ."	**P-5.** "A law may not restrain or abridge liberty of speech or press . . . except [obscenity, libel, slander]	**P-5.** Students have editorial control. Except for obscenity, libel and slander, or speech that incites students to create a clear and present danger of unlawful acts, students have right of free speech. Responsibility of advisors to maintain "professional standards of English and journalism."	**P-6.** "Educational mission outweighs [free] speech." Censorship Ok for valid educational purpose.	**P-8.** Film subject to same standards/rights as newspaper. **P-9.** Student publications are "limited public forum": State must show compelling state interest to censor.	**P-10.** Under sec. 48 students' rights are broader than under U.S. Constitution.
1. "Professional Standards"			**P-5.** It is the duty of school advisers to maintain "professional standards."	**P-7.** School may "disassociate itself" from certain speech.	**P-8.** Profanity violates "professional standards" under sec. 48.	
2. "Good taste"			Query. Included under "professional standards" in sec. 48? If so, permissible. But probably not.		**P-9.** Film/newspaper is "limited public forum." Compelling state interest required for restrictions.	

| MPT-Matrix™ *In re Gardenton Board of Education*, MPT, February 1998, *cont'd* ||||||||
Proposed Code	A. U.S. Constitution	B. Franklin Constitution	C. Sec. 48 Franklin Education Act	D. *Hazelwood* (U.S. 1988)	E. *Lopez v. Union High School District* (Franklin Sup. Ct. 1994)	F. *Leeb v. DeLong* (Franklin Ct. App. 1995)
3. "Accuracy"			Q. Students have editorial control. However, probably Ok. Use "Professional standards."			
4. Quotes/ permissions			**P-5.** Probably Ok: "Obscene, libelous," . . . and also under "Professional standards."			
5. No materials: a. Libel, etc.			**P-5.** Ditto.		**P-8.** Prior restraint Ok where material "violation" of sec. 48. Prior restraint Ok to forestall actions against school in defamation.	**P-10.** Prior restraint by school Ok to forestall actions in defamation. **P-10.** Must limit deletion to the offending material.
b. Profanity			**P-5.** Ok if profanity violates "professional standards"? Definitely Ok to prohibit it if it is "obscenity."	**P-7.** School may "disassociate" itself from profanity.	**P-8.** Sec. 48 permits prior restraint of profanity. **P-8.** Profanity violates "professional standards" under sec. 48. **P-8.** School also has interest in protecting students.	

MPT-Matrix™ *In re Gardenton Board of Education*, MPT, February 1998, *cont'd*						
Proposed Code	A. U.S. Constitution	B. Franklin Constitution	C. Sec. 48 Franklin Education Act	D. *Hazelwood* (U.S. 1988)	E. *Lopez v. Union High School District* (Franklin Sup. Ct. 1994)	F. *Leeb v. DeLong* (Franklin Ct. App. 1995)
c. Criticize public officials				**P-7.** School may refuse to associate itself with political positions.		**P-10.** *New York Times v. Sullivan* standard applies to public figures. So section not Ok.
d. "Not in school's best interest."			Ok under "professional standards"? But if provision is too broad, strike it.	**P-7.** School may "disassociate itself" from certain speech. However, this provision of the Code is probably too broad as written.		
6. Need prior approval of principal			Ok under "professional standards"?	**P-7.** Arguably permissible [?] because school may "disassociate itself."	**P-8.** Prior restraint Ok where material "violation" of sec. 48. Or to protect the students. **P-9.** Or where it is a limited public forum and there is a compelling state interest.	**P-10.** Prior restraint by school Ok to forestall actions in defamation. **P-10.** Must limit deletion to the offending material.

275

Perform Your Best™ Sample Answer for *In re Gardenton Board of Education*

MEMORANDUM

To: Frank Eisner
From: Applicant
Subject: Gardenton Board of Education—Proposed Communications Code for Gardenton High School
Date: _____

INTRODUCTION

For the Board's guidance as they prepare for a public meeting, the Gardenton Board of Education have asked us how to edit the proposed Gardenton High School Student Communications Code ("the Code") so that the school has the greatest possible latitude to censor objectionable material in student publications and productions. I conclude that the School Board should have little difficulty. Sec. 48 of the Franklin Education Act gives school boards authority to enforce "professional standards" of journalism, so most sections of the proposed code are unexceptionable. Most sections, furthermore, are also unexceptionable under constitutional, statutory, and case law. I provide a section-by-section analysis below, with suggestions for revision where necessary.

DISCUSSION

PREAMBLE OF THE CODE. The Preamble suggests that under the Communications Code the school can impose prior restraint on all official and extracurricular student publications and presentations, in all media, whether on campus or off. Legal issues: (1.) whether the Preamble is impermissibly broad; (2.) whether student films are subject to the same standards as student newspapers; (3.) whether off-campus activities are subject to the same standards as on-campus activities.

Is the Preamble permissible? Yes. Reasons: (1.) Sec. 48 of the Franklin Education Act does give students broader free speech rights than does the United States Constitution and limits prior restraint of speech. But sec. 48 also gives the school power to require "professional standards" of English and journalism. That means it may sometimes impose prior restraint.

(2.) The *Lopez* court says that student films are subject to the same standards as student newspapers.

(3.) If students' off-campus activities are what the *Lopez* court calls a "public forum," then critics might argue that the school cannot regulate them. If, on the other hand, they are a "limited public forum," then the school can regulate them, but only if it demonstrates (i) a compelling state interest and (ii) that the regulations are both narrowly drawn to achieve that compelling interest and sufficiently precise to withstand a challenge as void for vagueness.

Suggestions: If the School Board strikes the words "off campus," in specific cases the Board can support censoring off-campus productions using the "disassociate itself" language of *Hazelwood* ("a school may . . . disassociate itself . . . from speech that is . . . vulgar or profane, or unsuitable for immature audiences"), perhaps together with the "professional standards" language of sec. 48.

Perform Your Best™ Sample Answer for In re Gardenton Board of Education

Sec. 1. Is the requirement of professional standards of English language and journalistic style permissible? Legal issues. Whether this standard is clear, definite, and not too broad. Permissible? Yes. Reasons: Courts have upheld sec. 48 of the Education Act, allowing schools to require "professional standards."

Sec. 2. Is the requirement of good taste, having regard to the "age, experience and maturity" of the students permissible? Legal issues. Is the term "good taste" unconstitutionally void for vagueness? Is "age, experience," etc.?

Permissible? Yes. But term "good taste" should nonetheless be changed. Reasons: Critics will argue that "good taste" is too vague. Suggestion: To avoid fruitless controversy, this section should read: "avoid language and depictions that violate professional standards of taste . . . ."

Sec. 3. Is the requirement that accuracy of facts and quotations be verified permissible? Legal issues: whether this requirement violates the students' right to editorial control under sec. 48; whether it is an impermissible prior restraint. Permissible? Yes. Reasons: Sec. 48 requires, again, application of "professional standards." Responsible newspapers of general circulation do require accuracy of facts and quotations. The School Board can require accuracy of facts, and probably also that quotations be verified by the supervising teacher.

Sec. 4. Is the requirement permissible that no quotes or photos be used without prior permission of that person or of a parent or guardian of a minor? Legal issues: whether this Code section imposes an impermissible prior restraint. Permissible? Yes. Reasons: Sec. 48 makes "professional standards" the touchstone, and prior permission is consistent with professional standards. In the *Leeb* case, where a group photograph was used for a purpose for which the subjects had not given permission, the court upheld censorship.

Sec. 5a. Is the requirement to avoid libel permissible? Legal issues: whether this Code section imposes an impermissible prior restraint. Permissible? Yes. Reasons: Sec. 48 by its terms proscribes obscenity, libel, and slander. *Lopez* permits prior restraint to prevent a "violation" of sec. 48. The cases also permit prior restraint to forestall an action in defamation against the school. Note that the *Leeb* court stipulated that the school must limit the deletion to the offending material. Suggestion: The school may prefer to avoid controversy about what is libelous by using the "professional standards" language here instead.

Sec. 5b. Profanity. Legal issues: whether this Code section imposes an impermissible prior restraint. Permissible? Yes. Reasons: Sec. 48 does not by its terms proscribe profanity. The School Board can argue, however, that profanity in student publications violates "professional standards." The Supreme Court of the United States has said that a school may "disassociate itself" from profanity. *Hazelwood*. In *Lopez*, the Franklin Supreme Court held that sec. 48 permits prior restraint of profanity. The school may also cite Lopez to argue that it exerts its interest in protecting students when it censors profanity.

Sec. 5c. No criticism or demeaning of public officials. Legal issues: whether this Code section impermissibly limits freedom of the press under the First Amendment. Permissible? No. Reasons. The Franklin Court of Appeal in *Leeb* made it clear that when students criticize public figures the applicable standard is *New York Times v. Sullivan*. Accordingly, this provision must be stricken.

Sec. 5d. May the school suppress material deemed not in school's best interest? Legal issues: whether this Code section impermissibly limits freedom of the press under the First

Amendment. Permissible? Probably not. Reasons: Under *Hazelwood*, a school may "disassociate itself" from certain speech. "Not in the school's best interest," however, is a very broad standard. It may also be void for vagueness under the United States Constitution. Conclusion: The School Board should strike this section.

Sec. 6. Is the requirement of prior approval of the principal permissible? Legal issues: whether this Code section impermissibly limits freedom of the press under the First Amendment by imposing prior restraint. Permissible? Yes. Reasons: The Education Act and the cases all assume that student publications require prior approval of the school. Sec. 48 of the Education Act affirms the authority of the school to teach and enforce professional standards. The Franklin Supreme Court in *Lopez* held that the school may censor official school publications to protect the students. Both *Lopez* and *Leeb* asserted that prior restraint by the school is permissible to forestall an action in defamation.

CONCLUSION

I have examined the proposed Code and concluded that most parts of the Preamble and most sections of the Code are unexceptionable under constitutional, statutory, and case law. I have made suggestions for deleting, modifying, or adding items in the few instances where it is necessary to help the Board achieve its goal. The School Board should have little difficulty responding to critics.

Perform Your Best™ Note on Analyzing *In re Gardenton Board of Education*

Objective Memorandum
Code Analysis and Drafting
Analysis for partner: to use for advising client
Statutory interpretation, with suggestions for deleting, adding or re-drafting sections

In the MPT task called *In re Gardenton Board of Education,* the client, the Gardenton Board of Education, has asked how to draft the Gardenton High School Student Communications Code ("the Code") so that the school has the greatest possible latitude to censor objectionable material in student publications and productions. This task may appear especially challenging because it requires bar candidates to apply constitutional principles in assessing the proposed Code.

In fact, this task is straightforward, and both the legal format and the analytic pattern are familiar. The task calls for writing an objective memorandum to the partner, so the format is one of the familiar basic legal formats. In addition, this task is yet another instance of the familiar MPT pattern in which the student must analyze a code or a proposed code, one section at a time. And as always where the MPT asks the bar candidate to examine a code one section at a time, the File or Library contains a document that provides the standard for judging the sections. Here, sec. 48 of the Franklin Education Act is that useful document. Sec. 48 allows school boards the authority to enforce "professional standards" of journalism. When you test the code sections against the "professional standards" clause of sec. 48, almost every section of the proposed Code turns out to be permissible.

The main challenge of completing *In re Gardenton Board of Education* is finding your framework within the partner's instructions in the task memo and then using that framework efficiently to keep the material under control. As always, you must finish the whole task within 90 minutes, and the work product you hand in must be not only intellectually compelling but also visually clear and simple.

As always, again, the key to success on this MPT task is reading the partner memo with exquisite care. Having first stated the scope of the task in general terms, the partner memo then gives you your analytic framework. Read the partner memo with exquisite care and you will see what the parts of your analysis of each code section must be. I have underlined the key terms in the partner's framework below:

> Please prepare a memorandum in which you evaluate the preamble and each of the guideline provisions in the draft of the communications code that Dr. Kantor left with me. Identify the <u>legal issues</u> that can give rise to constitutional challenges to each of the provisions and analyze whether each such provision is likely to be found legally <u>permissible</u>. Make <u>suggestions for deleting, modifying, or adding</u> any items in order to help the Board achieve its goal. Be sure to state your <u>reasons</u> for concluding that each guideline provision is legally permissible or impermissible, as well as the <u>reasons for any suggestions</u> you make. Support your reasons with <u>appropriate discussion of the facts and law</u>.

Perform Your Best on the Bar Exam Performance Test (MPT)

The sample answer uses these key terms as a framework. For example:

<u>Sec. 4. Is the requirement permissible that no quotes or photos be used without prior permission of that person or of a parent or guardian of a minor?</u> <u>Legal issues:</u> whether this Code section imposes an impermissible prior restraint. <u>Permissible?</u> Yes. <u>Reasons:</u> Sec. 48 makes "professional standards" the touchstone, and prior permission is consistent with professional standards. In the *Leeb* case, where a group photograph was used for a purpose for which the subjects had not given permission, the court upheld censorship.

If you handle every section of the proposed code this way, you will submit a work product that will merit a good grade.

This MPT task does present one significant challenge of legal analysis. You must use exactly the same framework to handle it that you use for all of your other treatments of code sections. The problem here is chiefly one of exam-taking tactics. Managing time while completing the work product is always a primary consideration, and here, unfortunately, it is the Preamble of the proposed code, the opening section, that presents the challenge. Don't let yourself get bogged down, and don't let yourself be intimidated. I suggest that if you run into a challenging issue that concerns only one section of the code you are analyzing, as here, you should leave space in your bluebook, complete the rest of your work product, and return to the challenging issue at the end of your 90 minutes.

Here is the way the sample answer handles the potentially challenging legal issue in *In re Gardenton Board of Education*:

PREAMBLE OF THE CODE. The Preamble suggests that under the Communications Code the school can impose prior restraint on all official and extracurricular student publications and presentations, in all media, whether on campus or off. <u>Legal issues:</u> (1.) whether the Preamble is impermissibly broad; (2.) whether student films are subject to the same standards as student newspapers; (3.) whether off-campus activities are subject to the same standards as on-campus activities.

<u>Is the Preamble permissible?</u> Yes. <u>Reasons:</u> (1.) Sec. 48 of the Franklin Education Act does give students broader free speech rights than does the United States Constitution and limits prior restraint of speech. But sec. 48 also gives the school power to require "professional standards" of English and journalism. That means it may sometimes impose prior restraint.

(2.) The *Lopez* court says that student films are subject to the same standards as student newspapers.

(3.) If students' off-campus activities are what the *Lopez* court calls a "public forum," then critics might argue that the school cannot regulate them. If, on the other hand, they are a "limited public forum," then the school can regulate them, but only if it demonstrates (i) a compelling state interest and (ii) that the regulations are both narrowly drawn to achieve that compelling interest and sufficiently precise to withstand a challenge as void for vagueness.

<u>Suggestions:</u> If the School Board strikes the words "off campus," in specific cases the Board can support censoring off-campus productions using the "disassociate itself" language of *Hazelwood* ("a school may . . . disassociate itself . . . from speech that is . . . vulgar or profane, or unsuitable for immature audiences"), perhaps together with the "professional standards" language of sec. 48.

Perform Your Best™ *Note on Analyzing In re Gardenton Board of Education*

As always, in the Conclusion of the memorandum you will restate the partner's assignment, state that you have completed it and say what general conclusions you have reached:

> I have examined the proposed Code and concluded that most parts of the Preamble and most sections of the Code are unexceptionable under constitutional, statutory, and case law. I have made suggestions for deleting, modifying, or adding items in the few instances where it is necessary to help the Board achieve its goal. The School Board should have little difficulty responding to critics.

Perform Your Best™ Materials
for MPT Task 4J:
In re Steven Wallace

Perform Your Best™ MPT-Matrix™ In re Steven Wallace

Note to the Reader: Your MPT-Matrix™ will have only page numbers, not words. The words in this MPT Matrix™ simply show you the information you will be indexing and cross-referencing. Do not attempt to write words in your own MPT-Matrix™.

	\multicolumn{6}{c	}{MPT-Matrix™ *In re Steven Wallace*, MPT, July 1999}
	A. Meeting 2/26/99	B. Receipt 8/15/98	C. *Walker on Bankruptcy*	D. Franklin Commercial Code sec. 2-326, Franklin Civil Code sec. 3533	E. *First Natl. Bank v. Marigold Farms* (Franklin Ct. App. Undated)	F. *In re Levy* (E.D. Pa. 1993)
1. Asset of bkrpty estate 1. Bkrpy. Act b. Legal Basis			**P-6.** Trustee can avoid transfer of property after case begins; Assets include consignments.			
2. ii. Factual Basis	**P-2.** Painting was on consignment; Lottie attempted to transfer it after case began.	**P-3.** Receipt indicates painting on consignment.				
3. Franklin CC i. Legal Basis				**P-7.** FCC § 2-326. Goods on consignment are subject to creditors' claims.	**P-8.** Goods held on sale or return are subject to claims of creditors regardless of consignor's retaining title.	
4. ii. Factual Basis	**P-2.** Painting was on consignment.	**P-3.** Receipt indicates painting on consignment.				
5. Defense: Sign Law (i) How supports	**P-2.** (a) SW's label on back; (b) Sign in window?			**P-7.** Franklin Civil Code sec. 3533.	**P-9.** Must be generally known to all creditors, not just consignors.	**P-10.** Signs must impart knowledge to creditors, not just customers.
6. (ii) Add'l. Helpful Facts	\multicolumn{6}{l	}{Regarding other artists' signs: Would be evidence of notice. Regarding whether Lottie had a sign in the window: What do the neighbors of the shop say? What have the other creditors seen? Ask them.}

283

Perform Your Best on the Bar Exam Performance Test (MPT)

MPT-Matrix™ *In re Steven Wallace*, MPT, July 1999, *cont'd*						
	A. Meeting 2/26/99	B. Receipt 8/15/98	C. *Walker on Bankruptcy*	D. Franklin Commercial Code sec. 2-326, Franklin Civil Code sec. 3533	E. *First Natl. Bank v. Marigold Farms* (Franklin Ct. App. Undated)	F. *In re Levy* (E.D. Pa. 1993)
7. (iii) Why Helpful	Artists' signs would show general notice, if intended to give notice to non-customers. Lottie's sign would show that owner complied with the sign law.					
8. (iv) Possible Sources	The other consignors are the best source regarding artists' signs. Go to the shop: is the sign still there? Ask other shop owners on the same street. Ask person from whom Lottie bought the sign, or seller, if any, from whom she bought the shop. Beat cop. Letter carrier. Caterers who worked at gallery openings. Other creditors. Photographs.					
9. Creditors Know Selling Goods of Others	Name of shop, Artists' Excg.				**P-9.** Other creditors, not just the artists/ consignors.	**P-10.** Must be creditors, not just customers.
10. (ii) Add'l. Helpful Facts	Are most of the creditors in fact consignors? (If so, perhaps can distinguish *First National Bank*.) Is there evidence from Lottie's correspondence with creditors that Artists' Exchange was primarily engaged in selling the goods of others? Ask other creditors. Include bank, newspaper advertising department, advertising agency. Was there a sign in the window?					
11. (iii) Why helpful.	If we can find other non-artist creditors and customers who know that Lottie was selling the goods of others, this will satisfy the defense that she is "generally known" to be in the business of selling the goods of others.					
12. (iv) Possible Sources	Ask Lottie. Look at the property schedules filed with the court, which will contain the names and addresses of the creditors. Ask the banker, the cleaning service, the printers who do announcements of shows, the newspaper advertising department, the advertising agency. Question whether most art galleries deal on a consignment basis may call for expert testimony.					
13. Compliance With filing Provisions of UCC Art.	Would be complete defense under FCC sec. 2-326(3)(c). No evidence now. No record that Ms. Morales asked the question. Ask Steven Wallace. Look in Sec'y of State files, etc. Ask whether any other consignors complied with Art. 9. Would be constructive notice.					
14. Consignor used for personal/ family/ household.	If this can be shown, it will be a complete defense under the FCC. However, SW did sell his paintings. See footnote in *First National Bank*.					
15. (ii) Add'l. Helpful Facts	Has Steven Wallace kept other paintings for personal use? Has he ever refused to sell a painting in his personal collection? Make sure to check SW's personal files and records. What discussions did the Wallaces have at the time they bought the rug?					
16. (iii) Why helpful.	It would show that these paintings are for household use, not commercial stock in trade.					
17. (iv) Possible Sources	Steven Wallace's friends and acquaintances who might have tried to buy a painting. SW's own records: does he maintain separate records for the inventory of paintings he holds for sale and the ones he keeps for his family's use?					

Perform Your Best™ Sample Answer for *In re Steven Wallace*

MEMORANDUM

To: Eva Morales
From: Applicant
Date: _____
Subject: Steven Wallace—Painting Titled "Hare Castle"

INTRODUCTION

You have asked me to analyze the legal and factual bases for the trustee's claim that under the Bankruptcy Act and under the Franklin Commercial Code, our client Steven Wallace's painting "Hare Castle" is an asset of art dealer Lottie Zelinka's bankruptcy estate. You have also asked me to assess possible defenses under FCC sec. 2-326(3).

DISCUSSION

IA. Since Lottie Zelinka held the painting "Hare Castle" on consignment, and since she returned the painting to Steven Wallace only after she filed for bankruptcy, the Bankruptcy Act provides legal bases for the trustee to avoid returning the painting to Steven Wallace.

Under the Bankruptcy Act, the assets of the bankruptcy estate include goods left with the bankrupt on consignment. In addition, the trustee can avoid any transfer of property made after the case begins. *Walker on Bankruptcy*, sec. 4.08.

Here, Steven Wallace reports, and the receipt indicates, that he placed the painting with Lottie Zelinka on consignment. Wallace Interview; Receipt; Appraisal. In addition, the facts show that Lottie did attempt to transfer the property, i.e., the painting "Hare Castle," back to Wallace after she filed for bankruptcy. Ms. Zelinka came to Wallace's house with the painting, 10 days or so before he spoke with Ms. Morales, saying that she wished to return the painting to him. Wallace reports learning that Ms. Zelinka had already filed for bankruptcy protection on the date when she tried to return the painting to him. Wallace Interview.

Therefore, if the painting was an asset of the bankruptcy estate, then the trustee has legal and factual bases for his claim. If, that is, Steven Wallace has no effective defense, the trustee can avoid Lottie Zelinka's transfer of the property back to Steven Wallace after the bankruptcy filing.

IB. Since Lottie Zelinka held the painting "Hare Castle" on consignment, the Franklin Commercial Code provides legal bases for the trustee's claim that Steven Wallace's painting is part of the bankruptcy estate.

Under the Franklin Commercial Code, goods on consignment are subject to creditors' claims. FCC sec. 2-326. Under *First National Bank* and *In re Levy*, it does not matter that the consignor retained title.

Here, the interview notes and the receipt Lottie Zelinka gave Steven Wallace show that the painting "Hare Castle" was delivered on consignment. Wallace Interview; Receipt.

Therefore, again, unless Steven Wallace can assert an effective defense, the trustee has legal and factual bases under the Franklin Commercial Code for his claim.

II. Depending on how our factual investigations turn out, Steven Wallace may possibly assert one or more of the defenses available under FCC 2-326, and oppose the trustee's claim.

Depending on the facts, Steven Wallace may be able to assert an effective defense under FCC 2-326(a). The best defense may be the defense of use for "personal, family, or household purposes."

  (a) Defense of compliance with the sign law. Under FCC 2-326(a), goods delivered to another person for sale are not subject to the claims of the latter's creditors where the person making the delivery "complies with all applicable law providing for a consignor's interest or the like to be evidenced by a sign."
- (i) How the facts we already know support this defense. First, Steven Wallace had a label on the back of his painting, saying that it was the property of Steven Wallace. Wallace Interview. Other artists may have done the same. Second, Lottie Zelinka's sign in the window of the shop—if there was one, as Steven Wallace thinks—may have indicated the consignors' interests in their art work. Note that these two supports are entirely different from one another.
- (ii) Additional helpful facts.
- (ii)(a) Artists' signs would show notice to customers.
- (ii)(b) Lottie Zelinka's sign, if any, would show that the owner complied with the sign law, if it stated that she was dealing in property in which others had an interest. FCC 3533.
- (iii) Why helpful:
- (iii)(a) If most artists had signs on the backs of their paintings, that might arguably constitute adequate notice to customers, even if it would not notify non-customers.
- (iii)(b) If Lottie Zelinka had a sign in the window, it would show that she complied with the sign law.
- (iv) Possible sources. The other consignors are the best source of information about their own signs. As to the possibility of a sign in the window, we can send an investigator to the shop. Ask other shop owners on the same street whether they ever noticed a sign. Ask the person from whom Lottie Zelinka bought the shop, if any. Ask the beat cop. Ask the letter carrier. Ask the caterers who work at gallery openings. Ask other creditors. Find out if there are reliably dated photographs of the front of the shop, perhaps in municipal archives.

  (b) Defense of creditors' knowledge that the gallery sold on consignment. Under FCC 2-326(b), the person making the delivery has a defense if he establishes that "the person conducting the business is generally known by his creditors to be substantially engaged in selling goods of others." Under *First National Bank*, these creditors must persons other than consignors. Under *In re Levy*, these creditors must not be just customers of the bankrupt.
- (i) How the facts we already know support this defense. We can argue that the name of the shop, "Artists' Exchange," Inventory Receipt, indicates that the gallery was selling the goods of others. And if galleries everywhere work on consignment, as Steven Wallace believes, then creditors probably know it.
- (ii) Additional helpful facts. Find out whether creditors such as newspaper advertising departments know that Lottie Zelinka was operating on consignment.
- (iii) Why helpful. All we need is evidence that Lottie Zelinka was "generally known" to be selling goods on consignment.

(iv) <u>Possible sources.</u> Ask Lottie Zelinka. Look for a list of creditors with the petition in bankruptcy. Ask the banker, the cleaning service, the printers who do announcements of openings, the newspaper advertising department, the ad agency. Send an investigator to talk to them.

(c) <u>Defense of compliance with Article 9 of the UCC.</u> Check the Article 9 filings in the Secretary of State's files. If artists filed, this would be constructive notice.

(d) <u>Defense of use for "personal, family, or household purposes."</u> If this can be shown, it will be a complete defense under the FCC. However, note that Steven Wallace did sell other paintings. See footnote in *First National Bank*.

(i) <u>How the facts we already know support this defense.</u> First, at the meeting of July 26, 1999, Steven Wallace reported that he had never thought about trying to sell "Hare Castle." Second, it was "one of his favorite paintings and had been hanging in his dining room since he finished it a couple of years ago." Third, Steven Wallace and his wife "had recently purchased a new rug for their dining room that coordinated with the colors in the painting." Fourth, up until now, Steven Wallace has been working out of a spare room at home. Wallace Interview.

(ii) Additional helpful facts. Does Steven Wallace keep separate inventories of paintings for sale and paintings for personal use? Has he ever refused to sell a painting because for family use?

(iii) Why helpful. Such facts might prove that "Hare Castle" was for family use only.

(iv) Possible sources. Look at Steven Wallace's personal and business records. Arrange for interviews with friends who might have tried unsuccessfully to buy his paintings.

CONCLUSION

My research indicates that the trustee has sound legal and factual bases, both under the Bankruptcy Act and under the Franklin Commercial Code, for claiming that our client Steven Wallace's painting "Hare Castle" is an asset of Lottie Zelinka's bankruptcy estate. Depending on the results of our factual investigations, however, our client may be able to assert one or more defenses under FCC sec. 2-326(3). If the facts turn out to support it, the best defense may be that Steven Wallace used the painting for family and household purposes.

Perform Your Best on the Bar Exam Performance Test (MPT)

Perform Your Best™ Note on Analyzing *In re Steven Wallace*

Objective memorandum
Possible litigation
Advise client on best response to a demand from trustee in bankruptcy
Structure of work product: Statutory and case law analysis and application,
with suggestions for factual investigation

In this case, the firm represents Steven Wallace, a professor recently retired from the University of Franklin who now intends to turn being a painter from an avocation into a full-time career. A year ago he consigned one of his paintings, called Hare Castle, to a local art gallery owned by his friend Lottie Zelinka. She returned the painting to him, but only after she had filed for bankruptcy. Now the trustee of Ms. Zelinka's estate in bankruptcy seeks to claim the painting as part of her bankruptcy estate. The Partner Memorandum asks the associate to write a memorandum evaluating the trustee's claims under both the Bankruptcy Act and the Franklin Commercial Code. The associate is also to analyze the client's factual defenses under the statute and to propose additional factual research. Both evaluating the trustee's claim and analyzing the client's defenses are objective tasks. You will examine both sides of the issues.

How to Read and Outline the Instructions in the Partner Memo. Nothing is more important on the MPT than understanding the main issues in the case and meticulously following the instructions in the Partner Memo, painstakingly outlining the instructions by dividing and sub-dividing the topics. Here, the instructions say,

Please draft for me a two-part memorandum:
- First, analyze the legal and factual bases of the trustee's claim that the painting is an asset of the bankruptcy estate under the Bankruptcy Act and the Franklin Commercial Code (FCC).
- Second, for each of the four defenses under FCC § 2-326(3), discuss how the facts we already know support the defense, identify additional facts that might be helpful to us, state why they would be helpful, and indicate from what sources we might be able to obtain them.

Outlining the instructions for Part I, which ask for analysis of legal and factual bases for the trustee's claim under the Bankruptcy Act and the Franklin Commercial Code, is straightforward. As usual, you must tear each instruction apart into the smallest possible elements. Clearly, you will have separate lines in your MPT-Matrix™ in which you will note the page numbers of items in the File and the Library that are useful for analyzing the Bankruptcy Act and the Franklin Commercial Code. But note that the Partner Memo says, "analyze the legal and factual bases of the trustee's claim." For each code, that is, under both the Bankruptcy Act and the Franklin Commercial Code, you must assign one line in the MPT-Matrix™ to "legal" bases and one line to "factual." For Part II, in addition, careful reading is required to note that the Partner Memo asks four questions as to each of the four possible defenses. That is sixteen questions in all.

So far as practical, you will use the same four-part analysis to look for facts that would support each of the four defenses the statute provides. You cannot simply skip anything the Partner Memo asks you to do, although in this case, some of the partner's questions about possible defenses will lead in more promising directions than others. Accordingly, you will try to answer the same four questions in the Partner Memo for each of the four defenses:

288

(i) How the facts we already know support this defense.
(ii) Additional helpful facts.
(iii) Why helpful:
(iv) Possible sources.

The four defenses are as follows. You will apply all four questions from the Partner Memo to each of the four defenses, in some cases more successfully than others. You have a practical option. You can either assign 16 separate lines to this analysis in the MPT-Matrix™ or you can note these four topics on a separate sheet of paper to one side, and consider each one in relation to the four questions the Partner Memo poses.

(a) Defense of compliance with the sign law.
(b) Defense of creditors' knowledge that the gallery sold on consignment.
(c) Defense of compliance with Article 9 of the UCC.
(d) Defense of use for "personal, family, or household purposes."

For step-by-step, treatment of how to outline the instructions for *In re Steven Wallace* in your MPT-Matrix™, consult Part 3 of this book, above. It treats *In re Steven Wallace* in detail.

<u>How to Apply the Rule of Three.</u> The instructions in the Partner Memorandum for *In re Steven Wallace* tell the applicant to draft a two-part memorandum. Where the Partner Memo tells you to write a two-part memorandum, you have no choice. You must write a two-part memorandum. Here, you will nonetheless apply the Rule of Three, since you will sub-divide the first part of your memorandum, applying two different statutes, into two parts.

In the first main part, the partner has asked you to apply both the Bankruptcy Act and the Franklin Commercial Code and to analyze the legal and factual bases for the claim of the trustee in bankruptcy that your client Steven Wallace's painting "Hare Castle" is an asset of art dealer Lottie Zelinka's bankruptcy estate. In the second main part of your Discussion you will assess the possible defenses under FCC sec. 2-326(3).

Your strong persuasive headings, which you will underline in your work product, might read as follows:

IA. Since Lottie Zelinka held the painting "Hare Castle" on consignment, and since she returned the painting to Steven Wallace only after she filed for bankruptcy, the Bankruptcy Act provides legal and factual bases for the trustee to avoid returning the painting to Steven Wallace.

IB. Since Lottie Zelinka held the painting "Hare Castle" on consignment, the Franklin Commercial Code provides legal and factual bases for the trustee's claim that Steven Wallace's painting is part of the bankruptcy estate.

II. Depending on the results of our factual investigations, Steven Wallace may assert one or more of the defenses available under FCC 2-326, and oppose the trustee's claim.

The second part of this memorandum often causes bar candidates trouble. It requires responding to four factual questions as to each of four code sections. Thus, on the one hand, it is like the other tasks in this book in which the MPT requires analyzing code sections, one after the other. In this instance, however, applying the code sections requires suggesting avenues for factual investigation, rather than applying a rule of law. To do this task, you must apply your street smarts to the bar exam. You must think about the facts,

Perform Your Best on the Bar Exam Performance Test (MPT)

and then think about how to obtain more facts. Students who try to substitute book-learning for factual proof will do an unsatisfactory job on this part of the task. See Part 3 of this book for further discussion of the use of facts for *In re Steven Wallace*.

Observe that in the MPT-Matrix™ for *In re Steven Wallace*, this book has included some notes about where one might look for the needed facts.

As usual, the Conclusion of your objective memorandum will summarize the partner's instructions and briefly summarize your conclusions. Here is the Conclusion from the sample memorandum for *In re Steven Wallace* in this book.

CONCLUSION

My research indicates that the trustee has sound legal and factual bases, both under the Bankruptcy Act and under the Franklin Commercial Code, for claiming that our client Steven Wallace's painting "Hare Castle" is an asset of Lottie Zelinka's bankruptcy estate. Depending on the results of our factual investigations, however, our client may be able to assert one or more defenses under FCC sec. 2-326(3). If the facts turn out to support it, the best defense may be that Steven Wallace used the painting for family and household purposes.

Perform Your Best™ Materials for MPT Task 4K: *Kantor v. Bellows*

Perform Your Best on the Bar Exam Performance Test (MPT)

Note to the Reader: Your MPT-Matrix™ will have only page numbers, not words. The words in this MPT Matrix™ simply show you the information you will be indexing and cross-referencing. Do not attempt to write words in your own MPT-Matrix™.

\multicolumn{7}{	c	}{MPT-Matrix™ *Kantor v. Bellows*, MPT, July 1999}
	A. Interview Notes	B. Expert opinion on value of BB's law degree	C. Franklin DRL secs. 3-6	D. *Morgan v. Morgan* (Franklin Ct. App., 2d App. Div. 1998)	E. *Sooke v. Sooke* (Franklin Ct. App., 4th App. Div. 1999)	F. *Sooke v. Sooke* Dissent
1. Argument: Linda K. should receive share/ H's enhanced earning capacity						
A. Legal principles.			**P-5, P-6.** DRL secs. 3-6. Nothing limits meaning of "property."			
				Cases agree. **P-7.** *Morgan*: Will grant an award to wife. Professional [MBA] degree.	Cases agree. **P-11.** *Sooke*: Will grant an award to wife. Professional license.	
				Cases differ. *Morgan*: **P-7.** Degree not property. Not physically equitably distributable.	Cases differ: *Sooke*: **P-11.** License is property. Valuing license like valuing any professional practice:	**P-12.** *Sooke* dissent: Not property. Not capable of sale, etc. Personal. Cumulative "product of many years of previous education, combined with diligence and hard work."
					P-11. *Sooke*: Expert testimony— present value of *enhanced earning capacity*	

292

	A. Interview Notes	B. Expert opinion on value of BB's law degree	C. Franklin DRL secs. 3-6	D. *Morgan v. Morgan* (Franklin Ct. App., 2d App. Div. 1998)	E. *Sooke v. Sooke* (Franklin Ct. App., 4th App. Div. 1999)	F. *Sooke v. Sooke* Dissent
					Cases differ. *Sooke*: **P-11.** Evaluate . . . interest in a *profession*. DRL Sec. 5.	
					Sooke: **P-11.** Investment in license created *enhanced earning capacity*.	
					Sooke: **P-11.** Wife entitled to "distributive award." DRL secs. 6(e), 5(d).	
				P-9. Cases differ. *Morgan*: Wife entitled to "reimbursement maintenance."	Cases differ. Theory. *Sooke*: **P-11.** Economic partnership concept. Wife entitled to fruits of the investment.	
				Cases agree. *Morgan*: **P-9.** Does not decide appropriateness of traditional maintenance under DRL sec. 6.	Cases agree. **P-11.** *Sooke*: Reject traditional maintenance under DRL sec. 6.	
B. Facts.	**P-2, P-3.** Linda: Delayed schooling; did 75% of child- and housework; contributed all of her earnings, $85,000, to family.	**P-4.** Present value of Bill B's law degree is $520,000 if he remains in gov't, and $820,000 if he enters private practice.				

MPT-Matrix™ *Kantor v. Bellows*, MPT, July 1999, *cont'd*

	A. Interview Notes	B. Expert opinion on value of BB's law degree	C. Franklin DRL secs. 3-6	D. *Morgan v. Morgan* (Franklin Ct. App., 2d App. Div. 1998)	E. *Sooke v. Sooke* (Franklin Ct. App., 4th App. Div. 1999)	F. *Sooke v. Sooke* Dissent
	P-3. *Bill*: Paid tuition ($25,000 plus $10,000). Earned $3,000, plus 1/2 of $3,000 savings.					
2. Address counter-arguments.	*Counter-argument*: Linda anticipated that she would share in possible enhanced future earnings of her husband, so case is on all fours with *Morgan*. *However, in distinction to Morgan*: Linda anticipated a future benefit for her *own* career.			**P-9.** *Morgan*: Wife anticipated sharing possible enhanced earnings of MBA husband.		
	Counter-argument: As *Sooke* dissent suggests, Bill's future earning capacity results from his own hard work. (**P-2.** work award) *However*, without Linda's contributions, Bill would not have been able to attend law school.					

	A. Interview Notes	B. Expert opinion on value of BB's law degree	C. Franklin DRL secs. 3-6	D. *Morgan v. Morgan* (Franklin Ct. App., 2d App. Div. 1998)	E. *Sooke v. Sooke* (Franklin Ct. App., 4th App. Div. 1999)	F. *Sooke v. Sooke* Dissent
	P-2, P-3. *Counter-argument*: Linda is earning as much as Bill is ($35,000). *However*, at least under *Sooke*, the issue is not whether the share to which she is entitled is needed, but rather that she shares in a partnership entity.					
3. Specific dollar demand justified by these arguments.				Under rule in *Morgan*: Linda receives minimum 50% of $85,000 she contributed.	Under rule in *Sooke*: Linda receives maximum of >50% of expert's high valuation of $820.000.	
					Sooke: Linda receives fees and costs.	

<u>Base figure.</u> The average of the high and low present value figures is $670,000. Concede Linda's demand limited to 50%, notwithstanding her greater contribution. This puts the demand at $335,000.

<u>Pay-out.</u> Propose Linda willing to accept payment over time ("Distributive award" under *Sooke*). Requires substantial up-front payment for immediate needs. Proposes $42,500, the lump-sum award she would in any event receive under *Morgan*. Balance over 10 years.

<u>Suggestion.</u> If settlement is reached, Linda will be willing to bear her own fees and costs.

Perform Your Best on the Bar Exam Performance Test (MPT)

Perform Your Best™ Sample Answer for *Kantor v. Bellows*

Crystal, Hughes & Bernstein
Attorneys at Law
47 Bridge Street
Oakton, Franklin 33311

Date: _____

Shawn Martin, Esquire
Name of Law Firm
Oakton, Franklin 33000

Dear Shawn Martin:

We represent Linda Kantor, who seeks a divorce from your client Bill Bellows. This letter describes the one contested issue in the case and proposes terms of settlement.

1. Bill Bellows's law degree is property, and Linda Kantor is entitled to share in the enhanced earning capacity it creates, because Kantor and Bellows entered into a partnership of equals, expecting to advance both careers, not just one.

The Franklin Domestic Relations Law uses but does not define "property." Our client believes that the enhanced earning capacity created by Bill's law degree is marital property under DRL secs. 3-5. It is therefore subject to division. While our client would like to reach an amicable settlement, she is also prepared to litigate this issue.

Franklin courts, both in *Morgan v. Morgan* (Franklin Court of Appeal, Second Division, 1998), and in *Sooke v. Sooke* (Franklin Court of Appeal, Fourth Appellate Division, 1999), state that where one party to the marriage has contributed to the other's gaining a professional degree or license, that second party is entitled to an award. Both courts rejected traditional maintenance.

The differences between the cases are key to our client's argument. We believe that a court will follow *Sooke*. The *Morgan* court held that the husband's MBA degree was not property under the DRL, because no value could be established. But in the more recent *Sooke* case, another Appellate Division court held that a professional medical license is property. According to *Sooke*, valuing a license is like valuing any other professional practice. *Sooke* allowed introduction of expert testimony as to the present value of *enhanced earning capacity*.

The measure of the wife's recovery, moreover, is drastically different in *Morgan* and *Sooke*. The *Morgan* court held that the wife was entitled only to "reimbursement maintenance," that is, the dollar amount that she contributed to the marriage. The *Sooke* court, by contrast, gave the wife an interest in the husband's *enhanced earning capacity* and made the wife entitled to the *fruits of the investment*.

Our client believes that *Sooke* applies to her situation, which is distinguishable on its facts from *Morgan*. Linda Kantor did not merely look to her husband's enhanced income to support her in the future. On the contrary, Linda Kantor and Bill Bellows entered into an agreement of equals, a partnership, by which they would advance not just one career, but both careers. They would take turns going to school, and they would take turns looking after the household.

Thus, because Bill Bellows entered school first, Linda Kantor endured delays and made sacrifices in her own career, but with the expectation that her sacrifices would be repaid by her own career advancement later on. She also gave up educational opportunities and conferences that would have advanced her career, because her turn would come later.

2. <u>Bill Bellows's arguments seeking to deny or diminish Linda Kantor's share are untenable, because she expected to benefit her own career, because he might not have attended law school without her contributions, and because the issue is not her current income, but rather how she can share in the partnership entity.</u>

Thus, Linda Kantor did not merely expect a higher standard of living resulting from Bill's law practice, as your client might argue. She expected, on the contrary, that she would benefit in her own career, as she and Bill took turns.

Your client might also argue that much of his future earning capacity resulted from his own hard work. Without Linda Kantor's contributions, however, your client would have had to get a job, and he would not have had the leisure to study so hard. He would have had to assume debt beyond the already substantial sum of $25,000 he already owes. He might not have attended law school at all.

Your client might argue, finally, that with an annual salary of $35,000, Linda Kantor is earning as much as he is. Under *Sooke*, however, the issue is not whether our client needs money to live; the issue is how she can share in the partnership entity.

3. <u>Linda Kantor makes a specific dollar demand of $335,000, plus fees and costs, that is, fifty per cent of your client's enhanced earning capacity, as reflected in expert testimony.</u>

As to settlement, we are making a specific dollar demand of $335,000, plus fees and costs. Linda Kantor is willing to limit her demand to fifty per cent of your client's enhanced earning capacity, notwithstanding her greater contribution.

Linda Kantor did seventy-five per cent of the child-rearing and the housework in the marriage. She also used her entire salary for the household, contributing $85,000 to the support of her family. In contrast, your client's contributions were $3,000 from part-time work, $10,000 from his parents, and $25,000 in loans. Some $36,000 of that went to pay his law school tuition over three years. In all, your client contributed barely $2,000 to his own support and that of his child.

The maximum recovery under *Sooke* is fifty per cent of the expert's high valuation of the present value of Bill Bellows's law degree if he goes into private practice, or half of $820,000. Instead of starting with $820,000, however, we are willing to start with a base figure that is the average of the high and low present-value figures, his potential income in private practice or government work, that is, $670,000. Accordingly, our demand is $335,000.

We believe, in addition, that in following *Sooke*, the court will award Linda her fees and costs.

Our client is willing to accept payment over time (a "distributive award" under *Sooke*). As a substantial up-front payment for immediate needs, we suggest $42,500, which is the lump-sum award she would receive if *Morgan* applied. She is willing to receive the balance over 10 years. If the parties reach a settlement, in addition, our client will be willing to bear her own fees and costs.

Please send your response at your early opportunity.

Yours very truly,

Pat Moore
Attorney at Law

Perform Your Best on the Bar Exam Performance Test (MPT)

Perform Your Best™ Note on Analyzing *Kantor v. Bellows*

Type of Task: Persuasive letter to opposing counsel
Context: Litigation
Purpose: Explain client's case to opposing counsel, and make settlement proposal
Structure of Work Product: Case law and factual analysis

The partner in *Kantor v. Bellows* tells you that the firm represents Linda Kantor, who seeks a divorce from Bill Bellows, and that there is only one contested issue in the case. You are to draft a letter explaining your firm's view of that single issue and proposing terms of settlement.

How to apply the Rule of Three. In this MPT task, the partner memo tells you that your work product must have three parts, so completing the task is easily compatible with applying what this book calls the Rule of Three. The partner says:

As the first step in the negotiation process, I want to send a letter to Shawn Martin that:

- argues that Linda is entitled to a share of Bill's enhanced earning capacity;
- addresses counter-arguments that would deny or diminish her share; and
- includes a specific dollar demand that is justified in light of these arguments.

Please draft such a letter for my signature. Be sure to discuss both the legal principles and the facts of our case in making the arguments.

As to format, although this task calls on the bar candidate to draft a letter, each of the three parts of the work product is headed by a strong persuasive heading, numbered and underlined. This device for revealing the structure of the work product is as useful in a letter as it is in a memo or brief. Strong persuasive headings, including both law and facts, are not optional on the MPT, they are necessary if you want to score as high as possible.

The sample answer to this task shows you how to overcome the three main challenges bar candidates face with *Kantor v. Bellows*. One challenge for many bar candidates is to keep from answering this Franklin case with the domestic relations laws of their own states. Easy as it is to read this task carelessly and assume that you already know about the issue it presents, in fact, you are unlikely ever to have encountered the issue in *Kantor v. Bellows* before, and the law of your own state won't help. This case is simply not about achieving the objective many bar candidates carelessly choose, namely, making sure that in a divorce a non-working spouse gets compensated for contributions to the household. That is not in issue here. Period.

The second challenge is to keep from applying your ready-made habits of analysis to this case. The task memo tells you flatly not to try to distinguish the two leading cases just on their facts. You cannot score high by ignoring the Partner Memo.

The third challenge is to come up with a proposed settlement figure and proposed settlement pay-out. Many bar candidates try to avoid dealing with numbers. But creating a settlement figure and pay-out is part of the assignment here, and to score high on this task, you must do it.

Perform Your Best™ Materials
for MPT Task 4L:
Franklin Asbestos Handling Regulations

Perform Your Best on the Bar Exam Performance Test (MPT)

Note to the Reader: Your MPT-Matrix™ will have only page numbers, not words. The words in this MPT Matrix™ simply show you the information you will be indexing and cross-referencing. Do not attempt to write words in your own MPT-Matrix™.

	Perform Your Best™ MPT-Matrix™ *Franklin Asbestos Handling Regulations*, MPT, July 2000					
	A. Franklin Environ-mental Protection Code, Title 6, Chapter 13	B. 29 C.F.R. sec. 1926 Asbestos	C. *Gade v. National Solid Wastes Management Association,* (U.S. 1992)	D.	E.	F. *Chamber of Commerce v. Noter* (15th Cir. 1995)
1. Best case for why statutory and regulatory scheme not preempted in its entirety.	**P-2.** State law purpose (1) to safeguard public health; (2) to ensure that workers handling asbestos receive training to protect public health.		**P-10.** Congressional intent determines preemption. No preemption if there is (i) no federal standard, or (ii) approved state plan. *Implied preemption.* (a) *Field preemption.* Congress has left no room in the field for states to supplement. (b) *Conflict preemption.* Impossible to comply with both, or else state law interferes. **P-11.** *Dual impact law.* Absent approved state plan, OSH Act preempts state law that in a *direct, clear and substantial way*, is regulation of worker health and safety. But state law may regulate workers as members of general public.			**P-13.** Where dual purpose, state law preempted only if it has a "direct and substantial" effect on the federal system of regulation. **P-13, P-14.** Sections of surveys re workplace hazards–not environmental hazards–are in conflict with methods of federal government to promote hazard communication.

300

	A. Franklin Environ-mental Protection Code, Title 6, Chapter 13	B. 29 C.F.R. sec. 1926 Asbestos	C. *Gade v. National Solid Wastes Management Association,* (U.S. 1992)	D.	E.	F. *Chamber of Commerce v. Noter* (15th Cir. 1995)
2. Discussion re whether each provision of Section 8 of Franklin regulations can survive preemption challenge. Section 8(a): Employees must complete 5-day course and 2-hour exam.		Sec. (m)(iii). Training program takes at least 8 hours. No exam. State can argue dual purpose: objective to protect public.				
(b) Course must cover (1) Physical characteristics of asbestos		Sec. (iv)(A) Methods of recognizing asbestos. Same: no conflict.				
(2) Worker protective equipment		Sec. (iv)(D) Respirators. Clothing. Sec. (iv)(E). Purpose, use, fitting, limits/ respirators. Same: no conflict.				
(3) State-of-art practices for abatement and remediation.		Sec. (iv)(F). Appropriate work practices for performing asbestos job. Same: no conflict.				

Perform Your Best on the Bar Exam Performance Test (MPT)

	Perform Your Best™ MPT-Matrix™ *Franklin Asbestos Handling Regulations*, MPT, July 2000, *cont'd*					
	A. Franklin Environmental Protection Code, Title 6, Chapter 13	B. 29 C.F.R. sec. 1926 Asbestos	C. *Gade v. National Solid Wastes Management Association,* (U.S. 1992)	D.	E.	F. *Chamber of Commerce v. Noter* (15th Cir. 1995)
(4) Procedures for collecting samples to minimize airborne fibers.		Sec. (iv)(D), (F). Work practices. Same: no conflict.				
(5) Personal hygiene pertaining to asbestos handling.		Sec. (iv)(D). Housekeeping. Hygiene. Same: no conflict.				
(c) Required one-day biennial review course to renew certificate.	Sec. 3(b). Workers handling asbestos material need valid asbestos handling certificate.	Training to be provided prior to or at the time of initial assignment and at least annually thereafter. **Possible conflict.**				
(d) Certificate on completion of course/fee of $100.		No cost to employee. **Direct conflict.**				
(e) Employer provides to DEP names of all employees with certificate, plus $600 each per year.		[Silent.] No conflict.				**P-14** Funding system that does not interfere with compliance with federal law is permitted. Funding provision a logical means to accomplish community health and safety purpose.

302

Perform Your Best™ Sample Answer for *Franklin Asbestos Handling Regulations*

Office of the Attorney General
State of Franklin
Environmental Protection Division

MEMORANDUM

To: Colin Dillard, Deputy Attorney General
From: Applicant
Date: _____

INTRODUCTION

You have asked me for the best arguments that the statutory and regulatory scheme of the Franklin Asbestos Handling Act (AHA) is not preempted in its entirety by the federal Occupational Safety and Health Act (OSH Act) and the implementing federal regulations. The best argument why the AHA is not preempted in its entirety is that it is a dual impact law, affecting both workplace safety and public health. In addition, most aspects of the Franklin regulatory scheme should survive challenge, as either complementary to federal law or concerned with public health. The DEP training-and-certification requirement under section 8(a) and the $100 training-and-review course fee under section 8(e), however, are in conflict with the federal regulations and will probably be preempted.

DISCUSSION

<u>1. The best argument that the Franklin Asbestos Handling Act is not preempted in its entirety is that it is a dual impact law, addressing both workplace safety and public health.</u>

In *Gade v. National Solid Wastes Management Association* (1992), the Supreme Court stated that whether a state act is preempted by federal law is a question of congressional intent. Congress intended the OSH Act to preempt regulations related to workplace safety, but it did not intend the OSH Act to prevent state regulation of any occupational safety or health issue "with respect to which no Federal standard is in effect." 29 U.S.C. 667(a)

In the absence of an approved state plan, a state dual impact law may be permissible. A dual impact law addresses workplace safety and some other field. Where such a law is not in a direct, clear and substantial way a regulation of worker health and safety, and where it does not burden commerce, such a law is not preempted. One part of a statutory and regulatory scheme may be permissible, while another part is not. *Chamber of Commerce v. Noter*. Nonetheless, "conflict" preemption may occur where a section of a state code conflicts with or occupies the same field as a federal regulation. *Gade*.

Perform Your Best on the Bar Exam Performance Test (MPT)

The Franklin Environmental Protection Code is a state dual impact law. Its purposes are (1) to safeguard public health; and (2) to ensure that workers handling asbestos receive training. Therefore, portions of the Franklin law that are intended to safeguard public health, and that are not regulation of worker health and safety, may be permissible.

<u>2. Some provisions of the Franklin Asbestos Handling Regulations will stand, either because they are intended to protect public health rather than workplace safety, or else because they are similar to the federal requirements. Other provisions are in conflict with the federal regulations and will be preempted.</u>

Logically, there are four possibilities:

(i) A state regulation is not a workplace safety measure, but has some other objective: it is not preempted;
(ii) The effect of the state regulation is similar to that of the federal regulation: it is not preempted;
(iii) A regulation conflicts with the federal regulation: it is preempted;
(iv) A regulation is a workplace safety measure: it is preempted.

Comparison of the Franklin AHA and regulations with the federal OSH Act and regulations yields the following results:

(a) The Franklin employee certification requirement will probably not be preempted, because the purpose is not to regulate workplace safety. The Franklin statute is a dual-purpose statute, protecting both workers and the general public. The State of Franklin may argue that the purpose of the certification requirement in Section 3(b) of the Franklin statute and Section 8 of the regulations is not to regulate workplace safety, but to protect the general public.

Section 8(a) of the Franklin regulations, however, requiring a 5-day course and an examination, will probably be preempted. The federal regulations require an 8-hour training program and do not require an examination, 29 C.F.R. 1926 sec. (m) (iii), while Section 8(a) of the Franklin regulations requires a 5-day DEP-approved course and a 2-hour examination for certification. While the State of Franklin can argue that the longer course and the examination are not in conflict with the federal regulations because they support public health, not worker safety, these regulations do not clearly on their face concern public health. They will probably be found to be both workplace regulations and in conflict with the methods specified by the federal regulations.

Section 8(b). There is no preemption of the required topics for the course. Where the topics regard worker safety, the Franklin requirements and the federal requirements are similar if not identical. There is therefore no preemption. As to the training requirements related to public safety issues, the DEP requirements do not fall within the ambit of the OSH Act and are not preempted.

Section 8(c). As to the biennial review course, there is preemption of the topics dealing with worker safety, but no preemption of the topics dealing with public health.

Section 8(d). The Franklin requirement of a $100 certificate fee is preempted. The federal regulations state that there must be no cost, while the AHA regulations are in direct conflict, requiring that the handler's certificate have a fee of $100.

Section 8(e). The Franklin requirement that the employer must provide DEP with names of all employees, and must pay $600 per year for each employee, is not preempted. Neither reporting names of employees nor paying a fee for each one is required under the OSHA regulations, and the State may argue that the DEP requirement is intended to safeguard the general public, not to assure workplace safety. In addition, a funding requirement is permissible under *Noter* where it is a "logical means for accomplishing a broad community health and safety purpose," without conflicting or interfering with the OSH Act.

CONCLUSION

The best argument that the Franklin Scheme as a whole should survive a preemption challenge from OSHA is that the scheme has a dual effect: it protects public health in addition to worker safety. Some aspects of the scheme as touching workplace safety should also survive challenge, either as complementary to federal law or as also concerned with public health. The DEP training-and-certification requirement under section 8(a) of the regulations and the $100 training-and-review course fee under section 8(e), however, are likely to be preempted.

Perform Your Best: *Perform Your Best on the Bar Exam Performance Test (MPT)*

Perform Your Best™
Note on Analyzing
Franklin Asbestos Handling Regulations

Type of Task: Persuasive *and* objective memorandum
Context: Litigation
Purpose: Frame best arguments *and* evaluate regulations section-by-section
Structure of Work Product: Statutory interpretation and case law analysis and application

The author of the task memo for *Franklin Asbestos Handling Regulations* is a Deputy Attorney General. He tells the applicant that he anticipates a challenge to the recently-enacted Asbestos Handling Act (AHA), which requires the Franklin Department of Environmental Protection (DEP) to implement health and safety programs to train and certify workers who handle asbestos. The DEP has asked his office to review the proposed regulations it has drafted. He anticipates that the AHA statutory and regulatory scheme will be challenged as preempted by the Federal Occupational Safety and Healthy Act (OSH Act) and the implementing federal regulations. The instructions ask you to draft a memorandum that answers two questions. Most MPT tasks are either persuasive or objective. This MPT task is unusual in that the memorandum must be both persuasive and objective. The part of your memorandum in which you respond to the first instruction will be persuasive, while the part in which you respond to the second will be objective.

<u>How to Outline the Instructions in the Partner Memo</u>. The task memo provides the following instructions:

Please prepare a memorandum for me that:

States the best case for why, in light of the absence of a State Plan, the statutory and regulatory scheme is not preempted in its entirety; and
Discusses whether each provision of Section 8 of the draft regulations can survive a preemption challenge.

The first instruction is straightforward. To take it apart into its component parts, you will first note that it says "in the absence of a State Plan." The main point, however, is that the statutory and regulatory scheme is not preempted in its entirety. So you must figure out the relevance of the fact that Franklin has no State plan. The first row in your MPT-Matrix™, will be devoted mainly to noting page numbers of materials in the File or Library that bear on whether the AHA is preempted in its entirety. It will include the page number for the Supreme Court case *Gade v. National Solid Wastes Management*. *Gade* stated that where there is an approved State Plan, there is no preemption. Constructing the MPT-Matrix™ for the first instruction thus requires both tearing apart the instruction and teasing apart the cases.

The second instruction, asking for section-by-section assessment of draft regulations, introduces a standard MPT task. As usual, to respond to that instruction, you will analyze each section of the draft regulations one at a time. Your MPT-Matrix™ will list each section of the Franklin regulations separately down the lefthand column. Your job is to discuss whether each provision of Section 8 of the draft Franklin regulations is preempted or not. You will compare each section of the Franklin regulations with the corresponding section of the federal regulations, one after the other.

Perform Your Best™ Note on Analyzing Franklin Asbestos Handling Regulations

How to Use the Rule of Three. Where the task memo contains two clear-cut instructions, but they ask for two such different types of writing, you may wish to divide the Discussion section of your memorandum into two main parts. Whether the Discussion section of your memo has two or three parts, however, the first part of your Discussion must be persuasive, arguing only one side of the case and answering this question:

> What are the best arguments that the statutory and regulatory scheme of the Franklin Asbestos Handling Act (AHA) should not be preempted in its entirety by the federal Occupational Safety and Health Act (OSH Act) and the implementing federal regulations?

Your answer the second question must be objective, analyzing both sides:

> Will each provision of Section 8 of the Franklin draft regulations survive a preemption challenge?

Answering the second question requires using the classic MPT structure where you examine the sections of a code one at a time. Your starting point must always be the MPT File and Library, where you will find, somewhere, the standard against which you can test the proposed code sections one-by-one. Here, the standard for testing each section of the proposed Franklin regulations is found in the Code of Federal Regulations, 29 C.F.R. sec. 1926. As always with such MPT tasks, as a matter of test-taking tactics, you must first calculate the amount of time available for critiquing each of the code sections, then take care not to exceed the time available for each section. Note that for convenience, the sample MPT-Matrix™ in this book includes a note about the conclusion as to each comparison, e.g., "No conflict" or "Probably preempted."

Logically, there are four possibilities:

(i) A state regulation is not a workplace safety measure, but has some other objective: it is not preempted;
(ii) The effect of the state regulation is similar to that of the federal regulation: it is not preempted;
(iii) A regulation conflicts with the federal regulation: it is preempted;
(iv) A regulation is a workplace safety measure: it is preempted.

How to Apply the Rule of Three. The Partner Memo clearly divides the task into two parts. Using the Rule of Three is entirely optional. You may wish to divide your memorandum into the two parts suggested by the partner's two questions, without further sub-division. The sample answer in this book illustrates a Discussion divided into two parts. Alternatively, you may wish to employ the Rule of Three and divide your memorandum into three parts as follows:

1. The best argument that the Franklin Asbestos Handling Act is not preempted in its entirety by the Federal Occupational Safety and Health Act (OSH Act) is that it is a dual impact law, intended to address not only workplace safety but also public health.

2A. Some provisions of the Franklin Asbestos Handling Regulations will survive challenge, either because they are intended to protect public health rather than workplace safety, or else because they are similar to the federal requirements.

a. There is probably no preemption of the Franklin employee certification requirement. The federal regulations do not require employee certification. But the Franklin statute is a dual purpose statute. The State's best argument that there is no preemption is that the purpose of the Franklin certification requirement is not to protect the workers as a matter of workplace safety, but rather to protect public health.

b. There is no preemption of the required topics for the course. Where the topics regard worker safety, the Franklin requirements and the federal requirements are similar if not identical. There is therefore no preemption of those requirements.

As to the training requirements related to public safety issues, moreover, the DEP requirements do not fall within the ambit of the OSH Act and are therefore not preempted.

c. As to the biennial review, again, the Franklin statute is a dual-purpose statute. There is no preemption of the topics dealing with protection of the public.

d. The Franklin requirement that the employer must provide DEP with names of all employees, and must pay $600 per year for each employee, is not preempted.

2B. Other provisions are in conflict with the federal regulations and will be preempted.

a. The requirement of a 5-day course and an examination in Section 8(a) of the Franklin regulations will probably be preempted. The federal regulations require an 8-hour training program and do not require an examination. 29 C.F.R. 1926 sec. (m) (iii). Section 8(a) of the Franklin regulations requires a 5-day DEP-approved course and a 2-hour examination for certification. The Franklin regulation will probably be found to be both a workplace regulation and in conflict with the methods specified by the federal regulation.

b. As to the biennial review, there will be preemption of the topics dealing with worker safety.

c. The Franklin requirement of a $100 certificate fee will be preempted, as directly in conflict with the federal regulations. The federal regulations require that there be no cost, while the AHA requires a $100 fee for the handler's certificate. This is a direct conflict, and the Franklin requirement will be preempted.

The sample answer in this book proposes the following Conclusion:

> The best argument that the Franklin Scheme as a whole should survive a preemption challenge from OSHA is that the scheme has a dual effect: it protects public health in addition to worker safety. Some sections of the code as touching workplace safety should also survive challenge, either as complementary to federal law or as concerned with public health. The DEP training-and-certification requirement under section 8(a) and the $100 training-and-review course fee under section 8(e), however, are likely to be preempted.

Displaying the structure of your work product visually is an important aid to the grader. Notice how in the analyses above, this book has indented the parts of the analysis and numbered and lettered them. Visual presentation counts on the MPT. "it's all in there" is an unsatisfactory defense of not presenting your logic in a way the grader can see on the page.

Part V:

Conclusion

In this book you have learned to write well-organized work products on the performance test, and to present them on the page so that its visual appearance reflects the logic of your work. You have learned how to use a four-step system to research and organize a lawyerlike work product. You have learned to create a graphic device, the MPT-Matrix™, to organize your research, focus your attention on responding to the Partner Memo, and structure your work product.

The most important element of success on the performance test is understanding and following the instructions in the Partner Memo ("task memo"). You will read and outline the Partner Memo at the beginning of your work. You will check the Partner Memo before your begin writing your work product to make sure that you remember the instructions and that you can follow them. When you are in the last five minutes of preparing your work product you will check again to make sure you are responding to the instructions in the Partner Memo.

You must have a time plan and stick to it. Whatever else happens, you must finish the work product within the time allowed.

Exercise all of the skills you have learned here, and you will present the bar exam graders with a lawyerlike work product. *Best of success!*